WAR IN THE FAR EAST

VOLUME 1

Storm Clouds over the Pacific, 1931–1941

PETER HARMSEN

CASEMATE

Philadelphia & Oxford

Published in the United States of America and Great Britain in 2018 by
CASEMATE PUBLISHERS
1950 Lawrence Road, Havertown, PA 19083, US
and
The Old Music Hall, 106–108 Cowley Road, Oxford OX4 1JE, UK

Copyright 2018 © Peter Harmsen

Hardback Edition: ISBN 978-1-61200-480-8
Digital Edition: ISBN 978-1-61200-481-5 (epub)

A CIP record for this book is available from the British Library

Printed and bound in the United States of America

Typeset in India by Versatile PreMedia Services. www.versatilepremedia.com

For a complete list of Casemate titles, please contact:

CASEMATE PUBLISHERS (US)
Telephone (610) 853-9131
Fax (610) 853-9146
Email: casemate@casematepublishers.com
www.casematepublishers.com

CASEMATE PUBLISHERS (UK)
Telephone (01865) 241249
Email: casemate-uk@casematepublishers.co.uk
www.casematepublishers.co.uk

Contents

Acknowledgements

As World War II recedes into history and the number of living witnesses to those momentous events sadly diminishes, the number of historians specializing in the biggest conflict in the history of mankind continues to increase. One advantage of this is the emergence of several international networks of scholars bringing together different approaches and traditions for a more complete understanding of events that continue to reverberate to this day.

In preparing this book, I have been the beneficiary of two such networks. The Second World War Research Group at King's College London, is a new branch on the rapidly growing tree of international scholarly exchange, and the two conferences I have been able to attend have offered the opportunity for immensely fruitful and stimulating discussions. The same is true for the many international gatherings that the Institute of Modern History at the Chinese Academy of Social Sciences, where I have been fortunate enough to be invited.

Many individuals also contributed to making this volume what it is. Special thanks go to Franco David Macri of the University of Hong Kong and Jokull Gislason of Iceland for reading the manuscript and providing invaluable, detailed feedback. Any errors or omissions in the book are, of course, mine alone. In addition, I wish to thank, for various forms of help, advice, and encouragement, Professor Gao Shihua of the Chinese Academy of Social Sciences, Ricardo Trota Jose of the University of the Philippines Diliman, Zafrani Arifin from Malaysia, and Stephen Hands from Britain.

At Casemate, I have benefited from the tireless support of a dedicated and professional staff headed by group publishing director Clare Litt. Sophie MacCallum edited this volume with an eagle-eyed attention to detail while keeping a keen focus on the overall narrative. I am also indebted to Ruth Sheppard, Isobel Nettleton and Katie Allen for their valuable contributions as the manuscript was turned into a book.

Finally, my family: my wife Hui-tsung once again offered her attention and support, and our two daughters Lisa and Eva were always understanding even during the many evenings and weekends when work on this book required my undivided attention. I suspect their forgiving attitude reflects our common love of books, a passion I am happy to have passed on to them.

Taipei, June 2018

Preface

In late summer 1939, a 22-year-old man in the uniform of a Wehrmacht officer was on his way to Germany's border with Poland. His mission was to attach himself to a German division as an observer during the invasion that was only days away. The young man must have attracted considerable attention since his features were anything but Aryan. His name was Chiang Wei-kuo, and he was the adopted son of China's leader, Chiang Kai-shek. For the past two years he had undergone advanced military training at the War Academy in the south German city of Munich. In that capacity, he had even taken part in Germany's peaceful occupation of Austria in March 1938.[1]

Chiang Wei-kuo's story was a reflection of how close Sino-German ties had grown in the 1930s, as Germany's resurgent armament industry was exporting vast quantities of military equipment to the Nationalist Chinese regime, whose efforts at building up a large modern army were also assisted by a corps of experienced German advisors. The assistance had proved particularly useful since 1937, after full-scale war broke out between China and Japan. By 1939, however, Germany was growing friendlier with Japan and was busy distancing itself from Chiang's regime. As a result, Chiang Wei-kuo's presence was beginning to appear out of place, and when he passed through Berlin *en route* to the Polish border and paid a visit to the Chinese embassy, he received new orders: he was to travel to the United States for military training there.

Consequently, by the time German panzers rolled into Poland in the early hours of September 1, Chiang was already on a ship bound for America, which was emerging as an important new ally for China. He would soon commence studies at the Armored Force Center, Fort Knox, before returning home three years later, his brain filled with the latest military knowledge. He was not the only one in his family to travel widely. His stepbrother Chiang Ching-kuo had spent 12 years in the Soviet Union. He had a Belarusian wife and even a Russian name, Nikolai Vladimirovich Elizarov.

The two stepbrothers formed just a corner of a corner in the immensely complex web of relations and interactions that characterized Chinese and Asian politics and society during the 1930s, the decade that saw the Sino-Japanese War flare up and, little by little, set in motion events which would eventually lead to Japan's conflict with an array of Western powers. What the Chiangs do exemplify, however, is the extent to which the war in the Asia Pacific was, right from its earliest origins, a global affair, involving both indigenous actors and actors from thousands of miles away.

The war that raged in and around the Pacific in the first half of the 1940s has traditionally been seen as a struggle pitting the United States against Japan. It is indeed true that the ambitious Japanese Empire was halted, then defeated and destroyed at the expense of primarily American blood. Names such as Guadalcanal, Saipan, and Hiroshima are milestones on the way to Japan's complete surrender in August 1945. The contribution of the British in Burma or the Australians in New Guinea are also important, and still remembered.

However, secondary parts were played by a host of other nationalities, some of them appearing in roles largely forgotten by posterity. Examples include Russian exiles in Japanese uniforms acting as auxiliaries in the service of Hirohito in northeast China, or Mexican pilots participating in the liberation of the Philippines. Events in Asia also saw strange alliances, and even stranger enmities. The Vichy French government, under German control, consulted frequently with the US government over developments in Indochina in 1941, and in the same year French forces in Laos and Cambodia found themselves involved in a brief, brutal border war with Thailand.

Just as a deeper understanding of World War II in Asia is gained by involving a wider range of actors than usual, it also makes sense to expand the period under review. This volume, the first in a series of three, does not begin on December 7, 1941. It ends on that day. To appreciate the deep animosities that drove the immensely destructive war and cost the lives of millions of people, soldiers and civilians alike, it is necessary to go decades, indeed centuries, back in time. First and foremost, it is important to explore the strange love-hate relationship between East Asia's two oldest civilizations, China and Japan, and how it was conditioned by shifting geopolitical winds, most crucially the arrival of the Western powers from about 1600.

It is a history whose earliest beginnings can be traced to the time when Europe was mired in the Dark Ages, or even further back, to the time when two great empires ruled much of the known world: the Roman in the west, and the Chinese in the east. It is also a history which has still not ended. Three generations after World War II many of the rivalries that led to bloodshed on the beaches of Micronesia, in the jungles of Malaya, and in the villages of Manchuria are still alive. This trilogy is written in the firm conviction that a better understanding of the past will contribute to a more dispassionate and level-headed approach to the problems of our present age.

CHAPTER ONE

Ancient Foes

China, Japan, and Asia until 1931

In August AD 663, two large navies clashed on the western side of the Korean Peninsula. The huge wooden ships, some several stories high and brimming with soldiers in heavy armor, met on the lower reaches of the Paekchon River,[1] near the spot where it emptied into the Yellow Sea. One fleet had been sent by China's powerful Tang emperor, while the other fleet was fighting for Japan's Yamato dynasty. They were supporting rival kingdoms in Korea, and this was their final showdown. As the two floating armies approached each other, catapults sent heavy projectiles whistling through the air, while archers tried to take out individual soldiers on the decks of the opponent's vessels.

When the distance was short enough, boarding parties climbed onto enemy ships, and the clang of iron against iron filled the air, as if the battle were taking place on land. Soon, the Chinese superiority in ships and men became evident, and the Japanese were surrounded on all sides. The *Nihon Shoki*, one of Japan's classical works of history, described the scene: "In a brief space of time, the Japanese imperial force was defeated, and many fell into the water and drowned. The ships were unable to maneuver either astern or ahead. The Japanese general Echi no Takutsu faced heaven and swore in anger and despair. He gnashed his teeth, and in his rage he slew dozens of men. He died fighting."[2]

It was a decisive Chinese victory and the earliest Sino-Japanese battle on record, but by the time their fleets fought to the death on that fateful summer day, the two ancient civilizations had already known about each other's existence for nearly a millennium. There were vague reports, shrouded in mystery and myth, that China's first emperor, Qin Shihuang, who lived around 200 BC and was thus the contemporary of the Carthaginian general Hannibal, had sent people to the Japanese isles in search of the elixir of youth, and in the year AD 57, the Chinese court had started exchanging emissaries with a kingdom located in what is now Japan.

Right from the earliest times, China jealously defended its position as the proud center of the known world, or as its people said, "all under heaven." Japan sometimes

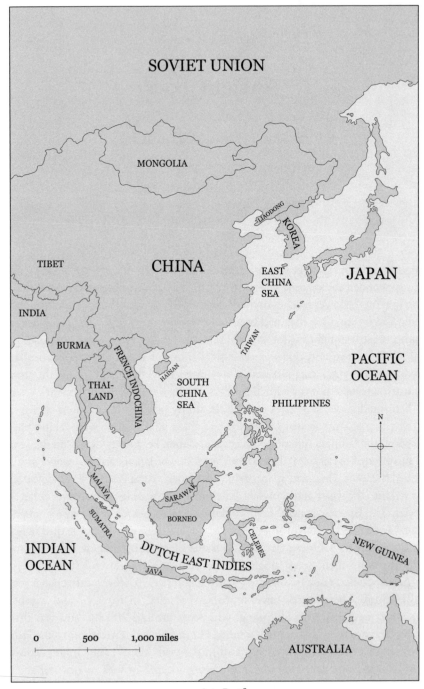

Asia Pacific

seemed to forget this, signaling that it lacked an understanding of its own position in the hierarchy of states. In the early 7th century, a Japanese prince, acting on behalf of the imperial court, infuriated China by dispatching a message suggesting equivalence between the two civilizations: "The emperor of the land where the sun rises sends a letter to the emperor of the land where the sun sets."[3]

The Chinese sense of superiority was not unfounded. All neighboring cultures, including that of Japan, were to a significant extent derivative of China's. The mere fact that the region's writing systems were mostly based on the Chinese script was sufficient indication of this massive one-way influence. China impacted its neighbors, not the other way around. In Japan, as elsewhere, China left an indelible mark in areas as diverse as philosophy, poetry, and architecture, as well as in the crucial area of religion. Buddhism, one of the most profound strands in Japanese thinking, was introduced mainly via China and the tireless efforts of missionaries such as the 8th-century Chinese-born monk Jianzhen.[4]

An era of growing suspicion and hostility between Japan and the Asian mainland began in the 13th century. In the 1280s, the rulers of China's Yuan dynasty, the descendants of the Mongolian world conqueror Genghis Khan, attempted an invasion of the Japanese islands. This could have spelled the end of Japan as an independent civilization, if it were not for an unforeseen event. A large part of the Chinese-Mongolian fleet was destroyed by a *kamikaze*, a "divine wind" or, in modern parlance, a powerful typhoon. As a grateful Japanese official wrote a few years later, "a green dragon had raised its head from the waves" and as a result, on the Japanese island of Kyushu, "the coast was piled high with corpses."[5]

The humiliating disaster did nothing to diminish China's arrogance and its sense of entitlement manifested in a tributary system that required the Japanese to send envoys at regular intervals in order to demonstrate submission. In the cases where Japan's rulers, once again, failed to demonstrate a sufficient degree of deference, the wrath from China's court was predictable. A letter from the 15th-century emperor Zhu Yuanzhang suggests the general atmosphere of the relationship: "You stupid eastern barbarians! Your king and courtiers are not acting correctly; you have disturbed neighboring countries in all directions."[6]

This set the tone for the uneasy relationship between China and Japan in late medieval times. Full-scale war broke out at the end of the 16th century. As had been the case nearly a millennium earlier, Korea formed the battleground. A samurai army landed on the peninsula and was harboring plans to enter China as well. China was huge, and the Japanese commanders asked, not for the last time in history, if they might have set their sights too high. "I wonder," a Japanese officer wrote in a letter home to his family, "if we will be able to provide enough men to enter and rule that country."[7]

Just as the political relationship changed throughout the centuries of conflict and cooperation, the Chinese views of Japan also underwent transformation. In Chinese texts from the first millennium AD, Japan was occasionally described as "a country of gentlemen" and a "society appreciating decorum."[8] An official dynastic history praised the Japanese, saying that "by nature, they are honest. They have a refined manner."[9] Over time, this was to change, and the positive depictions of the Japanese were, in the Chinese mind, to yield to more sinister images.

One much-feared figure did more than any other to transform Chinese perceptions: that of the Japanese pirate. For centuries, seaborne Japanese raiders were a threat to Chinese communities along the coastline, reputed to "arrive like a typhoon and leave like a flash of lightning."[10] The pirates lived by a strict law which required that "they all fought to the death," a Chinese chronicler notes.[11] Their code of conduct also allowed a staggering degree of cruelty. In a particularly notorious episode in the mid-15th century, a gang of Japanese pirates surrounded a village in east China's Zhejiang province, killing most of the inhabitants and looting their homes before setting them ablaze. A contemporary account explains what happened to some of the survivors: "They guessed the gender of the fetuses of the pregnant women they had captured, then slashed the women's bellies open to see who was right since they had made bets of wine on the outcome."[12]

One source describes an assault by Japanese pirates on northeast China's Liaodong peninsula in 1419 and their attempt to seize the riches of the city of Wanghaiguo: "The Commissioner-in-Chief, Liu Rong, taking charge in person, sped his crack troops to Wanghaiguo. The pirates, numbering several thousand men, came in twenty ships … and lay siege to city. "Liu sprang the trap, engaged them in battle and deployed troops to block their retreat route … Liu Rong threw in all the forces to attack them. Altogether 742 heads were taken and 857 men were captured."[13]

The scourge of the pirates continued for centuries and at times forced the Chinese empire to expend enormous resources as it boosted coastal defenses. The pirates came to include a variety of nationalities and, according to some historians, they may at times have numbered more Chinese than Japanese.[14] This did not change the fact that most people in China saw them as originating from the mysterious Japanese archipelago to the east and came to think of the strangers across the ocean as only partly human. "They are as wild as wolf cubs," a 16th-century Chinese author wrote. "It is their basic nature to hurt others."[15]

Technology progressed, cultural habits changed, and dynasties waxed and waned, but the basic pattern of Sino-Japanese interaction remained roughly the same for a millennium and a half. China formed the center of gravity of international politics in East Asia, and Japan mostly accepted this, although intermittently it showed itself in a defiant mode. This pattern might well have continued indefinitely were it not for the arrival of a completely new set of actors on the scene. They were

Europeans, and they were the vanguard of a force that would change the world. That force was Western imperialism.

When the Portuguese explorer Francisco Zeimoto set foot on the Japanese island of Kanegashima in the 1540s, he brought with him an invention which captured the local imagination more than any other. It was a firearm capable of plucking birds from the sky with almost supernatural ease. The island's ruler, who doubtless imagined other uses for this device, was said to show a particular interest and secured a weapon for himself. Soon, the technology was copied throughout the island and elsewhere in Japan and, little more than a decade later, when another Portuguese adventurer passed through the isolated country, he was told that there was now a total of 300,000 muskets in the Japanese islands. "From this alone," he wrote, "it is easy to understand what kind of people they are and how naturally they take to military exercise, which they enjoy more than any other nation that is known to date."[16]

Zeimoto and his shipmates were few in numbers, and with their light skin and their brown and red hair, they were little more than exotic curiosities to the people they encountered. Soon the sailors and merchants of the European powers would be arriving in East Asia in much greater numbers, bringing about the first era of true globalization, with the economies of all continents bound together in a tight network of maritime trade. Both China and Japan were affected, but their vastly different sizes determined the ways in which they reacted.

For a century after the arrival of Zeimoto and his contemporaries, Japan allowed trade not just with the Portuguese, but also with the Dutch and the British and, in addition, it allowed Catholic missionaries to seek converts among the Japanese. It was a spectacular success for Christianity, with half a million baptized souls speaking their own language about spiritual needs being met by the new religion. It was not to last. Fearing the fate of the Philippines, which had recently become a Spanish colony, the Japanese rulers decided to crack down on the foreign faith. In 1597, a total of 26 Roman Catholics, both European missionaries and local converts, were crucified. Over the coming decades, the persecution continued, with unabated ferocity, until Christianity was extinguished or forced entirely underground.

Japan's political masters went even further in their zeal to protect their civilization and keep it undiluted by alien influences. By the middle of the 1600s, in a dramatic move that is almost unique in the history of mankind, they decided to turn their backs to the world and seal their country off entirely from Europe. For the next two centuries, Japan was inaccessible to virtually all Western powers, allowing only trade with the Dutch, who were permitted to maintain a regular presence on a man-made islet in Nagasaki harbor.

China also saw occasional and sometimes violent outbursts of xenophobia, but it never experienced a sweeping anti-Western revolution of anything resembling the consequence and completeness seen in Japan. China was too vast and too preoccupied with the challenges of governing a continent-sized empire to feel threatened at any existential level by the few European missionaries, advisors, and merchants making it to its shores. Rather, it signaled a sense of complacent indifference to anything the West might have to offer.

This was made abundantly clear in 1793 when Britain sent its first official mission to the imperial court in Beijing, headed by George Macartney, an experienced colonial administrator. Hoping to open China for trade, the British delegation had brought 600 boxes of presents, including elaborate clocks and globes. None of it made any impression on the Chinese emperor, Qianlong. "We have never valued ingenious articles, nor do we have the slightest need of your country's manufacturers," he said in a letter addressed to Britain's King George III. "You, O King, should simply act in conformity with our wishes by strengthening your loyalty and swearing perpetual obedience."[17]

Although the letter was sure to cause anger among the confident British, the Chinese emperor did have something of a point. China was at the time probably still the world's largest economy,[18] and while its technologies were beginning to lag seriously behind, the gap remained narrow. Even so, Qianlong's empire was weaker than he was able to imagine. A disappointed Macartney dismissed China as "an old, crazy first-rate man-of-war," which, when ruled by incompetent people would "drift for some time as a wreck, and will then be dashed to pieces on the shore."[19] His description was not far off. Qianlong and his officials failed to realize one crucial fact. The kind of Western imperialism they were encountering now was qualitatively different from the imperialism of preceding centuries. It was much more powerful, and much deadlier for those unable to come up with an efficient response.

Qianlong's descendants were to learn that, to their chagrin, half a century after the Macartney mission. The British mission's failure did not stop trade between China and Britain, but the commerce was one-sided. While European consumers coveted a variety of Chinese products, British merchants really only had success with selling one item to the Chinese: opium. The Chinese empire decided to ban the trade in the drug, triggering a British reaction in the form of the dispatch of the Royal Navy. In a series of humiliating defeats inflicted on the Chinese, the superiority that Western military technology had now gained was exposed for anyone to see.

Epitomizing the British predominance was the steamship *Nemesis*, recently completed as the nation's first ocean-going warship made almost entirely from iron. Against this, what innovations was China able to muster? Attack-monkeys, for example. At the eastern port city of Ningbo, one of the Chinese strongholds, defenders had prepared 19 monkeys with firecrackers tied to their backs. The intention was to throw them onto moored British ships, but the plan never came to fruition, as no Chinese soldier was able to get within flinging distance of any of the enemy vessels.[20]

The Opium War ended in 1842 when British and Chinese envoys signed the Treaty of Nanjing. It opened five Chinese ports to foreign commerce, and it granted extraterritoriality to British citizens in China, meaning that if they committed crimes on Chinese soil, they were entitled to have their case heard in a British court of law. The treaty also ceded to Britain a modest piece of Chinese territory. In the words of Foreign Secretary Lord Henry John Temple Palmerston, it was a "barren island with hardly a house upon it." Its name was Hong Kong.

Britain kicked the Chinese door in, but other colonial powers soon followed suit. The Nanjing agreement became a model for other "unequal treaties" signed with Western powers. In the course of the ensuing decade France, Russia and even Sweden entered into similar agreements with China. More were to come. It was the start of a period later known to the Chinese as "the century of shame" which saw the once-proud empire reduced almost to a semi-colony, and only really approached its end during World War II and its immediate aftermath.

Amid the rush to open up China, the islands of Japan remained hermetically closed to Western influences. It would take a special effort to unlock them, and when it was eventually done, it was accomplished not by any of the old European powers, but by a nation whose youthful energy made it stand out. In stark contrast to the Chinese and Japanese civilizations, it was barely a century old, but in due course it would have a more profound impact on the history of East Asia than any other. America was about to burst onto the world stage.

On a misty July day in 1853, four dark ships appeared off the town of Uraga in Japan's Edo Bay. The Americans had arrived. On board the steam frigate USS *Susquehanna*, the flagship of the small but powerful fleet, was Commodore Matthew C. Perry. He was not the first American to visit the secretive Japanese islands, but he had studied the previous attempts at prying open the hermit nation, and he was determined to succeed where others had failed. A large man with a commanding presence, he was carrying a letter from his government, not asking but demanding that Japan open up to foreign trade.

In a way, Japan was not even the main objective. The longer-term US goal was to establish it as a station towards the much vaster Chinese market, but few if any Japanese appreciated this. The appearance of the American vessels—the "Black Ships," as they quickly became known, partly through the medium of rapidly spreading and easy-to-learn ballads—set off scenes akin to alien invasion movies of a much later age. In the capital of Edo, now Tokyo, a contemporary account reported that "the whole city was in an uproar. In all directions were seen mothers flying with their children in their arms, and men with mothers on their backs."[21]

The Americans, as French political thinker Alexis de Tocqueville had already remarked two decades earlier, were "called by nature to be a great maritime people," and while commerce was the main impetus drawing them to the sea, they were able and willing to put force behind efforts to open up new markets.[22] When Japanese boats manned with fierce-looking samurai warriors surrounded his fleet, Commodore Perry did not waver. Aiming for the largest impact possible, he ordered blanks to be fired with the state-of-the-art Paixhans guns on board his ships. The samurai kept up appearances, but they had been given a lesson in the crushing technological superiority of the new arrivals. After a little more than a week, the fleet left Japan, but with a firm pledge to be back the next year.

The following months were filled with tense discussions among the feudal lords who held most of the political power in Japan. Few of them welcomed the foreigners, but virtually all understood how powerful they were. Through their sparse contacts with the outside world, mostly the Chinese and the Dutch, they were somewhat informed about the growing might of the West, and they also knew the fate that had befallen China in the Opium War little more than a decade earlier. Despite the odds, a handful of Japanese strongmen advocated outright resistance to show off "our martial vigor to the whole world."[23] This boded ill for the second meeting with the Americans, but in fact it went surprisingly well.

The presents that Perry brought on his return in March 1854, including a quarter-size model locomotive big enough for people to ride astride, were not all that different from the ones that had accompanied Macartney on his fruitless mission to the Chinese emperor's court six decades earlier. They served the same purpose and were intended to showcase Western ingenuity and mechanical skill, but while the Chinese had contemptuously dismissed the British gifts as insignificant playthings, the Japanese delighted in them. As the model train was set up on the beach near Yokohama, samurai in flowing robes lined up for a trip on the steam-spewing marvel.[24]

The Japanese fascination with technology was much more than just a fling. It revealed a willingness to change and turned out to be essential for Japan's decision for the wholesale adoption of Western ways. Reformists within the Japanese establishment understood that their nation needed a revolution in its relationship with the outside world. In order for that to happen, a corresponding revolution in domestic affairs was required. In late 1867 and 1868 they succeeded in wrestling power from the elite that had held sway for two centuries, and reassert the emperor as the center of political authority.

The emperor, still only a 15-year-old boy, was posthumously known as Meiji, and the sweeping reforms that took place under his reign have been given the name the Meiji Restoration. It changed Japan profoundly. A constitution was drafted, a professional bureaucracy trained, and a parliament elected, all following a European model. Modern roads and railways were built, and harbors capable of handling the largest steamships of the age were constructed. Crucially, the educational system was thoroughly revamped.

A person born into the feudal Japanese society of the 1840s would hardly have recognized the industrialized nation-state he grew old in around the turn of the

20th century. The Japanese who had seen the "Black Ships" appear over the horizon had worn the same clothes as their ancestors had half a millennium earlier. Now, they adopted the hats and suits—and often also the mannerisms—of the West. Other, more profound changes may have taken place on the inside. At the start of the reforms, an English-language newspaper could still write that "the Japanese are a happy race, and being content with little, are not likely to achieve much."[25] That was not to last. Modernization had far-reaching consequences for the Japanese people, giving rise to traits that would later be considered part and parcel of the Japanese national character. Punctuality was one of them. Public clocks began appearing everywhere, reminding people that every minute counted.[26]

The Japanese response to the West marked a stark and illuminating contrast with China's reaction. China had tried to take on Britain during the Opium War, failing miserably as it simply did not have the material wherewithal to confront the world's most advanced power. Japan opted for domestic reforms first, before even thinking about a more assertive foreign policy. Just as important, China was fearful of the consequences of abandoning its millennia-old culture and therefore attempted an *à la carte* approach to modernization, picking only the elements that could be immediately useful, such as industrial and military technologies. The technologies were of little use without a modern mindset, but they resisted any kind of Westernization.[27]

While China was still struggling to come up with an adequate response to the West, Japan embraced it much more fully, impressed by the evidence of strength and vigor its officials had witnessed during long fact-finding missions in Europe and North America. In Japan in the late 19th century, foreign meant progressive. Mori Arinori, the Japanese chargé d'affaires to the United States, even advocated abandoning the complicated Japanese language in favor of the wholesale adoption of the simpler English tongue, and he was not alone in making that recommendation.[28]

It would be wrong to assert that Japan did not have its fair share of traditionalists who wanted nothing to do with the outside world, but they were in the minority and, in the end, they were unable to turn the tide of history. It was an advantage for Japan that, unlike China, it was not misled by delusions about being the center of the world, and as a result it faced fewer obstacles to accepting the modern international system of nation-states.[29]

Japan found a convenient partner in the United States. Many Americans felt a special bond with Japan in the late 19th century, as they were both nations undergoing rapid industrialization. At the same time, however, there was an unmistakable tenor of missionary zeal in the American efforts. "No one expects the nations of Asia to be awakened by any other influences than our own from the lethargy into which they sank nearly three thousand years ago, under the spell of superstition and caste," Senator William Henry Seward, later secretary of state under Abraham Lincoln, told an audience at Yale University in July 1854.[30]

The missionary impetus was also active in a quite literal sense. American missionaries fanned out across Japan faster than the missionaries of any other Western country, reviving the Christian faith which had been practiced in secrecy by a few devotees since the crackdown in the mid-1600s, while also seeking new converts. It was an uphill struggle, and the Japanese population was influenced by generations of anti-Christian propaganda. The *New York Times* reported about a Christian family with a female servant from the countryside who "used to fly past the door like an arrow if the family knelt at prayer; they were weaving a charm, she thought, that would bewitch her."[31] Still, by the end of the 1880s, it was believed by many, including some Japanese, that Japan would "soon be a Christian nation."[32]

To be sure, there was an undercurrent of mutual suspicion throughout the encounter between the Japanese and the Americans. It had been there right from the beginning. Commodore Perry and his fellow officers had noticed it, complaining about two sides of the Japanese character. Their local interlocutors came across as being perfect, polite gentlemen capable of telling abject lies with a straight face. In the words of one US observer, these first impressions, superficial as they might have been, "helped to set a pattern of American thinking about the Japanese that has persisted for a century: courtesy and hypocrisy."[33]

China was all too aware of the Japanese successes, and foresighted statesmen close to the emperor understood this could eventually become a major national problem. "Although the various European powers are strong, they are still 70,000 *li*[34] apart from us," wrote Li Hongzhang, China's most influential official, in 1874. "Japan is as near as in the courtyard, or on the threshold, and is prying into the weaknesses of our defense measures. Undoubtedly, she will become China's permanent and great anxiety."[35]

By the late 1800s, Japan was sufficiently modernized that it could begin thinking about foreign policy. Following the conventions of the time, this meant creating an empire. In turn, this required establishing a powerful modern military. In the course of two decades from the early 1870s onwards, Japan ticked off all the requirements for entering the ranks of the world's foremost military powers, including universal conscription, a General Staff modeled after the Prussian example, and advanced education for officers.[36]

The opportunity to see if it all worked in practice came in the First Sino-Japanese War of 1894 and 1895. Similar to the conflict that had caused the wooden fleets of the two nations to clash on the Paekchon River 12 centuries earlier, Korea was the *casus belli*, and the main theater of war. In the summer of 1894, China's waning Qing dynasty sent troops to the peninsula to prop up the Korean king in a time of local rebellion. In reaction to this move, Japan decided to go to war. It did so in a way that was to form a pattern in later wars, with a surprise naval attack. Without a declaration of war, in late July three Japanese cruisers attacked two Chinese warships returning from Korea. In the same operation, the Japanese force sank the Chinese troop transport *Kowshing*, killing hundreds.[37]

In the following days, as it formally declared war on China, Japan moved quickly to push the Chinese enemy out of the Korean peninsula. This was accomplished by the end of September, after a bloody battle over the northern city of Pyongyang. Pursuing the retreating enemy, the Japanese marched into northeast China, winning one battle after another. The war ended with a treaty signed in March 1895, imposing an onerous burden on China. Most painfully, it had to cede the island of Taiwan in the southeast and the Liaodong peninsula in the northeast "in perpetuity." European powers, unsettled by the sudden triumph of the Japanese, demanded that they relinquish the Liaodong peninsula, while allowing them to keep Taiwan.

The Japanese troops were contemptuous of their Chinese foes—or "pig-tails," as they called them with reference to the long cue that most were wearing. "It really is laughable," a doctor serving at a Japanese field hospital wrote home in a letter. "They fight for a moment then run a hundred miles so our real problem is chasing after them."[38] Similarly, the Chinese civilians were subjected to Japanese ridicule. "They see our troops and ask which country they are from," a war correspondent wrote. "Upon being told they are forces of the Japanese Empire, they still do not understand and ask where is this country Japan."[39]

The Japanese disdain for the Chinese translated into brutal treatment of those no longer able to fight. A much-published instance of this was the fate of the survivors of the transport vessel *Kowshing*. As the Chinese ship was listing and slowly filling with water, a witness saw a boat filled with armed sailors lowered from one of the Japanese warships. He believed it was coming to the rescue of the defeated enemy. "He was sadly mistaken," a newspaper reported. "They fired into the men on board the sinking ship, and they fired at the swimming men."[40]

Later in the war, a soldier of the Japanese 1st Division, Okabe Makio, described in his diary what happened after his unit entered the Chinese city of Port Arthur on Liaodong peninsula and encountered the head of a Japanese soldier displayed on a wooden stake: "Anyone we saw in the town, we killed. The streets were filled with corpses, so many they blocked our way. We killed people in their homes; by and large, there wasn't a single house without from three to six dead. Blood was flowing and the smell was awful."[41] A foreign observer reported the streets littered with perhaps thousands of bodies, "some with not a limb unsevered, some with heads hacked, cross-cut and split lengthwise, some ripped open, not by chance but with careful precision."[42]

With the benefit of hindsight, one can say that the end of the First Sino-Japanese War pointed directly towards Japan's next war, with Russia, ten years in the future. Among the Western powers that forced Japan to give up the Liaodong peninsula, none

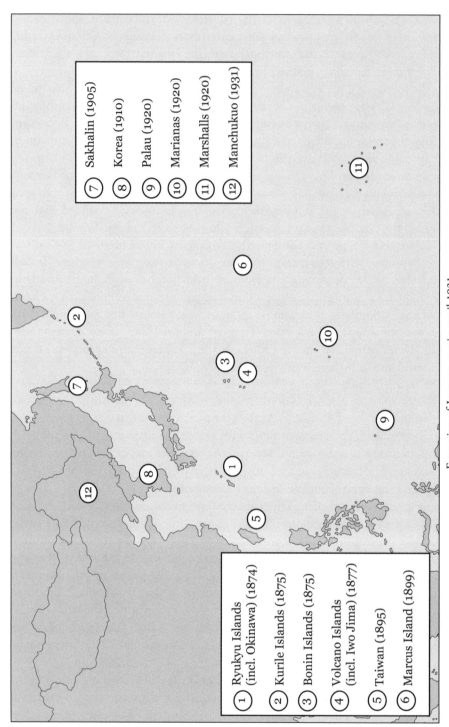

7 Sakhalin (1905)
8 Korea (1910)
9 Palau (1920)
10 Marianas (1920)
11 Marshalls (1920)
12 Manchukuo (1931)

1 Ryukyu Islands (incl. Okinawa) (1874)
2 Kurile Islands (1875)
3 Bonin Islands (1875)
4 Volcano Islands (incl. Iwo Jima) (1877)
5 Taiwan (1895)
6 Marcus Island (1899)

Expansion of Japanese empire until 1931.

was more active than the Czarist empire to the north. There were ulterior motives for this, as became clear three years later when Russia was able to secure a lease of Port Arthur on the same peninsula, strengthening its strategic position in northeast Asia immensely. Russo-Japanese rivalry was heating up, and Japanese planners went literally from the triumph against China to planning how to take on Russia.

Japan had won its war against China by being successful both on land and at sea, but it had been victorious with what was undeniably a second-rate navy, coming out on top only because China's navy was so much worse off. A war with Russia would be an entirely different matter, and Japan spent the years around the turn of the 20th century funding its largest naval expansion project to date, including the commission of six state-of-the-art battleships ordered from British yards.[43] It was no coincidence that the ships were built there. In 1902, in a strategic move aimed at isolating Russia, Japan entered into an alliance with Great Britain—its only formal treaty of this kind until the pact with Germany and Italy in 1940.[44]

The ambitious build-up coincided with a growing realization in Japanese strategic circles that, in the future, naval power would be of paramount importance, not least because of Japan's special conditions. According to Admiral Satō Tetsutarō, president of the Naval War College and a leading naval theorist, geography had created a clear parallel between Japan's strategic situation and that of the two Anglo-Saxon powers. "Among the powers in the world," he wrote in a seminal text, "there are only three countries that can defend themselves primarily with navies. They are the United Kingdom, the United States and Japan."[45]

Given the turn that events would take later in the 20th century, it is ironic that Japanese strategic thinkers were inspired by an American. Alfred Thayer Mahan, an officer in the US Navy, had published *The Influence of Sea Power Upon History* and other pioneering works in the 1890s, and while he had followers across the globe, nowhere did his ideas find a more receptive audience than in Japan. Mahan argued that "command of the sea" was a pre-requisite for great power status, referring to the need for a nation such as the United States to protect global trade routes. Japanese adherents transformed his ideas into a more modest view that a strong navy was needed to protect and defend a dangerously exposed island nation.[46]

Despite this fundamentally defensive mindset, Japan was prepared to burst into sharp, aggressive action when called for. This was how the war with Russia started. The Japanese government had sought to divide northeast Asia with the Czarist regime, offering to give up any claims in Manchuria—a territory in northeast China roughly the size of modern France, Germany, Italy and the United Kingdom combined—in return for control of Korea. Russia declined, and Japan responded the way it had a decade earlier in the war with China, by launching a naval attack without prior warning.

Shortly after midnight on February 9, 1904, a group of ten Japanese destroyers entered the Russian Pacific fleet's base at Port Arthur, firing off torpedoes. Although the operation lacked any coordination due to the darkness, it left two Russian battleships and one cruiser damaged.[47] A full day later, on February 10, Japan declared war on the Russian empire. "We have unhappily come to open hostilities against Russia," the Japanese emperor said in a message to his armed forces. The streets of Tokyo filled with people shouting "*Banzai!*"[48]

The enthusiasm was somewhat misplaced, since the war had only just started. The Japanese Navy blockaded the Russian fleet at Port Arthur, while Japanese land forces laid siege to the area. Meanwhile, Japanese soldiers marched into northeast China from Korea. Russia dispatched parts of its powerful Baltic Fleet, which would, however, be months underway. This created a situation in which Japan pushed for a quick resolution on the battlefield, while Russia played for time, until the Baltic force could arrive.

In January 1905, Port Arthur fell to the Japanese. The Baltic Fleet was still thousands of miles away and did not reach Far Eastern waters until spring. On May 27 and 28, the main naval forces of the two sides met in a deadly clash in the Tsushima Strait between Japan and the Korean peninsula. It was a resounding victory for the Japanese, who, led by Admiral Tōgō Heihachirō, benefited from superior gunnery and higher-quality ordnance. It was also a victory of the naval program that Japan had undertaken over the preceding decade. "Though the decisive battle took such a short time," Tōgō wrote, "it required ten years of preparation."[49]

The action at Tsushima may have been brief, but it was filled with terror for the participants. A British naval observer, Captain William C. Pakenham, described the scene on board the Japanese battleship *Asahi* after it had been hit by Russian shells. The explosions sent scraps of human flesh spraying through the air, and he himself was hit by one of the flying pieces. "It was the right half of a man's lower jaw, with the teeth missing," he wrote in a report to the Admiralty in London. "Everything and everybody for twenty yards round was bespattered with tiny drops of blood and minute particles of flesh that adhered to whatever they struck."[50]

On land, the Russo-Japanese War was a harbinger of the world war that was to erupt a decade into the future. It showed what happened when infantry charged in thick waves against heavily fortified defenses, running into artillery barrages and machine-gun salvoes. In the battle of Nanshan, not far from Port Arthur, the Japanese armed forces sustained 4,300 casualties, more than during the entire war with China. A young Japanese captain, critical of the way his army had attempted to rush to victory at Nanshan, warned against "shortcuts." The cost, he said, is paid in "unexpected quantities of blood."[51]

Despite the heavy losses, there was no question that Japan had achieved a crushing victory. In peace negotiations brokered by US President Theodore Roosevelt, Russia handed over its lease of Port Arthur and the surrounding areas, and it also gave Japan control of part of the strategically crucial Manchurian railroad. In addition, Russia acknowledged Japan's dominant position in Korea. For a generation of Japanese military men who had taken part in the key battles, it was a formative experience. Among those injured at Tsushima was a 21-year-old junior officer by the name of Yamamoto Isoroku, who lost two fingers on his left hand. The son of a samurai, he would much later go on to plan the attack on Pearl Harbor.

Abroad, the outcome of the war reverberated because it was the first time in generations that a European nation had been beaten by a non-white people, forcing many Westerners to readjust their views about the Japanese. The Canadian poet E. Pauline Johnson wrote about the "brave little Jap, who fights for Chrysanthemum Land."[52] The generally positive view of Japan was reinforced by reports that its armed forces had treated prisoners leniently, even with kindness. The International Red Cross remarked on this, and captured Russian officers admitted that "the Japanese were doing everything that the situation allowed for."[53]

This contrasted with Japan's behavior during both the First Sino-Japanese War and the so-called Boxer Rebellion, an anti-foreign insurgency in China in the years 1899 to 1901 which had got its name because of the calisthenics practiced by the rebels, reminiscent of "shadow boxing." Japan, along with other colonial powers, had sent troops to suppress the rising, and had often proceeded with great brutality. The same was true for Japanese troops' behavior towards civilians in Korea, which Japan was soon to annex and turn into a colony. In short, Japan was humane only towards fellow imperialists.

Japan in the early 20th century still identified with the European, "white" brand of colonialism and therefore was keen to project the idea that the Japanese, even though they were embedded in Asia geographically and culturally, were more Western than their neighbors. A leading Japanese Buddhist argued in May 1904 that "the Japanese have a white heart underneath a yellow skin. It is the Russians who are the Yellow Peril because they have a yellow heart under their white skin."[54] Still, not everyone believed the Japanese would remain entrenched in the Western camp. "I have no doubt," US President Roosevelt wrote in a letter, "that they include all white men as being people who, as a whole, they dislike, and whose past arrogance they resent."[55]

Nations that were under the yoke of Western imperialism did indeed interpret the Japanese triumph as a triumph for all non-Westerners. In July 1905, Chinese revolutionary Sun Yat-sen was on a ship *en route* from Europe to Japan. Passing through the Suez Canal, he met an Arab who asked him if he was Japanese. "I told him, no, I was a Chinese," Sun later recalled. "He told me he had observed vast armies of Russian soldiers being shipped back to Russia from the Far East, a fact which seemed an undeniable sign of Russia's admission of defeat. The joy of this Arab, as a member of the great Asiatic race, seemed to know no bounds."[56]

Despite the humiliation in the war with Japan in 1894–95 and again during the Boxer Rising, it was not unusual among Chinese at the time to find inspiration, and a sense of pan-Asian solidarity, in the growing importance of Japan. Among the Chinese who rooted for Japan was a young primary school pupil in China's southern province of Hunan. He would later reminisce how he enjoyed the song *The Battle of the Yellow Sea*, written in honor of one of Japan's many successes. "At that time I knew and felt the beauty of Japan," he later explained, "and felt something of her pride and might, in this song of her victory over Russia." The student's name was Mao Zedong.[57]

The admiration of Japan was mixed with envy and with a feeling that China could and should do better. "Take a look at Japan," Sun Yat-sen wrote. "They opened their markets to the West later than China and began their westernization later, too … but their achievement today is considerable."[58] More importantly, for many Chinese, admiration was soon to yield to anger, distrust, and even hatred as suspicions grew that in the age of imperialism, Japan was not a friend but an enemy. This antagonism was to prove lasting and become one of the main factors in pushing East Asian history down a violent path during the entire first half of the 20th century.

"Tsingtau Has Fallen" the German newspaper *Berliner Tageblatt* reported in huge Gothic letters across its front page on November 8, 1914. The day before Japanese soldiers had captured Germany's Chinese enclave—in today's rendering of Chinese words usually written as Qingdao—on the mainland's northeast coast. The final Japanese assault, taking place after a six-week-long siege, had been bloody for both sides. "Since the Japanese could constantly bring up reinforcements and fill the gaps emerging in their line, the heroic German defenders were forced to yield," the paper wrote.[59]

Japan's victory in China, achieved with British help and at a cost of 1,445 Japanese soldiers killed against 200 dead Germans, was the direct outcome of its alliance with the United Kingdom and the other Entente Powers in the Great War that had just erupted in Europe. In a series of operations, Japan swiftly gained control of Germany's possessions in the East. It was eventually forgotten, overshadowed by the German-Japanese partnership in the next world war, but it enabled Japan to consolidate the foothold in northeast Asia that it had been establishing over the previous decades. It also gave it access to a number of strategically located islands in the Pacific that had so far been held by Germany. Finally, it boosted Japan's confidence and prompted it to take a decisive step towards a role as the paramount power in the region.

This meant pushing aside China, the sick man of Asia. The timing seemed opportune. In 1911 and 1912, more than two millennia of imperial rule in China had come to an end when the Qing dynasty had collapsed and a new republican government, initially under Sun Yat-sen, had been installed. Against this backdrop, in early 1915 the Japanese government handed over a list of 21 demands to the new Chinese government in Beijing. They were wide-ranging, stretching from formal acceptance of Japanese control of the former German areas to the employment of Japanese advisors to assist the Chinese government at the highest levels. It was clear from the outset that the demands were unacceptable to China, even in its weakened state.

Especially at the public level, resistance was intense, and a wave of anti-Japanese rhetoric filled the papers, while protesters poured into the streets. Individual episodes highlighted the extent of the Chinese humiliation, since it was now being pressured by a fellow Asian nation that it had only recently considered inferior. In May 1915, a man by the name of Qin Lijun committed suicide in the province of Shandong in east China. He left a letter to his employer, a Japanese railway company. "The Japanese language I studied in Japan for ten years has completely disappeared from my mind," he wrote. "I was therefore not able to serve the company anymore. I could not provide food and clothes for my family, so I had to die."[60]

The demands signaled the emergence of a more assertive Japanese stance in continental northeast Asia. General Terauchi Masatake, the Japanese governor of Korea at the time, was a chief proponent of what he himself called "an Asian Monroe Doctrine," referring to US President James Monroe's decision in 1823 to declare the western hemisphere off-limits to interference by the imperialist powers of Europe. "Although we will not insist upon excluding Europeans and Americans," he wrote in a letter to an acquaintance, "it is proper to inform the Westerners that, up to a point, Asia should be under the control of Asians." [61]

Statements such as this made it evident that Japan wished to become the primary power in China to the partial exclusion of other foreign powers and sent jitters through Western capitals. It ensured foreign support for China's resistance to the 21 demands, and in the end, the Japanese government was forced to back down and sign a much-reduced list of 13 demands. All in all, it was a diplomatic setback for Japan which left governments in the West wondering what the long-term implications of Japanese ambitions might be for the region. Britain was led to question its alliance with Japan, and a few years later it abrogated the treaty, moved also in part by American pressure.

Even at this early stage, some clear-headed observers identified China as the key to relations between the United States and Japan. "In the Far East, peace can be permanently secured only if the two great Powers lying on either side of the Pacific work together in harmony and understanding," said Thomas Lamont, J. P. Morgan's operating head in Japan, as early as 1920. "The first evidence of this should be in their common attitude towards the Chinese nation."[62] Two decades later, when the United States and Japan clashed over China, these words would sound almost prophetic.

China would not have offered itself as an object of Japanese voracity had it not fallen so precipitously low in the preceding decades. With the removal of the Qing emperor, the proud old civilization had no unified, central authority in charge. It was what would later be known as a failed state. Some believed that after three millennia of turbulent history, it had no future. "Fifty years from now, there won't be any China," an American diplomat predicted in 1915. "Some of its provinces may continue to exist as independent states, together or separately, but there will be no Chinese nation as there is now."[63]

Sun Yat-sen's dream of a unified republic under the leadership of his Nationalist Party gradually fell apart, as power increasingly lay in the hands of local strongmen, who sometimes commanded areas larger than European countries and were locked in fierce rivalries and internecine battles. These individuals, known as warlords, quickly established a reputation at home and abroad for their eccentric and flamboyant behavior. A case in point was Feng Yuxiang, nicknamed the "Christian general," who reputedly baptized his troops by water hose to save time. Despite these somewhat comical antics, the wars people like Feng engaged in were no laughing matter. One of these, the Second Zhili-Fengtian War in late 1924, cost tens of thousands of casualties. As usual in this kind of conflict, civilians were the first to pay. Warlord troops would enter into villages "evicting peasants from their homes and forcing their womenfolk to remain as domestic servants and worse." Sometimes, the peasants fought back, pushing the warlord troops out of their villages in small-scale battles that almost became civil wars within the civil war.[64]

The anarchy was not to last. The Nationalist Party in its power base in south China gradually became stronger and was able in the early 1920s to secure assistance from the Soviet Union, which provided both advisors and financial backing. In return, Moscow demanded an alliance between the Nationalists and the Communists, a fledgling but growing force in Chinese politics. This coincided with the rise within the Nationalist ranks of a young and ambitious officer by the name of Chiang Kai-shek. He was intensely patriotic, but at the same time deeply influenced by Japan, having entered a military preparatory school in Tokyo when he was still in his late teens. After Sun Yat-sen died in 1925, Chiang eventually emerged as his heir and used the power put at his disposal to embark on a long-anticipated military campaign to unify all of China under the Nationalist banner. The campaign, which began in the summer of 1926 and ended up lasting two years, came to be known as the Northern Expedition and would evolve into what has been called the largest military operation anywhere between the two world wars.[65]

At the start of the campaign, Chiang and his commanders led an army of a quarter million troops north, defeating local warlords on their way and incorporating their lands into the growing territory under Nationalist control. His troops made progress not just because of better training, morale, and equipment, but also because they often had the civilian population on their side. Usually the peasants were forced to sell their produce to warlord soldiers offering money not worth the paper it was printed on. The Nationalists had a reputation for paying real money for their food, relieving them of many of the supply problems they would otherwise have had.[66]

Chiang was a pragmatist when he had to be one, and despite serious ideological differences, he initially acquiesced in the alliance with the Communist Party. However, it was a marriage of convenience, and in the spring of 1927, Chiang decided to cut the link, brutally. Allying himself with the conservative wing of the Nationalist Party, he struck once the Northern Expedition had reached Shanghai, a hotbed of labor movement activism. On April 12, Nationalist soldiers in cooperation with local gangsters rounded up leading members of the Communist party in the city, carrying out summary executions.

In the reign of terror that followed, any signs of protest were met with lethal force. The purge of Communist elements soon spread to other big cities, pushing the Communist movement almost to the edge of extinction. The survivors fled to the countryside. There, they reorganized and rethought their strategy. They concluded that revolution in the cities was not viable for the time being, and they turned themselves into a largely peasant movement. They would stay that way for the next two decades.

As Chiang's Northern Expedition continued after a pause of several months, it pushed onwards and in April 1928 it reached Jinan, a city of about 400,000 people and the capital of east China's Shandong province. A minor incident led to a clash between Chiang's troops and Japanese soldiers, who had rushed to protect their nation's consulate and business interests in the city. The confrontation escalated, with atrocities committed on both sides. A group of Japanese captives were castrated and killed, while a ranking Chinese official was blinded and put to death. The Japanese eventually pushed out the Chinese troops with the use of massive force that led to the deaths of thousands, including fleeing civilians.[67]

The American newspaper reporter Hallett Abend arrived in Jinan in the aftermath of the carnage, shocked to observe for the first time "death from violence in the mass." Lying scattered in the streets, he saw "human flesh blasted by shrapnel, the dead too long untended in the dust or in slimy gutters, the mangled bodies of children gnawed by rats the night before."[68] It was Chiang's first hostile encounter with the Japanese, and recognizing his own weakness, he decided to back down, even apologizing to Japan for the incident. Privately, in his diary, he vowed to write each day "a way to kill Japanese." But for the time being, patience was called for. Before "one can settle scores," he wrote, "one must be strong."[69]

The first order of the day was national unification, and Chiang came significantly closer to that aim when he brought the Northern Expedition to a successful completion later that year. As one of his first steps, he moved the national capital from Beijing to Nanjing. This was fraught with symbolic meaning as it marked a clear break with past Beijing-based regimes, which had not been able to put China back on the path towards former glory. It also had more practical explanations, as it enabled him to be closer to Shanghai and the heartland of economic power.

From Nanjing, Chiang set about reforming China and pushing it into the 20th century. His government started spending heavily on roads, bridges, and telecommunications. It began modernizing the schools and universities. To finance this, it took steps to improve the taxation system. It set up a central bank and introduced a new national currency. The military also embarked on an effort to modernize itself, with the eager help of European military officers who found employment hard to come by in the general pacifist mood of the 1920s. The press, while by no means completely free, was under fewer constraints than ever before or since in Chinese history.[70]

Chiang was onto something. For the first time since the fall of the Qing dynasty in 1911 and 1912, most of China was under the leadership of a man with a coherent vision for its future, and with the means to bring it about. It was almost a golden age, and it would later be known as "the Nanjing decade," for in the end it lasted no longer than that. Moreover, even during this brief period, China was virtually never entirely at peace. Time and again, Chiang was forced to divert his attention towards rebellious regional leaders, or the Communists, not for some minor skirmishes, but for full-scale civil wars, with tens of thousands of casualties. Likewise, the borders were continuous hotspots of trouble, and while Japan was the biggest challenge, it was not the only one.

The Sino-Soviet conflict of 1929 was serious enough and involved sufficient combatants on both sides that some historians do not hesitate to call it a war.[71] Contemporary newspaper reports bear this out. For example, this dispatch describes a pre-dawn Soviet attack on Chinese forces at the mining city of Dailur in Manchuria, which involved not just infantry and artillery, but also aircraft: "Shortly after daybreak Soviet planes joined in the attack, dropping incendiary bombs … causing serious fires which are still burning."[72] A few days later, another border city was reported in flames, as it fell to a force of Soviet cavalry and tanks.[73]

Parallel with the purely military operations, marauding bands of Soviet cavalry moved around the countryside inside Chinese territory, terrorizing the civilians, especially ethnic Russians who had fled the revolution 12 years earlier and now lived precarious lives on the Chinese side of the border. The *Chicago Daily Tribune* reported on a massacre in a village where all men and boys above the age of 12 were ordered to gather in the street: "They were then marched out of the village to a meadow, where they were mowed down by machine guns. The women and smaller children of the village dropped on their knees and begged for the lives of their husbands and fathers. But the appeals were of no avail… Those who were not killed by the machine guns were finished off by bayonets stabs or revolver shots."[74]

The immediate cause of the Sino-Soviet war was an attempt by a north Chinese warlord, Zhang Xueliang, known as the Young Marshal because he had not yet turned 30, to seize hundreds of miles of Russian-owned railways laid in Manchuria during the pre-revolutionary period, but now maintained by the Czar's Soviet successors. An inept performance by the undisciplined and poorly trained Chinese warlord armies made the job easy for the Soviet forces, and the conflict ended in an agreement reinforcing Soviet control of the railroads. It reflected a steep decline in bilateral relations compared with earlier in the decade, when the Soviet regime had supported radical nationalist movements in China.[75]

In the mid-1920s, the Soviet Union had temporarily seen its interests overlap with those of China, as they were both opposed to the existing international system dominated by imperialist powers. By the end of the decade, however, Moscow had in many ways returned to the traditional great power politics of the Russian empire. This entailed keeping the neighbors weak, and as a corollary of this thinking a strategic asset such the Manchurian railway had to stay in Soviet hands. Another way of preventing China from emerging as a threat, both in the 1920s and later, was to make sure the Chinese civil wars continue indefinitely. The Soviet government did this by supporting not just the Communists but also various warlord armies.[76]

The 1929 border war was a warning of growing international turbulence in northeast Asia. That year, the relative stability that had existed for most of the decade was coming to an end. The groundwork for that order had been made in Washington in 1921 and 1922, when the United States, Japan, Great Britain, France and other great powers had met and signed a series of agreements designed to limit the scope for great power rivalry in East Asia and the Pacific. Among the agreements was the 1922 Washington Naval Treaty, which kept a lid on the expansion of Japan's Navy.[77]

It did so by setting a limit on "capital ships," meaning ships of more than 10,000 tons or guns with a caliber exceeding eight inches. The ratio was 5:5:3 for the United States, Great Britain, and Japan, respectively. The acceptance of these numbers, dismissively described by some Japanese as the "Rolls-Royce: Rolls-Royce: Ford" ratio, caused severe anger at home in Japan. In fact, it secured Japanese superiority in the Pacific, since the two Western powers had to worry about other oceans as well, primarily the Atlantic.[78]

Since the Russian defeat in the war of 1905, the United States had been in no doubt that the only possible enemy in the western Pacific would be Japan.[79] By the same token, Japan had initially been playing with the thought of Imperial Germany as its main rival in East Asia, but soon concluded that the United States was the most important potential foe.[80] As a result, since early in the century, both powers began preparing for a war which many believed was likely or even inevitable. One of the proponents of this thinking was an officer by the name of Ishiwara Kanji, who held a series of talks at Tokyo's Army Staff College in the late 1920s, predicting the advent of what he called "the final war." The United States would be the main adversary in this hugely destructive conflict, but in the end, Japan would emerge victorious, and the world would "enter an era of peace under the guidance of the imperial throne."[81]

Interestingly, both the Japanese and the Americans based their planning for war on the same assumptions, which in due course would turn out to be severely flawed. Like naval planners elsewhere, they believed that victory at sea would be decided by battleships, just as the Battle of Tsushima had decided the Russo-Japanese War. On the US side, this was manifested in the so-called War Plan Orange[82], which foresaw a future war along these lines: early in the conflict, Japan would be on the offensive and assume control of the waters and territory off the Asian mainland, including the Philippines, an American colony. The United States would dispatch a fleet, which would make its way across the vast Pacific and clash with the Navy of Japan somewhere in the western part of the ocean.

Few were able to imagine the kind of war that would eventually be fought in the Pacific. It was a war in which the submarine and the aircraft carrier would prove far more decisive than battleships. The submarine had been tested thoroughly in combat in the Great War between 1914 and 1918, and the German Navy had actually made it the centerpiece of an entire strategic campaign aimed at bringing Britain to its knees. The carrier, by contrast, had still only been in its infancy during that conflict, but both the American and the Japanese navies saw the potential in naval aviation, and spent the 1920s improving their capabilities in that area. For example, Japan gained valuable lessons with the small experimental carrier *Hōshō*.[83] Still, by the end of the decade, Japanese naval planners, like their American counterparts, considered naval aviation only as a complement, and not the essence of war at sea. The battleship and other large surface vessels were still seen as decisive.[84]

The naval development took place within the constraints set by the 1922 Washington Treaty, and the 1920s were a decade in which Japan seemed to be gradually coming to terms with an international regime favoring stability and the preservation of the status quo. This accommodating approach to foreign affairs was matched by a more liberal atmosphere domestically. The 1920s were Japan's liberal decade. Jazz was becoming popular, and modern Western fashion was appearing in the streets of the big cities. In a sign of growing cosmopolitanism, star status was conferred on foreigners such as Russian-born Victor Starffin, a tall, blond baseball player who became one of the most popular members of the Tokyo Giants.[85] Even the Military Academy opened to the winds of change. The cadets listened to lectures about socialism, anarchism, and communism, and they were allowed to join tennis teams and smoke in their canteen.[86]

Some might look back at the 1920s with a sense of nostalgia and regret about the "Japan that might have been" if crass nationalism had not gained the upper hand the following decade. It is questionable if this makes any sense. To some extent, the manifestations of modern Western culture emerging among urban Japanese were surface phenomena. More importantly, perhaps, were developments such as the adoption in 1925 of the Draconian Public Security Preservation Law. Although to a great extent it was meant to keep socialism and communism under control, it had potentially much wider application, as it prescribed long prison terms for anyone planning, or even discussing, ways to alter the national polity or the form of government.[87]

At the same time, right-wingers within the Japanese military were deeply frustrated by what they saw as the erosion of traditional values, and angered that the nation's diplomats had agreed to a system preventing their empire from developing its full potential. This was particularly the case in China, where Japan, along with eight other major powers, had signed an agreement ensuring that no single country assumed a predominant position. The arrangement was in direct contravention of the wish expressed by many Japanese leaders to secure absolute control of northeast Asia.

Towards the end of the 1920s, conditions gradually shifted in favor of the hard-liners, as international and domestic factors combined to brew up a perfect storm. In 1929, the crash on Wall Street plunged the US economy into a depression, and soon the economic crisis became global. Japan, too, was hit hard. Unemployment rose, and the economic rug was pulled from under millions of families, especially in the farming sector. Most new university graduates could not find jobs.[88] Those affected had a voice, since a recent reform had given all Japanese men the right to vote, quadrupling the electorate and paving the way for populist policies. The Japanese Army was also stirring and meddling in politics with increasing frequency.

At the same time, in China the situation was coming to a head. Members of the Nationalist government were growing bolder and were beginning to challenge Japan's position in Manchuria. At a conference in Nanjing in May 1931, Chiang Kai-shek called for the return to China of the South Manchurian Railway, the rail network taken over by Japan after its war with Russia.[89] The main Chiang-allied warlord in the area, Zhang Xueliang or the Young Marshal, even executed a Japanese officer for espionage, triggering immense rage in Japan's Army and setting off calls for action to defend the nation's interests and honor.[90] The time was ripe. The hawks decided to strike.[91]

CHAPTER TWO

The Road to War

Asia, 1931–37

In the evening of September 18, 1931, Lieutenant Kawamoto Suemori of the Imperial Japanese Army led a sergeant and a group of soldiers to an isolated point on a railroad just north of Mukden, the capital of Manchuria's Liaoning province.[1] Under the cover of darkness, the lieutenant placed packages of explosives wrapped in yellow paper along the track.[2] Shortly afterwards, a sharp bang rang through the night, already freezing from the approach of the region's harsh winter. The damage to the railway line was limited. An express train that reached the spot just minutes after the explosion was seen to "sway and heal over to one side, but it recovered and passed on without stopping."[3] Still, it was good enough as a pretext for starting a war.

Lieutenant Kawamoto was part a group of officers, some of them quite junior, who were convinced that Japan needed a bigger empire. Their actions on that September evening served a carefully laid plan to conquer all of Manchuria. They immediately blamed Chinese rebels for the sabotage, and within minutes, two 24cm siege howitzers placed inside Mukden's Japanese district began shelling the city's airfield as well as a Chinese military barracks located in the northern suburbs. It was not yet midnight when Japanese infantry entered the Chinese part of Mukden, firing at random. Some bullets went through the Mukden Club in the International Settlement, where Westerners were having a dance. The Japanese soldiers also ambushed a car belonging to a Chinese general, killing both him and his driver.[4]

As Japanese infantry stormed the Chinese barracks, quickly executing those who did not flee, civilian diplomats at Japan's consulate in Mukden, who were not in on the plot, advocated a peaceful solution. They were met with the threat of physical violence. A major, perhaps inebriated after waiting for news about the railroad sabotage over a *sake*-filled dinner at a local Japanese restaurant, drew his sword and shouted, "I'll kill anyone that interferes."[5] When dawn broke on September 19, Mukden was under Japanese control. More than 300 Chinese soldiers had been killed or injured, against 24 on the Japanese side. In a sense, they were the first casualties of World War II.[6]

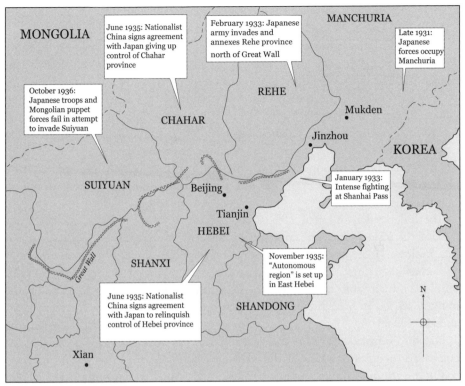

China 1931–1937

It was all the work of Japan's Kwantung Army, a military unit that had been set up a quarter century earlier to defend the South Manchurian Railway and other territorial spoils gained from Russia in the war of 1904–05. In the 1920s the Kwantung Army had become a hotbed of radical nationalist views, and since the end of that decade, its officers strove ceaselessly to place Manchuria under Japanese control. One of the leaders of this conspiracy was Ishiwara Kanji, the officer who had held speeches about his visions of a "final war."[7] All of this had taken place without the knowledge of the government back in Tokyo. The Japanese had a word for that kind of maverick behavior. It was *gekokujō*, an ancient practice of surpassing one's superiors when required to by circumstances.

If the Kwantung Army officers had worried in September 1931 about the reaction of their immediate superiors in Tokyo, they did not have to. As telegrams started arriving at the Army General Staff in the Japanese capital, "a peculiar psychology" took hold of the officers there, according to a confidential history compiled about the incident later. The oldest among them had not been in a "real war" since the showdown with Russia three decades earlier. The youngest had never been tested in battle, and they felt something was lacking. Now was their chance. At the first senior-level General Staff meeting at 7 am on September 19, no one contradicted Military Affairs Bureau chief Koiso Kuniaki when he said, "The Kwantung Army's action is entirely just."[8]

The political leadership was less enthusiastic. The Cabinet also met on the same day and, looking through the evidence, was not convinced that the situation in Manchuria had really warranted a response of such magnitude. It ordered a policy of "non-expansion," a decision which was supported by Emperor Hirohito when he was informed shortly afterwards. Nevertheless, in the field, no one was listening. As caution was urged in the Japanese capital, the Kwantung Army was dispatching troops to attack Chinese garrisons in other parts of southern Manchuria.[9] With equal disregard of opinion in Tokyo, the senior officer responsible for the army on the Korean peninsula even prepared on his own initiative to send troops to Manchuria.[10]

The independent-minded officers could claim that there was a legal basis for this line of action, since the constitution introduced under the Meiji ruler stated that military forces operating in national emergencies abroad were not subject to parliamentary control but were responsible only to the emperor.[11] For his part, Hirohito initially told the Cabinet to "stick to the containment policy," but as the military actions in Manchuria took on their own momentum in the following days, and the Kwantung Army went on to occupy ever larger parts of the region, the politicians eventually gave up and accepted the *fait accompli*. They persuaded the emperor to acquiesce, which he did, reluctantly.[12]

On the ground in Manchuria, a Japanese force, which at most numbered 30,000 troops, was able tackle a Chinese defense force totaling 160,000 men.[13] For the Chinese, it was a humiliating "David and Goliath" scenario, except David was the aggressor. Apart from a handful of bloody clashes in the big cities, Zhang Xueliang, the Young Marshal, did not put up much of a fight, withdrawing his Manchurian army ahead of the advancing Japanese. As the extent of the Japanese offensive became clear, he asked Chiang Kai-shek how he should proceed. Chiang's reply was not very helpful: "Do what you think appropriate." Given this leeway, the Young Marshal opted for a general retreat.[14]

Within just days, only a small part of southern Manchuria remained in Chinese hands, including the city of Jinzhou, where the Young Marshal had moved his government. It became the target of a Japanese aerial raid on October 8. The bombing appears to have been carried out more or less indiscriminately, as the Kwantung Army's air division lacked skill and sophistication, and the aircraft crews reportedly had to drop their bombs by hand.[15] "The military barracks were in fact not touched at all," said an American citizen who visited shortly afterwards. "A multitude of bombs fell everywhere in the town, even on the hospital."[16] The Kwantung Army initially denied that there had been any air attack on Jinzhou at all. In reaction, a Swiss journalist traveled to the city and returned to Mukden with a large collection of Japanese shrapnel that he had picked up from the railway yards. When he placed it in front of the Japanese Army spokesman at a press conference, the officer "nearly had a heart attack."[17]

The southern part of Manchuria may have been a push-over, but the vast, freezing northern part was a completely different matter. This was country controlled and defended by one of China's most capable warlords, the Muslim General Ma Zhanshan. Advancing Japanese columns encountered his troops in November, and saw the fiercest combat of the entire Manchurian campaign when they tried to dislodge him from the city of Qiqihar. In a howling Siberian gale with temperatures plunging to minus 20 degrees Fahrenheit, roughly 6,000 Japanese troops faced 30,000 Chinese. By the time they had pushed the Chinese out of Qiqihar, the Japanese, who were not equipped for winter, had lost 400 men killed outright, while more than twice that number had suffered frostbite.[18]

With Japanese forces entangled on several different fronts, all hopes that Japan's politicians could bring about a compromise solution in Manchuria had become extinct. Japanese decision-makers were under pressure from domestic public opinion, stirred into a frenzy by a jingoistic press. Shidehara Kijūrō, Japan's moderate foreign minister, explained the limited options available to him: "To suppress unnecessarily radical national opinion could play into the hands of the extremists, and bring about an explosion of anti-Chinese sentiment at home, inviting a dangerous situation."[19]

The paralysis in Tokyo set a fateful precedent, and in the coming years allowed field officers to make decisions with far-reaching political implications, without adequately consulting their superiors back home. The full ramifications of this would only become clear much later but, even at this early stage, perceptive observers in Japan understood the consequences. "What is most worrisome is the fact that the will of the senior officers is not thoroughly observed by their subordinates," Prime Minister Inukai Tsuyoshi wrote in a letter to a senior officer in early 1932. "It might become customary to act single-mindedly upon the belief that should those who hold direct command over regiments unite and cause a disturbance, the superiors would finally give *ex post facto* approval to all matters."[20]

Shortly after New Year, the crisis in China escalated dangerously, even as fighting in Manchuria gradually ceased after the Muslim General Ma had been convinced that continued resistance was pointless and that he served national interests better by cooperating with the Japanese.[21] The scene was now Shanghai. It was China's largest and most prosperous city, and while most inhabitants were Chinese, its advantageous position at the Yangtze estuary had attracted thousands of foreigners. Many had made Shanghai their home, and two large Western districts, the International Settlement and the French Concession, had emerged in the center of the city. One could walk down streets with names such as Edinburgh Road and Avenue Joffre and easily forget this was not some European capital.

Japanese merchants and settlers had also established their own district in Shanghai, in an area that had come to be known among the locals as "Little Tokyo." It was guarded by a small garrison unit, just as American and British soldiers were protecting their nations' interests in the city. Japanese commercial interests in this part of China were considerable, but they had come under pressure from anti-Japanese sentiments for several weeks, and calls had grown for the government in Tokyo to act.[22]

On January 18, 1932, five Japanese monks were attacked by a Chinese mob as they were chanting sutras near the Chinese-owned San Yu towel factory, a known hotbed of anti-Japanese activism. One of the monks died and two were seriously injured. Japanese vigilantes retaliated by burning down the towel factory. The situation could no longer be reined in. On the surface it seemed like a clear-cut case of tempers boiling over but, in fact, foul play was involved. The entire incident was precipitated by the Japanese themselves. A military attaché employed at the Japanese diplomatic representation had paid the Chinese mob to carry out the attack on the monks. Japan needed a high-profile, local conflict in the east of China to divert attention from events up north in Manchuria.[23]

The tension quickly spiraled, and within days, Shanghai's small Japanese garrison was involved in intense urban combat with Chinese forces. The situation was similar to the one in Manchuria insofar as the Japanese force was numerically far smaller than its Chinese adversary. Initially, 30,000 Chinese soldiers, including battle-hardened veterans from the 19th Route Army, were confronting fewer than 2,000 Japanese. They were from the Japanese Navy's Special Naval Landing Force, an amphibious unit similar to the American Marines, and despite the unenviable odds, their superiors back in Tokyo were welcoming the opportunity to cover themselves in glory. "It is now the Navy's turn to get to work," said Vice Navy Minister Sakonji Seizō in relief that he and his colleagues no longer had to play second fiddle to the Army in the north.[24]

During the first days of the battle, however, the Japanese soldiers displayed an amateurish behavior that would be unthinkable in later years. They were seen marching in an orderly fashion towards the Chinese positions at night, with two men in each squad carrying torches, allowing snipers to take them out one after the other.[25] They quickly recovered, and managed to hold back the Chinese. One of the hotspots was Shanghai's North Railway Station, where, according to the *North-China Herald*, "the Japanese brought seaplanes into use and commenced intensive bombing." The Chinese fought back, firing at the aircraft with machine guns. An armored train also weighed in on the Chinese side before being the object of too much return fire and steaming away again.[26]

At times, the battle assumed an almost surreal character. In the International Settlement and the French Concession, people continued their daily business, going to work and school while the war was happening just blocks away. The constant noise of battle was the only reminder that anything was amiss, along with the odd shell landing inside the borders of the foreign areas. For some, it was an opportunity for adventure. American journalist Hallett Abend described how one of the early skirmishes attracted a crowd watching from the relative security of the foreign district: "They stood around the sloppy streets, smoking cigarettes, occasionally drinking liquor from bottles and enjoying sandwiches and hot coffee procured from nearby cafés which had not yet closed their doors."[27]

As the battle progressed, the Japanese shipped in reinforcements and, in the end, fielded close to 50,000 men, roughly on a par with Chinese numbers.[28] While the Japanese soldiers sometimes showed lack of tactical skill, they added to their emerging reputation for suicidal bravery in the service of the emperor. At Miaohang, a village outside Shanghai, they faced Chinese barbed-wire defenses and were unable to move forward. Three engineers carried a heavy load of explosives to the barbed wire in a hail of enemy gun fire. The explosives detonated, and all three were killed, but they had created a hole in the barrier. Their action was greeted in the Japanese newspapers as an example of heroism, and the Three Human-Bomb Heroes were nearly turned into "military gods." In fact, the three had never intended to kill themselves, as a Japanese war correspondent explained later on: "The truth is that they simply didn't make it back as fast as they had intended."[29]

Although the Japanese Navy had initially hoped to show off its war-fighting capacity at Shanghai, the admirals quickly realized they needed help. After all, it was almost exclusively a land war, and Shanghai eventually became the Japanese Army's show. Desperate to find an end to the battle, the Japanese side launched a surprise move at the end of February. Striking behind the Chinese lines, they landed a division on the Yangtze bank north of Shanghai, and a series of fierce engagements followed. The Chinese commanders were now faced with the prospect of fighting on two fronts, and in early March they accepted a ceasefire.[30]

The Chinese had lost the battle, but they had left a favorable impression on the foreigners who had witnessed it. "Though they lacked planes, they were well equipped with mortars, machine guns and small arms. With what they had, they were just as capable as the Japanese in combat," a foreign correspondent wrote.[31] The battle also brought to the attention of the world a Chinese war hero, General Cai Tingkai, who had led his country's forces. Cai had a talent for oratory, which he often displayed in front of the international media. "I hope," he said on one such occasion, "our resistance will awaken China to the Japanese peril and help develop our national spirit of defiance. If we don't fight here in Shanghai, the Japanese will be like fierce tigers and swallow up our country in a few years."[32]

Immediately after the Manchurian Incident broke out in September 1931, there was guarded optimism in Western capitals that the situation could be contained. Some Western observers understood correctly that the crisis had originated within jingoistic circles of the Japanese military, but they overestimated the civilian Japanese government's ability to form a counterbalance to the officers. US Secretary of State Henry L. Stimson, who had been governor-general of the Philippines in the late 1920s and confidently declared that he knew "something about the attitude of mind of those peoples," believed Japan's civilian government was "sincerely trying to settle this matter."[33]

Washington's reaction may also have been tempered by the fact that US forces had only recently intervened in Nicaragua, Haiti, the Dominican Republic, and Panama.[34] US editorial writers directly made that point: "With what face," asked the *New York Times*, "could our State Department independently, and with an air of superior virtue, assail a Japanese action which is so nearly on all fours, at least in appearance with previous American action?"[35] An American officer with extensive experience in Central America also privately told a Japanese counterpart that he "took the same measures of self-defense in Cuba."[36]

Indeed, there was an undercurrent of thought among decision-makers and opinion leaders that Japan, an honorary member of the club of Western imperialist powers, might do some good in China. *The Times* of London, while critical of Japan's methods in settling the Mukden incident, opined that in Manchuria it had "created a flourishing oasis in a howling desert of Chinese misrule."[37] This was mixed with the opinion that it would be beneficial for the West if Japan became occupied in Manchuria. "Well, just between ourselves," US President Herbert Hoover said, "it would not be a bad thing for us if Mr. Jap should go into Manchuria, for with two horns on his side—China and the Bolsheviks—he would have enough to keep him busy for quite a while."[38]

The willingness to give the Japanese a free rein or at least the benefit of the doubt quickly receded, especially after news of the bombing of Jinzhou in early October 1931 reached Washington. "The situation … seems to be getting rapidly bad," Stimson now wrote in his diary. "I am afraid we have got to take a firm ground and aggressive stand toward Japan."[39] For people like Stimson, the concern may have had little to do with the welfare of the Chinese people and the integrity of the Chinese state, and rather reflected concern about the survival of post-Great War order in the Pacific as it was manifested in the Washington system.[40]

Later that month, The League of Nations in Geneva discussed the Manchurian Incident, and on October 24, its council voted on a resolution giving Japan until November 16 to pull back its troops to where they were before the railway sabotage. The resolution was passed with a vote of 13 to 1, with Japan itself providing the dissenting vote. "Never," the *New York Times* wrote, "was a nation in an international dispute made to feel her isolation and the force of combined disapproval as Japan was in the closing debate."[41]

If Western politicians had believed that the embarrassment of becoming the target of near-universal criticism would be enough to bring about a Japanese cave-in, they were to be sorely disappointed. The November 16 deadline passed with no signs that the Japanese had any intention of withdrawing to their original positions, as they continued their advance throughout Manchuria. Faced with this direct demonstration of its own impotence, the League decided to establish an investigative commission, headed by the second Earl of Lytton, going some way towards dispelling any fears that it was not doing enough to end the crisis in the Far East.[42]

Stimson, meanwhile, was enraged, especially after the fall of Jinzhou in January 1932. After a restless night, he arose in the morning and wrote out in longhand a note which, with some modifications, was passed on to both Japan and China. The note, which was soon called the 'Stimson Doctrine,' explained that the United States would not recognize any change of status quo which Japan might cause in Manchuria.[43] The doctrine had no more direct effect than any other diplomatic attempts at pausing the Japanese expansion in Manchuria, but it lived on in a note sent by the League of Nations to Japan in February, stating that no member of the organization ought to recognize any result of actions that had violated a nation's territorial integrity. This had long-term consequences, since in the years that followed only a small handful of states ever approved of the changes that Japan had brought about in Manchuria.[44]

Stimson's changing views of Japan were symptomatic of a broader shift in Washington and other Western capitals. The Manchurian incident marked a turning point in international politics in East Asia and a reappraisal of the roles played by Japan and China in the regional power dynamics. The Western governments increasingly considered Japan the unpredictable rogue whose actions tended to challenge the Washington system and the East Asian order that had been established on this basis. China, which had still been seen as a destabilizing force almost on a par with the Soviet Union in the 1920s, was beginning to be viewed as a supporter of the status quo.[45]

These subtle changes took place despite Japan's efforts to give its actions in Manchuria a veneer of legitimacy. The officers behind the Mukden incident had planned for the recruitment of local Chinese for work in a puppet administration that was to run the area under the strict supervision of their Japanese minders, but the endeavor had met with difficulties from the outset. In some areas of Manchuria, Chinese officials had fled before the area they served was occupied, leaving the Japanese with no choice other than filling the positions themselves. Still, the Japanese eventually managed to pull off a real coup by enlisting the assistance of none other than the last Emperor of China.

Henry Puyi, who had been removed from the imperial throne at the tender age of five, when the Qing dynasty was forced out and the Republic founded, had lived for the preceding seven years in the Japanese district of Tianjin, a northern port city near Beijing. He was persuaded to move to Manchuria with promises of regaining his old imperial title, leaving at the end of 1931 despite a Chinese decision to declare him a traitor. On March 8, 1932, Puyi was installed as the new titular leader of Manchukuo, initially receiving the less-than-exalted title of "chief executive," rather than being reinstated as emperor. Dressed in a Western suit, he read out his first declaration in his new role: "I am founding a new State based on virtue and benevolence," said the text, prepared by others, going on to promise "Paradise on Earth."[46]

Few were fooled, and the legitimacy of Puyi's regime received a further blow in October, when the Lytton Commission, having spent a lengthy period of time in East Asia, published its final report. Although it was cautious in its wording, it concluded that the Kwantung Army's actions on the evening of the railway sabotage could not be regarded as "measures of legitimate self-defense."[47] Even more devastatingly for Japanese designs in the region, the report dismissed the Manchukuo government as a puppet regime directed and controlled by Japanese advisors with no general support among the Chinese population.[48]

In February 1933 the League's Assembly voted on a set of recommendations formulated on the basis of the conclusions of the Lytton report. The recommendations called for an autonomous Manchuria under Chinese sovereignty and for the Japanese troops to be pulled back to their original positions. China and Japan were to start negotiations, and members of the League were urged not to recognize Manchukuo. The recommendations were passed by a vote of 42–1, with Japan providing the only dissenting vote.[49] A furious Japan formally left the League of Nations the following month, citing "irreconcilable" differences with the organization over Manchuria.[50]

The official Japanese view was that the League was the worse for it. The *Asahi* newspaper argued that Japan's departure had turned it into essentially a European organization, as it also did not count the United States or the Soviet Union among its members.[51] Privately, however, many Japanese had severe misgivings. "The people act as if by withdrawing we have achieved something great," Hirohito's chief advisor Makino Nobuaki wrote in his diary. "All of this shows the shallowness of thought in the Japanese public. As time passes, they will surely come to realize how superficial they have been."[52]

Still, the defiant Japanese reactions were right in one regard: the Manchurian crisis had dealt a fatal blow to the League of Nations from which it would never entirely recover, contributing to the downwards spiral of international relations that was to characterize the rest of the decade. The powerlessness that had been put on display would be further underlined with Italy's invasion of Abyssinia, the Spanish Civil War, and eventually, full-scale war between China and Japan. The Western democracies were also left, after the Mukden incident, with a lingering feeling of helplessness in the face of determined action by maverick regimes. "The power does not exist to prevent or restrain a determined aggression like that of Japan in Manchuria," the influential American commentator Walter Lippmann wrote.[53]

The upshot of the Manchurian crisis was a Japanese territorial victory, helped by a situation where Western nations were weakened by economic crisis, and China by internal disunity. It was a time of nationalist pride. A senior Japanese officer and main instigator of the incident boasted: "Even if Japan has to face the entire world, she can't be beaten."[54] Maybe the pride was misplaced. At the same time as it was gaining territory through aggression, Japan was beginning to lose the battle for international public opinion and, even more importantly, the sympathy of the Western governments. Civilian diplomats tried to delay and mitigate this deterioration in their country's international reputation, but in vain. Japan was inexorably sliding into pariah status. At home, the modest liberal aspirations were swept aside by a strong authoritarian wave.

Charlie Chaplin arrived by steamer in Kobe harbor, Japan, on May 14, 1932, receiving a tumultuous welcome from thousands of fans waiting for him on the quay. The Tokyo express had to add extra carriages for the huge numbers who wanted to pay for the privilege of traveling on the same train as the world-famous comedian.[55] If anyone wanted evidence that the Japanese people had latched on to American and European culture and were gradually becoming almost "as Western as the Westerners," this was it. Still, Chaplin was not adored everywhere in Japan. On the second day of his stay, he was nearly assassinated.

In the evening of May 15, Chaplin was to have attended a reception in his honor held at the residence of Prime Minister Inukai Tsuyoshi, the man who had only recently expressed concern about the undisciplined behavior of junior officers. A group of young Naval officers had planned to use this event to kill not just the actor and Japan's political leader, but also a number of other dignitaries expected to be present at the event. Only a last-minute schedule change meant that when they stormed Inukai's dwelling in the early evening of that day, Chaplin was watching a sumo match elsewhere. The prime minister, however, was at home and was mortally injured by two gun shots.[56]

The entire plot, a Quixotic design to bring down the existing political order in Japan, quickly unraveled. Investigations turned up a cabal of young firebrands who had wanted to kill Chaplin in order to facilitate war with the United States and bring about national revival.[57] Their practical planning was as amateurish as their logic was flawed, and they were quickly court-martialed. Still, their trial showed that, although they were few in number, they represented views and emotions shared by large numbers of other Japanese. The judges received 110,000 petitions for clemency, including one that was accompanied by a jar containing the petitioners' little fingers preserved in alcohol.[58]

During their trial, the defendants revealed stark opinions about the world and Japan's place in it. In their view, the real Japan and its traditional virtues were disappearing, defeated by the corrupt political parties, while the livelihood of the people was threatened by the forces of modern capitalism as represented in the *zaibatsu* business conglomerates. "In utter disregard of poverty-stricken farmers the enormously rich *zaibatsu* pursue their private profit," one of the defendants said. "Meanwhile the young children of the impoverished farmers ... attend school without breakfast, and their families subsist on rotten potatoes. I thought that to let a day go by without doing anything was to endanger the Army for one day longer."[59]

The coup plotters were treated with the utmost leniency, considering the harsh punishments that Japanese courts could otherwise mete out. All received light prison sentences and were pardoned and released before time, some as early as the following year. War Minister Araki Sadao said he was moved to tears by what the "pure and naïve young men" had done: "They are not actions for fame, or personal gain, nor are they traitorous. They were performed in the sincere belief that they were for the benefit of Imperial Japan."[60] It was the worst possible signal for anyone in a position of authority to send out. Japan in the early 1930s was marked by increasingly unstable politics, as assassinations and coup attempts added an element of unbridled violence.

Only 18 months earlier, one of Inukai's predecessors as prime minister had narrowly escaped an assassination attempt. In March 1931, officers had laid detailed plans for a palace revolution, but had been stopped at the last minute by the secret police, and in February 1932, just before the "Chaplin plot," nationalist radicals had planned a series of murders of liberal politicians and leading businessmen, but in the end killed only two. In July 1933, another failed coup attempt involving a naval pilot plotted the aerial bombardment of parliament and the prime minister's residence.[61]

This all happened while Japan's political system, never a real democracy, became increasingly authoritarian. The politicians targeted by many of the coup plotters for their corrupt practices and unsavory links to the *zaibatsu*, were becoming increasingly irrelevant. Their parties continued to exist, and the voters continued voting for them, but they were no longer picked for executive power. Inukai was to be the last prime minister with party affiliations to lead the country until 1945. Over the next years of both peace and war, all prime ministers would be chosen from among nationalist circles or the officer corps.

In the army, two main factions vied for influence. One group considered the Soviet Union, rapidly strengthening and internationally active, to be the overwhelming threat facing Japan, and it wanted to concentrate all available resources on countering that particular challenge. The other group was less focused and advocated a rejuvenation of the nation under the benevolent leadership of the emperor, cleansed of the corrupting influences of modern life. The ideological differences were important, but underlying them were traditional enmities dating back to the Meiji period.[62]

The rivalry of the two factions came to a head in February 1936, when 1,500 officers and soldiers belonging to the group viewing the Soviet Union as the main priority attempted a coup, turning Tokyo upside down for a numbers of days. As the plot got underway, the rebels occupied a series of key positions in the capital, and carried out assassinations of a list of pre-selected officials. One of the targets, 78-year-old Admiral Saitō Makoto, was murdered in a hail of bullets in his bedroom wearing his night kimono. His wife threw herself onto him, crying: "Kill me instead!" The assassins pulled her away and poured yet more bullets into the old man's dead body.[63]

The coup had no more luck than the other attempts earlier in the decade, even though it involved a larger number of conspirators. Emperor Hirohito was instrumental in bringing the uprising to an end. Furious that some of his closest advisors had been killed by the mutineers, he ordered the Army to crack down "and turn this misfortune into a blessing." Within four days, the leaders of the coup had been placed under arrest, and the soldiers they had commanded, many of them recruits with just weeks of training behind them, had returned to their barracks.[64]

Unlike earlier coup attempts, the legal aftermath of the February 1936 rising was severe. A total of 124 people were prosecuted, and of these 17 were sentenced to death. They were executed by firing squad in the back yard of Tokyo's Yoyogi Prison, having been allowed, as custom required, to write farewell poems beforehand. A light drizzle was falling as they faced their executioners and shouted *"Tenno Heika Banzai!"* "Long Live the Emperor!"[65] With them disappeared the practice of effecting political change by coup and assassination. From now on, stability set in, but it was a stability built on the Army's tightening grip on the politics of the nation.

Despite the growing role of the military, Japan in the 1930s was not a dictatorship comparable to Nazi Germany or even Fascist Italy. A censorship system with roots in the Meiji period did prevent the uninhibited flow of opinions, but throughout the decade it remained possible to publish articles in mainstream magazines criticizing the government's policies in mainland Asia.[66] The majority of the press, however, remained staunchly patriotic. Mass-circulation newspapers such as *Asahi* and *Mainichi* and broadcaster *NHK*, modeled on the BBC when it was formed in 1925, fanned the jingoistic flame with reports from the front in Manchuria, shuttling correspondents back and forth by plane to ensure their audience got the latest news.[67]

After the fighting had subsided, and the Manchukuo puppet regime had been established, the Japanese news organizations stayed on, and dutifully reported back to their audience at home about efforts to build a new society. They tried to present it as a boon to the local population, but in fact it was crass colonialism. Many farmers in Manchuria were forced off their land to make way for Japanese settlers and as a result became a ripe recruiting pool for the Communists. In tactics resembling those adopted by the Americans in Vietnam three decades later, they were concentrated in collective villages to prevent Communist insurgents from reaching them.[68]

The occupation of Manchuria had come at a convenient time. Japan was severely threatened by overpopulation in the 1920s and 1930s, with about two million births annually.[69] This had led to concern among observers abroad that Japan would sooner or later embark on a major war to gain the territory it needed. The influential American demographer Warren Thompson warned that population pressure in Japan might "become so great that it will be easy to suggest to the mass of the people that it would be as well to die fighting as to sit at home and starve."[70] Counterproductively, government and military authorities in Japan considered a large population a source of strength, causing knowledge about birth control techniques to be suppressed.[71]

It would be easy to call Manchuria Japan's *Lebensraum*, but it would also be misleading. Unlike the Nazis, Japan did not contemplate the full-scale slaughter of the local population to make room for its own people. In another major difference, the Germans never considered in detail how they would be able get large numbers of German farmers to move thousands of miles east to till the conquered Soviet lands, whereas the Japanese government took the task of engineering mass migration to Manchuria very seriously. Surveys suggested that as many as 17 percent of young Japanese males wanted to emigrate, but far fewer actually took the step.[72] To stir up a pioneer spirit among the young, the government launched propaganda campaigns featuring rousing speeches to spread Japanese civilization on the mainland. "Go! Go and colonize the continent!" one such speech said. "For the development of the [Japanese] race to build the new order in Asia!"[73]

The Great Wall had stood as a barrier between Chinese civilization and the barbarians for millennia. Countless battles had been fought with swords, spears, and bows. In early 1933, it became the scene of a war waged with modern weaponry—machine guns, tanks, and airplanes. The Japanese in Manchukuo only had access to the easternmost part of the wall, at the narrow Shanhai Pass between the mountains and the sea, but they wanted control of a larger area around the 10,000-Mile Wall, as it is called in Chinese. They needed it as a buffer zone between Manchukuo and the potential threat of a unified and stronger China, and they set about reaching that objective by the usual *modus operandi*: a staged incident.

After dark on New Year's Day, Japanese troops stationed at the Shanhai Pass lobbed hand grenades into the back yard of the Japanese military police detachment, and also threw grenades on a rail track running past the Japanese garrison. Two hours later, Japanese garrison commander Major Ochirai Jinkurō, who had actually engineered the attack in the first place, presented the neighboring Chinese garrison with a series of demands, including a request that the Chinese withdraw and leave control of Shanhai Pass to the Japanese side. The Chinese refused, and by the morning of

January 2, a tense situation had evolved, with Chinese soldiers placed on the Great Wall taking potshots at Japanese inside the pass.[74]

The standoff was resolved the day after, when the Japanese side had brought up reinforcements in the form of extra infantry backed by a small number of aircraft. In the sea off Shanhai Pass, the contours of warship *Hirado* and the 16th Destroyer Squadron emerged. Before dawn on January 3, the Japanese launched a combined land, air, and sea attack, pushing out the Chinese defenders, who were numerically superior but deficient in weaponry. They withdrew back to a position south of the Great Wall, licking their wounds and waiting for the next Japanese move.[75]

That move, when it did happen, took place elsewhere. The Japanese officers in Manchuria had long coveted the Inner Mongolian province of Rehe, north of the Great Wall. It had a strategic location vis-à-vis China and was also of great economic significance, producing most of the opium consumed in Manchukuo. Not wasting any time, the Kwantung Army had spent most of 1932 preparing an invasion of Rehe, even transferring an entire division from Japan for that explicit purpose, while following past practice and not heeding warnings from the high command in Tokyo.[76] A sense of urgency was added when in the second half of the year Zhang Xueliang, the Young Marshal, still hoping to regain his lost Manchurian lands, moved tens of thousands of troops to Rehe.[77] Hirohito did not oppose the operation, but told his generals to exercise caution. "We have been very lucky so far in Manchuria," he said. "It would be regrettable if we should make a mistake now."[78]

After last-minute delays caused by concern in Tokyo, the Kwantung Army invaded Rehe with two divisions in late February 1933. It was *Blitzkrieg* before the coining of the word. One city after the other fell, as the modern Japanese troops overwhelmed poorly equipped warlord armies. The Japanese had an extra advantage in the form of their air force, which raked the open Chinese trenches with machine-gun fire, causing what an eyewitness described as "frightful" casualties.[79] It all went smoothly for the Japanese, right until the middle of March when they encountered the same obstacle that had defeated numerous invading armies in the past, the Great Wall.

At three gateways through the wall, Chinese soldiers manned bastions which in some cases had been built by the Ming emperors half a millennium earlier and were still able to hold off the Japanese, inflicting a heavy toll. Some of the Chinese defenders were carrying ancient but fierce-looking broadswords, and from their advantageous positions above the Japanese, they hurled abuse and displayed banners with anti-Japanese and anti-Manchukuo slogans.[80] Intelligence suggested that the Chinese were assembling more forces in the rear, leading the Japanese commanders to the conclusion that the wall had to be breached in order to prevent a dangerous and blood-consuming stalemate.[81]

During the first days of April, Japanese troops succeeded in punching through several gates on the Great Wall, advancing into Hebei province on the other side, and getting close enough to Beijing to form a credible threat to the old Chinese capital.

At this point, Hirohito intervened, ordering the troops to withdraw immediately back behind the Great Wall.[82] While he was almost certainly not unhappy with the territorial gain in Rehe, he may have been concerned that by moving beyond the wall, the Kwantung Army could set in motion events that could not be easily contained. This was not like Manchuria, which had only been an integral part of China for three centuries. The area around Beijing was an ancient part of China, and invading it could stir dangerous patriotic emotions among the Chinese.

Chinese and Japanese delegates signed a truce at Tanggu, a district near the port city of Tianjin, in late May, marking the temporary end of more than 20 months of intermittent hostilities. It was a humiliating peace for China. The text of the truce forced it to acknowledge the loss of Manchuria, as well as the Japanese annexation of Rehe. The eastern part of Hebei province was to be a demilitarized zone but Japanese planes and observers were allowed to patrol the area to ensure that Chinese forces stayed out.[83] It was a highly unsatisfactory arrangement for the Chinese, but they deemed themselves too weak to do anything about it for now. The truce was meant "to slow down Japan a little," Chiang Kai-shek told a group of officers. It would buy time "to regain North China, recuperate, and figure out what to do next."[84]

"Hands off China." This was how Tokyo-based Western diplomats interpreted a series of statements made by Japanese foreign ministry spokesman Amō Eijirō in April of 1934. If foreign powers were to use force to "disturb the peace in Asia," he told correspondents in Tokyo, "Japan herself may be compelled to resort to force." Japan reserved the right itself to determine when such drastic action was needed, he added. His remarks triggered concern in Western capitals, but received widespread support in the Japanese press. "Japan does not need the help of other powers to maintain peace in Asia," one headline read.[85]

While senior government figures in Tokyo sought to downplay Amō's remarks[86], there was little doubt that Japan was becoming more assertive following its recent military victories in northeast Asia. Japanese officials such as the former governor of Korea, General Terauchi, had raised the prospect of an Asian "Monroe Doctrine" before, but they had done so in private letters. Now they were talking about it openly, to foreign journalists. Even relatively moderate diplomats argued that Japan should be the primary power in charge in China. It was as if Japan were developing its own version of America's manifest destiny.

The year 1934 also saw growing consensus within the Japanese Navy that the limits imposed on its size by the Washington Treaty system were becoming unbearable. So far, the United States, Japan's most likely foe in case of war, had refrained from building up to treaty limits, but new American legislation now required that the US Navy make up for the shortfall by building 102 new ships within an eight-year period. If the existing limitation system were continued, there was a real possibility that within a foreseeable future, Japan would be irreparably behind the United States in warships. Therefore, when a new treaty was up for negotiation with the United States and Great Britain in London in late 1934, the Japanese asked for parity among the three navies. Heading the Japanese delegation to the British capital was a vice admiral and former naval attaché at the embassy in Washington DC, picked mainly because of his participation in a previous round of talks in 1930, Yamamoto Isoroku.[87]

"Japan does not want naval competition," Yamamoto told his British and American counterparts in idiomatic English honed not only by his stint in Washington but also by a stay at Harvard. "She simply asks for a new agreement for reduction or limitation that is fair to her."[88] Privately, Japanese naval officers acknowledged that they did not actually seek a new agreement, but wanted to be released from treaty obligations altogether. They estimated, correctly, that the two Western powers would not accept the demand of parity or the even more far-fetched demand, made as a bargaining tactic, of a complete elimination of battleships and aircraft carriers. As a result, the talks ended up in deadlock, and in December 1934, Japan declared that it renounced the treaties.[89]

Japan's more assertive behavior posed a challenge to all powers with an interest in Asia and the Pacific, and each nation addressed it in a different manner. Great Britain, now rapidly relinquishing its former role as the most important power on a global scale, was in no doubt that an emerging Japan could undermine its position in East Asia and in the long run pose a threat to Hong Kong and even Singapore. Indeed, beginning in 1931, Japanese militarism had displaced Chinese nationalism as the main challenge in the Far East, in the eyes of British diplomats.[90]

The rise of Adolf Hitler in Germany had the twin effects of occupying London with matters in Europe while encouraging Japan to make bolder moves in Asia. In the words of Robert G. Vansittart, the chief diplomatic advisor to the British government, "Japan would take advantage of the complications in Europe to erode our position in the Far East."[91] There was little Great Britain could do other than to lie low. As a senior British official phrased it, "it is a major British interest not to antagonize Japan, and still more not to be made the spearhead of opposition to her aims."[92]

In this unenviable situation, the British strategy was to seek direct bilateral cooperation with Japan on the question of China, where a great deal of British business interests were concentrated. A mission to the Far East in 1935 headed by Frederick Leith-Ross, the British government's top economist, aimed to bring about a joint British-Japanese loan to China, but met a cold shoulder in Japan. Representatives of the Japanese military gave interviews to the press where they declined any joint efforts at helping China, urging Great Britain to recognize, as foreign ministry spokesman Amō had said the year before, that Japan was now the "sole stabilizing influence" in East Asia.[93]

Paradoxically, given the future history of World War II alliances, the nation most willing to openly defy Japan in Asia was perhaps Germany, which had a thriving relationship with China. It was driven mainly by economics, since China had many of the raw materials, such as antimony and wolfram, that Germany needed in its effort to rebuild its armed forces.[94] In turn, Germany was a major supplier of military equipment to China, with the result that the elite forces of the Chinese Army were gradually equipped with steel helmets and stick grenades of German make or design. An experienced corps of German advisors, most of them veterans of the Great War, also traveled to China to train its officers and soldiers. Nazi racist ideology was, of course, a problem for the Chinese, and German diplomats had to discreetly reassure them that nothing their propaganda said about the superior Aryans was meant to discriminate against "old cultural races of the Far East, in particular the Chinese."[95]

While defying Japanese warnings against active involvement in China, the Nazi leadership was actively considering ways to secure better relations with Japan. This effort, sanctioned by Hitler himself, was chiefly motivated by a wish to contain the Soviet Union, a common ideological foe. At the same time, there was an undercurrent in Nazi thinking which found affinities with Japanese culture. "We too are battling to destroy individualism," Deputy Fuehrer Rudolf Hess said, comparing Nazi thinking with Japanese collectivism. "We are struggling for a new Germany based on the new idea of totalitarianism. In Japan, this way of thinking comes naturally to the people."[96]

Ideally, Germany would want to stay on good terms with both China and Japan and actively encouraged measures to decrease tension between the two Asian rivals.[97] In practice this balancing act proved difficult, and, as Germany's envoy to China Oskar Trautmann put it, German policy in the Far East "moves like a pendulum, sometimes to the Chinese and sometimes to the Japanese side, and a strong inclination to one side causes bad feeling on the other."[98] One such pendulum swing came in the form of the signing of a pact between Berlin and Tokyo in November 1936 in opposition to the Communist International, or Comintern, a global organization directed from Moscow with the aim of fostering revolution worldwide. The Anti-Comintern Pact caused concern in China when it was announced, and although it was not obvious to everyone at the time, it constituted the first major step towards Japan's wartime alliance with Nazi Germany.[99]

The tension with Moscow was a cold war that threatened to turn hot. Tension was growing on the border between Japan's puppet Manchukuo and Mongolia, a Soviet satellite. For powerful circles within the Soviet Army, the growing presence of Japan on the Asian mainland was a source of grave concern, and there were calls to strike at Japan now, when the Soviet side retained an undeniable technological advantage. Some officers who had careers stretching back before the 1917 revolution had memories of the humiliating defeat in the 1904–05 war, and they were frustrated at what they saw as the Communist rulers' greater reluctance to enter a fight. "It is very lucky for Japan," said one of these officers, "that the Soviet Union is not Tsarist Russia."[100]

Whereas the Soviet threat was the main preoccupation of the Japanese Army, the Japanese Navy stayed focused on the United States throughout the 1930s. This became even more salient after the White House was occupied by a self-declared "big navy man."[101] US President Franklin D. Roosevelt had been assistant secretary of the navy during the Great War, and soon after he assumed office in March 1933, he was instrumental in the largest shipbuilding program since 1916, serving his New Deal agenda at the same time, as an estimated 85 percent of naval spending went to labor.[102]

The American naval buildup in the 1930s still revolved around the basic assumption that the battleship would remain the core of any modern navy, reflecting expectations that the next big war at sea would be decided in a line-of-battle action similar to Tsushima or its Great War counterpart, Jutland.[103] The US Navy did, however, experiment with innovative designs, most importantly the aircraft carrier, such as the USS *Enterprise*, launched in October 1936. In the words of an American naval historian, few disagreed that "a fast, high-flying airplane would be a far better observation platform than the crow's nest of a 30-knot cruiser." In addition, a growing number of far-sighted officers realized that airpower was revolutionizing naval warfare and had considered themselves vindicated as early as 1921, when an exercise saw an aircraft drop 2,000-pound bombs on a captured German battleship and cruiser off the coast of Virginia, sinking both.[104]

In Japan, which was now freed from the constraints of the Washington Treaty, the situation was roughly the same: conventional wisdom dictated a focus on the battleships, but a growing number of people in high places were realizing that the future belonged to the carrier. A ship-building program launched after Japan had exited the treaty included the construction of *Yamato* and *Musashi*. They were "superbattleships" with nearly twice the displacement of any battleship afloat at the time of their design. Secrecy was extreme. In the port city of Kure, where *Yamato* was being built, a huge fence was erected, and on trains that passed by the windows facing the harbor were covered.[105]

In parallel with these efforts, innovative minds within the Japanese Navy worked tirelessly on developing carrier capabilities, led in large part by Rear Admiral Yamamoto, who played a key role in the Naval Aviation Department, eventually becoming the department's leader.[106] As the decade progressed, Japanese carrier doctrine gradually evolved until it settled on two main principles. First, fleet maneuvers and map exercises convinced planners that Japan's carriers should move into battle in dispersed formation to avoid being annihilated in one mass attack. Second, they agreed that the carriers' aircraft complement should consist mainly of attack planes, with torpedo planes given priority over dive bombers. Fighter aircraft, mainly for defensive purposes, received lower priority.[107] This would prove of great significance in the future.

In the 1930s, Japan was even more of a pioneer in the field of amphibious operations, a type of warfare that would prove almost as decisive as the aircraft carrier, especially in the Pacific. The Japanese military had put infantry on shore to devastating effect in the conflicts with both China and Russia and, during the Great War, landing forces had captured the German stronghold at Qingdao as well as a number of the Kaiser's islands in the South Pacific: Saipan, Palau and Truk.[108] Doctrines and technologies had continued to evolve over the next decade and a half, and in the 1930s, in a rare example of inter-service cooperation, the Japanese Army and Navy built the world's first ship designed exclusively for amphibious operations.[109] At the same time, the Japanese Navy was forming a unit trained specifically for amphibious operations, the Special Naval Landing Force, which first saw major action in Shanghai in 1932.[110]

The naval build-up that Japan carried out in the 1930s, especially after abandoning the Washington Treaty system, facilitated a fundamental adjustment to its national strategies in the form of a commitment to expand into the Pacific Ocean. The change was meant to prepare Japan for the much-anticipated decisive clash between surface fleets. The Japanese believed that the US Navy would send all its major battleships westward across the Pacific Ocean, seeking out its Japanese counterpart, and then try to defeat it, before proceeding to blockade the Japanese home islands. Japan could brace itself for this eventuality by setting up a defensive perimeter well into the vast ocean. The American Plan Orange for war with Japan foresaw a similar scenario. The irony was that both navies misinterpreted the very essence of the war that waited a few years down the line.[111]

The adjustment towards the Pacific strategy was made easier by the defeat of the anti-Soviet faction within the Japanese armed forces in the coup attempt of February 1936, allowing the Japanese military to move away from a one-sided focus on the Soviet threat.[112] The intensified interest in the Pacific Ocean was ratified in two official documents that were completed in the middle of 1936, and approved by members of the Cabinet. Japan was set on a path that would eventually lead to Pearl Harbor, and both the military and political establishments supported it.[113]

Japan was knocking on China's door, but the country's Nationalist leader Chiang Kai-shek never budged in his deep-seated conviction that the Communist rebellion was by far the bigger threat to his rule and to the continued existence of the Chinese state as he knew it. As he told a group of foreign reporters: "The Japanese are a disease of the skin; the Communists are a disease of the heart."[114] Based on this analysis, he spent most of the 1930s on a prolonged effort to annihilate the Communist movement, even as calls multiplied within China, especially among the educated young, for a more proactive stance vis-a-vis Japan.

After they had been purged in Shanghai and other large cities in the late 1920s, many of the Communists had retreated to the countryside. They had established themselves in what they called "rural soviets" or "base areas," autonomous zones spread throughout the vast nation which virtually functioned as states-within-the-state with their own government and administration, and sometimes even their own money. One of these areas, in southwest China near the French colony of Indochina, was a training ground for a minuscule revolutionary who had recently returned from abroad, Deng Xiaoping. The Communist forces in this area assisted partisans beyond the border in Vietnam, and in retaliation they were bombed by French aircraft.[115]

The largest Communist area, however, was located in southeast China's Jiangxi province and at its height had a population of three million, gradually augmented as party members were driven out of the cities, where police and informers made life untenable. While defending its outer boundaries against attack from Chiang Kai-shek's Nationalist armies, the area built up popular support by parceling out landlord estates to poor peasants. The area's leader was Mao Zedong, the young man who had admired Japan three decades earlier in its hour of triumph against Russia. Now, as one of the founding members of the Chinese Communist Party, he cut a charismatic figure, combining a penchant for romanticism, which mainly found expression in a steady stream of poems, with ruthlessness. Intense in-fighting took place, and in one such face-off between rival factions, from which Mao emerged victorious, thousands were executed.[116]

Chiang Kai-shek was intent on wiping out the base areas and carried out a series of encirclement campaigns that combined economic blockade and military suppression. He did so with the help of his German advisors, a group whose influence in Nationalist China was growing at the time. In 1934, Chiang kicked off the most ambitious of these campaigns yet, seeking to annihilate the Jiangxi area once and for all. By late summer of that year, the campaign had become so effective that Mao and the other leaders decided to evacuate the area in search of safer territory. Leaving behind a rearguard of mostly injured soldiers, altogether 80,000 men and women set out in separate columns in October. It was the beginning of a 6,000-mile retreat through some of China's most inhospitable terrain, later to be known as the "Long March." After more than a year, the troops, which now numbered one tenth of their original size, following death and desertion, ended the march in a remote corner of rural northwest China. The main body of the Communist movement would remain there for the next decade, until 1945.[117]

By the middle of the 1930s, Chiang Kai-shek was nominally in charge of roughly half a billion people in the world's most populous country, but he was far less powerful than he looked. True enough, from his capital Nanjing, which was under rapid reconstruction, he led an ambitious effort to modernize the ancient society, and some institutions, such as the army, saw impressive changes. While the

Chinese armed forces added to their weaponry with the expensive acquisition of everything from American airplanes to British tanks and Czech machine guns, it was also building up a nucleus of tough and well-equipped divisions, with the help of the German advisors. A professional officer corps was also in the making, and the educated sons of wealthy families often opted for a career in the armed forces. There was no longer much truth in the old adage that "good iron is not beaten into nails, and good men are not turned into soldiers."

Other parts of traditional Chinese society were much more resistant to change. Foreign visitors were shocked by the ways in which the most backward aspects of the imperial period remained in full view. Opium smoking was rampant, and on every street one could see women with bound feet. The most troublesome inheritance from the past was not even visible. Centrifugal forces had caused a decentralization of power since the mid-19th century, and much authority rested not in the capital but with local warlords. Some were loyal to Chiang, many were not.

The warlords had many reasons to distance themselves from Chiang, but for some the main grievance was his reluctance to face the Japanese threat while the Communist rebellion was still on. Every new Japanese provocation, every incremental Japanese victory caused dissatisfaction to grow to new heights. Two agreements with Japan following in rapid succession in the summer of 1935 forced the Chinese government to relinquish effective control over two major provinces, Hebei and Chahar, in the north of the country.[118] The following year, Chinese puppet armies, partly consisting of ethnic Mongolians and supported by the Japanese, sought to push inland and take over the province of Suiyuan, but were beaten back by Nationalist Chinese forces.

In China's southern provinces, the original birthplace of the Nationalist movement which now ruled the country, criticism of Chiang Kai-shek's policy of patience towards Japan was particularly strong, and mixed with more mundane lust for power. By the summer of 1936, this part of the nation found itself in a state of open rebellion, with calls for Chiang to step down in favor of a new regime more inclined to resist Japan. Chiang loyalists only succeeded in putting down this southern insurgency after months of maneuvering and cajoling. It was just a short reprieve for Chiang, and did not quell the growing criticism of his "soft" Japan strategy. At the end of 1936, tensions came to a head.

In December, Chiang visited the northern city of Xian, where he met the Young Marshal.[119] He was unhappy with the Young Marshal's efforts in putting down the Communist rebellion, and wanted him to pursue this more enthusiastically. After a heated exchange, the Young Marshal and another general present in Xian, Yang Hucheng, decided to arrest Chiang in order to force him to make peace with the Communists and concentrate his resources on the struggle against Japan. Before dawn on December 12, men sent by the Young Marshal burst into Chiang's local residence, but met with resistance from his bodyguards. In the melee, Chiang managed to escape through the back door and jump over a wall, hurting his back in the process.

He hid on a hillside, but was found within hours. "We will not shoot you," said the officer who apprehended him. "We only ask you to lead our country."[120]

News of Chiang's arrest soon reached the isolated Communists, triggering a jubilant mood. Mao is said to have laughed wildly. The initial impulse among the Communist leadership was to see to it that Chiang was executed, disregarding whatever promises his captors might have made, but eventually they decided to go with the Young Marshal's demand for an alliance between the Nationalists and Communists similar to the one that had tied them together in the 1920s, but this time targeting the Japanese. This was what resulted after days of tense negotiations, and Chiang was eventually released and allowed to leave Xian. It was a startling result. After all, the Communists had held complete power over the man who had hunted them for years, and caused the deaths of close friends and family. That they did not have him killed might have been due to Moscow. The Soviet Union was now openly implementing a more anti-Japanese policy and considered Chiang the only person capable of leading a unified China into war with Japan.[121]

Once back in Nanjing, Chiang soon got busy seeking revenge against his former captors. The Young Marshal, who had accompanied Chiang to the capital, was apprehended but escaped execution. Instead he was put under house arrest, a fate that he would not escape for another half century.[122] Chiang, however, did not forget his pledge to channel all his resources into the battle against Japan. With the backing of the Communists, and perhaps more importantly their Soviet masters, he now felt confident about facing up to the Japanese enemy. The long-awaited showdown was approaching, and most believed it would happen in the new year. Then, unexpectedly, a last chance of peace emerged.

The year 1937 was to be of pivotal importance for Asia. It began on a note of cautious optimism. Chinese Vice President H. H. Kung in his published "New Year reflections" said the Chinese nation was standing together, ready to face new challenges. "If the same spirit of unity can be maintained, the future of China will indeed be encouraging," he said.[123] In a traditional New Year's message, Japanese Foreign Minister Arita Hachirō admitted that relations with the rest of the world were not "completely satisfactory," but added that "Japan today is facing no problem that cannot be settled through diplomatic channels."[124]

As winter turned into spring, the optimism grew. In early February, a new Japanese cabinet under Hayashi Senjūrō, a former war minister, assumed office. One of his most important early decisions was to pick Satō Naotake, a career diplomat who had spent 25 years in Europe and was now ambassador to France, to become his foreign minister. Satō was known for the view that the key to Japanese greatness was a liberal economic policy and an open attitude to the outside world. Japan's solution to its population problems lay not in conquest and colonization, but in industry and trade, according to Satō, who, unknowingly, anticipated some of the policies that would ensure Japanese prosperity after 1945.[125]

Satō also advocated policy changes in China, seeming to move away from the insistence in previous years of a Japanese version of the Monroe Doctrine that would have minimized the role of other nations in Chinese affairs. In a speech held in March, he even went so far as to suggest that "difficulties in Sino-Japanese relations have been due to Japan's sense of superiority over China." He proposed to rectify this by negotiating with China "on the basis of equality" while taking into consideration "China's demands and vital interests."[126] Meanwhile, Japan's ambassador to China was rumored to be in negotiations with the government in Nanjing about the abolition of the puppet governments set up in the north of the country.[127]

Foreign diplomats quickly picked up on the changed atmosphere, and the US ambassador to China reported in May that there was hope that "the Japanese policy of armed invasion of China may be laid aside for an indefinite period."[128] A softening approach was indeed in evidence within the military ranks. Ishiwara, the officer who had helped orchestrate the Manchurian Incident, now suggested in a policy paper prepared for the ministry of war that the Japanese military should abandon its divide-and-rule policy in China, and that the two nations should step up economic cooperation for the sake of common prosperity.[129]

This was not a consensus view, however, and it was more than the conservative cliques within the Japanese armed forces could stomach. As a result, the slender hope that had been kindled in early spring was extinguished. Hayashi's stint as prime minister lasted only until June, and when he departed, so did Satō. Instead, the premiership went to Konoe Fumimaro, the scion of an ancient family with the rank of prince. The Chinese foreign ministry put up a brave face, saying Konoe's appointment was "a matter of congratulation not only for Japan, but for China," but the upbeat mood was misplaced.[130]

Konoe was already known for his eagerness to change the international system in Asia in Japan's favor. "We must overcome the principle of peace based on the maintenance of the status quo, and work out new principles of international peace from our own perspective," he had written.[131] He chose as his foreign minister Hirota Kōki, a former premier. A ranking Japanese foreign ministry official described Hirota as "a peace lover from the bottom of his heart," but at the same time also "a man with weak resistance to the military and the right wing."[132] He was the wrong man at the wrong time, since the hawks in the Japanese military were soon to get a chance for renewed belligerence in China. It came in the form of an incident near the ancient capital of Beijing, at a small hitherto obscure location that would soon become world-famous. Its name was Marco Polo Bridge.

CHAPTER THREE

Blitzkrieg

China, 1937

Captain Shimizu Setsurō had a strange feeling of foreboding as he walked the banks of the Yongding River near Beijing early in the evening of July 7, 1937. He was inspecting the area in preparation for night-time maneuvers to be conducted by a company of the Japanese Army's Ichiki Battalion a few hours later, and he noticed that Chinese positions near the water's edge had been newly reinforced. "Something might happen tonight," he thought with growing apprehension as he finished his simple supper, sitting near Marco Polo Bridge, so named because the medieval Italian traveler had seen and reported about its elaborately carved stone lions more than 600 years earlier.[1]

The Beijing region was in a state of lingering tension in the summer of 1937. The Japanese China Garrison Army, a brigade-sized force of roughly 5,600 men, had been stationed near the old Chinese capital since the turn of the century to protect Japanese citizens and property, as part of the settlement after the anti-foreign Boxer Rebellion. Since then, the number of Japanese nationals had grown rapidly, and there were now 12,000 in Beijing and the nearby port city of Tianjin. The garrison army's soldiers were becoming bolder and more arrogant, often driving their trucks at great speed through Beijing's narrow lanes, with no regard for local residents' safety. Adding to the tension, the 75,000 soldiers of the Chinese 29th Army were stationed throughout the area, and anti-Japanese feelings were growing in its ranks.[2]

There was enough to worry about, but Shimizu kept his premonitions to himself when he led his company, about 135 men, out of its compound in the Beijing suburb of Fengtai that evening. Moving through the hot and humid night, the soldiers embarked on the maneuver, which took place around the Marco Polo Bridge and the adjacent walled town of Wanping, home to a moderate-sized garrison of Chinese soldiers. At about 10:40 pm, after the first stage of the maneuver had been completed, and the soldiers were getting ready for much-needed rest, they were startled by the sound of two shots aimed at them from somewhere in the pitch black. Shimizu had

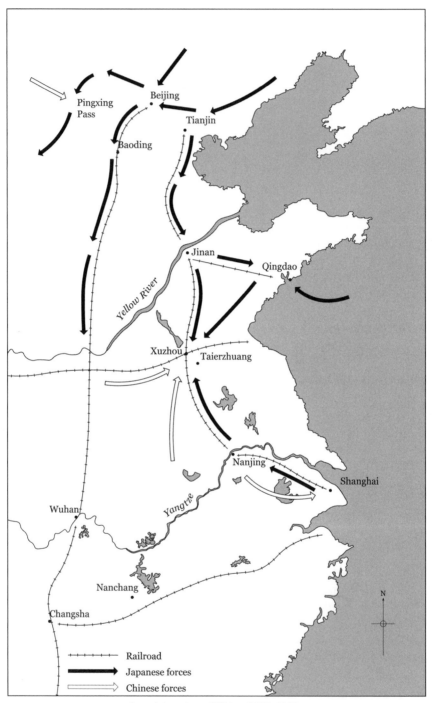

Japan's invasion of China 1937–1938.

no idea where the fire had come from, and immediately ordered a roll call. His worst fears were realized when one of his soldiers turned out to be missing.[3]

Shimizu reported the situation to his battalion commander, Itsuki Kiyonaho, back in Fengtai. The news about the missing soldier caused particular alarm, and Itsuki sent reinforcements to Marco Polo Bridge with special orders to gain access to Wanping and search for him there. By this time, ironically, the missing soldier had reappeared elsewhere, but events were spinning out of control, and they could not be stopped. The Japanese force appeared at Wanping's city gate, and when the Chinese garrison turned down its request to enter, a skirmish broke out. It began as an exchange of rifle fire, but shortly before dawn, the Japanese rolled up artillery and blasted at the city's ancient walls. They still did not manage to enter the city, and an uneasy quiet settled in the area around Marco Polo Bridge.[4]

As the sun rose over Asia on July 8, both the Chinese and Japanese governments had been alerted to the incident. A radioed message reached Chiang Kai-shek, who was at a military conference at Mount Lu, a resort in central China where he often spent his summers. Chiang ordered the 29th Army to enter into negotiations, while insisting on not giving up "one iota of sovereignty."[5] Chiang felt it necessary to emphasize this, since the commander of the 29th Army, Song Zheyuan, was a former independent warlord of somewhat uncertain loyalties. There was a certain risk that he could reach some kind of accommodation with the Japanese that would weaken Chiang in the north.

At the same time in Tokyo, the Army Chief of Staff, Prince Kan'in Kotohito, ordered the Beijing garrison to "avoid further use of force so as to prevent extension of the conflict," but was prepared to dispatch more troops to seek a quick solution if need be.[6] Following these instructions, the field commanders near Beijing initiated talks, and in the morning of July 9 after intense discussions, they reached a tentative agreement, calling for the Chinese troops in the area to be withdrawn and the Chinese soldiers in Wanping to be replaced by a paramilitary force.[7]

The situation around Marco Polo Bridge remained tense, and fire fights erupted intermittently. Later on the same day, Joseph Stilwell, the military attaché at the US embassy in Beijing, got a taste of this when he tried to make his way to the scene in a car. Five hundred from Marco Polo Bridge both sides started shooting at the approaching vehicle, forcing the driver to make an abrupt U-turn. "We got out on two wheels," Stilwell said.[8] Despite the trigger-happiness displayed at the bridge, it seemed that the entire incident was now manageable, and that a more formal agreement could be signed within hours. This was when things started going wrong.

In Chinese government headquarters, Chiang and his commanders decided on the same day, July 9, to dispatch four divisions north to the border of Hebei, the province next to Beijing. This was not necessarily in order to take military action, but a means of putting pressure on the Japanese forces in north China and dissuading them from creating a second Manchukuo.[9] "We will not shy away from war," Chiang wrote in his diary. The following day, he aired suspicions that the incident at Marco Polo Bridge was a pretext to expand Japan's clout: "Maybe their objectives go further than this. Perhaps by proactively sending troops up north, we will be able to rein in their ambitions."[10]

At the same time, hawks in the Japanese military leadership in Tokyo argued that troops should be ordered to China to protect national interests there. On July 11, they succeeded in pushing through a decision to send three whole divisions from Japan, only to see the decision rescinded almost immediately when hopes reappeared for a negotiated solution. Then the pendulum swung back once again. Within just hours, reports arrived in Tokyo about China's dispatch of reinforcements to the border of Hebei. This news tilted the balance in favor of the hawks, and the final decision to send the three divisions was made. "If we, on the basis of a mere oral agreement, should trust the Chinese, we would only be deceived by them again," the Japanese Army ministry spokesman said. His statement ignored the fact that the agreement had now, in fact, been signed, and was no longer just verbal. Perhaps it was deliberate and an attempt to escalate the situation. If so, he got what he wanted.[11]

"Should we open fire, or shouldn't we?" This was the question that occupied Colonel Cui Zhenlun of the Chinese 29th Army's 38th Division for several hours after the Japanese turned up. Cui's regiment was garrisoned in the city of Langfang, midway between Beijing and Tianjin, and a military train with a company of Japanese soldiers had arrived at about 4 pm on July 25 and rolled into Langfang's train station. The soldiers had poured out and begun setting up positions around the station building. Their task, or so they said, was to repair a telephone line, but Cui and his fellow officers suspected that they might be the vanguard of a much bigger Japanese force.[12]

During the fortnight that had passed since the crisis over the Marco Polo Bridge incident, tensions had remained high around Beijing and Tianjin. While the Japanese generals had received the go-ahead to send extra troops to the area, it took time to prepare and dispatch the reinforcements, and in the meantime, moderating forces inside the Japanese establishment attempted to get the decision reversed, warning that China could develop into a quagmire similar to Napoleon's campaign in Spain.[13] Nanjing remained belligerent in its rhetoric, but negotiations between local commanders continued and left hope that the situation could be defused.[14]

Therefore, it could go either way that July afternoon in Langfang, and it was not a foregone conclusion that the Japanese incursion would end in bloodshed. One of Colonel Cui's officers, an ethnic Korean with excellent Japanese, had walked from Langfang's military barracks up to the front of the train station and demanded that the Japanese leave. Not only had the Japanese refused, they had arrogantly required that the Chinese troops in Langfang pull out, and for good measure they had slapped the Chinese-Korean officer in the face. Cui had sent a message to his superiors in Tianjin hoping for instructions, and had received a simple, unsatisfying answer: "Be patient. Do not escalate." Many of Cui's younger officers were spoiling for a fight. "Let's strike them now," said a company commander. However, Cui was not ready to move just yet.

Cui went to see his brigade commander, but he seemed paralyzed by the situation, sitting by his desk with lowered head, smoking one cigarette after the other. While he was trying to drag a decision out of his superior officer, both men heard the sound of guns and explosions coming from near the train station. Cui rushed back, and was informed that one of his company commanders, the one who had expressed impatience earlier that day, had authorized machine guns to be fired at the Japanese line. Soldiers from another Chinese company had heard the automatic fire and had lobbed hand grenades into a Japanese position. The battle had started.[15]

The Japanese troops around the train station only had small arms at their disposal, while the Chinese had a variety of weapons and used them all. The battle dragged on into the night, when a terrible wailing from the Japanese injured emerged from the station area. The Chinese had the upper hand, and they tried to use their advantage to clear the entire railway station of enemy troops. They hoped to get the job done before daybreak on July 26, when the Japanese side was bound to bring in reinforcements, but they failed. The Japanese had made good use of the buildings inside the station area to set up strong defensive positions and beat back all Chinese assaults.[16]

As expected, when the sun rose the reinforcements arrived in the form of nine Japanese airplanes. Dividing themselves into three groups, the aircraft circled over Langfang and then attacked, dropping bombs on the Chinese military barracks and strafing personnel caught in the open. The barracks was surrounded only by mud walls and offered very little in the way of protection. The Chinese soldiers fled out into the surrounding countryside, hiding in the high vegetation. At the same time, the Japanese infantry poured out from the station building, taking over all main points in the city. Late that morning, the Chinese troops were ordered to withdraw. The battle for Langfang was over.[17]

Now the situation began to change fast. Japan's China Garrison Army had received a new commander shortly after the Marco Polo Bridge incident, the belligerent General Kazuki Kiyoshi, who regarded the rest of his staff as "a bunch of cowards"[18] for not having acted more decisively. Eager to teach the Chinese a lesson, he was a representative of the "culture of disobedience" among field commanders willing to make wide-ranging decisions on their own authority. Without waiting for the green light from Tokyo, he ordered a regiment to Beijing and sent an ultimatum to the Chinese commander, Song Zheyuan, to abandon the city voluntarily or be forced out.[19]

The Japanese regiment arrived on trucks at Guang'an Gate in Beijing's ancient city wall at 7 pm on July 26. As the vehicles rolled into the old capital, troops of the Chinese 29th Army posted on top of the wall opened fire. The Japanese shot back, and a fierce battle raged for the next three hours. At this time, as darkness enveloped the city, one part of the Japanese column that had managed to get inside the wall continued on to the area near the Japanese consulate close to the old Forbidden City. The rest of the column withdrew back out of Beijing.[20]

With the clashes at Langfang and Guang'an Gate, the hawks in the Japanese military had what they needed to demand retribution against the Chinese. While the skirmish at Guang'an Gate was still underway, General Kazuki decided singlehandedly "to chastise" the Chinese troops in the area around Beijing and Tianjin and issued a detailed plan of attack.[21] On July 27, his plan was approved in Tokyo, and Hirohito, who was becoming impatient and wished to put a swift end to the fighting in north China, sanctioned an imperial order to "bring stability to the main strategic places in that region."[22] The Japanese attack was set for the following day, July 28.

The main objective in the Beijing region was a compound south of the city, next to Nanyuan civilian airfield, which served as the headquarters and main barracks of the 29th Army. The Japanese 20th Division prepared to attack the area from the south, while a brigade set up positions north of Nanyuan, cutting off the only retreat route back to Beijing. The attack began at 8 am with air raids and artillery shelling of the compound. The 20,000 officers and men trapped inside the barracks had no chance against the superior Japanese weaponry, and when the Japanese infantry moved in three hours later, they were reduced to offering resistance from the scant cover provided by the smoking ruins.[23]

The battle for Nanyuan was short, and by early afternoon the survivors in the Chinese garrison tried to escape north along the road to Beijing. This was exactly what the Japanese had expected them to do. The Japanese brigade that had moved in earlier the same day had commandeered local farm buildings, before ordering everyone indoors and placing machine guns on the rooftops.[24] Lying in ambush as the retreating Chinese passed by, they caught them in crossfire from which there was no escape.[25] The road became an avenue of death, as described by an eyewitness, who arrived shortly afterwards: "The cars still stood in a crazy line, each one packed with corpses. The chef d'oeuvre was a staff car under which a dead horse, inexplicably wedged, was swelling and jacking upward a cargo of dead men," he wrote. "Still all agreed that none of these sights or even the smells were as harrowing as the sounds which hung over the scenes of battle, for the moans and screams of the wounded hidden in the crops were still unceasing."[26]

At 2 pm on July 28, Song Zheyuan called a meeting of his commanders to decide what was next for the 29th Army. Everyone agreed the situation was critical. The Japanese had attacked not just at Nanyuan, but in a number of locations, and everywhere they had won. A defeatist mood gripped the Chinese officers bent over their maps, and General Song made a decision to retreat along with his main force to the city of Baoding south of Beijing. With no defenders left, China's old capital had fallen to the Japanese, virtually without a fight.[27]

The need to supply troops for the Beijing offensive had forced the Japanese commanders to leave the port city of Tianjin precariously exposed, with only about 5,000 soldiers defending this key hub. The Chinese troops in the Tianjin area were themselves becoming increasingly isolated, especially after the withdrawal from Beijing, but nevertheless launched an attack on the Japanese positions on July 29. They were able to inflict considerable losses at first, but Japanese planes brought in to offer tactical support turned the tide. Later the same day, the Chinese commanders in Tianjin opted for pulling out. By doing so, they conceded defeat in the entire Beijing area.[28]

This was not the main reason why July 29 was to be remembered. Events on this day would take on a special significance for quite another reason: the Tongzhou incident. Tongzhou, a walled city east of Beijing, was the seat of government of a collaborationist regime known as the East Hebei Autonomous Council, which had been set up in late 1935. It housed a fairly large Japanese garrison, as well as both Japanese and Korean civilians. It was also home to a force of Chinese auxiliary police which secretly harbored a deep hatred for its Japanese masters. When a large number of Japanese soldiers left the city to take part in the general assault on Chinese forces near Beijing, the auxiliary police decided to strike.

On July 29 they stormed out into the streets, attacking the remainder of the Japanese garrison as well as the government building. Civilian homes were also razed. "Heads were hung in wicker baskets from the parapets above the closed town gates," according to a report. "Mutilated bodies were left where victims fell in the muddy streets for hungry dogs and flies."[29] A total of 27 soldiers and officers died, as well as 223 of the city's 385 civilian Japanese and Koreans. Many women and children were among the victims.[30]

Sakurai Fumio, a 27-year-old Japanese platoon leader, entered the city the following day, encountering what he would later describe as a "picture-scroll of hell." Walking from house to house, the soldiers shouted out, "Are there no Japanese?" Then the survivors started crawling forward from their hiding places in garbage bins, trenches, behind walls: "a child whose nose was pierced crosswise with wire as an ox, an old woman whose one arm was cut off, a pregnant woman whose abdomen was stabbed with bayonets." One family of six had been thrown into a well, the hands tied together and pierced with steel wire like "beads on a rosary."[31]

The Japanese payback was swift and brutal. It was said that the Japanese Army killed 600 uniformed men and a large number of civilians in a revenge orgy that did not limit itself to Tongzhou.[32] A highly biased version of events at Tongzhou was reported widely in the Japanese press, causing intense fury to spread through society. In the weeks and months that followed, "Avenge Tongzhou" became a rallying cry for Japanese soldiers and served as the flimsy justification for yet more atrocities committed against innocent Chinese. This would be especially clear further south, along the mighty Yangtze river, a part of China that was soon to see the brunt of the fighting.

★   ★   ★

In the evening of August 9, 27-year-old Sub-Lieutenant Oyama Isao of the Japanese marines rode in a car chauffeured by First Class Seaman Saitō Yozo to the entrance of Hongqiao Aerodrome on the western outskirts of Shanghai. It was a military air base and guarded by Chinese paramilitary soldiers. What the two Japanese wanted will probably never be fully understood. An altercation ensued, and someone opened fire. The Chinese soldiers released a hail of bullets that ripped through the Japanese vehicle, killing both marines. The scene looked too much like an assassination, and the Chinese officials in charge understood it could not just be left like that. They quickly fetched a prisoner from a local jail, hauled him to the airport and dressed him in a Chinese uniform before executing him.[33]

Within hours, investigators from both sides as well as neutral representatives from the Western powers descended on the airport, trying to disentangle the facts. The incident had come at a precarious time, when the Chinese Army had sent its elite forces to the vicinity of Shanghai. They had avoided entering the city proper in accordance with an agreement reached after the battle over the city five and a half years earlier, but they could move at any time. Similarly, the Japanese high command had dispatched reinforcements to bolster the tiny garrison in Shanghai. It was an explosive situation, and only cool minds and careful negotiation could de-escalate it. Instead, the Chinese side decided to strike.

On August 14, the elite of the Chinese Army was thrown against the Japanese marines along the boundaries of "Little Tokyo." They were from the 87th and 88th Divisions, the result of years of training and investment in state-of-the-art weaponry. Their advisors were German, as was much of their equipment, including the signature M35 German helmet. They attacked the Japanese head-on, but by doing so, they proved that in modern war, personal valor in itself is rarely sufficient. The Japanese marines had spent the past several days strengthening their already impressive defenses, greeting the attacking Chinese with rows of barbed wire and well-oiled machine guns. Their field artillery was supported by the heavy guns of warships anchored in Shanghai's Huangpu River which fired indiscriminately into the Chinese districts of the city. It was clear after the first couple of days of fighting that the attempt to push the Japanese marines into the river was going to be far harder than expected. The streets around "Little Tokyo" had been turned into a slaughterhouse.[34]

It was inevitable that a large battle taking place in a city of Shanghai's size would result in huge civilian suffering. This fact was driven home just hours after the first shot was fired. August 14 was later to be known as "Bloody Saturday" due to a fatal error committed by the inexperienced Chinese air force. When its airplanes took off on that day, their primary objective was the Japanese cruiser *Izumo*. Built in the 1890s, it was approaching retirement but still possessed formidable firepower. Anchored near the Shanghai waterfront, it provided crucial tactical support for the marines fighting inside the city by raining down shells on the Chinese lines in the densely populated streets.

Several waves of Chinese planes descended on the Japanese vessel, and not one of them hit its target. Most of the bombs ended up in the Huangpu River without doing any damage, but one plane released its bombs far too early, dropping two over the Cathay and Palace Hotels, two of Shanghai's swankiest establishments. The result was a bloodbath.[35] "Here was a headless man, there a baby's foot, wearing its little red-silk shoe embroidered with fierce dragons," a Western journalist wrote about the horrific scene. "One body, that of a young boy, was flattened high against a wall, to which it clung with ghastly adhesion."[36]

Exactly why Chiang Kai-shek decided to open a second front at Shanghai remains a subject of dispute. Perhaps, some historians have argued, the decisive factor was the presence in the city of a sizable foreign community. Crucially, many Western journalists were also there, ready to record what everyone could see was world history in the making. Chiang may have hoped that by waging the battle in front of a large international audience he would be able to gather sympathy abroad. He might even be able to obtain foreign intervention, if the battle spilled over into the International Settlement or the French Concession.

If so, it was a highly risky gamble and one unlikely to pay off. The probability was low that the Western powers would want to get involved in the complexities of Sino-Japanese affairs. A certain aloofness also prevented many Westerners from investing any emotion in the war. As one British financier quipped, "It's just the natives fighting."[37] More likely, Chiang may have genuinely thought that by concentrating his best troops in a shock attack on the meager Japanese garrison in Shanghai, he would be able to score a quick, dramatic victory that could rally the nation.

Japan, on the other hand, only entered the battle reluctantly. The army already felt overstretched in the north of China, and for the wrong reasons. Many Japanese generals considered the Soviet Union to be the main threat and the one that most resources had to be directed towards. The Chinese themselves understood this was the case, and on occasion admitted so in public. "Japan had no wish to fight at Shanghai," Chinese General Zhang Fakui, one of the top field commanders during the struggle for the city, said in a post-war interview. "It should be simple to see that we took the initiative."[38]

Despite the lingering doubts, Japan continued to pour in reinforcements as the battle progressed. In a sense, events were taking on a momentum of their own. Once a sizable number of troops had been deployed at Shanghai, it would have entailed considerable loss of prestige, and constituted major logistic challenges, to extricate the soldiers. Also, unlike the Manchurian Incident, the Japanese side during and after the Marco Polo Bridge Incident had no clear plan about what was to be achieved. This meant that there were no predetermined objectives that negotiators in the field knew they should aim for, and local settlements were hard to achieve. As a result, the conflict in 1937 was effectively open-ended.[39]

For the first few days, the Chinese forces held the initiative, but this changed roughly one week into the battle. On August 23, two entire Japanese divisions started landing in separate areas north of Shanghai, hitting the Chinese forces in the flank. Supported by the naval guns and ship-based aircraft, they made rapid progress inland. It came as a complete surprise to the Chinese, although they probably should have anticipated the move, since Japan had performed almost the exact same operation during the 1932 battle. The Chinese commanders had to swiftly regroup and assign some of their best forces to deal with the new threat.

From this point onwards, the battle for Shanghai changed. The Chinese side was forced into the defensive, and would stay that way for the remaining ten weeks of the battle. Counterattacks carried out against the Japanese, often at huge cost in lives, did not change this fact. The Japanese landings in late August also caused the battle's center of gravity to move to the rural areas north of Shanghai. While Chinese and Japanese forces remained locked in a deadly embrace in the ruins of the downtown districts, most of the fighting and the killing now took place in the villages and rice fields outside the city limits.

The battle was slowly but surely turning in favor of the Japanese. As late summer morphed into fall, the Japanese leveraged their technological advantage, slowly pushing back the Chinese on all fronts. The Chinese air force, never a major factor in the battle, was shot out of the sky, and eventually the Japanese gained air superiority, making any movement in the daytime a highly dangerous business for the Chinese. In late October, they decided to pull out of their positions in central Shanghai, setting fire to large parts of the city's working class neighborhoods as they moved west, in a scorched earth campaign that was at least as costly to the civilian inhabitants as to the Japanese.

In one final act of bravado, a battalion was ordered to make a dramatic last stand in the Chinese district near Suzhou Creek, which formed the border with the International Settlement. The battalion prepared positions inside a sturdy building known as the Sihang Warehouse, putting up determined resistance against the advancing Japanese. Militarily, it made no difference, but as a propaganda exercise it was highly successful, and before the battalion withdrew after four days of fighting, its soldiers had triggered the admiration of large numbers of compatriots, standing across Suzhou Creek in the safety of the international district as they watched the battle unfold. Foreign journalists, too, were present, referring to the defenders as "the suicide battalion" or "the lost battalion."[40]

For the Japanese, the time had come to put an end to the protracted battle. They delivered their final devastating blow in early November, when they succeeded in hitting the Chinese in the rear once more with a second amphibious operation. This time the landing took place south of Shanghai, on the shores of Hangzhou Bay where the Chinese coastal defenses were weak or, in some places, non-existent. Three divisions disembarked and waded ashore in circumstances that for some seemed as safe as a maneuver back in the home islands.

Reports suggested that the sudden deterioration pushed Chiang Kai-shek close to a nervous breakdown.[41] He had engaged in a highly risky gamble and staked his army's German-trained elite, many of whom had become casualties in the Shanghai meat-grinder, and all for nothing. Now he faced the very real danger that the remnants of his army would fall victim to a giant Japanese pincer movement. He had no choice but to order a full retreat. While a few scattered troops were left in the south of the city to carry out rearguard actions, tired and dirty columns of Chinese soldiers trudged out, mercilessly bombed and strafed by the Japanese air force along the way. On November 11, the 19th anniversary of the end of the Great War in Europe, the battle of Shanghai was over. The Japanese triumph was total.

The combat in and around Shanghai was in many ways similar to the positional warfare that the world had come to know only too well two decades earlier in the trenches of France and Flanders. Some aspects, including the use of mounted troops on both sides, were a reminder of even earlier periods in the history of warfare. In other ways, however, the battle for the city also pointed into the future, with the introduction of weapons and tactics that would become typical of the approaching global conflict. In particular, armored and amphibious tactics were tested on the Shanghai battlegrounds.

For China, the development of a tank arm had been part of the ambitious effort to build up a modern army in the preceding years. As was the case with the air force, the Chinese opted to rely on foreign expertise and technology, acknowledging that their country had not yet reached a stage in its industrial development where it could realistically sustain a tank construction program of its own. In the 1930s, the Chinese government had imported light tanks and armored cars from several countries, mostly Great Britain and Germany.[42] In Shanghai, the Chinese Army deployed British-built 6-ton, one-turret Vickers tanks, and lost nearly all in futile frontal attacks against sturdy Japanese positions.

Japanese armor proved superior to its Chinese counterpart in Shanghai. This said more about Chinese shortcomings than Japanese excellence. Japan's Army was conservative and averse to innovation, much more so than its Navy. This was particularly clear in tank design and doctrine, an area that was to fundamentally alter land warfare in World War II. Japan did introduce some novelties in the 1930s, including the world's first diesel-powered tank, the Type 89B, but in general it was lagging behind other industrialized countries.[43] Unfortunately for Japan, these shortcomings did not become immediately apparent in the China theater because of the general lack of efficient anti-tank weaponry available to the Chinese forces.[44]

By contrast, Japan was a pioneer in amphibious warfare and had improved its capabilities since it had put troops ashore at Shanghai in 1932. The two major landing operations near Shanghai in August and November 1937 had a decisive impact on the outcome of the battle, and other countries were watching attentively. For example, Dutch Colonel Henri Johan Diederick de Fremery, who was officially an advisor to the Chinese military, sent detailed reports to the authorities in the Netherlands East Indies about the vessels used by the Japanese.[45] To be sure, the landings had been mainly unopposed, and therefore did not fully reflect the challenges of storming a fortified coastline.[46] Still, the amphibious experience Japan gained in China in the late 1930s meant it was as well prepared as the United States in this particular form of warfare by the start of World War II.[47]

"The very foundations of civilization are seriously threatened," President Roosevelt told an audience in Chicago in the morning of October 5, 1937. His topic: how a world that had emerged from devastating global conflict less than a generation earlier was now again threatened by aggression. "It seems to be unfortunately true that the epidemic of world lawlessness is spreading," he warned. "And mark this well: When an epidemic of physical disease starts to spread, the community approves and joins in a quarantine of the patients in order to protect the health of the community against the spread."[48]

Roosevelt did not name the nations that were to blame for the state of affairs, but no one could doubt that he was referring to Germany for its proxy war in Spain, Italy for its very conspicuous invasion of Abyssinia, and Japan for its bloody campaign in China. Indeed, in a private conversation a few weeks earlier, he had directly referred to them as the "three bandit nations." In the same conversation, however, he had also made it clear that his idea about "quarantining," or isolating, aggressor nations was a plan for future contingencies. It was too late for China. Japan was already so deeply involved that nothing could be done about the situation, he believed.[49]

The president was well into his second term, and as the leader of the world's largest democracy he was hoping to gradually shift the strongly isolationist mood of the nation in favor of engagement abroad. He was pushing for only moderate change, remaining of the opinion that US involvement in global affairs, for now at least, should not be in the form of military action, or even sanctions.[50] These caveats were not enough to change the isolationist leanings in the American public. Reactions to the "quarantine speech," according to a close colleague, were "quick and violent—and nearly unanimous."[51] There were dissenting voices of internationalism among the public and in the media, but the *Wall Street Journal* summed up the feelings of many when it called on the government to "Stop Foreign Meddling; America Wants Peace."[52] As Roosevelt stated candidly in a message to the British Foreign Office, "I cannot march ahead of our very difficult and restive American public opinion."[53]

In other words, the conditions for more active US diplomacy were not ideal when on October 6, the day after Roosevelt's speech, representatives of the world's governments at the League of Nations in Geneva started moving on the crisis in East Asia. A committee which had been charged with finding a response to the ongoing undeclared war in China issued a denunciation of Japan and called for an international conference to enable "full and frank communication" about the situation.[54] It suggested that the conference should take place within the framework of the so-called Nine-Power Treaty, which had been signed by China and a group of major powers in 1922, mainly in an effort to secure equal rights of foreign nations inside China while also paying due respect to Chinese sovereignty.[55] Choosing this forum was a pragmatic option, since it allowed the participation of both Japan and the United States, which were not members of the League but both among the nine signatory governments.[56]

After some delay, the meeting was convened in Brussels on November 3, with the active participation of a number of involved powers, including China, the United States, and even the Soviet Union, but Japan was conspicuously absent. The Japanese government was encouraged twice to send a representative, but turned down both invitations, arguing that it was conducting its operations in China as "a measure of defense against Chinese acts of provocation."[57]

The US representative at the conference, experienced diplomat Norman Davis, was eager to explore ways to apply pressure to Japan, arguing that this was the only language Tokyo understood. "We learned at school," he told a journalist in an off-the-record press briefing, "that the only way of restraining a bully is to knock him down."[58] Still, cables sent by Davis to the State Department soliciting support for a tough stance on Japan got a cool reception. The opposition to any kind of foreign entanglement was too strong.[59]

The firm US stance against sanctions was a key factor behind the toothless declaration passed by most of the participating nations on November 15. "Force by itself can provide no just and lasting solution for disputes between nations," the text said, urging that "hostilities be suspended and resort be had to peaceful processes."[60] The Chinese delegation was visibly disappointed that nothing harsher emerged from the conference. As Davis said frankly in a telephone conversation with Secretary of State Cordell Hull, the Chinese were keenly aware that the statement "doesn't stop Japan from killing their people."[61]

The Brussels conference made little real difference, but it did consolidate the growing coordination between the foreign services of the United States and Britain, also vis-à-vis Japan. Both governments had entered the conference with few hopes that it would be much more than a public relations exercise, but at the same time, both were gratified to end up on the same page during the talks, as the US and British representatives took great care not to work at cross-purposes. In the words of one British diplomat, "as international cooperation declined, Anglo-American cooperation would arise."[62] In the following months, the State Department and Foreign Office increasingly shared information about Japanese intentions in the Far East, even at the risk of exposing their intelligence sources to each other.[63]

Meanwhile, the lack of concrete results in Brussels forced Chiang Kai-shek to look elsewhere for assistance. For attempts to seek a palatable diplomatic solution, he increasingly pinned his hopes on Germany, which had not participated at the Brussels Conference, partly out of general hostility towards the League of Nations or any initiatives associated with the organization.[64] Oskar Trautmann, the German ambassador to China, became a key figure as a liaison between Nanjing and Tokyo, trying to move the belligerents to talk, but it was an uphill battle. Even after the fall of Shanghai, Chiang Kai-shek was reluctant to consider any agreement with Japan which might entail political cost, especially in the form of further loss of control of north China.[65]

Germany's Nazi regime was not an obvious choice for a peace mediator, but it was put in an awkward situation by the ongoing conflict in Asia, since it had significant commercial interests in the region. More importantly, it considered both China and Japan potential partners in an attempt to contain the Soviet Union, whereas a Japanese empire tied down by war with China would be less able to exert pressure on the Russians from the east and allow them to allocate more resources to Europe.[66] As Herman Goering, the president of the *Reichstag,* told a Chinese visitor, "the Sino-Japanese War has placed Germany between Scylla and Charybdis."[67]

The Soviet Union, for its part, was becoming an increasingly active player in East Asia. It welcomed war between China and Japan for the same reason that Germany opposed it, and since late 1936 it had been aiming quietly to nudge Chiang Kai-shek towards a firmer stance against Japan. In the summer of 1937, as war was approaching, the Soviet ambassador to China had directly promised "armed support" if Chiang was to resist Japanese aggression.[68] British diplomats had tried to warn Chiang that the Soviet Union only had its own interests in mind, but this did not significantly change the Chinese leader's high hopes for his Russian connection.[69]

If Chiang had expected Soviet entry into the war, he was disappointed. However, he did achieve a major diplomatic triumph when, in August, his government was able to sign a non-aggression treaty with Moscow, which in fact implied cooperation in a number of areas—political, economic, and military.[70] In the fall, Soviet supplies of military equipment started moving overland to China, and at the same time, Soviet military aircraft arrived, flown by Soviet pilots. By the time Shanghai was captured by the Japanese in November, the aviators had taken to the skies over the lower Yangtze, and the Soviet Union had become an inconspicuous but important part of the war.

While the battle of Shanghai was raging, absorbing the lion's share of international interest, fighting also continued in the north of China. After the fall of Beijing and Tianjin, the victorious Japanese troops attempted to build on their momentum, fanning out in several different directions in pursuit of the remaining organized resistance. Much of it came from warlords who in many cases felt little loyalty to Chiang and might defect to the Japanese side if properly motivated. The Japanese did the same as the Chinese armies had done during the civil wars in the preceding decades, concentrating their efforts on securing the major cities and the railroads that connected them.[71]

The main Japanese force moved south out of the Beijing area in September with two armies supported by a well-equipped tank complement, advancing along two major rail lines. Their initial objective was the city of Baoding, the seat of an advanced medical college and one of modern China's most influential military academies. It had robust defenses in the form of a 60-foot city wall, surrounded by two moats and rows of barbed wire.[72] A siege could take weeks or months, but instead the Japanese captured the city in less than a day. After a one-hour shelling of the city wall in the morning of September 24, the Japanese stormed the city, and found it deserted. The defenders had moved out the night before, deciding to preserve their strength rather than being caught in an unwinnable battle.[73]

Baoding was among the first cities to witness the depth of depravity that the Japanese Army could sink to when savoring a triumph over a defenseless foe. The population was subjected to a week of alcohol-induced rape and murder. "The library and laboratories of the medical college went up in roaring flames, into which a number of screaming students and instructors were thrown for good measure," according to one account.[74] Territorial conquest was on the minds of the Japanese commanders, and they instilled in their armies a spirit of unbridled ambition. "The officers and men shouldn't return without filling their canteens with water from the Yellow River as a souvenir," said General Terauchi Hisaichi, the commander of Japan's newly formed North China Area Army.[75]

The Japanese columns marched through Chinese villages that had been quick to adapt to the new times. In some areas, nearly every farmhouse sported a makeshift Japanese flag, usually just a white rag with a splash of red paint or a crudely cut disc of red paper.[76] Foreign missionaries were also among the witnesses of the rapid Japanese advance across the north Chinese countryside. Some had seen so much turbulence in their lifetimes that even a foreign invasion left them unfazed. "When you've been here as long as I have," said an American missionary who had spent her entire life in China and now resided in the city of Kalgan[77] near Beijing, "you'll realize these flare-ups come and go. They always have. But the voice of God is heard above them all."[78]

In the north of China, the Communist forces played a more important role than elsewhere. After all, this was where the Long March had taken them earlier in the decade. They fielded a unit referred to as the Eighth Route Army, consisting of three divisions with a total of 46,000 soldiers. They were loosely linked to the overall war effort directed from Nanjing, as a result of an agreement reached by Chiang Kai-shek and the communist leadership under Mao Zedong in the summer. This was the latest offshoot of the united front against Japanese aggression that the two former mortal enemies had reached following the Xian incident.

One of Mao's most capable field officers was the 29-year-old offspring of a wealthy merchant family by the name of Lin Biao. As the commander of the Eighth Route Army's 115th Division, he orchestrated a battle that was eventually to take on nearly mythical proportions. The battle originated in the situation that emerged when a Japanese army moved west out of the Beijing area, seeking to gain control of a railroad stretching from the ancient capital towards Inner Mongolia. Lin Biao saw his chance when one of the slow-moving Japanese supply columns following in the footsteps of the infantry entered into a desolate area near the Great Wall known as Pingxing Pass.[79]

It was an area that had been traveled by caravans for centuries, and in this particular spot, camel hooves had gradually carved a narrow ravine in the soft loess terrain, with no exit except at the beginning and the end. It was the perfect spot for an ambush, and Lin Biao ordered his troops on a forced march to the area to prepare positions prior to the arrival of the Japanese. He sprang the trap on September 25 at the appearance of the Japanese column, a few hundred mostly lightly armed troops with pack animals and vehicles weighed down by their cargoes. Nested on the sides of the ravine, Lin Biao's troops poured bullets into the trapped column and dropped hand grenades, then moved in to finish off the wounded with bayonets. The scene was one of utter destruction. A Japanese eyewitness described "cars charred on the roadside with their burned drivers still at the steering wheel."[80]

The casualties were relatively limited, and recent research has suggested that fewer than 200 Japanese soldiers were killed.[81] Even so, the battle quickly became a staple of communist propaganda, and its significance was also greatly exaggerated by foreign sympathizers. American journalist Anna Louise Strong claimed that the triumph at Pingxing Pass helped prevent Japanese convergence on Nanjing from the north. Otherwise, it would have cornered the Chinese government, she argued, adding implausibly that "it would have meant that complete surrender to Japan must have followed."[82] Clearly, it was good for the Communist Party's image, but Mao Zedong was not happy. He had emphasized that the war had now entered into a new phase characterized by guerrilla tactics rather than big conventional battles. The Pingxing

Pass battle defied this order, and he subsequently sent repeated messages to his field commanders reminding them that risks such as these were not worth taking.[83]

All through the last weeks of fighting in Shanghai, when it became ever clearer that the Chinese forces would be defeated, the Japanese commanders both in the field and in Tokyo had been debating the question of what to do next. Two distinct camps had emerged. One group of officers was wary of an entanglement in China from which there would be no easy escape and wished to limit operations to the Shanghai area. The other group was in favor of "teaching Chiang Kai-shek a lesson" and advocated with growing vigor a campaign to conquer the Chinese capital Nanjing.

By late November 1937, the group of "China hawks" had gained the upper hand in Tokyo, and on December 1, one of the top decision-makers at the General Staff, General Tada Hayao, arrived by plane in Shanghai with orders for the two armies in the field, the Tenth Army and the Shanghai Expeditionary Force, to take Nanjing. Shortly afterwards, Tokyo made a fateful change. It promoted the commander of the Shanghai Expeditionary Force, which had been in uninterrupted combat for months, and replaced him with Prince Asaka Yasuhiko, an uncle of Hirohito's. Prince Asaka had displayed insufficient loyalty during the coup attempt of February 1936 and was eager to redeem himself. The combination of an ambitious officer and an army of battle-weary soldiers would prove fateful.[84]

The campaign to take Nanjing was qualitatively different from the battle for Shanghai. While the soldiers in the muddy trenches around Shanghai often found themselves fighting for inches of territory at the time, not unlike the conditions on the Western Front a generation earlier, the rapid advance towards Nanjing, when armored columns often took the lead, was to some extent a foreshadowing of the German *Blitzkrieg* to take place two years later in Poland. The Chinese defenses did manage to halt the Japanese on several occasions, but the advantage gained was invariably local and could not stem the Japanese offensive until, a week into December, Hirohito's army was standing at the ancient stone walls surrounding Nanjing.

As the Chinese defenders turned down an offer to surrender, the Japanese units arrayed along the southern and eastern perimeter of the city went about seeking the weakest parts of the city wall. Intense battles developed around the main gates, which were towering, fortress-like structures, ingeniously designed to make it almost impossible for an attacker to enter forcibly. In some sections along the wall, Japanese units aptly named "dare-to-die" troops sought to gain access to the top with unstable, wobbly ladders. An unofficial contest was underway among the various units to be the first to plant the banner of the Rising Sun on the wall.

The city gates became the scenes of battles within the battle, as Japanese infantry supported by tanks, artillery and often aircraft sought to gain entry by storm. At one section of the city wall, the Japanese attackers were under explicit orders to take the city gate. They were to achieve that objective, even if it meant fighting to the last man. Facing them was a Chinese unit under even more direct orders to keep the city gate at any cost: "If you don't carry out the order," was the menacing command the Chinese soldiers had received from higher up, "we want to see your severed heads."[85]

In the final analysis, Nanjing's fate was decided not by what happened on the Japanese side, but what took place among the Chinese. Chiang Kai-shek's government had made a decision to move the capital to the large but isolated city of Chongqing in the southwest, but he himself and many of his closest aides had set up a temporary new headquarters in the city of Wuhan up the Yangtze River. From this location far from the battlefront, Chiang started issuing contradictory orders to Nanjing's commandant Tang Shengzhi. Initially, he suggested that the capital would only have to be held for a short while, in order to prevent a senseless waste of men and materiel on a lost battle. Later, he urged Tang to defend the city for weeks or even months, reflecting hopes that the Soviet Union might step up its support of China. In the end, however, Chiang ordered a full-scale retreat.

This final order to abandon Nanjing was promptly obeyed by Tang and his staff, but it was not passed down the ranks in a timely and consistent manner. As a result, rumors started spreading among the Chinese rank and file that the top brass had already departed, causing panic to erupt. As large parts of the city wall were left unguarded, a great number of Chinese soldiers started moving towards the banks of the Yangtze, hoping to find ways to escape to the other shore. Soldiers of the elite 36th Chinese Division, stationed near the river port, allegedly opened fire on the mass of soldiers, killing many, but it failed to stem the stampede. At the Yangtze docks, indescribable chaos reigned, as soldiers and civilians fought over the few spaces available aboard vessels going to the opposite side.

While the Chinese defenders struggled to get out of the city, the Japanese attackers marched in. The first soldiers inside the wall encountered what seemed almost a ghost city. In fact, those among Nanjing's population who could afford it had left long ago, while those without money or connections were cowering behind boarded-up windows and doors, hoping for lenient treatment at the hands of the city's new masters. Those hopes were entirely in vain, as was soon to become tragically obvious.

Within hours of the Japanese occupation of Nanjing, the bodies of killed civilians appeared in the streets. The occupation was also only a few hours old when Japanese soldiers started running through the alleys, rounding up Chinese soldiers. Those caught in uniform were killed on the spot or collected into larger groups, led to the Yangtze, and machine-gunned. Soon, the search expanded, and the Japanese also went on the lookout for any young male of military age. People with calloused hands, a supposed sign of weapons handling or work with entrenching tools, were taken aside and shot. That such hands might be the sign of any manual labor was ignored.[86]

The Japanese went on a rampage through the once prosperous city, pillaging both businesses and private homes. To a certain extent this was a reflection of the desperate logistical situation in the Japanese Army. Time and again, its soldiers found themselves deprived of supplies and were expected to live off the land or, put more bluntly, loot the towns and villages they passed through. This also happened in Nanjing, but with an added element of destructiveness. Soldiers would top off ransacking a building by setting it on fire, and within a few weeks of conquering the city, they had reduced large parts to ashes.

Perhaps more than anything else, it was the treatment meted out to the city's women that gave Nanjing's dark winter its particularly sinister hue. The Japanese Army unleashed an orgy of rape, exempting virtually no one. Any female, whether a preteen or an octogenarian, could become a victim of sexual violence. Pregnant women were not spared either. Ginling College, which was exclusively for girls and had been included in a larger safety zone meant to protect civilians, was repeatedly visited by Japanese soldiers on the prowl.

The reign of terror lasted for six weeks and only ended in January 1938. No one knows exactly how many were killed in what was soon to be known as the Rape of Nanjing. The official Chinese figure today is 300,000, while some scholars estimate a figure less than half of that. Regardless of the exact number, there is no doubt that a transgression quite out of the ordinary had taken place. It was clear even to the Japanese High Command, which sent an order, resembling a reprimand in tone, to the senior officer in Nanjing to get his soldiers under control. Grotesquely, China and Japan still had diplomatic relations at the time of the massacre, maintaining ambassadors even as civilians were killed by the tens of thousands in Nanjing.[87]

The massacre attracted attention in the West, causing some uproar, especially among those already opposed to Japanese imperialism, but it is possible that another, significantly smaller, incident did more to alienate Western governments because of the identity of the victims. On December 12, the day Nanjing fell, Japanese planes attacked the US gunboat *Panay* in the Yangtze. The assault cost three American lives, and although it was most likely an error, anger in the United States was intense, albeit brief. The Japanese rushed to apologize, and the *Panay* incident was eventually solved, but it served to ostracize Japan further in the international community.[88] Why the harsh tone this time? A likely reason was that the victims at the *Panay*, unlike those in Nanjing, were Caucasian.

Nanjing served as a warning that the Japanese were capable of mind-boggling acts of cruelty, a pattern of behavior that would persist until the end of hostilities in 1945. The cruelty may have been partly a tactic meant to intimidate their Chinese opponent. Rumors of Japanese cannibalism and the killing of well-fed peasants for food caused many Chinese soldiers to abandon their positions.[89] However, far more often than not, the crimes committed by the Japanese in the field seemed to defy any rational purpose. Indeed, the brutality frequently interfered with wider strategic aims. If anything, it served to further strengthen Chinese resistance to the Japanese invasion.

For those who had been in personal touch with Japanese in peacetime, and had been struck by their friendliness and politeness, this was particularly puzzling. Some put it down to the ambiguity of the Japanese character. In the words of American anthropologist Ruth Benedict, who wrote an analysis of the Japanese mind a few years later, after most of the world had been engulfed by war, "the Japanese are, to the highest degree, both aggressive and unaggressive, both militaristic and aesthetic, both insolent and polite, rigid and adaptable, submissive and resentful of being pushed around, loyal and treacherous, brave and timid, conservative and hospitable to new ways. They are terribly concerned about what other people will think about their behavior, and they are also overcome by guilt when other people know nothing of their misstep. Their soldiers are disciplined to the hilt but are also insubordinate."[90]

CHAPTER FOUR

Defiance

China, 1938

In January 1938, Russian pilot F. P. Polynin was still only a recent arrival in the central Chinese city of Wuhan, the de facto capital after Chiang Kai-shek had left Nanjing, and the Japanese invaders had still not got used to the idea that now they also had to fight the mighty Soviet Air Force. The 31-year-old officer's squadron of high-speed, twin-engine Tupolev SB bombers was part of the Soviet aid that was beginning to trickle into China. On a cold morning shortly after New Year, his unit was put to the test with a difficult and dangerous mission into the heart of enemy country.

Polynin's plane took off from the airfield before dawn, followed by 25 other bombers. Only they and a few other military personnel knew where they were heading: a Japanese air base near Nanjing, where a large number of aircraft had been assembled for a planned offensive. Secrecy among the Russians and Chinese had been tight, due to an all-pervasive fear of spies. The briefing of the crews had taken place behind closed doors protected by armed guards, to make sure no one was listening in.

The bombers crossed the Yangtze River under the dim light of the moon and reached their target just as dawn was breaking. The attack came as a total surprise to the Japanese. "Apparently they were still sleeping, because nothing was moving on the airfield," Polynin wrote in his memoirs. "The Japanese aircraft were lined up as if for a review. Soon the bombs started falling. Fires broke out, and people were running back and forth among the flames."

The operation went completely according to plan. Intelligence later showed that 48 Japanese airplanes had been destroyed in the raid. It was just one of many successes scored by the Soviet pilots assisting China in its desperate war against Japan.[1] The aviators, part of the military aid to China promised in the wake of the bilateral Sino-Soviet agreement of the year before, had started making an appearance on the battlefield during the autumn 1937, and by 1938 their presence was of such a scale that it made up for some of Japan's crushing superiority in the air.

A few weeks later, Polynin and his fellow airmen took part in an even more daring raid. This time the target was Formosa, a Japanese colony that the Chinese referred to by the old name of Taiwan. A total of 28 Tupolev SB bombers took off from Wuhan and crossed the narrow Taiwan Straits heading for the ocean north of the island. Once the aircraft had reached that area, they abruptly changed course due south, in the direction of Taiwan's main city, Taihoku,[2] and its military airport.

Once again, Polynin was struck by the lack of preparation by the Japanese. "We could clearly see two lines of airplanes next to the hangars," he wrote. "The enemy had done nothing to conceal the area. Obviously, he felt completely safe." Polynin was in the lead plane, and releasing his bombs, he saw to his satisfaction one explosion after the other unfold like flowers in the middle of the airfield. The other planes followed suit, dropping a total of 280 bombs. Japanese anti-aircraft batteries opened up, but too late. All Soviet aircraft returned safely.

The day after, a banquet was held in honor of the Soviet pilots. The hostess was Madame Chiang Kai-shek, China's beautiful, arrogant and eloquent First Lady. "The raid on Taiwan has made a big impression throughout the world. The newspapers are full of dispatches describing these events," she told the aviators.[3] This was true—even the *Japan Times and Mail* put the news on its front page[4]—and it was testimony to Madame Chiang's obsession with public relations that she cared more about the amount of newspaper copy that the attack generated than about the actual damage that it inflicted.

It did, however, serve as more than just propaganda. As time went by, Soviet pilots came to play a pivotal role in Chiang Kai-shek's war effort. "We depended on the Russians," a Chinese general said later. "Our pilots had been too brave at Shanghai. Our air force had been dealt too severe a blow."[5] The Russians were known for their courage and their devotion, spending most of their days in their cockpits, ready for take-off at seconds' notice. Wherever they showed themselves in the big cities, they were treated as celebrities. In the countryside, they could not count on the same level of recognition. On the back of their jackets, Chinese characters stated: "I am a Russian. I am here to help you fight Japan." It was a safeguard, perhaps even a life insurance, if they were shot down and parachuted down among suspicious Chinese peasants.[6]

The deepening Chinese relationship with the Soviet Union came at a time when its formerly close cooperation with Germany was falling apart. By early 1938, it was becoming clear to the Nazi leaders that the policy of maintaining good relations with both China and Japan at the same time was untenable. Joachim von Ribbentrop, a fast-rising star in Germany's foreign service, wrote a memorandum to Hitler in January, arguing that the main priority of Nazi diplomacy should be to build an alliance against Britain by "strengthening our friendship with Italy and Japan and in addition winning over all countries whose interests conform directly or indirectly with ours."[7]

Ribbentrop, who was soon to become foreign minister, approached Japanese diplomats in Berlin to sound them out about the feasibility of closer friendship. Rather than talking to the ambassador himself, he deliberately sought out Ōshima Hiroshi, the military attaché, believing that he would get a more sympathetic audience in Japanese Army circles. He was both right and wrong. The Japanese Army officers were not opposed in principle to developing German ties, even if it meant antagonizing the Soviet Union and Great Britain. The problem was with the timing. First, they had to tend to the festering business in China.[8]

A tense meeting took place in Tokyo in the morning of January 15, 1938. A liaison conference between the military brass in the High Command and the civilian officials in the Cabinet had been called to discuss a hugely important topic: should the behind-the-scenes talks with Chiang Kai-shek continue in the hope of a negotiated settlement that could end the carnage, or should they be abandoned, extinguishing the best hope of peace? The background was Chiang's continued rejection of Japanese demands, including war reparations and recognition of Manchukuo.

The participants at the meeting were divided in ways that might have seemed odd to outsiders. A group of officers from the Army High Command insisted that talks be continued, fearing that open-ended conflict in China would see all their resources disappear into a bottomless hole. "Once this opportunity is lost, Japan is in great danger of being dragged into a protracted war," said General Tada Hayao.[9] Foreign Minister Hirota Kōki, a civilian, was adamantly against wasting any more time on Chiang. "In light of my long experience as a diplomat," he said, "it is obvious, judging from its handling of the matter, that China lacks good faith for reaching a peaceful settlement."[10]

The discussion was so heated that Prime Minister Konoe Fumimaro ordered a two-hour recess over lunch to calm down tempers. General Tada and his allies moved fast, hoping to sway Emperor Hirohito in favor of keeping the talks alive. Prince Kan'in Kotohito, a senior officer and an uncle of the ruler, made a prompt visit to the palace asking for an audience, but was turned down. In this situation, Tada felt he had no other option but to bow to the hawks.[11] At the same time, he remained hopeful Hirohito would order a continuation of talks.[12]

That did not happen, because it could not happen. The emperor was firmly in favor of forcing a decision in China by means of war, as he made clear when Prince Kan'in finally managed to see him in the evening.[13] The next day, Tokyo issued a statement declaring that "the Imperial Government will from now not regard the Nationalist government [of China] as a negotiating partner."[14] Two days later, Prime Minister Konoe rubbed it in by saying he wanted to "eradicate" Chiang's government.[15] It was not quite as definitive as it sounded. There was a great deal of diplomatic grandstanding involved, as the future would show. Ahead was a series of behind-the-scenes dialogues, taking place in neutral third-party territories.

Nevertheless, the stern announcements coming out of Tokyo brought to an end the strange state of affairs in which China and Japan had been at war only unofficially, meaning that amid all the horrors of Nanjing and innumerable other nameless places they had been able to maintain diplomatic relations. Within days, their respective ambassadors had been recalled, and there was no longer a direct line of communication between the two governments.[16] By severing diplomatic ties, Japan behaved in a way comparable to Germany and Italy in Europe when they dismissed the Republican government in civil war-torn Spain. The difference was that Berlin and Rome could rely on a charismatic alternative in the form of Fascist leader Francisco Franco. Japan would find, to its chagrin, that China had no Franco.[17]

On the face of it, the Japanese statement on January 16 was a manifestation of strength, but it also indirectly demonstrated a source of weakness: a tendency among its leaders to make suboptimal decisions. At best, the decisions radically limited their options. At worst, they laid the groundwork for future defeats. The Japanese policy of non-recognition forced Chiang to concentrate single-mindedly on resisting the invaders, as he had no alternative. The Chinese military and political elite came to the same conclusion, throwing in their lot with Chiang. In the words of a modern historian, the Japanese decision to end negotiations with China was "one of the greatest foreign policy blunders of any Axis power."[18]

This was evident to many top Japanese decision-makers, and there were second thoughts almost instantaneously. Even though a consensus had been enforced on the proper policy in China, the top military officers continued voicing fears that it was the wrong war, waged against the wrong enemy, for the wrong reasons. A mere fortnight after the Japanese government had loudly proclaimed to the world its willingness to carry on in China for the long term if need be, the General Staff issued a memorandum calling for an early end to hostilities in order to focus on the real threat emanating from the Soviet Union.[19] At this early stage, at least, the Army was inclined to cut its losses and back out of the Chinese cul-de-sac.

At that exact time, China offered Japan an opportunity to step back from the brink. Even though talks had been called off and diplomatic relations severed, lower-level officials in both camps refused to give up all hopes of a revival of talks. A quiet dialogue continued throughout the first months of 1938, and in February a Chinese Foreign Ministry official even visited Japan. In April, a series of Sino-Japanese talks went ahead in Hong Kong, and China declared its willingness to reach a ceasefire followed by peace talks.[20] This did not have any real consequences, since the Chinese conditions, including a restoration of control in north China, were considered too extravagant by Tokyo. Still, it highlighted the fact that almost a year into the outbreak of full-scale war in China, a negotiated peace was arguably within Japanese reach.

History could have taken a much different path, had the opportunity been seized. Instead, the killing continued with undiminished ferocity.

On January 24, 1938, Chinese General Han Fuju, just one day short of his 48th birthday, was being summoned to a meeting with Chiang Kai-shek in Wuhan. General Han could be in no doubt that his end was drawing near. He had been put on a court-martial and had been found guilty of dereliction of duty after he had allowed the strategically important province of Shandong, along with its capital Jinan, to fall into the hands of the Japanese without a fight. The sentence had been no surprise: death. As Han Fuju, stripped of all rank and dressed in simple civilian clothes, was facing Chiang one last time, there was no point in false pretenses or begging for mercy. Instead, Han picked a defiant note: "I lost Jinan, but who," he said, staring straight at Chiang, "lost Nanjing?" Minutes later, Han Fuju was dead, his bullet-riddled corpse lying in a pool of blood. He had just become the highest-ranking general in modern Chinese history to be executed for failing to fulfill his duty.[21]

The severe punishment meted out to Han Fuju was a reflection of the grave situation faced by the Chinese Army in early 1938. Due to his failure in Shandong, a potentially fatal breach had developed in the Chinese line of defense. The province was sitting as a buffer between Japan's victorious armies in the north and its equally triumphant troops in the Yangtze area. To the people around Chiang, it was an inauspicious start of the year, but it would turn out to have surprising ramifications. Even though no one could have known it at the time, it actually set the stage for a battle that would go down in history as the first major Chinese victory of the war.

South of Shandong was the city of Xuzhou, in the middle of an area that had played an important role in Chinese military history since ancient times. It had been the scene of numerous epic battles, and perhaps the most celebrated general of any age, Zhuge Liang, had been born there.[22] Xuzhou was near the Grand Canal, a partly artificial waterway which had been used to transport grain to the Beijing area for centuries, and in modern times it had derived its strategic importance from its key location at the intersection of two major railroads, one going north-south, the other east-west. In a war such as the one being fought with Japan, where transportation networks mattered immensely, control of this particular point on the map was essential.

In early 1938, the Japanese forces in the north and those in the south, having recovered somewhat after the long and costly campaigns in Shanghai and Nanjing, set out in an attempt to converge at Xuzhou. The plan was to link up the two armies and create one continuous area of Japanese control stretching from the Korean border to the Yangtze. Once that had been achieved, the Japanese command planned to move inland towards Chiang Kai-shek's government in Wuhan and force an end to the war. Just as in the Nanjing campaign, the Japanese Army was keen to wrap up the China affair as soon as possible.

The Chinese generals were fully aware of Xuzhou's importance, and even though the armies they commanded had been severely depleted in recent months, they sent their most valuable reserves to the area, close to half a million officers and men. Overall command went to General Li Zongren, one of China's most capable and experienced officers. There was one problem: Chiang Kai-shek and Li Zongren had fallen out repeatedly in the preceding years, and early in the decade, they had been on the brink of going to war with each other. Li Zongren only won the command due to the intervention of Zhou Enlai, a prominent communist who had been seconded to the Nationalist headquarters in Wuhan. Zhou understood the importance of a unified command. In return, he promised support from communist guerrillas to harass Japanese troops going into battle at Xuzhou.[23]

In the course of a four-month campaign beginning in February 1938, a series of battles raged in the entire area around Xuzhou. One of the towns in the region, Taierzhuang, achieved legendary status. Chinese and Japanese troops clashed there during a terrible fortnight in late March and early April, locked in a deadly embrace very similar to the costly urban battles that Europe was soon to see. A participant described the brutal conditions at Taierzhuang: "The battle continued day and night. The flames lit up the sky. Often all that separated our forces from the enemy was a single wall. The soldiers would beat holes in the masonry to snipe at each other. We would be fighting for days over a single building, causing dozens of fatalities."[24]

Conditions at the Taierzhuang front were so uniquely horrendous that the Chinese believed they had to enforce discipline by the most Draconian of means. Junior officers who had seen large numbers of their men consumed in the inferno repeatedly asked for permission to retreat, and had their requests turned down. Those who asked for reinforcement after intense fighting had depleted their ranks were told to personally fill the empty spots themselves. Li Zongren warned one of his key commanders that if he did not carry out his duty with the necessary vigor, he would "be treated as Han Fuju had been."[25]

The Japanese used large amounts of armor at Taierzhuang, and they left behind a tank cemetery. The testimony of one of the Chinese participants described the situation that evolved when a combined force of Japanese tanks and infantry was advancing towards the Chinese lines: "The officers and men got very nervous and loudly called out for artillery support. The battalion commander personally ran over to the artillery battery ordering the captain in charge to fire or risk losing the position. The captain insisted to wait until the very last moment. Just when the advancing Japanese were about to overrun the Chinese positions, he ordered the guns to fire. The sudden barrage caused great confusion among the Japanese. Some of the shells ripped up the tracks of the tanks, others caused them to catch fire. The Chinese infantry opened up, and the Japanese were forced on a chaotic retreat."[26]

In early April, after having suffered about 20,000 casualties, the Japanese decided reluctantly to pull out. True, the battle had nearly leveled Taierzhuang to the ground, and the Chinese too suffered casualties of a similar magnitude, but in the context of the campaigns of the preceding months, where the Chinese had invariably sustained significantly larger losses than the foe, this was considered a victory. "It was the first happy occasion since the war of resistance had started," Li reminisced later, saying that Taierzhuang had become "a symbol of national renaissance."[27] The rare triumph triggered days of jubilation on the Chinese side. Feng Yuxiang, "the Christian general," published a long narrative poem in the *Ta Kung Pao* newspaper comparing the trapped Japanese with "soft-shelled turtles in a closed jar."[28]

The Japanese, of course, would be back. Once the initial shock at being beaten by the supposedly inferior Chinese had dissipated, the Japanese commanders assembled 400,000 fresh troops in the Xuzhou area. Supported by artillery and aircraft, they converged on Xuzhou from three sides, initiating a giant pincer movement which threatened to trap the Chinese. Eventually, in May, following consultations with Chiang Kai-shek, Li Zongren ordered a full-scale retreat from the area. In one of the war's most skillful Chinese maneuvers, he and his aides succeeded in extricating 200,000 men in 40 divisions from the battlefield, moving at night and hiding in the wheat fields in the day time.[29]

The campaign around Xuzhou had a sinister last act, one that would reverberate for decades. Once the Japanese understood that their Chinese adversary had left the battlefield, they started the pursuit. A quick look at the map convinced the Chinese commanders that precious little lay between the advancing Japanese and Wuhan. They reasoned that the city would fall, bringing the Nationalist regime one step closer to collapse, unless drastic measures were undertaken. They did indeed opt for unusual measures, perhaps unique in the history of modern warfare.

Twice in early June 1938, Chinese soldiers breached the dykes along the Yellow River, causing the stemmed-up water masses to inundate the surrounding countryside. Xiong Xianyu, a young captain with the 8th Division, watched as soldiers under his command worked day and night to break down the sturdy dyke walls, spurred on by the promise of money if it could be done in time. Once the dyke was breached, it took just a few hours for the hole to widen and cause a massive, unstoppable stream to pour out into the flat countryside. "It looked like an ocean as far as the eye could see," Xiong wrote in his diary. "We have done this to stop the enemy, and to salvage the situation as a whole. We must accept even large sacrifices in the interest of final victory."[30]

It was a desperate act designed to slow down the Japanese offensive, and it may not even have caused a delay. In the words of a modern Chinese historian, at this point "the Japanese did not have the capacity to carry out further strategic offensives." Therefore, according to the same historian, the breaching of the dykes "did not make much strategic sense."[31] A more immediate result was the devastating impact on China's own farmers living along the river. Half a million civilian Chinese are estimated to have died in the resulting flood, and perhaps millions more lost their homes:[32] there was a reason why the Yellow River had traditionally been called "China's Sorrow." The breaching of the Yellow River dykes, according to Japanese spokespeople, revealed "ruthless contempt for human life."[33] For once, the verdict of the Japanese propaganda seemed apt.

An unusual encounter took place in Hong Kong on June 16, 1938. The Japanese Consul General Nakamura Toyokazu met with Jiao Fusan, a Chinese official. Although largely unknown in public, Jiao was not just anybody. He was the personal secretary of H. H. Kung, China's prime minister and Chiang Kai-shek's brother-in-law. Only a ranking official would do, since the topic of the meeting was to find ways to end hostilities between the two Asian nations.[34] It was the first in a series of negotiations, which ran for the next two and a half months and was the cause of considerable hope among circles in Japan still aspiring to step back from the brink. At one point, the Japanese Navy even prepared a warship for a mission to transport Kung to Nagasaki for high-level meetings.[35]

Kung's visit to Japan, sensational as it would have been, never happened, but the fact that it could even be considered reflected a sudden bout of optimism, erupting despite the continued slaughter on the China front. There was a very specific reason why the Hong Kong meetings could take place. They were made possible after a new Japanese foreign minister, General Ugaki Kazushige, assumed office in late May. He was convinced that the war in China needed to end, and he had entered government on the condition that peace talks be resumed.[36] His views were widely known in China as well, and despite the state of war, former Chinese Foreign Minister Zhang Qun even sent a telegram to Ugaki to congratulate him on the appointment, calling it an "exceedingly splendid event."[37]

In Japan, too, Ugaki's appointment was greeted with relief and seen as an opportunity to halt the descent into total war. A certain degree of war-weariness could be detected among the Japanese public. The summer of 1938 was unusually wet, and many Japanese believed that the continuous heavy downpour was a mark of the displeasure of Heaven and a protest by the souls of the war dead.[38] In order to play down the extent of the involvement in China, authorities did away with the large-scale send-offs of reservists that had characterized the early days of the war, and lists of casualties from the China front were relegated to inconspicuous sections of the newspapers.[39] In this situation, the appointment of a foreign minister who might bring peace corresponded to the "deepest desires" of many Japanese, a prominent columnist wrote, continuing: "Our hopes were closer to prayers."[40]

Remarkably, Ugaki privately showed great sympathy for Chiang Kai-shek, the man reviled by the Japanese government as the main obstacle to peace. After decades of being bound hand and foot by the Western powers, China was now following a trend of national solidarity, and Chiang was "the one who had stepped forward to lead this trend," Ugaki noted in his diary.[41] Nakamura, the chief Japanese negotiator in Hong Kong, held similar views, stating that Japanese insistence on the January policy of demanding Chiang's resignation would cause problems.[42] This did not sway the Japanese Cabinet as a whole, which was adamant that a peaceful settlement was impossible with a China led by Chiang. On July 8, three weeks into the Hong Kong talks, it officially called for Chiang's removal from public life.[43]

This doomed the Hong Kong talks, and even though the negotiations were continued for the rest of July and into August they were going nowhere, with the question of Chiang Kai-shek's role as the main sticking point, but also with disagreement about the extent of future Japanese control in northern China. Meanwhile back in Tokyo, Ugaki was undermined by opponents who succeeded in removing China policy from the foreign ministry. Ugaki resigned in frustration in late September, abruptly ending the hopes that his appointment had triggered.[44] The Hong Kong talks had already wrapped up by then, with no result to show for them.

Ugaki was a dove not just on China policy, but also on the relationship with the Western powers, and his brief four months as foreign minister could potentially have set diplomacy moving along a completely different trajectory that had not ended in a Pacific War. Ugaki sensed a special kinship with Great Britain, one that he felt with no other nation. Unlike Japan and China, who were "sleeping in the same bed but dreaming different dreams," he argued that the Japanese and the British were "sleeping in different beds but dreaming the same dream" and that despite their geographical and cultural distance, they were at heart similar nations which could accommodate each other on the world stage.[45]

The Japanese foreign minister had found an eager interlocutor in Robert Craigie, the British ambassador to Tokyo, who argued in a message to his superiors in London that reestablishing the traditional friendship between the two nations "would afford the best hope visible today of weaning Japan from her foolish policy of armed imperialism."[46] The Foreign Office, while generally adopting a pragmatic stance towards Japan, considered this a rather naïve view, pointing out that Britain had achieved its position in China by means of war during the 19th century, and that it would only be able to keep that position "by the same or similar methods." The conclusion, as far as London was concerned, was clear: either Britain itself forced Japan to give up its conquests in China, or it made the Chinese do their fighting for them, exhausting Japanese national strength in a long unwinnable war.[47]

Once the risk of war in Europe was thought to have subsided, there was even less of a need for the British government to accommodate Japan, dooming talks that had bogged down over much the same sticking point as the Sino-Japanese dialogue:

Japanese insistence that any solution in China which included Chiang Kai-shek was unacceptable.[48] Even before Ugaki's resignation, therefore, there was little possibility of finding common ground. Indeed, the gap between the two sides was probably even wider than the Japanese knew. The British government was impressed by the resistance that China had been able to put up against the Japanese invasion, and some of the traditional British adversity to the anti-Imperialist Chinese Nationalists was being tempered by a view that cooperation might be possible. "Our interests in China," wrote a British diplomat in the summer of 1938, "have better chances of favorable treatment under a Chinese regime than under a Japanese."[49]

The United States had been watching on the sidelines as Craigie met with Ugaki, but just days after Ugaki resigned in late September, the US government stepped into the fray, issuing the strongest protest yet over Japanese conduct in China, with an exclusive focus on damage done to the business interests of Americans and other nationals.[50] While the protest explicitly refrained from criticizing the military campaign per se, this did not suggest American indifference to the plight of the Chinese, as subsequent events were to show. The Japanese behavior in China, especially the reports of mind-boggling crimes against civilians, had long mobilized left-leaning Americans, but was beginning to attract attention elsewhere as well.

Japanese air raids on the south Chinese city of Guangzhou in the first half of 1938 had been widely reported in the American press, triggering calls for some kind of US reaction. It was clear to many US officials that Japan's main weakness was its economy, but embargoes were a complicated weapon to use, as they would require political action at the highest level of power in Washington. Instead, the US government resorted to moral suasion. In July, 1938, the head of the State Department's Office of Arms and Munitions Control Charles W. Yost told the 148 airplane manufacturers and exporters listed by his office that he would issue new licenses for exports of military airplanes and their munitions with "great regret." The businesses took the hint, and within a month, the unofficial embargo was reported to be 95 percent effective.[51] It would not be the last time that the United States would seek to bring its economic might to bear on Japan.

Du Longji, one of the ranking officers at the Chinese river fortress of Madang, had been asked to attend a ceremony and subsequent banquet at a nearby military school on June 24, 1938, but he had turned down the invitation. Madang, designed to be a major obstacle against the Japanese advance up the Yangtze towards the temporary government seat of Wuhan, was simply too important to be abandoned even for a short period of time, Du Longji figured. Few of his colleagues felt the same way, and all other senior officers had departed, with the result that some military units

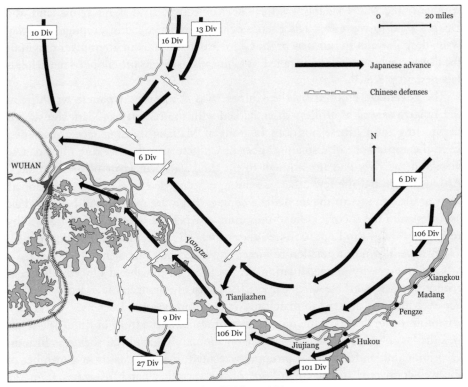

Battle of Wuhan 1938.

in Madang had no one in charge above the rank of platoon commander. As bad luck would have it, exactly on this day the Japanese decided to strike.[52]

The town of Madang was situated at a dramatic narrowing of the Yangtze, where the river was a mere 500 yards across. Since the outbreak of the war, Chinese engineers had built bamboo barriers and laid mines so that ships could now only pass along a designated route, one at a time. This was a major headache for the Japanese, who relied heavily on the support of the naval guns as their infantry pushed upriver towards Wuhan.[53] There was no other way for the Japanese commanders than to take Madang from the landside. They implemented the first part of this plan in the morning of June 24, while virtually all Chinese officers had deserted their posts to attend the ceremony.

Du Longji got his first inkling that something was amiss when at dawn his signals units tried to get in touch with a regiment located at the port town of Xiangkou, a few miles downriver. A messenger was dispatched and returned with the unsettling news that the entire town was crawling with Japanese. It was clear that they had landed in Xiangkou shortly before daybreak and had overwhelmed the defending regiment, and that Madang was their next objective. To make it across land, the Japanese had to wade through a series of inundated rice fields, groping their way waist-deep in water in full view of the Chinese defenders. Four attempts throughout the day at reaching Madang all failed, as Chinese small arms fire chopped the helpless Japanese to pieces.[54]

The advantage enjoyed by the Chinese was temporary. Japanese warships in the Yangtze as well as artillery disembarked with the infantry at Xiangkou started pummeling the Chinese positions in front of Madang, causing severe casualties. Even the appearance of a small number of Chinese aircraft attacking the Japanese vessels in the river was not enough to tilt the balance in favor of the defenders. As Du Longji and the few other remaining officers tried to alert the commanders away at the banquet to the immediate danger, they were met with disbelief. "Have you even seen the enemy?" one of the commanders inquired after being reached by telephone. "How can I not have seen the enemy," the officer in the frontline replied. "They have blown our position to pieces and killed half our men."[55]

Once the gravity of the situation became clear to the absent officers, they sent reinforcements, but these never arrived. The 167th Division, commanded by General Xie Weiying, was ordered to march to Madang and boost the defenses, but took a circuitous route that gave them no chance of reaching the front in time. The result was the loss of Madang late in the day on June 26. Chiang Kai-shek was furious. Division commander Xie was promptly executed. Even his status as a member of the well-connected military elite, one of the very first batch of cadets from the prestigious Whampoa Academy, did not help him.[56]

Meanwhile, Japanese naval forces accompanying the infantry up the Yangtze managed to blast through the barriers erected in the river at Madang. Once passage had been secured, the Japanese warships could bring their full firepower to bear on the Chinese opponents inland, facilitating a speedy Japanese advance. This enabled the Japanese to take the city of Pengze, upriver from Madang, followed by the city of Hukou.[57] At Hukou, a Chinese after-action report claimed, the Japanese had used poison gas. "Our troops had no chemical warfare equipment and no experience," the report stated. "As a result, there was widespread panic, affecting the soldiers' fighting ability."[58]

Next on the Japanese route was Jiujiang, the most important river port before Wuhan, and a key railway juncture.[59] It fell in late July, after five days of sometimes determined, but usually uncoordinated Chinese resistance. Following its capture, Jiujiang was subjected to what one Western historian has described as a "mini-Nanjing massacre."[60] Urban districts and nearby villages believed to harbor anti-Japanese sentiments were razed to the ground, while many of the male residents were put to death and the women raped. At the same time, the Japanese forces carried out a deliberate campaign designed to destroy the city's means of survival. Ceramics factories, a pillar of the economy for centuries, were destroyed and pieces of

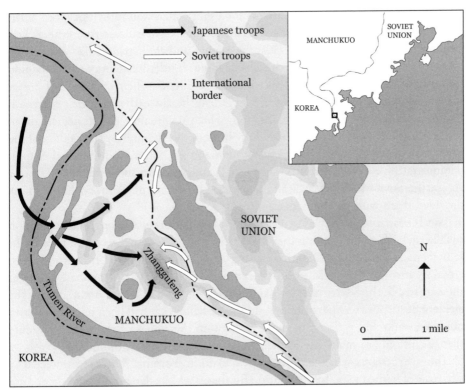

Soviet-Japanese battle at Zhanggufeng, 1938.

porcelain left scattered in the streets. The boats that the population used for most transportation needs were confiscated, wrecked, or left adrift on the Yangtze river.[61] It was the well-known Japanese combination of efficiency, ruthlessness and wanton cruelty. A year had passed since Marco Polo Bridge, and Japan was still fighting a successful war of movement against the Chinese. Further up north, the opposite was true. On the edge of Siberia, it was facing a different opponent: Stalin's Russia.

★   ★   ★

In the evening of July 15, 1938, a small Japanese reconnaissance patrol left a military police station on the northernmost border of Japan's colony, Korea. The soldiers crossed the Tumen River and moved up the slopes of a 149-meter-high hill named Zhanggufeng, which had recently been occupied by Soviet troops. The Russians on top of the hill spotted the approaching Japanese and shouted: "Halt!" Realizing they had been seen, the Japanese started running back. The Soviet soldiers opened fire, and one of them shot and killed a fleeing Japanese. When the Soviet troops searched his body, they found a camera, a notebook with descriptions of the patrol's observations, and documents identifying the dead man as Corporal Matsushima.[62]

The brief skirmish became the trigger for a short, sharp war fought between Japan and the Soviet Union in a poorly demarcated area of northeast Asia where their empires met. Throughout the 1930s, the Soviets and the Japanese had engaged in intense rivalry, and by the end of the decade minor border incidents were happening more than 200 times a year.[63] This time was different. When a handful of Soviet troops had taken up positions on Zhanggufeng hill in early July, their intention had been to acquire a vantage point from which to monitor the strategic Korean port of Najin as well as important railway lines in the vicinity. By the middle of the month, their strength had grown to 40 men and 30 horses, and they had dug in, demonstrating every intention to stay. The Japanese had to show the flag or simply accept the Soviet presence as a *fait accompli*. The killing of Corporal Matsushima provided them with the immediate impetus to act.[64]

Local commanders wanted to react at once and made preparations for an operation to take back Zhanggufeng, but they were held back for several days by more cautious senior officers in Tokyo. The initial hesitation ended when Soviet troops were seen crossing into Japanese-held territory, and early on July 31, the Japanese forces in the area struck the Soviet positions at Zhanggufeng in a dramatic night attack. The element of surprise was paramount, and the battalion that had been selected to carry out the assault was ordered to make its way up the slopes of the hill in absolute silence and only to make use of their firearms at the very last moment.[65]

The Soviet troops, which had now grown to number around 300, were protected by two rows of barbed wire. In preparation for the attack, the Japanese battalion had cut a breach in the first row, and at 1:15 am, its soldiers made their way through towards the next row. At this point, military dogs left in front of the Soviet positions started barking, exposing the ongoing attack. The Soviet soldiers began firing frantically, their loud cheers clearly audible over the continuous noise of their weapons.

Despite the heavy fire, the Japanese battalion pushed onwards up the slope and did not stop even after its commander was severely injured. Passing through the second line of barbed wire, the Japanese soldiers poured into the Soviet positions, and desperate combat ensued, some of it hand-to-hand. The Soviet defenders sent up reinforcements in the form of infantry riding on trucks and tanks, and for a few hours before dawn, the situation seemed to hang in the balance. The injured Japanese battalion commander directed the battle from a stretcher, but was killed by a Soviet hand grenade at about 4 am. This was exactly the time when the Japanese gained the upper hand. At 4:10 am, the battalion reported the capture of Zhanggufeng.

The fighting had been shockingly bloody so far, and it had only just begun. With surprising speed, a mere day after the initial battle the Soviet side amassed a large quantity of men and materiel in the area and embarked on an effort to retake Zhanggufeng. On August 1, Soviet fighters and bombers carried out eight waves of attacks on Japanese positions, and over the following six-day period, a total of 700 Soviet sorties were recorded.[66]

The Soviet aircraft even bombarded targets well behind Japanese lines, inside Korea. Risking the lives of Korean civilians was completely acceptable to Joseph Stalin, as he had explained to his hesitant Far Eastern commander, Vasily Blyukher. "I do not understand your fear of harming the Korean population," Stalin told him by telephone. "Who forbade you to harm the Korean population in the conditions of a military skirmish with the Japanese?" Blyukher, knowing very well the danger of appearing less than fully obedient to Stalin, complied.[67] Meanwhile, the Japanese, fearing an escalation, barred their own planes from taking to the air.[68]

On the ground, too, the Soviet forces were superior and eager to use their advantage, having deployed about 200 tanks and up to 120 artillery pieces near Zhanggufeng. The artillery especially was employed to great effect, with one Japanese artillery commander stating the Soviet batteries fired as many rounds in one day as the Japanese side did during the entire battle. The Japanese soldiers on Zhanggufeng paid the price, with reports of 200 killed and injured every day. Those left were saved by the Japanese ambassador to Moscow, who succeeded in negotiating a ceasefire effective from August 11, allowing the Japanese to withdraw from the hill.[69]

The battle of Zhanggufeng was a resounding defeat for Japan, who had no desire to enlarge the conflict at a time when its army had its hands full in China. It also showed the Japanese what a formidable foe the Soviet Union would become if full-scale war were ever to erupt.[70] Geographical distance had placed the Russians at a disadvantage in the Far East for centuries, but modern technology was helping them to make up for this rapidly. As late as 1935, British intelligence had described how the Soviet Army in the area remained dependent on "slow moving and vulnerable columns of horse transport," but in the second half of the decade the regional railroad network had developed significantly, improving Soviet chances of coming up with an adequate response to any eventuality along the border with the Japanese Empire.[71]

The triumph did not do Soviet commander Blyukher any good, however. In the toxic atmosphere at Stalin's court, steeped in suspicion and paranoia, he was accused of inadequate leadership in the battle and arrested. More than 20 years of loyal service to the socialist cause, including several years in China, counted for nothing. He was tortured badly in prison—one of his eyeballs was beaten out of its socket—and executed.[72]

The growing Soviet-Japanese hostility was one reason why Japan was emerging as a potential alliance partner for Germany. This would necessarily have to be at the expense of the hitherto close Sino-German relationship. A stark reminder that Germany could not possibly maintain amicable ties with both Asian nations had come as early as in February 1938, when Berlin announced its intention of recognizing Manchukuo. This was tantamount to giving the stamp of approval to Japan's attempt to carve up China into smaller pieces, and elicited a predictably harsh response from the Chinese foreign ministry, referring to Manchukuo as "an unlawful regime… born of Japanese aggression" and expressing disappointment at the German move, given "the very cordial relations heretofore existing between China and Germany."[73]

In fact, relations were to grow even less cordial. In May, Hitler issued an order recalling the German military advisors from China, and after some foot-dragging, Chiang Kai-shek allowed them to be released from their contracts.[74] As the Germans left on a train from Wuhan to the southern city of Guangzhou, *The Times* of London spoke highly of their impact, arguing they had transformed the Chinese Army "from a mass into something like a machine," while concluding that their recall was "a serious matter to China."[75] Many of the Germans, residents of China for years, agreed and departed only with great regret. "We thought the war was lost," one of the advisors said later. "Of course, we told our Chinese friends they had a good chance to win. What else could we have told them?"[76]

In the months that followed, negotiations began between Berlin and Tokyo on transforming the Anti-Comintern Pact into an actual military alliance. Much of the shift was attributed to the growing influence of Joachim von Ribbentrop, Germany's foreign minister since February 1938. Ribbentrop, who had long had Hitler's ear on foreign policy matters, was known in Berlin for his pro-Japanese views, which were, in fact, dictated more by his anti-Soviet inclinations than by any inherent love of Japan. In a speech to German officers a few months later, Ribbentrop explained the rationale for opting for Japan. China, he said, had been in deep sleep since time immemorial, and for the foreseeable future, "this weak China would not be able suddenly to dispose of a strong army against Russia or produce a fleet of Dreadnoughts. There was no choice for Germany other than Japan."[77]

Likewise, Japan saw a closer alliance with Germany and possibly Italy as a means to contain the Soviet Union. A reduction of Soviet and British influence in China could also assist in bringing the war there to a conclusion, some Japanese decision-makers argued, starting work on draft agreements with Germany. "The Empire," read a new policy approved at the highest political level, "wishes quickly to reach separate agreements with Italy and Germany, making even closer our mutual ties of alliance, and desires to strengthen each nation's power to resist the Soviet threat and to check Britain. By this means we wish to contribute to a speedy and beneficial settlement of the China Incident and to the advancement of our nation's leadership in East Asia."[78]

The war in China did indeed appear to be heading towards a conclusion in the summer of 1938. Following the succession of battles along the Yangtze River in the first half of the year, precious little stood between the Japanese and the prize they coveted, the large city of Wuhan. Victory seemed within reach for the Japanese commanders—and then suddenly and wholly unexpectedly their offensive stalled. Continued Chinese resistance was part of the explanation, but not the only one. Another reason was a sudden mass outbreak of dysentery in the Japanese Army, caused by drinking unboiled water.[79]

The Chinese defenders were unable to take advantage of this situation, as they themselves were hampered by a short supply of quinine, causing malaria to run rampant. The fact that the war came to a halt because of disease suggests the overall lack of ability to cope, especially on the Chinese side, with notoriously unhygienic conditions. "Their bodies are unwashed," said a report about the patients at a Chinese military hospital, "their hair long and nails uncut, and their quilts covered with lice. The dysentery and diarrhea cases lie in beddings soaked with excreta."[80]

To the Japanese foot soldier, the sudden epidemic was just the latest instance of intense physical misery. China to them was an inhospitable nightmare landscape where injury and subsequent evacuation to hospitals in the hinterland offered the only feasible escape. "China is very dirty with many mosquitoes and flies and I cannot take meals comfortably," a Japanese soldier wrote home to an acquaintance. "On the road, in the mountains, in the fields and everywhere, there are many corpses of Chinese and the stench is very bad."[81]

After weeks of stalemate, the Japanese troops recovered their momentum and resumed their advance towards Wuhan. Throughout much of September, a huge and bloody battle raged around the Yangtze city of Tianjiazhen. The Chinese defenders were unusually well prepared, as their engineers assisted by Soviet advisors and the muscle of thousands of local workers had built massive defenses. The Japanese only succeeded in overcoming the Chinese stronghold with copious use of poison gas.

At about the same time, Wuhan was threatened from a new direction, as a separate Japanese force managed to break through Chinese lines northeast of the city and move within striking distance of Wuhan's rail link with Beijing.[82] At this time, General Li Zongren, the hero of Taierzhuang, could have met an early end. He was stationed with his staff in a village near the railroad, but had a strange premonition. "I have a feeling we must leave at once," he told his staff, basing it on no more than a hunch. Two hours after their hasty departure, the village was swarming with Japanese cavalry. "This little incident reminds me of the many records in Chinese history of miracles that occurred at critical moments," Li later said.[83]

By early October, Chiang Kai-shek had decided to abandon Wuhan and move inland to Chongqing, long ago chosen as China's wartime capital. Unlike the situation at Nanjing, when Chiang had ordered a doomed fight for the sake of symbolism, there was no appetite for another expensive sacrifice at Wuhan merely for show. However, in a replay of what had happened in Nanjing less than a year earlier, rumors of the evacuation filtered through the Chinese ranks, causing panic. There was widespread concern that Chiang would prioritize saving his key supporters, mainly officers who had graduated from the Whampoa Military Academy. Despite the immediate national danger, old regional rivalries that had defined the warlord period still held sway.[84]

Japanese forces marched into Wuhan in October 1938, and at about the same time, the main city of south China, Guangzhou, was also conquered. There were atrocities in both places, but nothing resembling the protracted carnage of Nanjing. The commanders in both areas reportedly took pains to rein in their troops in a bid to preempt another massacre. Still, it did not do much to improve the tarnished reputation of the Japanese armed forces. The bombing that had preceded the capture of Guangzhou had spread death among the city's civilians and had been described widely to a disgusted public in the West, especially the United States.

With Wuhan and Guangzhou in Japanese hands, all major Chinese cities along the comparatively prosperous east coast were under Japanese control. On the face of it, the situation looked unmitigatedly bleak for the Chinese. It was as if the German Army had, after a year of war in 1942, taken all the major cities of the Soviet Union, including Leningrad, Moscow and Stalingrad. Paradoxically, however, it was in accordance with the long-term objective of Chiang Kai-shek and his commanders. They had at an early stage adopted a policy of exchanging space for time. China's territory was vast with large areas in the center and west remaining. Japan could not possibly conquer it all.[85]

Chiang's strategy worked, in a crude kind of way. Still, he also had to acknowledge that, one year into the war, the performance of his troops had been mixed. In some cases, they fought desperately against the approaching enemy, but in other instances they were happy to withdraw at the beginning of battles, especially if they knew that prepared positions were waiting for them in the hinterland. There were reports that some Chinese units had arranged unofficial truces with their Japanese foes and even engaged in trade with them.[86] After months of severe attrition, there was little question that the quality of the troops had declined. "It was inferior to the quality of our army at Shanghai," said Zhang Fakui, one of the Chinese commanders in the Wuhan area, in a post-war interview. "The men were not as well trained. Morale had declined but it was still alright."[87]

At the top of the hierarchy, morale was also not a given. It was of course true that Chongqing was so far inland that it was virtually out of reach to the Japanese. Nestled on steep hills squeezed in between the Yangtze and Jialing Rivers, and hardly linked to the rest of China by any roads, the Japanese would have to leave all their tanks and artillery behind to reach it. Moreover, Chongqing was located in the huge province of Sichuan, a breadbasket that could keep Chiang's regime self-sufficient for years. It was "a virtually impregnable redoubt from where in peace and quiet the Chinese government can direct the defense of the country against the invader," De Fremery, the Dutch observer with the Chinese military, wrote in a dispatch to his superiors in the Netherlands East Indies.[88]

"The Chinese government can harass the Japanese unpunished from this redoubt," De Fremery continued, and then turned almost prophetic: "As long as they are able to keep the armed resistance of the soldiers and the guerrillas plus the passive resistance of the civilian population at the present level, the Japanese will be obliged to maintain their present troop levels in China at enormous cost."[89]

The main urban area of Chongqing had been home to a quarter million people in the early 1930s, but the influx of new residents arriving with Chiang soon doubled that figure. Still, it was nothing like the sophisticated and cosmopolitan cities along the lower Yangtze that the Chinese ruling elite had been used to. The very virtue of inaccessibility also made it an isolated backwater with few redeeming characteristics.[90]

Many of the foreigners who were forced to relocate to Chongqing along with the Nationalist government were thoroughly unimpressed. "One of the most backward holes on earth," said US journalist Edgar Snow, otherwise a friend of China. Another American described it as "one large festering sore … the whole place is a mass of nondescript browns and dirty grays, here and there a smudge of sooty white."[91] This was where, for an indefinite future, Chiang and his government were to direct their country in its struggle for survival. For many of Chiang's closest aides, Chongqing was a welcome reprieve after long months on the run. For others, it was yet another sign that China under Chiang was headed in the wrong direction.

Early in the morning of November 13, 1938, people in the city of Changsha, roughly 200 miles southwest of Wuhan, woke up to the sound of desperate shouting. Chinese soldiers were walking through the streets methodically torching the buildings. Soon flames engulfed the entire city, trapping thousands of people. At the military hospital the sick and wounded tried to escape a grizzly death by crawling through doors and windows.[92] It was the result of a "scorched earth policy," ordered by Chiang Kai-shek in emulation of the Russian decision 126 years earlier to raze Moscow to keep the spoils from falling into Napoleon's hand. When the local defenders started implementing his order, they believed the Japanese were just hours away. In fact, they had halted well short of Changsha and had no immediate intention of moving in on the city.[93]

The city burned for three days and nights, falling victim to the largest man-made fire in Chinese history. At least 20,000 were buried in mass graves outside the city.[94] A Westerner who visited Changsha just weeks after the blaze reported that nine out of ten houses had been gutted: "Occasional solitary walls thrust up black distorted shapes, their windows staring at the sky with dead eyes. The streets showed mile upon mile of silent death. There was nothing left that was familiar and man-made, but only the twisted and grotesque, the gaping belly, the gray corpse of a city."[95] The same Westerner encountered scenes of horror in the local hospital, including a young girl who had recently been under surgery. "They have taken off so much of me!" she said. "My leg, my hand. It is very funny, I quite miss myself!"[96]

One person in particular was horrified by the ultimately meaningless destruction and suffering at Changsha. His name was Wang Jingwei, and he had been one of the leading members of the Nationalist movement for years, although he had been increasingly eclipsed by Chiang. As vice president, he had followed the government to its wartime location in Chongqing, but he was quietly of the conviction that an end must be found to the hopeless war. There was no way around a negotiated solution with the Japanese, Wang thought. He had become irreparably frustrated with Chiang's leadership, which he believed provided China with no realistic long-term vision for its future. News of the self-inflicted tragedy at Changsha may have been the last straw. Wang decided to take a fateful step.[97]

On December 18, he defected. Accompanied by a small entourage, he departed on a plane from Chongqing, flying to the southwestern Chinese city of Kunming, and continuing the day after to Hanoi in French-controlled Indochina.[98] Wang had been lured by a Japanese pledge to pursue a peace agreement which would, he was promised, eventually see the near-complete withdrawal of Japanese troops from China. The offer was irresistible at a time when China was facing disaster, having lost all its main national assets along the eastern seaboard. It was too good to be true. Once Wang had arrived in Hanoi, Japan signaled its willingness to continue peace talks, but the pledge to pull out of China had quietly been stricken from the list of commitments.[99] Wang was trapped. He could not return, even if he had wanted to. In Chongqing, he was branded a weak quitter, and on January 1, 1939, he was excluded from the Nationalist Party.[100]

CHAPTER FIVE

Attrition

1939

The rain was pouring down over Shanghai's French Concession in the evening of Sunday, February 19, 1939, the first day of the Chinese New Year. At 7 pm a group of eight men, split into two groups, walked at a brisk pace down Lane 668 of Yuyuan Road. They were heading for villa No. 25, the home of Chen Lu, foreign minister of China's Reformed Government, one of three pro-Japanese puppet regimes established in the Chinese provinces occupied by Japan. Chen, 61, and his wife were having a dinner party for the former Chinese ambassador to Denmark, and only a single bodyguard was standing at the gate.

The bodyguard was quickly overpowered, and four of the men, now wielding hand guns, proceeded into the building, while the others waited at the gate as lookouts. Walking through the kitchen, the four men threatened the cooks and servants into silence and burst into the living room, where the party was just getting ready for dinner. The assassins quickly spotted Chen Lu, who was sitting in a sofa. One of the men fired his gun at the foreign minister, grazing his ear. Chen Lu picked up an embroidered pillow and covered his head, while rolling to one side.

Another of the men stepped forward and fired two shots at Chen Lu's face. Chen slumped onto the floor in a pool of blood, and the assassins fired yet more bullets into his gradually lifeless body. Then they pulled out a piece of white paper with a message they had prepared beforehand: "Death to the collaborators! Protect the motherland! Long live Generalissimo Chiang Kai-shek! Long live the Chinese Republic!" Leaving behind a room full of shocked and shivering dinner guests, the assassins hurriedly exited the villa, disappearing into the rain.[1]

The man who had fired the lethal bullets was an operative named Liu Geqing. The 27-year-old son of a southeast Chinese family, Liu Geqing had been dispatched to Shanghai by the innocuous-sounding Bureau of Investigation and Statistics, which was in fact the main clandestine service of Chiang Kai-shek's government. The head of the organization was a sinister figure by the name of Dai Li, who gradually earned himself the moniker "China's Himmler." Few foreigners had any fondness for Dai Li.

"He was the enemy of almost every ideal of American democracy," wrote an American agent who traveled to China. "He tried to unify China under Chiang by enforcing iron control. He was cold, crafty, and brutal."[2]

Dai Li's record made him a household name in China, and it was said that his name was even used to scare children. To an American associate, he confessed that he was actually fond of his reputation, as it had a remarkable preemptive effect on racketeers, smugglers, and defectors. "A righteous fear," he told the American, "works better than guns."[3] Dai Li possessed a flexible mind, and at the same time was steeped in Chinese tradition. This showed in the way he recruited young men and women into his service. He preferred people who were bold, tough, and able to think independently, in the mold of the knights-errant of classical Chinese martial arts fiction.[4]

The main opponent that Dai Li and his people faced was widely known as Organization No. 76. It was a reference to its address on 76 Jessfield Road in Shanghai, a compound notorious for its torture chambers. The unit routinely resorted to murder and other forms of terrorist tactics to suppress anti-Japanese sentiment. In particular, it targeted those in the press that were seen as fanning nationalistic flames. To silence a small anti-Japanese weekly in Shanghai, agents of the organization abducted its publisher, decapitated him, and placed his severed head on a pole in the street in front of his office.[5]

Similar to the violence in occupied Europe in the 1940s, when much of the fighting was between members of the resistance and local collaborators, the urban cloak-and-dagger conflict in Shanghai and other big cities was very much a matter of Chinese fighting Chinese. It could be argued that the Japanese had to rely even more on local help than the Gestapo in Europe a few years later, due to the way Chinese social networks worked. They were based on kinship and long-standing relationships and could rarely be penetrated by outsiders.[6]

One of the leading figures in Organization No. 76 was the former Nationalist agent Ding Mocun. "Little Devil Ding," who was only five foot one, topped his adversaries' hit list and was targeted for assassination several times. In the best-known of these cases, Dai Li's agents used Ding's young mistress to lure him into an ambush. She had divided loyalties, since she wished to help the Chinese cause but remained in love with Ding. That proved her demise: the ambush failed, and she was caught because she had placed a calling card in Ding's pocket with a Buddhist prayer asking that he would die peacefully. When she was led to her shallow grave to be executed, she asked to be shot in a way so her face was not harmed. Her wish was granted.[7]

In this world of backstabbing and betrayal, the spies even fought their own sides. An internal struggle among leaders of Organization No. 76 ended when one of the protagonists was poisoned with steamed cakes, a Japanese delicacy. He died after 24 hours during which his "perspiration poured out like rain."[8] Poison flowed freely, as did narcotics. It served as a particularly unpalatable aspect of Japanese occupation policy that Japan's military decided to finance its intelligence efforts in China partly by controlling the hugely profitable opium trade. This happened in direct collaboration with some of urban China's most notorious criminal organizations, such as Shanghai's Green Gang.[9]

While Shanghai was the heart of China's secret war, it was also waged in many other cities, and even in other countries. One of its potential targets was Wang Jingwei, the defector from Chongqing, who remained in limbo in Hanoi for several months in early 1939. Initially, Chiang Kai-shek attempted to get rid of Wang in a lenient manner, offering to let him go to Europe, where he would do minimal harm. When Wang refused, Chiang sent a team of killers across the border into Indochina.

At 3 am on March 21, 1939, an assassin armed with a submachine gun scaled the wall surrounding the two-story villa in the suburbs of Hanoi where Wang was staying. Entering the main room on the first floor, the assassin made out the silhouette of a man and fired a burst of bullets before turning around and rushing out of the building. The dying man he left behind was not Wang, but one of his close associates.[10] Still, this close brush with death convinced Wang that he could not stay in Indochina. Within a month, he had departed by freighter, and shortly afterwards, he turned up in Japanese-occupied Shanghai. Wang's long slide into what would become his historical role as China's Quisling had begun.[11]

In the same period that the drama around Wang Jingwei unfolded, the Japanese commanders were making strategic readjustments that changed the entire character of the war in China. The army completed a policy document which argued that one stage of the war had ended with the occupation of Wuhan and Guangzhou, and that "the expansion of the occupied area should be avoided unless imperative for security reasons."[12] The offensive spirit that had overtaken the Japanese Army for one and a half years since the Marco Polo Bridge Incident was now replaced by an almost defensive stance. The vast majority of Chinese territory was to be turned into "areas of peace and order" where the maintenance of stability was the top priority, and only in instances where the Chinese Army was concentrating in preparation for attack or otherwise presented itself as an opportune target were the Japanese forces to strike.[13]

The Japanese Army was to settle down and lay siege to Chiang Kai-shek's forces. The front turned quiet, relatively speaking. This was not to say that the war had ceased. Soldiers and civilians were still being killed by the tens of thousands, and battles were fought on a scale and with a ferocity on a par with what was to take place in Europe a few years later, but the high degree of mobility that had marked the preceding 18 months, when Japan conquered huge swathes of Chinese territory, was a thing of the past. Now, the conflict settled into a more stable pattern where frontlines might still change, but not to an extent that either side would consider decisive for the entire war as such.

The limited campaign to take the city of Nanchang in the spring of 1939 was an example of this new and more modest approach. The city, located 160 miles southeast of Wuhan, had escaped occupation by the Japanese the previous year, but remained a potential menace to the Japanese war effort. It had an airfield and, due to a railway line going south, it was an important transit center for supplies from the south Chinese coast. In other words, it would be an important hub in any Chinese counterattack to roll back Japan's recent conquests in the area. From the Japanese perspective, Nanchang had to be taken simply to maintain status quo.[14]

The Japanese generals planned the attack on Nanchang with great care. Two divisions, the 101st and the 106th, moved up to the city supported by a large number of guns of various calibers. After one of the most destructive artillery barrages of the entire war, the 101st marched straight into Nanchang and seized the city amid intense fighting. The 106th Division moved south and cut the railway line into the city.[15] As the battle ground to a close, it emerged that Japan's new, more low-key approach to the war in China continued to exact a heavy toll on the civilian population. "During the final assault and street fighting, large areas of the city were either badly damaged or burned," wrote American military observer Frank Dorn. "Several hundred thousand more terrified refugees straggled in a bewildered stream of uprooted humanity to the south and southwest."[16]

While the policy of "protracted war" that Japan adopted by early 1939 meant an end to massive offensives on the ground, it also entailed more activity in the air, as it introduced a methodical strategic bombing campaign against objectives in central China. Chief among these was the temporary capital of Chongqing. Orders issued from Tokyo made it clear that "strategic and political targets" were to be covered in future air campaigns, in effect sanctioning the bombardment of civilians.[17] It was an example of a school of military thinking in the late 1930s that saw strategic bombing as an efficient means to end wars. While the hopes for this new kind of warfare eventually proved exaggerated, it meant that the full terror of modern war was unleashed on civilian populations, as the fate of the people of Chongqing was soon to show.

The first few Japanese bombing raids against Chongqing's residential and commercial districts took place in January 1939. Following a more than three-month lull brought about by the foggy season, the Japanese bombers returned with a vengeance in early May. In the course of a few days of intensive bombing, approximately 3,700 civilians were killed, and thousands of buildings were destroyed. An additional horror came in the form of incendiary bombs that the Japanese aircraft rained down on the largely defenseless city and its many bamboo structures.[18]

Foreign witnesses watched in horror as 100 Chinese women, children, and elderly people who had sought refuge at the foot of the city wall were surrounded by flames and, unable to escape, burned to death.[19] After the Japanese had left, the fires continued to expand as bamboo exploded and walls came crashing down, spreading the flames.[20] In what was seen as an evil omen on the night after the first bombing, the city experienced a complete lunar eclipse. According to ancient folklore, the moon was being eaten up by a heavenly dog, which had to be driven away with loud sounds. As fires were still burning throughout the city, the eerie banging of drums filled the air under a blood-red sky. War had arrived in Chongqing.[21]

★ ★ ★

For Japan, the courtship with Germany was part of a larger reorientation of foreign policy and a final break with the regional order represented by the Washington Treaty system that had been in force since the end of the Great War. After the moderating influence that Ugaki had briefly exercised as foreign minister in Tokyo, his replacement by the more strident Arita Hachirō brought a radical, iconoclastic tone to Japanese diplomacy. In a letter to the US ambassador, Arita wrote that Japan was "devoting its entire energy to a new order based on genuine international justice throughout East Asia." Any attempt to apply the principles of the past, in other words the Washington Treaty system, would, he added, "not in any way contribute to the solution of immediate issues."[22]

The call for a new regime for Asia under Japanese leadership was emerging as a major theme in pronouncements out of Tokyo. Prime Minister Konoe made a landmark statement on the war in China, demanding a "new order for ensuring permanent stability for East Asia" and even a "new culture." China and Japan were to be part of this new culture, as were Korea and Manchukuo. This was the origin of a Japanese propaganda line that was to be sustained up until 1945, claiming that Japan was really operating for the benefit of all of Asia.[23]

The corollary of the Japanese ambitions for East Asia was a reduced role for the western nations. In the economic bloc that Japan aimed to build with China and Manchukuo, it was "imperative that the economic activities of other powers should be subject to certain restrictions," Foreign Minister Arita told foreign correspondents in December.[24] The Western response was immediate and unmistakable. Shortly after Arita's statement, the United States rejected it outright in a message handed directly to the foreign minister: "This Government reserves all rights of the United States as they exist and does not give assent to any impairment of any of those rights."[25]

The United States had ways to counter Japan. The United States had flexed its economic muscle with the voluntary restraint on the export of airplane technology, but with the picture that was now emerging of a Japan excluding other nations from the western Pacific, voices in Washington emerged in favor of much broader sanctions. Hawks in the State Department put together a list of potential measures, including the abrogation of a treaty of commerce and navigation signed by the United States and Japan in 1911. Scrapping the treaty would have pulled the rug from under most bilateral trade and could pave the way for sweeping export curbs, but the political will was lacking, and it did not materialize at this point. Still, a parallel scheme to extend loans to China passed inspection and was signed by President Roosevelt.[26]

There was, of course, the growing possibility that the Japanese challenge could not be solved by economic means alone. The military was expanding its capabilities in preparation for storms ahead. Congress had approved several naval expansion programs, and in 1938 it had given the green light for a "billion-dollar-a-year naval building program" in a direct response to the growing assertiveness of especially Japan.[27] Antipathy to foreign involvement remained strong in the American political establishment, but there were signs that isolationists were breaking ranks. Senator George W. Norris of Nebraska, for one, came out in support of a strong Navy, since "a war with Japan would be a war upon the sea." He based his change of heart on the behavior of Japan in China and the slaughter there of "hundreds of thousands of innocent people, many of them women and children."[28]

War Plan Orange for conflict with Japan was updated repeatedly in view of strategic and political changes. This was in contrast to most of the other "color" plans and showed that war with Japan remained a very real prospect for American planners.[29] Just three years after the most recent revision, Army and Navy planners concluded a new version of War Plan Orange in February 1938. Like all previous Orange plans, it foresaw hostilities in the Pacific triggered by a Japanese surprise attack without prior declaration of war.[30] The US Navy, with traditional offensive-mindedness, insisted on its right to launch a counterstrike as early as possible, moving west across the Pacific towards the Japanese home islands. This was over the objections of the US Army, which required more time to become combat-ready after the outbreak of war.[31]

One aspect of a coming Pacific conflict which was incorporated into the Orange plans of the 1930s was the rejection of the idea that every major Japanese island fortress had to be conquered on the way to Tokyo. The strategy of "island-hopping" from one strategic strongpoint to the next was fully accepted, as was the notion of leaving even major Japanese fortifications along the way to "wither on the vine," if their capture was not essential for the overall war aims. Surprisingly, and tragically, this understanding was forgotten in the early months of the Allied offensive during the war.[32]

Combined with preparations for war was an undertone of condescension towards the Japanese and their skills in battle. Doubtless there was some racial prejudice involved, but it was also a reflection of the difficulty of obtaining reliable intelligence. Lieutenant Commander Ralph A. Ofstie, assistant naval attaché for air at the embassy in Tokyo, found that he could obtain very little useful information on military matters inside Japan, and went to the China front to gain first-hand impressions there. He was not impressed. "I believe that there is no doubt that we are markedly superior to the Japanese in the air—in piloting skills, in material, and in ability to employ our aircraft effectively on the offense and the defense."[33]

While the US Navy considered its raison d'être to be a future war against Japan, the Army was looking towards Europe and remained in almost willful ignorance of conditions in Asia. When Claire Chennault, a veteran aviator advising the Chinese Air Force, visited the United States in 1939 and was to give a lecture on the Sino-Japanese conflict for senior staff at the Army Air Corps, a map of China was only found with great difficulty. "The one they finally produced," Chennault wrote in his memoirs, "had such scanty detail that I had to pencil in most of the locations that figured in the war."[34]

While US Army officers might have had problems locating even important Chinese cities, more and more Americans were able to put Japan on a map. Japan in the late 1930s was many different things. In great power politics, it was a bully. Ideologically, it was increasingly tending towards the European Fascist dictatorships. In the fields of economics, technology and culture, however, it was viewed in many parts of the world as an up-and-coming nation with a people of unusual talent and diligence. Just at the time when the diplomatic tone between the United States and Japan was worsening, officials in Tokyo were busy preparing the national entry for the World's Fair, held in New York in 1939. Aided by top names such as modernist designer Yamawaki Iwao, they aimed to "combine illustrations of the ancient classical civilization and the modern industrial phase of national life," foreign reporters were told.[35]

The world had got a taste of Japanese can-do spirit, when pilot Iinuma Masaaki and navigator Tsugakoshi Kenji had broken the world record for flight between Tokyo and London, making the trip in less than 100 hours. When the two aviators arrived in the British capital, a ranking Japanese official had gushed about the "fraternity of wings" that had always tied and would continue to tie Japan and Britain together. The airplane was another example of Japanese ingenuity, a Mitsubishi Ki-15, one of the fastest aircraft in the world at the time. In a perfect example of Japan's penchant for mixing the practical and technical with the poetical, the aircraft was named "Divine Wind"—*Kamikaze*.[36]

Japan's growing attraction—its "soft power," to use a modern expression—could be directly observed in the way it was perceived by otherwise dramatically different societies. In Australia, an emerging debate touched on whether the nation's future prosperity hinged on the British Empire or on the geographically closer economies of Asia. By 1935, Japan had replaced Great Britain as the top supplier of textiles to Australia, and the flow of goods also went in the opposite direction, as the Bank of New South Wales had said in a report a year before: "The industrialization of Japan promises to bring with it great possibilities for the development of markets for Australian foodstuffs and raw materials."[37]

Japan was also emerging as an obvious future partner for the Philippines. The archipelago was on its path towards nationhood, following a US act in 1934 guaranteeing independence within a 12-year period, and it was considering its options. The United States intended to maintain a strong presence even after independence, for example through the continued use of existing naval bases. However, Japanese economic involvement was growing, helped by a thriving Japanese business community. In Japan, adherents of the ideal of a close-knit Pan-Asian commonwealth also saw signs of kindred spirits in the Philippines. As a Japanese writer and supporter of the Pan-Asian cause wrote about Manuel Quezon, the Philippine president since 1935: "He can see that we are Oriental peoples, and as Oriental peoples, we finally have to understand that we must plan co-existence and co-prosperity."[38]

While nations such as Australia and the Philippines saw Japan as a partner, poorer societies viewed the emerging Asian giant as a role model. In one of the most remarkable international developments of the period, Abyssinia in faraway Africa had developed a love affair with Japan, since it offered an example of how a non-white nation could succeed in a world dominated by the West. "Let us follow this amazing and praiseworthy example of farsightedness and resoluteness of an entire people," one of Abyssinia's "Japanizers" had said.[39] Conversely, business in Japan had seen much potential in the African economy, especially as a buyer of cotton.[40] Rumors had even circulated of a marriage linking the Abyssinian royal family with Japanese nobility. "There was a nationwide atmosphere of friendship toward Ethiopia in the 1930s," a Japanese woman later recalled, referring to Abyssinia by its modern name. "I imagined that Ethiopia must be a wonderful country."[41] Still, the courtship came to an end after the Italian invasion of the African nation, when Japan decided its relations with Rome were more important.[42]

Even as Japan continued to project strength to the outside world, on the inside it was ailing. The very qualities that had caused it to become the envy of the nations of Asia and Africa were disintegrating, and a slow creep towards militarist rule was setting in. Something resembling a balance between the civilian and military establishments had prevailed in the early years of the century, but the officers had increasingly come to dominate politics. In 1936, an attempt by the political elite to co-opt the military had backfired spectacularly: by ending a ban on active-duty officers in the Cabinet, the politicians hoped to bring about a *modus vivendi*. Instead, they gave the top brass a veto power over all political decisions, as they could bring any civilian government down by ordering officers in a Cabinet position to resign.[43]

It was part of a more general trend for the military to take over control of all aspects of Japanese life. The passage in March 1938 of the National Mobilization Law had been a turning point, rolling back some of the modest but hard-won freedoms that the Japanese people had obtained for themselves in the course of decades of political evolution. It gave the government, now under growing military clout, far-reaching powers to control human and material resources during a prolonged war, by regimenting industrial workers, setting prices, and restraining the media. Although it was not obvious at the time, it was a decisive move towards the totalitarian state that Japan would eventually become.[44]

The circumstances under which the bill was introduced were a warning sign to those worried about the increasing role of the military. When Lieutenant Colonel Satō Kenryō of the War Ministry's Military Affairs Bureau turned up in the Diet, Japan's parliament, to explain the law, he had surrounded himself with uniformed soldiers, like a mafia don signaling power by bringing his bodyguards. Interrupted by a heckler, Satō shouted: "*Damare!*"—"Shut up!" Quickly gaining notoriety as the "Damare incident," it was symbolic of the new level of arrogance that characterized the officer corps and its lack of respect for civilian authority. The passage of the law, in the words of a modern historian, was "the beginning of the end of the Diet as a functional body capable of any meaningful opposition to the decisions of nonelected elites."[45]

The Japanese people did not uniformly approve of the way things were going. Lawmakers critical of the National Mobilization Law received letters of support from angry voters. However, the voices of dissent were to be gradually drowned out as a mood of belligerent conformity took over. "War is both the father of creation and the mother of culture," a military-backed pamphlet argued.[46] At the same time, conservatives in the education ministry issued a hugely influential treatise on the meaning of being Japanese, *Fundamentals of Our National Polity*. The document, directed primarily at teachers, urged absolute obedience to the emperor, identifying him as the direct descendant of Amaterasu Ōmikami, the goddess of the sun. "Offering our lives for the sake of the emperor," it argued, "does not mean so-called self-sacrifice but the casting aside of our little selves to live under his august grace and the enhancing of the genuine life of the people of a state."[47]

In the evening of April 9, 1939, visitors to the Grand Theater in the British district inside the north Chinese city of Tianjin were watching Cary Grant in the brand-new Hollywood adventure movie *Gunga Din*. Among the audience was Cheng Xigeng, superintendent of customs, manager of the Japanese-owned Federal Reserve Bank of North China and, many patriotic Chinese thought, an odious collaborator. Once the movie was underway, four shots could be heard. A Chinese man dressed in a Western outfit had shot Cheng from behind and killed him. As the assassin fled the theater, he fired yet more shots, killing a foreigner and injuring another, before escaping out into the streets, avoiding arrest.[48]

The perpetrator remained at large, but four Chinese men suspected of involvement in the plot were soon apprehended by Japanese police, who were in control of all areas surrounding Tianjin's foreign districts.[49] Possibly under torture, the four admitted to their participation in a plot to murder Cheng. They were subsequently handed over to Tianjin's British authorities, who in turn were expected to pass them on for judgment by the north Chinese puppet regime in nearby Beijing. At this point, the British ambassador to China, Sir Archibald Clark Kerr, put his foot down and refused to abandon them to an uncertain fate, citing his own conscience. He received sufficient backing from London to insist on this stance, even when the Japanese side gave him until June 7 to hand over the four suspects. When the deadline passed with no British concessions, Japanese forces imposed a blockade on Tianjin's foreign district, home to 120,000 people, including 5,000 Westerners.[50]

In the days that followed, British nationals passing the Japanese cordon were forced to undergo humiliating strip searches, while foreign guards were watching well-armed but powerless from behind their barricades. Reports of the situation incensed public opinion back in Britain. The Foreign Office initially assumed an unbending stance, refusing to hand over the four suspects, and when after a few days the British diplomats got second thoughts, it was too late to back down and lose face in front of the whole world. By now, the crisis had also assumed more gravity, as the Japanese no longer demanded just the suspects, but also an end to British assistance to the Chinese side in the war, including measures that helped prop up the Chinese currency. The standoff dragged on throughout the summer, as papers overseas showed ominous photos of Japanese and British soldiers staring down each other across barbed wire.[51] Eventually, a compromise was found as the British government promised to refrain from actions that ran counter to the Japanese war effort. Shortly afterwards the four suspects were quietly handed over to an uncertain fate at the hands of the Japanese.[52]

It was perhaps inevitable that British and Japanese interests were to collide in a spectacular fashion. Japan's ambition of turning the entire Northeast Asian region into an economic community with itself in the lead sat awkwardly with the fact that the West had deep entrenched interests in China. None were bigger than Britain's, with investments in the country worth 1.08 billion dollars, nearly five times as much as number two, the United States.[53] However, it was more than an economic issue. A growing number of ambitious Japanese officers were looking beyond Asia to the wider world. They saw what was happening in Europe, where Hitler's Germany was rising as the dominant power, and they sensed that huge changes were afoot. It was time to act, in the interest of national survival. Talks were going on with Berlin about a firm alliance, and humiliating its British rival in a high-profile crisis would be one way to gain favor with the prospective German partner.[54]

These were the topics of nearly daily meetings that were taking place in 1939 at the Tokyo residence of Japanese War Minister Itagaki Seishirō, a veteran commander of troops in the China theatre. The participants in the meetings were senior officials in the War Ministry, all concurrently ranking military officers, and the topic for discussion was the need to enter into an alliance with Germany, a challenger of the international status quo not unlike Japan.[55] The Japanese Army continued to see the Soviet Union as the main long-term threat to its security and made detailed plans for war with the Russians,[56] but now increasingly viewed its security in a global context. Japanese Army planners concluded from the growing tensions between Germany and the Anglo-American powers that war would break out in 1941 or 1942. It would mean a complete transformation of world politics, and the Japanese Army wanted to be on the German side in this coming clash of giants.[57]

The Japanese foreign ministry was strongly opposed to the Army's wish to cast Japan's lot with Germany in a too-definitive manner. So was the Navy.[58] Even so, Japanese naval officers in the first half of 1939 engaged in operations that brought it dangerously close to conflict with the Royal Navy as well as the French Navy. In a swift operation in February, it had invaded the large tropical island of Hainan 250 miles south of Britain's colony Hong Kong, and close to the Gulf of Tonkin off French Indochina.[59] The following month it had taken possession of the Spratly archipelago deep in the South China Sea, also claimed by France, and only 650 miles from Singapore, Britain's "Gibraltar of the East." While Japanese officers insisted that the aim was to facilitate a naval blockade of China,[60] British officials were not convinced. A look at the map was enough to convince them that the islands were simply too far away from the mainland to be of any real significance for the war in China.[61] Rather, to the Foreign Office it seemed to be part of a long-term scheme to reach the oil of the Dutch East Indies and the iron ore of Malaya, and thus a stepping stone towards final Japanese dominance of the Asia Pacific.[62]

France, too, had reason for concern, seeing its Indochinese possessions suddenly exposed from two angles, but neither London nor Paris did much to protest, and the only response to the Japanese thrust down the South China Sea came from the Netherlands, which reduced its purchases of Japanese cotton.[63] With the crisis in Europe reaching an apogee in the summer of 1939, there were limits to what Britain could realistically do to counter the Japanese, but Foreign Secretary Lord Halifax was adamant that appeasement of the Japanese would have counterproductive results. "It would lead to the downfall of China," he argued, "it would put Japan in a better position to undermine the British Empire in the East, and it would alienate America, whose goodwill is essential to us in the West as well as in the East."[64]

Although the United States was less heavily involved financially than Britain in China, it remained concerned and was exerting growing pressure on Japan. In July 1939, the Roosevelt administration decided to abrogate the 1911 commerce treaty which had narrowly survived the year before and had, for a generation, allowed companies from both sides to carry out business and given ships the freedom to come and go.[65] Little by little, Japan was sliding into the status of an international outcast, deepening the impact of its decision a few months earlier to sever the last remaining ties with the League of Nations.[66] Things were coming to a head in the tense summer of 1939. While in places like Tianjin an effective cold war was being fought between the West and Japan, further north Hirohito's Empire was involved in an actual hot war.

"I'll give orders that all the necessary things be packed for you for a long journey," a senior defense ministry official in Moscow had told Georgi K. Zhukov before sending him with a small group of experts to Mongolia.[67] Zhukov, a soldier since the Czar had ruled Russia, was now deputy commander in the key Byelorussian Military District and a rising star.[68] By sending him to Mongolia in the summer of 1939 the Soviet leaders showed that they considered the escalating situation on the border with the Japanese Empire a grave matter. The center of attention was a disputed part of the boundary between Mongolia, a Soviet satellite, and the Japanese-controlled state of Manchukuo.

The area, a bushless sea of grass with low, gently sloping hills, was known as Khalkin Gol to the Russians, who had named it after a river in the region. The Japanese referred to it as Nomonhan, after a village just east of that river. A skirmish had taken place there in May, after a group of Mongolian horsemen had trespassed into territory claimed by Manchukuo. Despite the small scale of the incident, tensions had spiked, and both the Soviet and Japanese armies had been sending reinforcements to the sparsely populated area.[69] On the Japanese side, much of the escalation had taken place at the initiative of the local officers of the Kwantung Army, with Tokyo acting as a concerned bystander.[70]

The main force on the Japanese side was the 23rd Division, formed just a year earlier and never tested before in battle. Its men were mainly from the southern Japanese island of Kyushu, famous for delivering soldiers of great physical strength and endurance, while the officers were considered of mixed quality, many of them reservists pulled in from their civilian lives.[71] Its commander, Komatsubara Michitarō, was a veteran of the brief campaign against German forces in China a quarter century earlier and one of the Japanese Army's leading experts on the Soviet Union. Unbeknownst to his superiors, as military attaché in Moscow he had compromised himself with his local mistress—in fact a spy—and had been vulnerable to Soviet pressure since then.[72]

The division was put to the test in early July, when it formed the main component of a 15,000-strong force attacking the Soviet positions. The assault was in retaliation for a Soviet air raid deep inside Manchukuo the month before. The objective of the Japanese offensive was to trap a Soviet force entrenched around a bridge across the rapid streams of the Khalkin Gol. This was to be carried out in the form of a

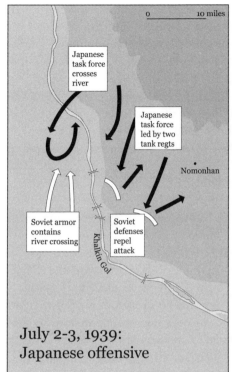

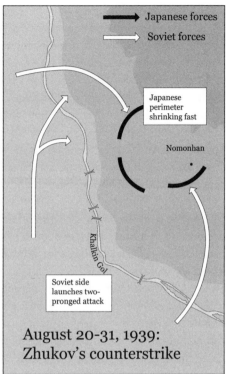

0 _____ 10 miles

Japanese
task force
crosses
river

Japanese
task force
led by two
tank regts

Nomonhan

Soviet armor
contains
river crossing

Soviet
defenses
repel
attack

Khalkin Gol

→ Japanese forces

→ Soviet forces

Japanese
perimeter
shrinking fast

Nomonhan

Soviet side
launches two-
pronged attack

Khalkin Gol

July 2-3, 1939:
Japanese offensive

August 20-31, 1939:
Zhukov's counterstrike

Soviet-Japanese battle at Nomonhan, 1939.

two-pronged attack. One Japanese force was to attack the Soviet position head-on, while another force was to move across the Khalkin Gol a few miles north and storm the Soviets from the rear.[73] The Japanese were so sure of victory that they had invited journalists and military attachés from foreign countries to witness the battle from up close.[74]

The operation kicked off on July 3 before dawn. The frontal attack on the Soviet bridgehead was led by two Japanese tank regiments. They made early advances but were soon bogged down. One of the most efficient Soviet measures turned out to be piano wire, strung up in front of their positions, which was entangled in the tanks' tracks and brought them to a halt, turning them into death traps at the hands of the Soviet artillery. The Japanese crews rarely escaped their burning wrecks, even if they could. They were under strict orders never to abandon their tanks, but to share their fates, like captains on board their doomed ships.[75] Nearly 60 percent of all Japanese tanks deployed in the attack were either disabled or destroyed completely.[76]

North of the unfolding carnage, the other Japanese force had made its way across the Khalkin Gol in the pre-dawn hours, setting up a pontoon bridge but finding to their chagrin that it was not sturdy enough to carry the accompanying tanks. As a result, the Japanese infantry was on its own as it marched down the western banks of the river and encountered a massive wall of Soviet armor rumbling towards them. The Japanese artillery took out some of the tanks, but the most efficient weapon turned out to be bottles with gasoline, the type of low-technology device that would soon be known worldwide as a "Molotov cocktail." Unlike their Japanese counterparts, the Soviet crews were permitted to bail out, but it rarely helped them. "The bodies of many were half-burned, and they would stagger a few steps in agony. Some tried to help wounded comrades; others sought to hide under blazing tanks," military historian Alvin Coox writes. "Japanese heavy machine gunners claimed to have cut down most of the escaping Soviet crews."[77]

Despite the successes against the Soviet tanks, it was clear that the advance on the western side of the Khalkin Gol was not going well either, and by the evening of July 3, less than 24 hours after the offensive had started, the Japanese commanders decided unanimously on a general retreat.[78] It proceeded throughout the night in great confusion, and probably at a far higher loss of life than necessary. This was especially true for the northern force, as it attempted to get back across the Khalkin Gol. According to Soviet sources, nervous Japanese engineers blew up the pontoon bridge too early, trapping many of their comrades on the wrong side of the river. Panic-stricken, the trapped soldiers jumped into the water in an attempt to swim across. Second Lieutenant Negami Hiroshi, an Olympic swimmer, was watching the desperate spectacle, knowing full well that they had little chance against the rapid stream. Many drowned that night.[79]

After the fiasco, the Japanese spent the rest of July seeking to challenge the Russians in smaller-scale operations, resorting to night attacks to minimize the Soviet advantage in military hardware. This was the mirror image of the situation less than two years earlier at Shanghai, where Japan's Chinese opponent had opted for the same solution. Night was the great equalizer when unevenly matched armies met. At Nomonhan, it did not do much to change the outcome of the battle but merely bled the involved Japanese units dry.[80] Shifting to another tactic, the Japanese commanders attempted to engage in artillery duels with the Soviet adversary, but soon learned that their guns were far inferior both quantitatively and qualitatively. "Underdog tactics may be fine for infantrymen, but not for artillery," as a Japanese officer later admitted.[81]

Many of the Japanese defenders were already doomed. Soviet dictator Joseph Stalin gave the order in early August to expel the "Japanese samurai" from the area.[82] Since then, Zhukov had been carefully planning the Soviet counteroffensive, amassing enough armor, artillery, and aircraft to be able to deal a shocking blow to his Japanese foe.[83] The nearest railhead was 400 miles away, and everything had to be carried by truck the last part of the way. Soviet drivers, hauling their cargoes day and night, performed "miracles," Zhukov said.[84] Concealment was of paramount importance. All units assembled for the attack were camouflaged and hidden from view. In order to disguise the inevitable sound of an army preparing for battle, the Soviets had come up with an ingenious plan. A fortnight before the attack, they had started using special sound equipment to imitate the noise of aircraft and tanks. Initially the Japanese had been annoyed, but eventually they got used to it, believing it was some kind of psychological warfare, which was, Zhukov pointed out, "exactly what we wanted."[85]

The Soviet general struck on August 20. As the sun rose over the grass-covered expanse, the Japanese positions were exposed to furious air raids and artillery bombardments. After the last round had been fired, the Soviet tanks—some equipped with flamethrowers making them look like mythical dragons made of steel—started rolling. Zhukov's plan was simple. Emerging from the bridgehead that the Japanese had tried to eliminate more than a month earlier, the main Soviet force engaged the enemy, pinning them down. At the same time, two separate thrusts were launched across the Khalkin Gol river both in the north and the south, cutting through the Japanese flanks and carrying out a double encirclement in almost as perfect a fashion as if it had been undertaken on the drill ground. For the Japanese, the shock was complete, but the officers were initially unwilling to acknowledge the extent of the disaster. A major was enraged when a junior officer reported to him that a unit occupying a key tactical position had been annihilated. "You fool," the major shouted into the face to the shaken younger man. "What do you mean by 'annihilation'? *You* are alive, aren't you?"[86]

No amount of sarcasm could hide the fact that casualties on the Japanese side were mounting, and that they were massive among both soldiers and officers. "We do not know how many wounded or killed we have," a Japanese soldier wrote in his diary. "The shelling does not stop."[87] The charismatic Colonel Morita Tōru, who was widely known as one of the army's leading instructors in *kendō* swordsmanship, prided himself on being invulnerable to bullets, and as his regiment was sent south in a futile attempt to contain the Soviet envelopment maneuver there, he was last seen standing erect in the midst of enemy fire to instill courage into his men. An eyewitness described the result: "He was shot down and killed instantly by three Maxim machine-gun slugs that hit him in the head and chest."[88]

As all Japanese counterattacks failed, in the course of five days and five nights of ferocious fighting, the Soviet forces were able to completely surround the 23rd Division and isolate its active units in three separate pockets.[89] Attempts by units of the Japanese Kwantung Army to penetrate through the Soviet lines and relieve their encircled comrades failed. The battle was lost for Japan, and by the end of August, Zhukov was in a position to declare the entire disputed area between Khalkin Gol and Nomonhan cleared of organized enemy resistance.[90] On the Soviet side, there was little doubt where credit was due. Grigori M. Shtern, a Soviet commander who was at Nomonhan and watched Zhukov's moves from up close, compared it to the classic encirclement battle of the ancient world, at Cannae when a Punic force had annihilated a Roman army: "I think it will become the second perfect battle of encirclement in all history."[91]

The battle was a rare defeat for the Japanese Army, which had fought for nearly a decade in China scoring one victory after the other. The humiliation was all the more profound because the 23rd Division had been virtually wiped out. Its commander, Komatsubara, had managed to slip through the Soviet lines in the closing moments of the battle and was now the target of severe criticism. "When the war situation gets difficult, he gets impatient, panics and takes it out on his subordinates," one of his officers said later.[92] In coming to terms with the debacle, however, Japan went far beyond pointing fingers at individuals. The entire idea of challenging Soviet power, essentially an army project, suffered a severe blow. This had consequences months and even years into the future, as the Japanese leadership discussed if the nation should direct its energies north towards the vast expanses of Asia or south towards the equally vast ocean.

The battle at Nomonhan had been waged against the backdrop of shocking changes in global politics. Perhaps the main reason why Stalin felt secure enough to order Zhukov's masterful counterattack in early August was confidence that he would have his back covered in Europe. Hitler was no longer a concern. German diplomats had warned their Japanese counterparts that unless they moved faster on plans for an alliance, Germany might turn to the Soviet Union instead.[93] The Japanese had continued to drag their feet, fearing that friendship with Germany could put them on a path towards conflict with the Western powers. An exasperated Italian foreign minister juxtaposed "the phlegmatic and slow Japanese and the dynamic Fascists and Nazis."[94] In the end, Germany, preparing for an invasion of Poland and a possible war with Britain and France, moved fast to neutralize the Soviet factor. The German efforts came to fruition in the form of a non-aggression pact with the Soviet Union which was signed on August 23.

The news startled the world, and nowhere was the surprise bigger than in Tokyo, which was already reeling from the US abrogation of the 1911 commerce treaty. Now, a potentially promising situation in Europe had been bungled, and a chance had been missed to form a common front with Germany against the Soviet threat. "The world of Europe is complicated and inscrutable," said Prime Minister Hiranuma Kiichirō, shortly before stepping down as a result of the twin humiliations of Nomonhan and the German-Soviet pact.[95] The disappointment with Hitler's "betrayal" was so profound that when Germany was briefly mentioned as a go-between for renewed peace talks with China, Japan turned down the proposal.[96] Relations between Tokyo and Berlin would not fully recover for another two years. In the meantime, events in Europe continued to influence the situation in Asia in profound ways.

On September 1, 1939, the very day that Germany attacked Poland, Chinese officers in the area south of the occupied city of Wuhan issued a war plan predicting how the new partnership between Berlin and Moscow would affect events in China: "The Nazi-Soviet Agreement has created great unease amongst Japanese officials and the public. In order to cover up their defeat and invigorate public morale, the Japanese militarists will again begin an offensive against China."[97] Another report was even more precise in its forecast: "The enemy will use the inability of the European powers to pay attention to the East to launch a rapid offensive on Changsha."[98]

This was indeed what the Japanese commanders were planning at the time. Changsha, a large city 180 miles southwest of Wuhan, lay astride a strategic railroad allowing the Chinese to transport troops and materiel from the south. It was also the main entrance into the vital province of Sichuan, the location of China's new capital Chongqing.[99] These were all sound strategic reasons for Japan to launch an offensive. In addition, the warlike Japanese officers felt a need to keep their troops busy. Colonel Miyazaki Shūichi, who was stationed in the area at the time, explained it in his post-war testimony: "As mosquito larvae hatch in stagnant puddles, troops become demoralized if they don't fight. Troops have to rest after an operation and work hard in training, but then they must fight again," he said.[100]

The Japanese kicked off their offensive on September 14. The 101st and 106th Divisions, previously in action during the battle of Nanchang, advanced from the east towards Changsha, while three other divisions moved in from the north. The Chinese defenders had decided beforehand on flexible, guerrilla-style tactics, rather than waiting for the Japanese in fixed positions. The objective, as ordered by Chinese General Chen Cheng, was "to lure the enemy into the vicinity of Changsha for a decisive battle."[101] When the Japanese reached Changsha at the end of September, General Chen sprang his trap. In a night attack on the last day of the month, the advance Japanese troops found themselves surrounded by "60,000 screaming Chinese on their front, rear and both flanks," as an American military observer reported. The Japanese beat a hasty retreat and were harassed by the Chinese every step of the way back.[102] The campaign lasted for about a month, and the Japanese had been uncharacteristically bloodied.

The almost pointless battle of Changsha brought home, once again, the fact that Japan's top concern remained the China quagmire. Escaping it was its primary foreign policy priority. Newly appointed Foreign Minister Nomura Kichisaburō warned that in the absence of a political solution that genuinely appealed to the Chinese "the only alternative course that could bring the war to an end would be the stationing of several million troops across China." Nomura, an admiral by profession and a moderate brought into government after the resignation of the previous Cabinet in August, went on to warn: "It would be conquest of China by sword alone. And such a course could endanger the future of the Empire."[103]

Nomura had spent time in the United States and belonged to a group within the Japanese foreign policy establishment who held out hope for some type of accommodation with the US government. In a series of meetings with US Ambassador Joseph Grew in late 1939, he sought to narrow differences by offering modest concessions, such as opening up the lower Yangtze, which had been closed since the hostilities two years earlier. It was a sign of the support in Japanese society for better relations with the United States that Grew also met with a representative of Japanese business interests in the shape of Aikawa Yoshisuke, the president of the Manchuria Heavy Industries Development Corp.[104]

Grew was highly sympathetic to people of Nomura's ilk. The Japanese government, he said in a dispatch to Washington, was "endeavoring courageously, even with only gradual success, to fight against a recalcitrant Japanese Army, a battle which happens to be our own battle."[105] Despite the good intentions, the efforts were doomed from the start. The basic demands were too far apart. Like almost all other Japanese, Nomura insisted on a continued Japanese presence in China, whereas the basic American endeavor was for a return to the situation existing prior to the outbreak of full-scale war between China and Japan in 1937.[106]

In stark opposition to Nomura, another group within the Japanese military and civilian elite was calling for closer ties with the Soviet Union. The way they saw it, the pact between Berlin and Moscow had set the scene for a global showdown between liberal status-quo powers and their anti-capitalist enemies, and they believed Japan belonged in the latter group.[107] It had been encouraged by Germany's Foreign Minister von Ribbentrop, who, on the way to Moscow and the signing ceremony for the non-aggression pact, had told a Japanese diplomat that "I, for one, believe that the best policy for us would be to conclude a Japanese-German-Soviet non-aggression agreement and then move against Britain."[108] As it turned out, this was the basic direction that Japanese diplomacy would take over the next year and a half.

CHAPTER SIX

Stalemate

1940

Li Jiefu was a private in the 200th Division, famed as China's only fully mechanized unit of that size, but he still did not have good shoes when he marched into battle shortly before New Year 1940. The objective was the strategically vital Kunlun Pass in China's deep south. The Japanese had taken it, and now his division had been ordered to take it back. At age 22, Li already was a hardened soldier, and he hated the Japanese. "We'd been told we'd receive a handsome reward if we caught a Japanese prisoner alive, but we were soldiers and could lose our lives in battle at any time, so what did we need money for? We killed the devils the moment we saw them," Li said.[1]

The battle of Kunlun Pass raged from mid-December 1939 until mid-January 1940. It was part of a larger campaign that began in November when a Japanese force consisting of the 5th Division and the Mixed Taiwan Brigade disembarked on the north shore of the Gulf of Tonkin, close to the Chinese border with Indochina. They marched north, aiming to take the city of Nanning and cut off a supply line that allowed a slender stream of materiel to reach Chiang Kai-shek's forces further inland. The weak local Chinese defenses crumbled before the Japanese forces, and the advance proceeded briskly. Within ten days, Nanning had fallen. Within another ten days, Japanese forces were in control of Kunlun Pass, the main transportation route from Nanning north into territory held by the Chinese.[2]

The Japanese had succeeded in opening a new front, and the Chinese high command clearly recognized the gravity of the situation. It decided to deploy one of its elite formations, the 5th Corps, consisting of the 200th Division and the 1st Honors Division, which derived its name from the fact that it consisted of officers and men previously injured in battle. The corps, commanded by General Du Yuming, had been training for a month in combined arms operations, involving infantry, armor, and aircraft.[3] If any unit in the battered Chinese army was capable of pushing the Japanese out of their positions at Kunlun Pass and back into the Gulf of Tonkin, it would have to be this one.

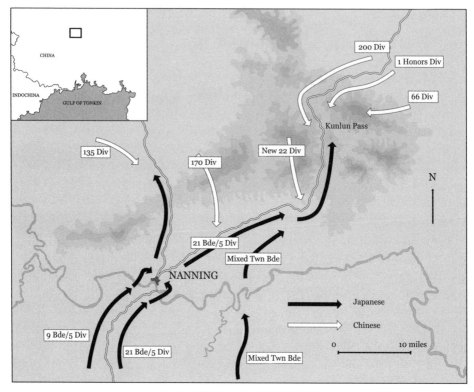

Battle of Kunlun Pass, 1939–1940.

The Chinese forces arrived in the middle of December. Initial reconnaissance showed that the Japanese had spent the intervening days wisely, strengthening their positions in the pass. They had set up camouflaged machine-gun nests providing interlocking fire while rolling out parallel lines of barbed wire to form seemingly impregnable fortifications on top of a number of hills that offered a perfect view of every inch of the pass. Du Yuming's plan for defeating the Japanese was to follow the stratagem of "closing the door to catch the tiger." While the 200th Division and the 1st Honors Division attacked Kunlun Pass head-on, the New 22nd Division, which had been rushed to the area from central China, would move by small roads to the south of Kunlun Pass and cut off the retreat route to Nanning, "closing the door."[4]

The battle for the pass began on December 18, when artillery on both sides engaged each other in a deadly duel, before the two divisions of the 5th Corps began their advance towards the enemy lines, supported by tanks. Usually, Chinese infantry would be easy prey for Japanese planes, but this time the Chinese anti-aircraft batteries forced them to keep a distance. The weeks spent in training paid off for the Chinese divisions, and within hours they had taken back Kunlun Pass. The New 22nd Division also succeeded in moving to the south of the pass, encircling the Japanese.[5]

The victory was brief. The following day, the Japanese launched a counterattack, and the pass changed hands again. Over the next ten days a seesaw battle evolved, and the Chinese side ended up taking the pass a total of three times. It was unlike any battle China and Japan had engaged in before. While the Japanese side had habitually prevailed because of technological superiority on the ground and in the air, the Chinese showed this time that they had learned from their enemy. Chinese tanks coordinated with infantry in storming the Japanese positions, and Chinese aircraft repeatedly descended from the sky to strafe Japanese soldiers.

Bai Chongxi, one of Chiang Kai-shek's best-known generals and a member of China's large Muslim community, was in overall charge of military operations in this part of the country and visited the frontline at Kunlun Pass to observe the unfolding battle. "I ordered a battery of French mountain guns and another battery of Soviet anti-tank guns to be moved to a hilltop on the enemy's left flank and fire into his flank, tearing up his barbed wire," Bai wrote in his autobiography.[6] While the artillery forced the Japanese to keep their heads down, Chinese units remained south of the pass to prevent supplies from reaching the Japanese, prompting them to airlift ammunition and other supplies to the encircled troops in the pass.

The end result, by early January 1940, was stalemate. Chinese troops held onto Kunlun Pass, while the Japanese remained in possession of Nanning. The original Japanese objective, to stop the supply from Indochina, was not met. The Chinese side simply moved the supply line to the west, allowing the traffic to continue.[7] Still, the battle was less about actual military gain, and more about symbolism. Kunlun Pass was a much-needed boost to Chinese morale, especially among the large and politically important population in the cities which kept informed through the newspapers and cared about the nation's future. "We have achieved a new belief in victory," wrote star Chinese reporter Fan Changjiang, who toured the battlefield shortly afterwards.[8]

The battle in the south in late 1939 and early 1940 had ripple effects elsewhere. Chiang Kai-shek and his commanders had planned a winter offensive across large parts of north and central China, and the assistance of the 5th Corps could have added firepower to what was one of the most ambitious operations to date. The offensive marked a departure from the past in that it saw the Nationalist Chinese forces seize the initiative and strike the Japanese at a time and place of their choosing, rather than passively waiting in prepared positions for the enemy to attack.[9] The Japanese were taken aback. "We have never seen the Chinese army undertake such a large-scale and determined attack," said an astonished Lieutenant General Okamura Yasuji, commander of the Japanese Eleventh Army.[10]

Paradoxically, even as Chinese and Japanese forces were engaged in protracted pitched battles in some parts of China, other sections of the Nationalist regime's long, fluid, and porous border with Japanese-controlled territory had settled into a strange state in between war and peace. For people who were willing to pay, it was actually possible to reach Chiang Kai-shek's Nationalist capital in Chongqing. The young American Graham Peck made the journey from the British colony of Hong Kong in the summer of 1940. He did so as one of several passengers on board a primitive vessel meandering its way through the south Chinese swamp, dodging not just Japanese fortresses and patrols, but also local pirates and Nationalist soldiers of somewhat dubious loyalty.

Peck was exposed to a post-apocalyptic landscape rendered nearly empty of people by the war: "In the heat and glare of the July weather, the emptiness gave the journey the quality of a dream," he wrote. "We would glide between the luxuriant banks for hours with no glimpse of human life except an occasional farmer in a field, who ran and hid when he saw us, or a quiet watcher in a thicket, staring out with enigmatic face." Floating by a village was like "passing a tableau of horror in a tunnel ride at an amusement park. The walls of mangrove and palmetto would fall away, revealing the decayed houses with their shabby people."[11]

It was not coincidental that an American would try to make his way by circuitous means to China's wartime capital. The United States had always considered itself as having a special relationship with China, and by 1940, America was China's closest foreign friend.[12] The partnership between the United States and China was not without serious problems. Corruption was a constant complaint among Americans exposed to Nationalist China. Herbert Yardley, an American intelligence professional who advised the Chinese government on espionage, discovered how large amounts of official gasoline was being embezzled. He told a Chinese friend about it. "Small thief if caught is executed," the Chinese said in broken English. "If successful he becomes honored official, and bigger theft becomes perquisite of office."[13]

China, on the other hand, was concerned about continued US exports to the Japanese of materials that they needed in order to carry on their war. Bea Liu, an American woman who was married to a Chinese and spent the war years in the heavily bombed southwest of the country, described how one morning in May 1940 on the way to work, she saw a lone plane circling above the city she lived in. A Chinese officer was watching it intently through his binoculars. The American woman asked him whose plane it was.

"Yours," he answered.

"What do you mean by that?" she shot back.

"Japanese."

"Then don't call it mine."

"I beg your pardon," the Chinese officer replied. "But it couldn't be up there without your country's gasoline."[14]

On March 30 1940, a new government of China was installed. Its name was far from catchy: The Reorganized National Government of the Republic of China. Its choice of capital was inauspicious: Nanjing, the scene of the worst Japanese atrocities to date. Its geographical reach was unimpressive: part of the eastern provinces conquered by the Japanese Army since 1937. Its mission, impossible: to convince the people of China that it was anything but a pliable tool in the hands of the Japanese empire. At its head was Wang Jingwei, the defector from Chiang Kai-shek's government in Chongqing, who had spent the past 11 months in long, frustrating negotiations with the Japanese on what kind of republic was to emerge on China's occupied soil.

Few guests at the inauguration of Wang's regime could help but notice that Nanjing was a city still not fully recovered from the slaughter of just a couple of years earlier. The organizers did their level best to put an optimistic face on the orchestrated event. For the first time since 1937, the streets were lined with the blue, red, and white flag of the Chinese Nationalist government, but with a narrow yellow pennant at the top to distinguish it from the flag flown by the rival regime in Chongqing. Security was abundant and conspicuous. The spacious building where the ceremony was taking place was strictly off-limits to the public, as Chinese gendarmes with cocked Mauser pistols were keeping a watchful eye. Wang read out a declaration, talking about a "post-war era" which had now begun: "China and Japan, like two brothers reconciled after unfortunate resort to arms, will be in everlasting peace and will jointly stabilize East Asia."[15]

Around the time of his inauguration, on a cold, windy and rainy day, Wang Jingwei went to the hilly outskirts of Nanjing to visit the tomb of Sun Yat-sen, the founder of the Chinese republic. Wang considered himself Sun's heir, and he saw it as his responsibility to history to enable the republic to live on, even under a new name. If in a time of extreme duress, it meant bowing to Japanese suzerainty, that was a price that had to be paid. Wang had made a similar visit to the tomb more than two years earlier, when Nanjing was about to fall to the Japanese Army, and Wang had still been on Chiang Kai-shek's side. Much had changed, and it filled Wang with emotion. "Now looking back on the intervening events, it seems like a dream," wrote an aide who accompanied him at the tomb. "Wang read Sun Yat-sen's will and cried, tears running down. I cried also. After we visited Sun Yat-sen's tomb, the sun came out. This seemed to me a kind of good sign for a bright future."[16]

Wang and his closest collaborators were very much alone in believing in this bright future. Not even the Japanese government had much faith in Wang's republic and took a leisurely eight months to recognize it diplomatically.[17] In an instance of unintended irony picked up eagerly by foreign reporters, the Japanese foreign ministry spokesman Suma Yakichirō told a press conference that the new regime was as independent as Manchukuo.[18] Other Japanese officials dropped all pretenses and spoke their minds about the weakness of Wang's regime. In a debate in the Japanese Diet, leading conservative lawmaker Saitō Takao criticized the Chinese puppet government as "shot through with bandits and defeated stragglers," and dismissed it as unable to enforce its own rule on Chinese territory.[19]

Some of the "defeated stragglers" actually began escaping back to Chongqing. Even before the inauguration, the career diplomat Gao Zongwu, who had been a key figure in planning Wang's defection, had grown disillusioned with the lack of real authority accorded to the new regime. In his despair, he wrote a poem in traditional Chinese style. "The north, the south, the sea, and the mountains," it began, and went on:

> None of them belongs to China.
> Where shall the Chinese people live?[20]

On New Year's Day, 1940, Gao Zongwu and an associate by the name of Tao Xisheng, helped by members of Shanghai's underground, stepped onto a passenger ship that took them to Hong Kong. Once in the safety of the British colony, the two started releasing secret documents on Wang Jingwei's negotiations with the Japanese. A furious Wang wrote in his diary: "The two beasts, Gao and Tao. I vow that I will destroy them."[21]

In fact, Wang destroyed himself. Wang's regime never succeeded in building up the legitimacy it was aspiring to. Its close association with Japan was a liability. Not only did it fail to reduce the Japanese military presence in China. It also took over some of the occupying power's most hated practices, inheriting the opium monopoly that the Japanese military had developed in China in order to finance its intelligence activities. It would be hard to think of a more unpopular cause among Chinese nationalists. Addiction to the drug had been the hated expression of Chinese weakness for a century since the First Opium War. Yet, Wang Jingwei's government was tempted by the huge revenues derived from the narcotics trade and also, with some justification, held that control of the trade would make it easier to rein it in over time.[22]

Arguably, the Japanese government used the existence of Wang's regime mainly as leverage in another doomed attempt to force Chiang Kai-shek to the negotiating table. Primary among these efforts was a series of low-profile talks taking place in Hong Kong, codenamed "Operation Kiri" by the Japanese side. The chief Chinese delegate in the discussions, T. L. Soong, the younger brother of Madame Chiang Kai-shek, made no effort to disguise the fact that Chongqing considered the Communists the main enemy.[23] "If peace is achieved," he said, "we are fully prepared, as fast as you can say 'truce', to launch a military operation against the communist bandits."[24] Despite a certain mutual sympathy, and a suggestion even that Chiang Kai-shek should meet with the Japanese in the city of Changsha, the talks did not produce a rapprochement with the Chinese Nationalists. The sticking point was Japan's insistence that the Nationalists recognize Manchukuo, which they refused to do, and probably would be unable to do, if they wanted to hold onto power.[25]

In this regard, Wang's regime was much more pliable, and on the same day in November 1940 that it established formal diplomatic relations with Japan, it also recognized Manchukuo. By then, the northeast Chinese puppet state under former Chinese Emperor Puyi had become an integrated part of the Japanese-led regional economy, and an appearance of normalcy was desperately maintained, even when conditions were anything but normal. At the same time as Japanese tourism officials met in the big city of Harbin, discussing ways to attract foreign travelers and give them "correct knowledge about Manchuria," ten miles to the south, in the suburb of Pingfang, members of the Japanese Army's Unit 731 were conducting sickening experiments, exposing prisoners to poison gas and other gruesome trials with complete disregard for their victims' suffering.[26]

This was the raw reality that official propaganda was designed to cover up, and it did so efficiently. Many Japanese accepted the official narrative of Manchukuo as the land of opportunity and emigrated to a new life as settlers. Some did it out of economic necessity, others because they were filled with missionary zeal. They were often shocked by the reality they encountered. "Manchurian kids ate such things as the peels of watermelon we had discarded on the streets," a Japanese settler said.[27] Another settler wrote in his diary about a visit to a local village and the state of the children: "Their faces, hands, and legs are all filthy. They probably have never cut their hair. I bet they do not bathe, nor wash their faces either ... I noticed a pig carcass and the bones of a horse scattered all over and sighted several Manchurians excreting in public under the eaves and by the roadside." The visit strengthened him in the conviction that "we should lead them into a better future."[28]

A Japanese-designed future, however, failed to inspire many of the original residents of Manchukuo. The military opposition to the Japanese invasion in the early 1930s had morphed into a partisan movement, which still was causing considerable trouble for the Japanese Army in 1940. By this time, the Japanese were employing all methods available to fight the insurgents. This included the introduction of strategic hamlets, which made it possible to isolate the partisans from the crop-producing population in an attempt to starve them into submission.[29] It seemed to work. When the Japanese killed a well-known partisan commander in early 1940 and opened his abdomen, they found grass in his bowels. He had eaten nothing else for a considerable period of time prior to his death.[30]

One ethnic group in Manchukuo was standing out: the Russians. Out of a total population of over 36 million, they amounted to no more than 115,000 officially registered residents.[31] Despite their small number, they were highly visible. The vast majority had arrived in northeast China as refugees in the years after the Bolshevik revolution in 1917 and were staunchly anti-communist, dreaming of a chance to return to the motherland they had lost. A few allowed these patriotic feelings to translate into Fascism, and the swastika emblem became a common sight in the 1930s and 1940s. Others decided to enter into military service, either to make a living or because they hoped they would eventually be able to fight the communists who had expelled them from their country of birth. Both Chinese warlord armies and the Japanese benefited from their willingness to serve.[32]

The most well-known Russian military unit in Manchukuo was the Asano Detachment, established in the spring of 1938 and named after its first commanding officer, Japanese Major Asano Makoto.[33] Although it was officially a part of the

Manchukuo Army, everything about the unit was Japanese including the outfit, offering the incongruous sight of Caucasians in Japanese uniforms. They initially numbered a few hundred and were primarily involved in guard duty and anti-partisan operations. An example of such a deployment was in August 1939, when a unit from the Asano Detachment was sent on a punitive expedition against a group of Chinese insurgents who had killed 14 ethnic Russian settlers in eastern Manchukuo. The Russians caught up with the rebels and engaged in an exchange of fire which yielded three Chinese prisoners.[34]

The ranks of the Asano Detachment filled up rapidly in the spring of 1940 after Manchukuo introduced compulsory military service for all ethnic groups, including the Russians. The attitude in the Russian community was ambiguous. Some families welcomed the opportunity to serve, or at least thought it was a necessary duty to perform for the state that offered them shelter. Others actively opposed it. Since students were exempted from military service, there was a sudden influx of young men into the North Manchurian University in Harbin, Manchukuo's only Russian university. There were stories of young men eating whole packages of dry tea leaves to look sick when appearing before the recruitment committees. An ethnic Russian who evidently belonged to the group reluctant to serve described his feelings when seeing members of the Asano Detachment returning home on leave: "They made an impression with their bearing and military uniform with Japanese swords on their sides. But their appearance did not tempt anyone."[35]

Besides the Nationalists and the array of puppet regimes poised against it, a third force was vying for the future of China in 1940: the Communists under Mao Zedong. Similar to Chiang Kai-shek, Mao had pinned his hopes on other nations coming to the aid of China in the war against Japan. Mao had said as early as 1936 that in the absence of foreign aid, the conflict could be a protracted one. "The war will be very long," he had said, "but in the end, just the same, Japan will be defeated, only the sacrifices will be extensive and it will be a painful period for the whole world."[36]

Also similar to Chiang, Mao was convinced that time was on China's side. A report issued by the Communist Party leadership was typical: "The more the enemy advances, the vaster becomes the rear area, the weaker his troop strength, the more favorable [it will be] to our strategy of turning the enemy's rear into his front, and the more advantageous to our development of a large-scale guerrilla movement."[37] This was not just wishful thinking, but based on solid historical precedence. China had invariably proven too huge for any foreign invader. Japan was merely the latest in the row of historical would-be conquerors who were forced to face this simple truth.

While believing in the inevitability of final victory, the Communists employed various tactics to hasten the defeat of the Japanese. Recognizing that they were no match for the Japanese in conventional battles, they resorted to tactics with a high element of surprise and deception. A senior Communist officer told New Zealand journalist James Bertram how this worked. During a battle for a mountain, the Communists built what appeared to be heavy fortifications halfway up the slope. The Japanese bombed the mountain massively, and then sent in its cavalry to finish off survivors. "Meantime," the officer explained, "our main force had been waiting in ambush at the foot of the hills—very much nearer the Japanese than the latter expected. We surprised their cavalry when they advanced, attacking from short range with machine-guns and hand-grenades; and inflicted very heavy losses on them before they retreated."[38]

In a war where prisoners were rarely taken, and, if so, often only to be mistreated and then killed, the Communists attempted to enforce new more humane practices. According to a detailed US Army report on the Chinese guerrilla movement, this had little to do with any sympathy for the Japanese foe, but reflected a deep understanding of the psychological effect it would have. "The regular [Communist] army forces use the prisoners for propaganda purposes to cause defection in enemy ranks," the report said. "They are given money, new clothes and good food. They are usually allowed to return if they so desire. Those who do return dispel the belief of their associates that they would be maltreated if captured; hence, according to the Communists, they surrender more easily when hard-pressed."[39]

Still, for all the ingenuity displayed by the Communist guerrillas, the future was beginning to look bleak for them in the north Chinese countryside by the middle of 1940. The Japanese Army and its Chinese auxiliaries had come up with an anti-partisan formula that seemed to be working, occupying fortified positions in the middle of Communist-held territory, and linking them up to each other by heavily guarded rail lines and roads. It was in many respects similar to tactics employed by the Nationalists in the 1930s to deal with the Communist insurgents in the countryside. The Japanese called it the "cage strategy," and their Chinese foes reluctantly agreed that it had that exact effect on them. Liu Bocheng, an influential Communist commander, concluded after an inspection tour that the Japanese were using "the rail lines as bars, the roads as chains and the strong points as locks."[40] Another reason for concern was speculation that Chiang Kai-shek's regime would enter into a peace agreement with Japan, giving him a free hand to move on the Communists.[41]

The situation was dire enough that the Communist leaders decided to launch one of their only conventional campaigns of the entire war. It stretched across five provinces of northern China, but was primarily targeting the railway network in the two key provinces of Shanxi and Hebei.[42] The operation would soon be named the Hundred Regiments Offensive, because it eventually involved 105 regiments on the Chinese side, although many were considerably smaller than standard regiments, and some were militia units of questionable quality.[43] They were commanded by Peng Dehuai, a seasoned general who had been a warrior his entire adult life and had risen through the ranks primarily fighting the Nationalists.

The campaign was meticulously prepared, and great efforts were made to ensure secrecy. Still, it was almost inevitable that the Japanese would sense that something was afoot. In the late summer of 1940, the Japanese commanders in north China received unsettling reports of new faces inexplicably showing up at village fairs in occupied areas,[44] while isolated garrisons saw unnerving signs of nighttime activity in supposedly pacified countryside—flickering torch lights and whispering voices. In fact, it was farmers guiding Communist rebels to their positions in preparation for attack.[45]

Despite the various signs of growing activity, the Japanese garrisons were taken almost completely by surprise when the offensive was unleashed at 8 am on August 20. They were extremely thinly spread on the ground, giving the Communist guerrillas a numerical advantage in virtually every battle they fought. The Jingxing coal mines, the source of fuel for a large part of the entire Japanese Army in north China, had a mere fourteen soldiers attached and could do nothing when the Communists launched their attack and flooded the shafts.[46] There were numerous other actions like that, and to the Japanese, it was "death by a thousand cuts," similar to the way that the Vietcong would launch the Tet Offensive in Vietnam in 1968 with a series of pinprick operations against American and South Vietnamese positions throughout the southern half of the country.

The offensive lasted for a total of three and a half months. The early successes led to an overestimation of what could be achieved, and eventually it backfired. The Communist leadership issued orders to expand the initial offensives, "thereby shrinking enemy-occupied territory, enlarging areas, breaking the blockade, and enhancing our strength." At the same time, the Japanese Army moved in reinforcements from the big cities and met their foe in regular battles, where the Communist armies were bound to suffer severe casualties due to their inferior equipment and training.[47]

The Japanese military was honest in its appraisal of the shock the offensive had inflicted: "These totally unexpected attacks caused serious damage, and it was necessary to expend much time and money in restoration work," an after-action report stated.[48] Even so, the infrastructure was rebuilt with some ease, and although large tracts of countryside were in the hands of Communist rebels, the Japanese were not prevented in the long run from extracting whatever resources they needed for their war economy.[49] More important, perhaps, the experience of the Hundred Regiments Campaign and the realization of the potential strength of the Communist guerrilla army prompted the Japanese to allocate more troops to the north of China, reducing their ability to fight elsewhere.[50]

Still, the campaign came at an immense cost to the Communists, not least in human life. As a Communist source stated about a part of the campaign carried out in a border area where several provinces met, "the big battle also inflicted very

Chiang Wei-kuo, the adopted son of Chinese leader Chiang Kai-shek, in the uniform of the German Wehrmacht in the late 1930s. Chiang Wei-kuo studied at a military academy in Munich for several years, while his stepbrother spent long years in Russia. Asian and European politics were intimately intertwined in the prewar years. (Wikimedia)

A Chinese naval vessel attacks a Japanese pirate ship in this Chinese painting from the 18th century. The Japanese pirate was a much-dreaded figure in the Chinese imagination throughout many centuries of hostility. (Wikimedia)

A modern Japanese Navy clashes with a less sophisticated Chinese foe during the war of 1894–95. The conflict between the two proud and ancient nations was a wake-up call for many Chinese as it showed how far they had fallen behind Japanese technology and know-how. (Wikimedia)

A Japanese Red Cross nurse tends to wounded Russian prisoners at a hospital in Korea in 1904. Japan's humane treatment of POWs during its war with Russia was widely recognized abroad. (Library of Congress)

German troops man positions near the enclave of Qingdao in China during the Japanese siege in 1914. As an ally of Britain, Japan entered World War I on the side of the Entente Powers, adding to its own empire in the Asia Pacific by seizing Germany's colonies in the region. (German Federal Archives)

A young Japanese naval captain Yamamoto Isoroku (left) during a visit to the United States in 1926. Fifteen years later, he would be the brains behind the Pearl Harbor Attack. Seated next to him is US Secretary of the Navy Curtis D. Wilbur. The other Japanese is Captain Hasegawa Kiyoshi, who went on to command naval forces in China in the late 1930s. On the right is US Admiral Edward Walter Eberle. (Library of Congress)

Three *modan gāru*, Japanese for "modern girls," in a department store advertisement from 1929. Japanese society saw a brief period of liberalism and Westernization in the 1920s before a conservative reaction asserted itself. (Wikimedia)

Japanese soldiers march past a dead body in the opening stages of the conquest of Manchuria, late 1931. The harsh winter proved costly for the Japanese. (National Digital Archive, Poland)

Japanese diplomat Matsuoka Yōsuke strikes a defiant note at a meeting on the Manchurian crisis at the League of Nations in Geneva. As foreign minister, Matsuoka would later play a key role in forming Japan's Axis alliance with Germany and Italy. (National Digital Archive, Poland)

Japanese postcard from the 1930s showing an idealized, cartoon-like version of life in Manchukuo, the puppet state established in the three Chinese provinces that made up Manchuria. (Author's collection)

The raw reality in occupied Manchuria: Two prisoners of the Japanese, probably guerrillas, await an uncertain fate. The young man on the right appears to have been beaten. (National Digital Archive, Poland)

Japanese troops stand triumphantly on top of the Great Wall in early 1933, peering south into the vast expanses of yet unoccupied China. Fighting broke out in the area around the ancient symbol of Chinese power as Japanese forces aimed to create a buffer zone to protect its conquests in Manchuria. (National Digital Archive, Poland)

Japanese soldiers, covered in layers of winter clothing, receive decorations for bravery during the battle of Shanhai Pass in early 1933. The pass was of strategic importance as a narrow entry point from Manchuria into the rest of China. (National Digital Archive, Poland)

„Nicht über unsere Schwelle!"

"Not Across Our Threshold!" The German satirical magazine *Kladderadatsch* on the formation of the Anti-Comintern Pact by the governments of Germany and Japan in 1936. The Comintern, a Soviet-led international organization pushing for global revolution, is depicted as a giant snake, which is being ordered to halt by a German knight and a Japanese Samurai. (Kladderadatsch)

One of the Chinese Army's elite formations during a maneuver in the 1930s. China's pre-war military modernization program received significant assistance from Germany, which was a main supplier of equipment and also allowed a corps of experienced officers to go to China as advisors. (National Digital Archive, Poland)

Soldiers from Japan's Special Naval Landing Force, a unit under the Navy that served as a counterpart to the US Marines. Japan was at the forefront of the development of amphibious technology and tactics in the interwar years. This would prove useful in the early stages of the Pacific War, when the empire expanded across large parts of the vast ocean. (Wikimedia)

China's leader Chiang Kai-shek (right) after his release from captivity in the city of Xian in December 1936. Standing to his left is his former captor, Zhang Xueliang, also known as the Young Marshal. The so-called "Xian Incident" presaged a period in which the Chinese Nationalists and their Communist rivals buried the hatchet to face the common Japanese enemy. (National Digital Archive, Poland)

After full-scale war broke out between China and Japan in the area near Beijing in the summer of 1937, the Japanese Army had a clear technological edge in areas such as armor. The campaigns across huge distances in China soon became a contest for the control of the major cities and the railroads that connected them. (National Digital Archive, Poland)

As the Japanese Army quickly emerged victorious in north China in 1937, the civilian population was left with little choice but to seek accommodation with their new masters. Advancing Japanese troops soon became used to the sight of hurriedly crafted Rising Sun flags in the villages they passed through. (Asahi Shimbun)

A Chinese soldier prepares to throw a hand grenade from his position near Shanghai in late summer or early spring of 1937. His equipment shows that he is from one of the elite German-trained divisions. (Photograph by Malcolm Rosholt. Image courtesy of Mei-Fei Elrick, Tess Johnston, and Historical Photographs of China, University of Bristol)

A Chinese squad await a Japanese attack in a position near Shanghai in 1937. In the course of just a few weeks of intense fighting, Chiang Kai-shek squandered a large portion of the troops that he had spent years training and equipping for the showdown with Japan. (Photograph by Malcolm Rosholt. Image courtesy of Mei-Fei Elrick, Tess Johnston, and Historical Photographs of China, University of Bristol)

Japanese infantry in house-to-house combat in downtown Shanghai. The battle for China's largest city turned into a meat-grinder in districts mainly inhabited by Chinese. The international areas nearby escaped largely intact but ensured that the events received worldwide attention. (Asahi Shimbun)

Nurses of the Red Swastika, a Chinese organization modelled on the Red Cross. The swastika was the ancient Buddhist symbol and had no connection with contemporary Fascism. (Photograph by Malcolm Rosholt. Image courtesy of Mei-Fei Elrick, Tess Johnston, and Historical Photographs of China, University of Bristol)

Chinese prisoners under Japanese guard. The civilian is probably a Japanese national serving in an auxiliary role, perhaps as a translator. The Japanese Army's brutal treatment of prisoners, culminating in the notorious Nanjing massacre, was in sharp contrast to its conduct during the war with Russia a little more than three decades earlier. (National Digital Archive, Poland)

A Japanese column moves through a devastated Chinese city. Japan entered the war in China with no clear concept of what it wanted to achieve, and its military involvement in the vast country soon developed into a quagmire. (National Digital Archive, Poland)

Female Chinese soldiers during drill practice. As the war dragged on, China showed that its recruitment pool was inexhaustible, giving its leaders confidence that they would prevail in the long run. (National Digital Archive, Poland)

Injured soldiers return to Japan from the front in China. As the war progressed and casualty figures mounted, the initial enthusiasm of the Japanese public waned somewhat. However, the seemingly endless string of victories on the China front was a continued source of pride to many. (National Digital Archive, Poland)

Members of the Hitler Youth during a widely touted tour of Japan in 1938. Germany and Japan grew ever closer in the late 1930s, and as a result the Nazi government abandoned its old ally, China. (Wikimedia)

Emperor Hirohito during inspection of his rapidly expanding army in the 1930s. In the pre-radar days, some nations were experimenting with acoustic devices such as this to aid in the early detection of incoming enemy aircraft. (National Digital Archive, Poland)

Japanese soldiers arrive in China in the late 1930s. The war devoured ever larger resources which Japan's Army had hoped to save for what it believed to be its real enemy, the Soviet empire to the north. (Author's collection)

Snapshot from a Japanese soldier's private photo album covering his stint in China. The picture either shows actual combat or a maneuver in rural surroundings. (Author's collection)

A group of Chinese men, probably suspected partisans, captured by the Japanese Army. After Japan occupied most of eastern China in 1937 and 1938, a brutal guerrilla campaign continued behind the frontlines. (Author's collection)

Somewhere in China in the 1930s. A Japanese supply column passes by human remains which no one has bothered to bury. Large parts of China became a wasteland after the Japanese invasion, haunted not just by war but also disease and starvation. (Author's collection)

Mocking in absentia: An oversized effigy of China's leader Chiang Kai-shek, set up in the Japanese-occupied part of the country. The figure representing a Japanese soldier in the top right hand corner is holding a hammer carrying the words "New Order." (Author's collection)

Japanese tank crews take a break in the summer of 1939, around the time of the battle of Nomonhan with Soviet forces. To their left is a Type 89 I-Go medium tank, which was becoming obsolete by the time of the battle. (Wikimedia)

The battle of Nomonhan ended in a crushing Soviet victory over the Japanese, marking the first time that Georgi K. Zhukov led large numbers of troops in battle. Coming just months before the debacle against Finland, it showed that the Soviet Army was a formidable force when under competent leadership. (Wikimedia)

Zen Buddhist monks undergo military training in Japan under the supervision of a professional officer. Japanese society became increasingly militarized during the 1930s, as the war took up an ever larger share of the available resources, while the army came to play a growing role in politics. (National Digital Archive, Poland)

Japanese citizens during a civil defense exercise in the late 1930s. Mass gas attacks on civil populations centers were among the scenarios that planners prepared for during the interwar years, basing their concern on the important role chemical weapons had played on the fronts during the Great War. (National Digital Archive, Poland)

Japanese, German, and Italian children gather in Tokyo to celebrate the establishment of the Tripartite Alliance, or the Axis. The gray-haired man in the center is Education Minister Hashida Kunihiko, who committed suicide after the war as he came under suspicion of war crimes. (National Digital Archive, Poland)

Japanese battleship *Yamato* under construction at Kure Naval Base in the fall of 1941. Along with its sister ship *Musashi*, it was the heaviest battleship in history. This building program only became possible after Japan abandoned the Washington Naval Treaty, which had placed strict limitations on the size of capital ships. (Wikimedia)

Aircraft carrier USS *Saratoga* with its interwar complement of biplanes. The carrier was a converted battlecruiser and played a pioneering role as the US Navy experimented with naval aviation, a form of war that would prove decisive in the coming struggle over the Pacific. (National Archives)

Japanese soldiers play baseball in occupied northern China, around 1940. The quintessential American game had a huge following in Japan in the interwar years, and players such as Babe Ruth were stars. The advent of war did not diminish interest much, and it remained a popular pastime among men in uniform. (Wikimedia)

The militarization of Japanese society sent ripple effects through colonies and puppet states under its control. Manchukuo introduced national military service in 1940, and even though students were exempted they did not escape military training completely, as shown by this group of young men from a technical college. (Author's collection)

Japanese Foreign Minister Matsuoka Yōsuke visits Berlin in spring of 1941, inspecting a *Luftwaffe* guard of honor with the head of the German air force, Hermann Goering. Matsuoka retained hopes that it would be possible to build an alliance between the Axis and the Soviet Union, ignoring intelligence that Germany actually planned an attack on the Communist giant. (National Digital Archive, Poland)

Japanese photo journalist Sasamoto Sunji (second from left) with German officers at a camp for Soviet POWs at the start of Operation Barbarossa in 1941. The German attack on the Soviet Union undermined lengthy Japanese efforts to build amicable relations with Moscow and Berlin simultaneously. (Wikimedia)

Japanese troops enter Saigon in the French colony of Indochina by bicycle. The Japanese advance triggered a US decision to introduce a comprehensive oil embargo against Japan, hitting the empire where it hurt the most. (Wikimedia)

The oil embargo against Japan may have been enforced more vigorously than intended at a time when President Franklin D. Roosevelt was absent from Washington and therefore unable to monitor its implementation. Roosevelt was away for a meeting with British Prime Minister Winston Churchill at Placentia Bay, Newfoundland, cementing the Transatlantic relationship. In this photo, taken on board HMS *Prince of Wales*, Roosevelt and Churchill are seen with numerous key aides, including US Army Chief of Staff George C. Marshall (second officer from left) and Chief of Naval Operations Harold R. Stark (fourth officer from left). (National Archives)

Two of the most important decision-makers in the critical period during the fall of 1941 when Japan decided to go to war with the United States: Emperor Hirohito, standing in the middle, and Minister of War Tōjō Hideki, soon to be appointed prime minister, to the right. (National Archives)

Japanese Ambassador to Washington Nomura Kichisaburō and Kurusu Saburō, a senior negotiator, are surrounded by inquisitive reporters after a visit to the State Department in Washington. The two Japanese envoys had numerous encounters with Secretary of State Cordell Hull in the fall of 1941, but the talks eventually proved futile. (National Archives)

Target: Pearl Harbor. Japanese Navy Type 99 carrier bombers, known to the Americans as "Val", prepare to take off from an aircraft carrier in the morning of December 7, 1941. In the background the carrier *Sōryū* can be seen. The Americans used common boys' and girls' names to identify Japanese aircraft. (National Archives)

A Japanese Type 97 carrier attack plane, also known as "Kate" takes off from aircraft carrier *Shōkaku*, in the morning of December 7, 1941. (National Archives)

Photo of Pearl Harbor during the attack, taken from a Japanese plane. Battleship row is on the far side of Ford Island. A geyser is rising in the air where a torpedo has just hit the USS *West Virginia*. (NH 50930 courtesy of the Naval History and Heritage Command)

USS *Arizona* on fire after an explosion in its forward magazines has shattered its hull and essentially doomed it. A total of 1,177 men were killed on board the battleship, accounting for half of all deaths at Pearl Harbor. In the background left, sailors on board USS *Tennessee* deploy fire hoses on the water to force burning oil away from their ship. (National Archives)

Two Japanese "Val" carrier bombers photographed from an American B-17 Flying Fortress aircraft as the raid on Pearl Harbor is still ongoing. The B-17s, arriving from California, had been expected, and when the approaching Japanese aircraft appeared on the radar screen that morning, they were initially confused with the scheduled planes from the American West Coast. (National Archives)

Two Japanese Navy planes circle around a downed US aircraft near Ewa airfield. The American plane is probably from the USS *Enterprise*, which was in waters near Pearl Harbor, but was lucky not to be trapped by the Japanese attack. (National Archives)

Marines and soldiers fire on low-flying Japanese aircraft during the attack on Pearl Harbor. (National Archives)

An unexploded Japanese bomb has been discovered on board the severely damaged USS *West Virginia*, and it must now be carefully removed. Salvage work of the battleship in early 1942 led to the grim discovery of 70 sailors who had survived in air pockets, some right up until December 23, more than a fortnight after the attack on Pearl Harbor. (NH 64305 courtesy of the Naval History and Heritage Command)

extensive casualties on our army (7,000 were wounded or killed among the border region's forces alone), and the morale was not easily restored for a while."[51] In another similarity with the Tet Offensive nearly three decades later, the military cost had been so staggering to the Communists that they opted to return to the smaller-scale operations that they had specialized in prior to the Hundred Regiments Offensive, with an emphasis on mining, booby-traps, and tunnels.[52]

The shift to lower-intensity warfare did not mean it became any less brutal. Local Japanese commanders developed what they termed "butcher knife tactics" in which overwhelming forces were prepared for surprise attacks against Communist strongholds. In the murky conditions of partisan warfare where combatants and non-combatants could often be impossible to distinguish, the result was bloodshed on a massive scale, usually targeting civilians with utmost ferocity. Foreign travelers would later say that it was rare to come across a village in Hebei and Shanxi province which had not been at least partially destroyed.[53]

In the spring and summer of 1940, Hitler's armies struck fear and awe into the world, achieving a series of major victories in northern and western Europe with shocking speed. In particular, the six-week campaign to defeat France, Europe's strongest military power next to Germany itself, was proof to some that the future belonged to totalitarian government. Among them was Matsuoka Yōsuke, a diplomat and businessman who took over as foreign minister in a new Japanese government formed in July 1940 under Konoe Fumimaro, who had also been prime minister when the war with China began three years earlier. From the US perspective, it was not a change for the better. Secretary of State Cordell Hull considered Foreign Minister Matsuoka "as crooked as a basket of fishhooks."[54] Matsuoka, on the other hand, was on record as saying that war with the United States was "inevitable."[55]

Matsuoka had spent long years thinking about Japan's future mission in Asia as president of South Manchurian Railway Co. and was known abroad for his desire to remake the international system, which he found to favor the old Western powers. He had been Japan's strident face to the outside world in Geneva in 1933, when he headed his country's delegation to the League of Nations and led its departure from the organization. By 1940, he found support for his views in the German successes. "In the battle between democracy and totalitarianism, the latter adversary will without question win and will control the world. The era of democracy is finished and the democratic system bankrupt," Matsuoka told an American correspondent. He went on to say that "Fascism will develop in Japan through the people's will. It will come out of love for the Emperor."[56]

Mixed with the enthusiasm for being on the side of a victorious Germany was a distinct feeling of dread among decision-makers in Tokyo that Japan might "miss the bus" if it did not act swiftly. There was concern that Germany might use its victory over the Netherlands and France to seize control of the defeated nations' colonies in Southeast Asia. This was potentially fatal for the Japanese war effort, not least because of rich oil fields controlled by the Dutch in Borneo and Celebes. If access to these areas were suddenly denied, it could paralyze the Japanese Navy, which consumed 400 tons of oil every hour.[57] "The construction of the new world order which Hitler advocated will proceed rapidly," said Satō Kenryō, the officer who had ordered a legislator to "shut up" in the "Damare' incident and was now dispatched to the army in south China. "If Japan is solely preoccupied with the Sino-Japanese War, Germany will come to East Asia and acquire the territories of Britain, France and the Netherlands, leaving no role for Japan to play in the region. Therefore, Japan has to advance southward quickly."[58]

In fact, Germany had very few ambitions in that remote part of the world, and just days after the fall of France it had made clear to the Japanese foreign ministry that it "had no interest in occupying itself with such overseas problems."[59] However, this message was not transmitted efficiently through the Japanese bureaucracy, and nearly a month later, civilian and military officials remained concerned about imaginary Nazi designs on Southeast Asia. "Japan should consider that Germany intends to take over French Indochina and the Netherlands East Indies, and must take measures to deal with this," Lieutenant Colonel Takayama Hikoichi said at a high-level meeting in the Japanese capital in the middle of July. "We need to be thoroughly prepared for this."[60]

The first clear public sign that Japan was sharpening its focus on Southeast Asia was the announcement on July 26 of plans to establish a "New Order in Greater East Asia." This was followed up the next day, when at a joint gathering of military and government leaders known as the liaison conference met for the first time in two and a half years, in reaction to the grave changes afoot. The conference confirmed that, in response to the altered global situation, Japan would have to advance southward.[61] The precise extent of the new order that Japan was to create in this way was left vague, although it was clear that its core would constitute the three "solidly united" nations of Japan, Manchukuo and collaborationist China. Other documents at the time suggested huge territorial ambitions, indicating a desire to control most of East Asia and the Western Pacific.[62]

A policy paper prepared under the guidance of Foreign Minister Matsuoka even included India in the planned New Order. More strikingly yet, the document expressed an interest in Australia and New Zealand, saying that "Japan does not want these countries to become territories of… any country outside East Asia."[63] To be sure, the consensus among Japanese decision-makers was to extend the Empire's clout into the furthest reaches of Asia by means of diplomacy rather than armed force, but war was never ruled out. Ominously, a background memorandum attached to the decision at the joint conference foresaw the possibility of clashing with the

United States over the resource-rich territories in the region. "We should make adequate preparation for war with the United States," it said.[64]

The Japanese decision to push southwards was about resources, but not just that. It was also about reining in the part of China not yet under occupation and cutting off the last transportation routes bringing vital supplies to Chiang Kai-shek's beleaguered regime. One of these routes was from the Soviet Union. Another one ran from British-controlled Burma and was closed for three months, beginning in July 1940, under Japanese pressure applied against a severely weakened Great Britain. Yet another route originated in Hong Kong and was a significant source of supplies even after Japan had conquered a large part of south China.[65] Finally, Chiang's regime was kept supplied via a conduit from French Indochina.[66] Japan had long wanted to seal it off, and with the fall of France, the colonial administration in Indochina was left isolated and thinly defended by 32,000 unenthusiastic soldiers and 17,000 unreliable local auxiliaries.[67] Like most other colonies of France, Indochina was controlled by the new French government, which was set up in the sleepy provincial city of Vichy and effectively served as a Nazi client state. It was time for Japan to act.

As early as June, the Japanese government had exerted pressure on the French governor general in the Indochinese capital of Hanoi, George Catroux, forcing him to close the border with China. It was highly effective, and by the middle of July all aid to Chiang Kai-shek via Indochina had ceased.[68] Unexpectedly, the Vichy government dismissed Catroux for this act of appeasement towards the Japanese, replacing him with Admiral Jean Decoux, commander-in-chief of French naval forces in the Far East.[69] This was, however, only the first of a series of ultimatums put to the colonial authorities in Indochina by Japan. They were evidently aimed at boosting its control in the area and included a demand for the permanent stationing of Japanese troops. It was clear who had the upper hand. At one point during talks, the top Japanese negotiator in Hanoi, wanting his French counterpart to move faster, told him "to stop sleeping, to get busy, or take the consequences."[70]

In late August, the Vichy government reached a tentative agreement with Tokyo permitting Japanese troops to be garrisoned in Indochina for the duration of the war in China. The details were to be worked out by the military representatives meeting in Hanoi.[71] In this tense situation, a strange alliance evolved between Vichy, officially pro-German, and the United States, unofficially anti-German. While talks were going on in Indochina, the US State Department instructed its ambassador in Tokyo to pass on the warning that the stationing of Japanese troops in the country would have "an unfortunate effect on American public opinion."[72] The Americans were speaking harshly while carrying a small stick, and the Japanese knew that. The only thing the French could hope for was a reduction in the number of troops Japan was to place in Indochina, and in the course of talks lasting most of September they managed to get them down from 25,000 men to 6,000.[73]

The French negotiators in Hanoi were under intense pressure. Japan had moved troops to China's border with Indochina and threatened to start a war if no agreement was reached. A Japanese ultimatum expired at midnight between September 22 and 23, and with just seven and a half hours to go, a Franco-Japanese agreement was signed.[74] *Time* magazine snidely reported that "the French out-Japanesed the Japanese" in praising the agreement, pointing out that Admiral Decoux called it "one of the greatest marks of confidence one country can give another."[75] If the admiral's words expressed relief that war had been averted, they were misplaced. The war started anyway, regardless of the agreement.

Late at night on September 22, Lieutenant General Nakamura Aketo, the commander of the 5th Japanese Division, was standing on the border of Indochina, peering into what was soon to become enemy territory. At 10 pm exactly, unaware that the Japanese and French negotiators had reached an understanding, he had the barrier torn down and ordered his division on the move. It was a formidable force, 31,000 well-equipped and battle-hardened men, their morale towering after three years of uninterrupted victories in China.[76] Poised on the other side was a motley assembly of French-led troops. Most were colonials with a core of French officers and soldiers, dispirited at being isolated in a colonial outpost while France was disintegrating half a world away. Their equipment was outdated, and many units had no armored vehicles or even radios. They were truly lost.

Despite the unenviable odds, the first obstacle on the Japanese path, the old fortress of Dong Dang just south of the border, offered robust resistance. Manned by just two battalions, the French fortification never had a chance, but it took hours of heavy fighting, and considerable loss of life on the French side, before it surrendered at 11 am on September 23.[77] While the shooting was still going on, 5th Division commander Nakamura and his staff received a much-belated message to the effect that there was actually no need for the military operation, since the French had already agreed to the Japanese demands. The Japanese officers, Nakamura later recorded, "were so shocked that no one uttered a word." After some back and forth with his superiors, Nakamura decided, apparently with their tacit consent, that a withdrawal back across the border would blemish the reputation of the Japanese Army and carried on with his essentially unnecessary campaign.[78]

As they fanned out from Dong Dang the Japanese encountered scattered pockets of French resistance. One Japanese column moving northwest from the fortress, was stopped 10 miles out at the town of Nacham, where a French captain had set up a spirited defense with his company of soldiers. While he ordered part of his troops to stay inside their prepared strongholds, two platoons moved out in front, taking up positions on rocky hills overlooking the route that the Japanese would take. When the Japanese arrived, they unleashed a barrage of murderous fire, inflicting heavy casualties.[79] However, this was almost a unique instance. In most places, the indigenous troops threw down their arms and fled the scene of battle, leaving their French officers to their own devices. The local residents also showed no particular affection for the French, often leading the Japanese troops to their whereabouts.[80]

The main priority for the Japanese 5th Division was the fortress of Lang Son, overlooking the river Song Ky Kong. Lang Son had been the scene of an abject French defeat against the Chinese during a short war in 1885, and, on paper at least, it was by far the most serious challenge facing the Japanese, with a garrison of four battalions, including the 2nd Battalion of the 5th Foreign Legion Regiment, as well as 155mm artillery and tanks, although these were somewhat dated. The French could never have won, but they could have put up resistance for a significant period of time. Instead they panicked. When during the day of September 24 it became clear to the French defenders at Lang Son that the Japanese were launching a pincer movement and that their position was about to be encircled, they lost their nerve. After dark, a jittery young officer believed he had seen mounted Japanese scouts just outside the defense perimeter. Receiving this news, the commander of the garrison ordered the breechblocks of his 155mm artillery thrown into the river, where they joined guns the French had dumped in their previous defeat in 1885. The commander then ordered a retreat.[81]

The French moved out of Lang Son by the only available route, a footbridge across the river. In the dark, some soldiers waiting to get on the bridge noticed movement on the other side of the river and believed it to be the Japanese. They opened fire, not knowing that their targets were in fact fellow Frenchmen who had already made it across. There were casualties, and tremendous confusion. The French commander now lost hope that even a withdrawal could be implemented without serious losses and decided to throw in the towel. At 10:40 am on September 25, the white flag was hoisted over the garrison.[82] No unit of the Foreign Legion had ever before given up without a fight. The commander of the legionnaires in the 2nd Battalion, clearly aware of the unfortunate historical significance, protested the decision to surrender "like a herd of sheep, before an enemy whom he has not even seen in front of him," but nevertheless walked into captivity. Some of the battalion's honor was saved when the Japanese found out the battalion included 179 Germans and Austrians and tried to enlist them, but met with their staunch refusal.[83]

Weeks of tough negotiations, followed by a brief, albeit unnecessary, border war, had brought Japan the influence in northern Indochina that it had been craving. Even though it was not widely understood at the time, this was a milestone. It marked the first instance that Japanese shots had been fired in anger in Southeast Asia and, as such, it was a harbinger of the aggressive spirit that the Japanese Army and Navy were to unleash in massive offensives little more than a year later. At the same time, it was also an example of one of the basic contradictions in the strategy pursued by the Japanese leaders. Almost anything they did to strengthen national security ended up having the opposite result.

On September 26, just a day after the French forces had hoisted the white flag in Indochina, the White House announced an end of exports to all destinations except Great Britain and the western hemisphere of scrap iron and steel.[84] It was an indirect but severe blow to resource-poor Japan, and the Japanese embassy in Washington promptly dismissed it as "an unfriendly act."[85] In fact, it was only the latest in a series of such acts. Earlier the same month, the US government had imposed restrictions on equipment used in the production of aviation gasoline, and in July it had halted the export to Japan and elsewhere of aviation gas of octane 87 and higher, putting an end to the shipping of fuel required by modern airplanes.[86]

The ever-tighter American restrictions highlighted the need for Japan to adopt a multi-pronged approach to securing access to energy resources. The decisions made in the summer of 1940 to "go south" also included plans for talks with the Netherlands East Indies on securing privileged Japanese access not only to the Dutch colony's oil fields, but also to its rubber plantations and mineral mines. Japan's first choice of chief negotiator, an army general, wanted to sail to the colony's capital Batavia[87] on a warship surrounded by a uniformed landing party. This was deemed unnecessarily pompous and aggressive, and the next candidate for the position adopted a more low-key manner. Still, the Dutch turned down his request for concessions in the East Indies' raw materials sectors, and instead he had to settle for modest increases in Japanese imports.[88]

The dwindling overseas sources forced Japan to take a second look at partners it had previously decided against. It had shied away from Mexican oil in the 1930s, considering it both more expensive and of inferior quality compared with oil from the United States. This gradually changed once the US government started closing the oil faucet, and by September 1940, Japan expressed an interest in developing Mexican oil fields of even marginal value. In the middle of the month, a contract was signed between the Mexican government and the oil drilling enterprise Compañía Petrolera Veracruzana, whose Spanish name disguised the fact that it was Japanese-owned. The contract granted the company the right to drill for oil in a 100,000-hectare area in the state of Veracruz. The area had already been explored, with minimal results.

The US government was convinced Japan had ulterior motives, and was planning to gain access to territory that could be used as a base for military operations against the US mainland in case of war. There is no evidence for such plans on the part of the Japanese, and it seems likely that they were genuinely looking for new sources of energy. Nevertheless, the US government instructed its ambassador, Josephus

Daniels, to seek ways to get the deal on the Veracruz oil field canceled. Applying the necessary pressure, Daniels moved the Mexican government to cooperate, and shortly afterwards, it had nullified the agreement on a technicality—ordering the Japanese-owned firm to pay a deposit that it could not possibly afford.[89]

Efforts to develop synthetic fuel and make up for Japan's lack of natural resources were not much more successful, despite towering ambitions: one of the world's largest petroleum research centers was scheduled to open up at the city of Ōfuna near Tokyo. The facility, run by the Japanese Navy, was to employ more than 1,000 workers and contain 37 laboratories spread across 100 acres.[90] The effort was guided by wildly optimistic production targets made explicit in a seven-year plan for the Japanese economy which the government had adopted in 1937. The plan foresaw the construction of a total of 87 synthetic fuel plants in the period until 1944, potentially providing a war-winning boost to the Japanese economy.[91]

The men behind the program exhibited a great deal of confidence and suggested a narrowing of the technological gap with the great role model in the field, Germany. "Japan ranks next to Germany in synthetic oil manufacturing," said Enomoto Ryūichirō, a vice admiral in charge of synthetic oil, hinting at the military significance: "The industry is responsible to a large measure for the success of [Germany's] military exploits in the present war."[92] In fact, the endeavor to build up a synthetic fuel industry lagged significantly behind the plan, and even though Japanese scientists and technicians were often close to world-class, they suffered from self-inflicted handicaps.

For the production of synthetic fuel, Japan relied on machinery from primarily Germany and the United States. When deliveries from Germany became more uncertain after the outbreak of the war in Europe in September 1939, the Japanese Navy sent a team of specialists to the United States to acquire plans for the processing of synthetic oil. The Japanese Army urged the team to buy American-made synthetic oil-processing equipment also, which is where inter-service rivalries kicked in: the Navy interpreted this as an underhand insult to its own endeavors, and refused. The Finance Ministry, worried about the cost, sided with the Navy.[93]

That decision soon proved wrong. The Navy was unable to produce synthetic fuel in sufficient amounts and of a good enough quality, partly because of excessive secrecy that prevented the free exchange of research results with civilian scientists.[94] Once the Japanese realized this and reversed their decision, hoping to buy the American machinery after all, it was too late. US sanctions against Japan now made it impossible. As a result, while the seven-year plan had called for synthetic oil production to reach 5.8 million barrels annually by 1940, the actual level achieved that year was a mere 151,000 barrels.[95] It was a clear-cut fiasco for Japanese efforts to become more self-sufficient.

★　★　★

For all its outward blustering, Japan's essential weakness was increasingly guiding its foreign policy and forcing some tough decisions on its leadership in the second half of 1940. Japan could no longer go it alone. Boiled down to the basics, it would have to make a clear choice between friendship with Germany and Italy on one hand, or with the United States and Great Britain on the other. No agreement with the United States, Foreign Minister Matsuoka warned, would leave Japan with the possibility of maintaining its ambitions for China, let alone for the entire East Asian region. "We should have to … obey Anglo-American dictates for at least half a century to come," Matsuoka said at a high-level meeting in Tokyo. "Would the hundred thousand spirits of our dead soldiers be satisfied with this?"[96]

To Matsuoka and a majority of decision-makers in Tokyo, it would be preferable if not ideal to forge closer ties with Germany, another likely future foe of the Americans. The chief German negotiator Heinrich Stahmer traveled to Tokyo in September to hammer out details of a pact, and in remarks prior to his arrival Matsuoka made it clear that he wanted a closer alliance with Germany to serve as deterrence against the United States. When Stahmer set foot in Japan, he expressed very similar views, talking about the need to realize the "magnitude of the danger that threatens from the western hemisphere" and the desirability of an agreement between Berlin and Tokyo that could preempt US entry into war with either nation.[97]

A small group within the Japanese elite had been against the pact, worrying that it might precipitate war with the United States, rather than forestall it. Navy Minister Yoshida Zengo had been in the cautious camp. "The Japanese Navy can fight the United States for only one year," he had said. "Going to war where battle could only be sustained for one year would be reckless—like a ferocious tiger rushing into a snare."[98] The minister essentially disliked politics, and as pressures on him to accept the pact had mounted, his health had taken a beating. In early September he had collapsed and entered hospital, and the next day, he had resigned. To succeed him, Prime Minister Konoe chose Admiral Oikawa Koshirō, picking him mainly for being the candidate most likely to "unconditionally support" the alliance with Germany and Italy. Oikawa accepted the post after a brief 16-minute meeting with Konoe.[99]

With Navy opposition out of the way, the scene was set for signing the Tripartite Alliance, which happened at a ceremony in Berlin on September 27. The text was in English, of all languages, since it was the medium in which diplomats from the three countries communicated most confidently with each other.[100] The creation of the Axis, as the alliance would soon be universally called,[101] triggered hopes in the circle around Foreign Minister Matsuoka that a broader range of foreign policy problems could be solved, such as Japan's strained relationship with the Soviet Union. This was what German ambassador to Tokyo, Eugen Ott, suggested on the very day that the pact was signed. "Germany will do everything within its power to promote a friendly understanding [between Tokyo and Moscow] and will at all times offer its good offices to this end," Ott wrote to Matsuoka.[102]

The most typical reaction to the Axis, however, was dismay. "I saw the constructive work of eight years swept away as if by a typhoon, earthquake, and tidal wave combined," US ambassador to Japan Joseph Grew said.[103] In Washington, Assistant Secretary of State Breckinridge Long saw a dismal future opening up, and was concerned that the United States was not yet properly prepared for that future: "And so we go—more and more—farther and farther along the road to war," he wrote in his diary. "But we are not ready to fight any war now—to say nothing of a war on two oceans at once—and that is what the Berlin-Rome-Tokyo agreement means. Nor will we be ready to fight any war for eighteen months in the future."[104]

The sparse text of the Tripartite Pact mainly stated that the three powers would respect each other's zones of influence and assist each other in case of future attack, but the ramifications were much wider. Japan had definitively thrown in its lot with the Fascist bloc. Even among the Japanese there was grave concern about how this would all end. "Germany has always been a poor ally," said Ishii Kikujirō, a senior advisor to Hirohito. "Every country that has concluded an alliance with it has, without exception, suffered unforeseen disasters."[105] Japan's ambassador to London Shigemitsu Mamoru, too, was worried: "I felt the alliance placed Japan in an international situation from which it could not be saved."[106]

CHAPTER SEVEN

A Distant Thunder

Late 1940 until summer of 1941

In the morning of November 11, 1940, the German merchant raider *Atlantis*, captained by legendary skipper Bernhard Rogge, sighted the British-owned 7,528-ton freighter *Automedon* in the Indian Ocean, 250 miles northwest of Sumatra. The *Automedon*, which was heading for the Malay island of Penang, was an obvious target, and Rogge carefully altered course to close in on it. Once the *Atlantis* had narrowed the distance to about 5,000 yards, Rogge ran up two flag signals in rapid succession—"Do not raise the alarm" and "Stop"—getting ready to seize the enemy cargo ship. Rather than obey, the *Automedon* started sending an alarm signal, hoping it would reach friendly vessels in the vicinity. The *Atlantis* immediately fired its guns. The salvo devastated all structures above the hull and brought the *Automedon* to an immediate stop. The ship's officers, who had been assembled on the bridge, were all killed.[1]

Rogge's adjutant Ulrich Mohr boarded the wrecked ship, encountering a scene of carnage and destruction unlike anything he had seen so far in the war. Sifting through the cargo, he found most of it of limited interest, but he did recover fifteen mail bags with the label "Secret," among them a green pouch with holes that would allow it to sink immediately if tossed overboard in an emergency.[2] It was meant for Sir Robert Brooke-Popham, the new British commander of the Far East, and contained top-level War Cabinet minutes of August 8, 1940, including a candid assessment by the Chiefs of Staff, which admitted that the British position in the Far East was weak. The assessment argued that since Britain was fighting for its life against Germany and Italy and was unable to send an adequate fleet against Japan should the need arise, "we cannot prevent damage to our interests in the Far East."[3]

After sinking the *Automedon*, Rogge ordered the top-secret documents to be sent off to Japan along with other booty. It arrived in early December. In Tokyo, the German naval attaché Vice Admiral Paul Wenneker initially held on to the papers, but after receiving an explicit go-ahead from Hitler, he handed them over to members of the Imperial Japanese Navy's general staff. The timid tone of the documents took the Japanese officers by surprise. They were astonished to see the once-proud British Empire state that "we must avoid an open clash with Japan." This showed more clearly than anything else that the tables had been turned in East Asia. It played into the hands of those in the Japanese military who argued that going south was a risk worth taking, first and foremost in order to gain control of the resource-rich Dutch East Indies. Rogge was later awarded a Samurai sword by the Japanese government for his service on this occasion.[4]

"Such a significant weakening of the British Empire would not have been identified by outward appearances," the Navy vice chief of staff, Admiral Kondō Nobutake, told Vice Admiral Wenneker. His remark suggested an inability to read the documents in their proper context. They reflected British thinking in the summer of 1940, during the proverbial "darkest hour." Since then, the Battle of Britain had been won, and the dreaded German invasion had not materialized. Prime Minister Winston Churchill's determination to fight on was widely supported by the British public, and help from the United States was growing. The renewed confidence felt in London was also evident in Asia and led to the decision in late 1940 to reopen the Burma Road over strong Japanese protests.[5]

Even if it was optimistic about the feasibility of taking Britain's possessions in East Asia, the Japanese Navy retained a sober attitude on the prospect of having to fight both Britain and the United States at the same time. This was considered a likely scenario among naval officers, as they did not believe the US government would sit idly by while Japan went on a war of conquest in the western Pacific. Among the doubters was Admiral Yamamoto Isoroku, the commander of the Combined Fleet, which included almost all Japan's warships. He had spent years in the United States as a naval attaché, traveling extensively in the country, and his verdict was clear: "To fight the United States is like fighting the whole world."[6]

The general opinion was that if war with the United States was inevitable, it ought to happen soon. Admiral Kondō voiced the view of many fellow officers when he opined that conflict with the United States would be risky at any time, but it would be riskier the longer Japan waited: "The United States will build more ships as time passes, and Japan will hardly be able to catch up with it in such a competition. On the contrary, the gap will become wider. In this sense, it is better to fight now."[7] Even Oikawa, the new navy minister who had got his job because of his willingness to go along with the plans to enter the Axis, agreed to some extent. "Today our fleets are completely equipped and in no way inferior to those of the United States," he said shortly after his appointment, hedging by saying that the war would have to be short, lest the Americans were allowed to bring to bear their industrial might. "If we aim at a quick war and a quick victory, we have a good chance to win."[8]

Yamamoto was thinking along similar lines when in early January 1941 he was sitting in the cabin of his flagship, the battleship *Nagato*, penning a proposal to Oikawa. The admiral was basically opposed to war with the United States, but if going south made it unavoidable, there was only one way to go about it and secure even a slight chance of coming out successful. On the very first day of the conflict Japan should, Yamamoto wrote, strike a violent, numbing blow straight at the heart of US naval power in the Pacific. "In case the majority of the enemy's main force is at Pearl Harbor, [we should] attack it vigorously with our air force, and blockade the harbor," he wrote. This would inflict serious material damage, but perhaps more importantly it would cause the morale of the US Navy and the American people to "sink to the extent that it could not be recovered."[9] The emphasis on morale was no coincidence. Given the huge differences in productive capacity, superior spirit was the only way that Japan could possibly hope to prevail in a war with the United States.

Yamamoto was not the first to broach the idea of targeting Pearl Harbor. As early as 1927, Japanese officers had played through the scenario of a raid on the Hawaiian port as a wargame at the Naval Staff College. The US Navy, too, had simulated attacks on Pearl Harbor by carrier-based aircraft on several occasions in the 1930s. The potential gains increased markedly after Pearl Harbor became the home base of the US Pacific Fleet in May 1940, taking over from San Diego. Yamamoto had initially dismissed the project as too hazardous, but he changed his mind towards the end of 1940, probably influenced by the successful assault by British torpedo bombers against a fleet anchored in the south Italian port of Taranto in November of that year.[10]

Yamamoto put his considerable prestige behind the Pearl Harbor plan, but in early 1941 it still remained one suggestion among many, and it had not yet received the final stamp of approval from the Naval General Staff.[11] Yet, it was studied avidly, and somehow its existence must have leaked. On January 27, 1941, US Ambassador to Japan Joseph Grew sent an ominous message to the State Department in Washington. The Peruvian envoy to Tokyo had passed on to Grew rumors that in the case of a crisis with the United States, the Japanese military planned to use all its available capabilities on a surprise mass attack on Pearl Harbor. "He added that although the project seemed fantastic the fact that he had heard it from many sources prompted him to pass on the information," Grew noted.[12]

Japan's main motivation for entering into the Axis alliance with Germany and Italy had been to avert war with the United States.[13] It was a miscalculation almost as bad as the one that led Japan to attack Pearl Harbor the following year. Believing that the resolve of America's democracy would evaporate in the face of a show of strength, the Japanese decision-makers found that the opposite happened. Leading members of the US government started talking about Japan and its allies as existential threats that had to be dealt with. Sentiment was also growing for strengthened cooperation with the powers that would soon become wartime partners—not just Great Britain, but also Australia, China, and the Dutch colonial authorities.

There was little doubt in the US government that America was facing a trial of unprecedented proportions, and it made an effort to communicate this somber message to the public. President Roosevelt, in one of his famous Fireside Chat radio broadcasts, on December 29, 1940, described the Tripartite Pact as a threat to American security like no other in history. "Never before since Jamestown and Plymouth Rock has our American civilization been in such danger as now," said his sonorous voice, filling millions of American homes which were, without knowing it, enjoying their last Christmas in peace.[14]

In one of the war's most memorable phrases, Roosevelt then called on America to help keep Great Britain in the fight by becoming "the great arsenal of democracy."[15] This was to take place mainly under the Lend-Lease arrangement, which allowed the United States to supply weaponry and other war necessities essentially for free.[16] This reflected the US conviction that Germany was the most immediate concern, while the Japan challenge would have to wait. As early as the summer of 1940, the priorities had been spelled out by General George C. Marshall, the chief of staff of the US Army. "Are we not," he had asked, "forced into a question of reframing our national policy, that is, purely defensive action in Pacific, with a main effort on the Atlantic side?"[17]

Still, China was not forgotten in the American endeavor to keep the enemies of the Axis supplied. How extreme the Chinese demand for war materials had become by the end of 1940 was exemplified by the lack of anti-aircraft weaponry, which in many cases gave Japanese pilots a free rein over much of China. Japanese aviators would touch down on airfields nominally under Chinese control, jump out of their planes, and set fire to Russian-supplied fighters lined up on the ground. In another display of impunity, the crews of Japanese bombers would circle three or four times over defenseless Chinese cities with their bomb bays open before dropping their deadly cargoes, simply to prolong the pain for the civilians huddled below. "The entire purpose of these performances was to impress the Chinese with the futility of their resistance and the certainty of their extermination from the air if they were foolish enough to spurn surrender," wrote Claire Chennault, the American advisor to Chiang Kai-shek.[18]

Chiang was beginning to sound a desperate note in his appeals to US officials. In talks with the American ambassador to Chongqing, Nelson Johnson, he said that he had now "virtually exhausted the strength of his nation in resisting aggression, in an effort as much in the interests of Great Britain and the United States as of China, and that it is now time for the United States to come to its help."[19] His entreaties were heard. The US government upped its loans to China, and crucially promised 50 pursuit planes along with a pledge to allow American citizens to go to China as pilots and instructors. This was the beginning of Chennault's legendary Flying Tigers.[20]

Strengthening the defenses against Japan also had a broader strategic purpose. According to the analysis in Washington, the Axis had removed Germany as a potential rival for the resources in Southeast Asia, paving the way for a Japanese advance. Stanley Hornbeck, a special advisor to Hull and one of the State Department's hawks, wrote in a memo in October 1940 that there was no longer any doubt that Japan was going south. "The Japanese will move southward unless and until they meet with or find interposed positive obstacles which they cannot overcome," he argued.[21] This was not only the view in Washington but also among Americans much closer to the unfolding situation in East Asia. In a report to his superiors in mid-November, the commander of the US Asiatic Fleet Thomas Hart stated his case bluntly: "There seems no doubt that Japan is resolved on a southward movement—employing force if necessary."[22] It also happened without the use of force. Japan was emerging as a major diplomatic player in Southeast Asia. This became clear when war suddenly erupted on a frontline most of the world had never heard about.

In early January, forces of the Kingdom of Thailand crossed the border into French Indochina in four different sectors from northern Laos to Cambodia. The attackers made swift progress in most places. Pockets of resistance were wiped out by overwhelming firepower. At the southern edge of the Thai advance, scattered fighting took place along the *Route Coloniale 1*, the main road connecting Bangkok to Phnom Penh and the other major cities of French Indochina. The French defenses, made up to a large extent of Indochinese recruits, considered the terrain near the road unsuitable for defense and pulled back, allowing the Thai forces to occupy large tracts of land virtually unopposed.[23]

The Thai offensive came as no major surprise to the French. Thailand, one of few Asian nations to escape Western colonialism, had been tempted by the speedy defeat of France in the summer of 1940 to request the return of territory in Laos and Cambodia that had been ceded to the French colonial power in the preceding decades. Part of the Thai motivation was also a desire to act fast and seek a strengthened position in this particular part of Asia before Japan moved in and made it impossible. Following the political fashion of the 1940s, Thailand carried out the drive for more land in the name of bringing "all Thai people" under one government, even though not all the areas claimed by Bangkok were inhabited by people that could justifiably be described as Thai.[24]

In addition, there were domestic reasons for Thailand's sudden aggressive demeanor. Militarism was growing in the country, and the civilian leadership was increasingly dominated, or rather threatened, by the Army's jingoistic top brass. Early in the crisis with France, while the United States was seeking to mediate, Washington's ambassador to Bangkok was visiting Thai Prime Minister Pibul Songgram at his private residence. The American envoy noticed that Army officers were sitting in an adjoining room, listening in on the conversation through an open

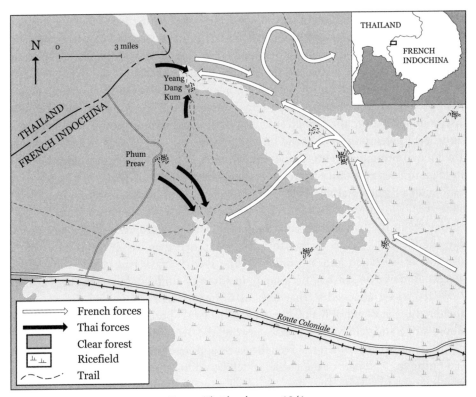

Franco-Thai border war, 1941.

door. "They might kill me if I do not follow their desires," the Thai prime minister told his American visitor.[25]

The mediation made little difference, and by late 1940 tensions between France and Thailand had built up. In December, all Thai nationals had left French Indochina, and in the end the diplomatic staff at the Thai consulate in Saigon had been ordered to pack up and sail for Bangkok.[26] In the same month, Thai airplanes dropped bombs over the French colonial city of Vientiane. French pilots who were scrambled to intercept the bombers were surprised to be faced with aircraft that were "extremely well flown." It seemed, they said, that the Thai pilots had "plenty of war experience."[27]

Once the land invasion in early January 1941 was a reality, the French military commanders in Indochina set in motion contingency plans prepared a few months earlier. It called for the concentration of the few forces available in a two-pronged counterattack in the forested area around *Route Coloniale 1* on January 16. One of the two French forces, consisting of three companies, was sent against the Thai-held village of Yeang Dang Kum. The attack got off to a bad start. The troops had been marching throughout the night, and intelligence about the Thai opponent was virtually non-existent. One of the companies got lost in the woods, while another did reach Yeang Dang Kum, but came under fire, and decided to withdraw. The French air force was nowhere to be seen, while Thai airplanes roamed at will, and by early afternoon the entire bid to seize the village was abandoned.[28]

Three miles further south, another French force of roughly comparable size attempted on the same day to take the village of Phum Preav, also occupied by the Thai military. Before the French soldiers had reached their objective, the defenders launched a preemptive strike, and intense fighting took place in front of the village. The French brought in anti-aircraft guns mounted on trucks, compelling the Thai air force to keep a distance from the battlefield. A column of Thai tanks intervened, tearing up a French platoon, before coming under fire itself from 25mm guns. Three tanks were shot up before the column retreated back towards Phum Preav.[29]

Neither of the two French counterattacks made any progress. At the end of the day, the French were no further forward than when they began the counterstrike, at a loss of 69 killed and 51 injured.[30] The French Navy had considerably more success. At dawn on January 17, a small squadron of gunboats led by the light cruiser *Lamotte-Picquet* attacked a Thai fleet of torpedo boats and coastal defense ships anchored at the island of Koh Chang, near Thailand's border with Cambodia. It was a bold strike and achieved complete surprise: the Thai sailors were in the middle of morning calisthenics when the French vessels appeared on the horizon at 6:15 am.[31]

During the first part of the battle, which lasted for about 45 minutes, the French vessels closed in on the Thai fleet, firing all guns and scoring several hits. The Thai vessels dispersed, and over the next hour, the two opposing sides were playing a deadly game of hide-and-seek among the numerous islets in the waters off Koh Chang. For the French, the main target was the Japanese-built coastal defense ship HTMS *Thonburi*, which managed to fend off the attacks with its four eight-inch cannon and escape to the northeast. At 8 am, the French fleet broke off the engagement and departed from the area. Sustaining no losses themselves, the French ships had managed to sink at least two torpedo boats, while the HTMS *Thonburi* was also reported beached later on. In a time that had got used to French defeats, this was a triumphant exception.[32]

Overall, however, the French military had been woefully unprepared even for a minor border war such as this. Requests that the colonial administration had sent to the Vichy administration for reinforcements had been turned down. About 90 American-made airplanes, including Brewster Buffalo fighters, had been languishing on the Vichy-held island of Martinique since the summer of 1940, unable to go to their originally intended destination of France. Appeals for these planes to be rerouted to Indochina had been received with "great irritation" by the Vichy government, which was, in fact, under pressure from Germany not to permit the planes to be shipped across the globe.[33]

Internal security was also a challenge for the beleaguered colonial administration in Indochina. As large parts of the military forces at its disposal were sent to the

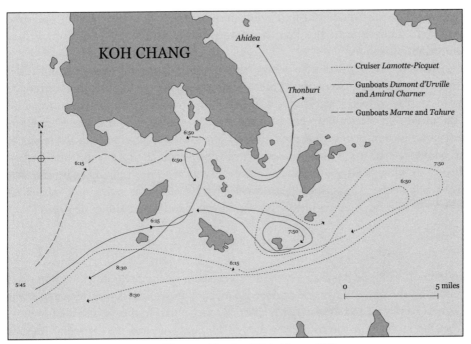

KOH CHANG

Ahidea

.... Cruiser *Lamotte-Picquet*

Thonburi

———— Gunboats *Dumont d'Urville* and *Amiral Charner*

– – – – Gunboats *Marne* and *Tahure*

N

6:50

6:15

6:50

7:50

6:50

6:15

7:50

8:30

6:15

5:45

8:30

0   5 miles

Franco-Thai naval battle of Koh Chang, 1941.

border with Thailand, it faced an uprising from the Vietnamese. They were put down with routine brutality. Airplanes were sent in to bomb lightly armed peasants. Those who looked suspicious were arrested. Those who attempted to flee were shot. "We were cruel," said a French soldier serving in Indochina. "The threat of [Thailand] haunted us, but above all we had to show our strength to those who remained loyal to us and to those who thought they could profit from our reverses."[34]

After the French forces had stopped the Thai invasion but no clear victory had been achieved by either side, Japan offered to host negotiations. This was in part to preempt a British attempt at mediation, and in case France declined, the Japanese government was prepared to carry out a show of force, sending warships to waters off Indochina or increasing the number of troops stationed inside the French colony for a period of time.[35] Japan had actually hoped a modest amount of saber-rattling would have been necessary as it would have helped underline its status as the dominant power in the region, but somewhat unexpectedly both Thailand and France agreed to talks mediated by Japan.[36]

The agreement that was signed after weeks of negotiations in Tokyo resembled a compromise, although it was clear that Thailand ended up with a net gain. While it did not get everything it had wanted, it was rewarded with territory in both Laos and Cambodia.[37] The loss of Cambodian soil infuriated the ancient nation's King Monivong, who defied his colonial masters and went into voluntary retirement, refusing to speak French during his last months before dying in April of the same year.[38] To replace him, the French administrators picked his grandson, Prince Norodom Sihanouk.[39]

Thailand also seemed a little too friendly with Japan for Washington's taste. This emerged when Secretary of State Hull was asked by his British counterpart Lord Halifax to help keep Thailand in line. "I myself," Hull replied, "am not at all convinced that the present Thai Government is a real friend of this Government or any other government except the Japanese. It went into collusion with the Japanese to secure Tokyo's aid which enabled it to obtain much territory from Indo-China. In my opinion Japanese-Thai alliances already exist in the military, political, and economic fields."[40] Significantly, a US war plan issued in the spring of 1941 placed Thailand among potential hostile powers in the Asia Pacific, alongside Japan.[41]

In January 1941, an American journalist received an assignment to go to China and report on the nation's struggle against Japan, now in its fourth year. Her name was Martha Gellhorn, and she was newly married to legendary author Ernest Hemingway. They both went on the trip, even though Hemingway had no particular interest in China, and the visit did nothing to kindle any slumbering passion. The famous couple received VIP treatment, but they were dismayed at the signs of heart-rending poverty that they saw everywhere. In an initially cordial meeting with Madame Chiang Kai-shek, Gellhorn raised the issue of lepers roaming the streets of China, forced to beg for a living. The Chinese First Lady exploded in anger. The Chinese were humane, she said, and unlike Westerners they would never lock lepers up in isolation from other people. "China had a great culture when your ancestors were living in trees and painting themselves blue," Madame Chiang concluded, referring to the war paint used by Britons in Roman times.[42]

For Hemingway himself, one of the highlights of the trip was a "booze battle"—the famous American drinker against 14 Chinese officers taking turns doing bottoms up. "Slowly officers grew scarlet in the face and slid beneath the table; others went green-white and fell as if shot," Gellhorn reminisced. Hemingway, by contrast, "was planted on his feet like Atlas."[43] These brief episodes, however, did not alter the overall disappointment that Gellhorn felt after seeing China close up. "An overlord class and tens of millions of expendable slaves was how China looked to me," Gellhorn wrote decades later in her memoirs. Hemingway was no big comfort, displaying an attitude of "I told you so."[44]

Hemingway and Gellhorn's experience was far from unique. A growing number of Western intellectuals felt disenchanted with Nationalist China and with Chiang Kai-shek in particular. Theodor White, a correspondent for *Time* magazine, described how his views of Chiang changed radically with the passage of time. "Rigid morality was locked in one compartment of Chiang's mind; while other compartments concealed animal treachery, warlord cruelty and an ineffable ignorance of what a modern state requires," White wrote in his memoirs. "Of his personal treachery there could be no doubt. I had come to China believing him a national hero. Then, incident by incident, as I accumulated notes, the hero became to me first an unlovely character, then an evil one."[45]

It is debatable how justified this criticism was. Some of the disappointment was based on unrealistic expectations of what Chiang could achieve with the limited resources at his disposal. Some was caused by the realization that China was not united in its battle against Japan, but that a state of tension persevered between the Nationalists and Communists. Soviet dictator Joseph Stalin, an expert on internecine power struggles, had no illusions about the tension threatening to tear China apart. "Instead of joining in a united front against the Japanese aggressor, Mao Zedong and Chiang Kai-shek cannot forget their old differences. The struggle goes on between them for influence and power. Mao fears Chiang and Chiang fears Mao," he told one of his senior officers shortly before he left for China as a military advisor.[46]

In an example of what this entailed, a pitched battle was fought in a valley in Henan province in east China in January 1941. It was a battle not involving the Japanese or any pro-Japanese troops. The only Japanese participation during the ten days of fighting was a lone airplane that briefly overflew the battlefield. Rather, it was fought between two large Chinese armies nominally allied in an effort to oust the foreign invader. One was Nationalist and the other Communist, members of the New Fourth Army. The Nationalist forces had been pursuing the roughly 10,000 Communists through the barren wintry landscape, until on January 9 the Communist force, starved and with uniforms in tatters, made its way down the valley into the tiny village of Shijing, where its soldiers prepared to make a last stand.

Over the next two days, Nationalist artillery bombarded the Communist positions, while Nationalist soldiers situated in the surrounding hills targeted anything that moved. On January 12, the Nationalist troops launched a major attack to dislodge the Communists completely. After seeing one position after the other overrun by the Nationalists, the Communists decided to make one last bid to break out. In the evening of that day, those who could still walk launched a strike against the Nationalist lines. A few managed to fight their way through. The vast majority were cut down in hails of machine-gun fire. A total of 9,000 Communist troops lost their lives.[47] The commanding officer, Ye Ting, was taken prisoner by the Nationalists, while his second-in-command was wounded in battle and killed by his captors.[48]

How had it come this far? Mutual suspicions between the Nationalists and the Communists had been growing for close to two years, fueled partly by Chiang's fears of Communist territorial expansion in north and central China. "The growing danger is not the Japanese, but most of all Communist expansion everywhere," Chiang had written in his diary in early 1939.[49] One of his main concerns was the New Fourth

Army, built on the foundations of scattered Communist troops that had been left behind in southern China after the main force under Mao had moved north in the Long March in the previous decade. "The Japanese and Wang Jingwei are absolute enemies," an advisor to Chiang had said. "The Communists are dispersed between their units and ours. They are even more difficult to deal with."[50]

In an attempt to separate Nationalist and Communist forces and minimize the number of incidents between them, Chiang had organized in late 1940 for the New Fourth Army to be moved north to link up with the Communist main forces beyond the Yellow River. The New Fourth Army initially acquiesced and started withdrawing along a pre-arranged route. On the way, all or some of the New Fourth Army troops suddenly changed direction, triggering Nationalist fears that it did not intend to leave. This kindled the Nationalist pursuit that resulted in the thousands of Communist dead in the mid-January battle in Henan.[51] For the Communists, it was a military defeat, but a victory in propaganda terms, as it enabled them to cast Chiang as a dictator more interested in killing his own people than fighting the Japanese. "Never before have we had such a mass of people on our side," a satisfied Mao told a Russian interlocutor.[52]

★ ★ ★

In early 1941 neither the American nor the Japanese people were eager to go to war with each other. The US government continued to be constrained by public opinion, which exhibited a strong isolationist propensity. A Gallup poll released in February 1941 showed 56 percent in favor of action "to keep Japan from seizing the Dutch East Indies and Singapore," but only 39 percent thought it worthwhile to risk war in this endeavor.[53] No similar polls were made in Japan, but when Japanese journalist Katō Masuo was traveling around the country in early 1941, speaking to people from all walks of life, a similar picture emerged. "As a result of these interviews," he wrote later, "there was not the slightest question in my mind that the people as a whole did not want war with the United States."[54]

Even without taking the pressure from public opinion into consideration, it was obvious to politicians in both Washington and Tokyo that a war would entail immense cost, and that everything should be done to prevent the friction from spinning out of control. One of the first indications that Japan was willing to talk was conveyed by two Catholic missionaries with extensive contacts in Japanese society, James E. Walsh and James M. Drought. The two men had met in Tokyo with Foreign Minister Matsuoka, who had told them that "if he could only see the president for an hour, he felt sure that he could bring about an improvement in relations."[55] Returning to the United States in early 1941, they conveyed this message to Roosevelt.[56]

In another sign that Japan was open to negotiations, Tokyo sent as its new ambassador to Washington Nomura Kichisaburō, the English-speaking former admiral who, as foreign minister, had constituted a moderating influence on his nation's diplomacy two years earlier. Nomura's friendly attitude towards the United States was well-known, and Germany was worried. A Japanese journalist who traveled to Washington at about the same time as Nomura in the spring of 1941 was greeted with a sarcastic question from one of his German colleagues: "Have you come here for the London-Washington-Tokyo Axis?"[57]

Nomura had his first meeting with Roosevelt in his capacity of ambassador on February 17. Receiving the Japanese envoy at the Oval Office, the American president was at his most charming, insisting on calling his guest "Admiral" and reminiscing on a previous encounter more than 20 years in the past. "There is plenty of room in the Pacific area for everybody," Roosevelt said. "It would not do this country any good nor Japan any good, but both of them harm, to get into a war." At the conclusion of the meeting, Roosevelt suggested that Nomura and Secretary of State Hull should start seeing each other informally to discuss problems in the relationship between the two countries and hopefully find solutions.[58]

After some hesitation and communication back to Tokyo, Nomura saw Hull for the first time on March 8.[69] This would eventually lead to a series of close to 50 meetings between Nomura and Hull, charting the last months of peace between their two nations. "They were invariably at night, in the study of my apartment, first at the Carlton and then at the Wardman Park Hotel," Hull wrote in his memoirs. "Nomura preferred to come to my apartment rather than to the State Department so as to keep our conversations as free as possible from publicity. During the course of these discussions many blunt words were spoken point-blank, but our voices never rose from the level of a conversational tone. Nomura was very gentlemanly."[60] The American secretary of state also doubted, however, that Nomura, who was no career diplomat, was up to the challenge. "I was never completely sure that Nomura understood our points," he wrote.[61]

Nomura's shortcomings were only part of Japan's problem. Another and much more serious difficulty from Tokyo's point of view was the US success and the Japanese failure at building coalitions. US and British coordination continued at a rapid speed, with staff officers from the two sides holding intensive talks in 1941, resulting in agreement on strategic priorities: the situation in Europe was paramount, while a defensive posture should be kept in the Far East, although the US fleet should be employed to weaken Japan and detract its attention from British possessions in Malaya. Gradually, the Dutch East Indies administration was also being involved in the planning. Along with China, a four-power alliance led by the United States was gradually emerging.[62]

Japan was aiming for its own four-power alliance, involving itself, Germany, and Italy, as well as the Soviet Union, but in contrast to America's diplomacy in the field, Japan's policy came up empty-handed. True, the friendship with Germany had been advantageous in small ways. The German veto against shipping the Vichy-owned planes from Martinique to Indochina was a case in point.[63] However, the kind of routine, detailed strategic coordination that the United States was developing with foreign allies remained out of reach for the Axis powers. When Foreign Minister Matsuoka visited Berlin in the spring of 1941, Germany was unable to get a firm commitment from him to attack British-held Singapore, while on the other hand the Japanese visitor could not get Germany interested in the plan for an expanded Axis including the Soviet Union—with good reason, since preparations for Hitler's offensive against Stalin were in full swing.[64]

In more efficient times, Japan's foreign policy establishment might have picked up the signals that relations between Germany and the Soviet Union had deteriorated rapidly by early 1941. The problem was that Japan's diplomacy was hampered by a thorough cleansing of the foreign ministry bureaucracy that had been carried out by Matsuoka when he took over at the helm.[65] As a result, he was happily unaware that his dreams of a four-power alliance were doomed, and went straight from Berlin to Moscow to sign a five-year neutrality pact with the Soviet Union. When Matsuoka was about the depart from the Soviet capital, Stalin made the rare gesture of seeing him off personally at the train station before he boarded the Trans-Siberian Express, exchanging compliments and embracing in warm hugs. The unusual honor was widely reported, although the significance might not have been entirely clear at the time. Most likely, Stalin was elated that Matsuoka had reduced the risk that Russia would have to fight a two-front war in the stand-off with Fascism that the Soviet leader might have seen coming.[66]

In the spring of 1941 a 27-year-old Japanese, Yoshikawa Takeo, arrived in Honolulu to join his country's consular staff there. In fact, he was an ensign in the Imperial Japanese Navy, and a spy. His task was to find out as much as possible about the Naval base at Pearl Harbor.[67] He was the right man for the job. For four years he had been an avid reader of everything from Japanese intelligence reports to *Jane's Fighting Ships* and the *US Naval Institute Proceedings*, pulling together information from all manner of sources to build a complete picture of Japan's likely main adversary in a future war: the US Navy.

"I was the Naval General Staff's acknowledged American expert," Yoshikawa wrote later. "I knew by then every US man-of-war and aircraft type by name, hull number, configuration, and technical characteristics; and I knew, too, a great deal of general information about the US naval bases at Manila, Guam, and Pearl Harbor."[68] Yoshikawa's main responsibility was to find out about the US Pacific Fleet's habits and routines. He wanted to know when the ships departed and returned, and in what combinations. He now had the opportunity to see the object of his study up close on nearly daily walks through Pearl City or occasionally by boat, taking girlfriends out on short cruises. He even rented a Piper Cub airplane to fly over Pearl Harbor. Given the large Japanese population in Hawaii, he did not arouse any suspicion.[69]

One of the best vantage points for Yoshikawa to do his spying was the Japanese restaurant Shuncho-ro, located on a hill above Pearl Harbor. There, he would spend the night in a simple Japanese room directly overlooking the Pacific fleet, peering through a periscope set up for curious tourists and chatting with the restaurant's *geisha*. "At nights, with the lights blazing, it was a magnificent sight indeed," Yoshikawa wrote. "From the *geisha*, too, who would have been entertaining US personnel earlier in the evening, I occasionally gleaned small bits of information—never with their connivance, however. It would have been too risky to confide in a woman, and, besides, the Japanese population of Hawaii we found essentially loyal to the United States."[70]

The Japanese espionage efforts went smoothly partly because US counterespionage was acting at cross-purposes.[71] For example, on February 15, 1941, the Japanese Foreign Ministry sent an encoded message to the Embassy in Washington, requesting information on a wide range of military matters, including "strengthening or supplementing of military preparations on the Pacific Coast and the Hawaii area."[72] US military intelligence was able to read this message because it had broken the Japanese codes, but it did not pass on the information to those who needed it most, the spy-hunters at the FBI, for fear that the Japanese would realize their codes had been compromised. "The FBI was never informed of this vital information necessary to the success of its work, despite the fact that the closest liaison was supposed to exist among the FBI, Naval Intelligence, and Military Intelligence," the post-war investigators stated. "It appears the *fact* the Japanese codes had been broken was regarded as of more importance than the *information* obtained from decoded traffic."[73]

Contingency planning continued apace in Japan as well. Yamamoto's proposal of striking at Pearl Harbor was still only a future scenario that might or might not materialize if diplomacy failed but it had arguably already led to the creation of the First Air Fleet, a powerful force of carrier-based aircraft, and soon an intensive training program in the dropping of torpedoes from airplanes was to follow.[74] Still, the entire concept of a Pearl Harbor raid remained the subject of controversy. Since it was to take place at the same time as Japan struck south, it implied a division of the Japanese Navy, with one fleet going to Hawaii, another fleet heading to Southeast Asia. An influential group of officers considered the risk too high—a typical brainchild, they said, of the inveterate gambler Yamamoto—and preferred the risk involved in leaving the US Pacific Fleet intact and banking on a decision by America to turn a blind eye while Japan occupied Malaya and the East Indies.[75]

Even if Japan struck early, it could still not afford a prolonged war. Warnings to this effect abounded in Japanese government circles. A report issued by the Army Ministry's War Preparations Section in March 1941 painted a sobering picture of

Japan's chances in a conflict with the combined forces of the United States, Britain, and the Netherlands: "While we have munitions to defeat the enemy within a period of two years, by the end of the second year liquid fuels will become short at least temporarily, and should the war be further prolonged, our economic capabilities might be strained."[76]

The issue would have to be settled soon. A war with America would have to happen now, or not at all. The window of opportunity that the Navy's top brass had been talking about previously was now clearer than ever, and most analyses showed that 1941 was the crucial year. In America, the so-called Two-Oceans Naval Act had been passed in June 1940. It called for a 70 percent increase in US naval expenditures and meant that the numerical balance in American favor would grow precipitously until the mid-1940s. A tough alternative was beginning to emerge for the Japanese planners: they would have to go to war in a matter of months, with all the huge risks that entailed, or condemn themselves to perennial subordination to the United States. It was one of the many ironies of World War II that a Congress Bill meant to enhance American security in fact served as a main factor in driving Japan to enter into the war.[77]

As war was becoming a real possibility, the Japanese intelligence service was producing assessments of each of the foes that the emperor's warriors were likely to encounter. The US soldier got a mixed review: "Although the character of the Americans is generally excellent, they are bothered by the tropical climate, they have a tendency to take it too easy both mentally and physically, and they lack in sincerity."[78] The Japanese spies also had both good and bad to say about British soldiers: "Their performance is not good. But their endurance in defensive battle is significant." The verdict on the Australians was the least positive: "Their quality is bad. The troops are composed chiefly of jobless men and rough individuals."[79]

The Japanese assessment of the Australians may have reflected contemporary stereotypes more than anything else, since Australian reinforcements arriving in Malaya in early 1941 were met with very similar prejudices. "We learned that we had been given the reputation of being unholy terrors where women and children were concerned," according to one Australian source. He went on to note that the prejudices were soon dispelled: "As soon as a convoy of troops was sighted approaching a town or village, the streets became lined with shouting youngsters holding up their thumbs and crying out 'Hello, Jo'."[80]

A different and more serious culture shock hit the Australians when they encountered members of Singapore's and Malaya's white colony. The peaceful atmosphere startled the newly arriving troops, and some started questioning the wisdom of having been posted in this corner of the globe when the world was aflame seemingly everywhere else. As one of them commented later: "We were being sent to a war station. We were equipped—even if only 50 percent equipped—for war. Yet the first sight that met our eyes on the first evening was officers in the mess dress and fashionable women in evening dress. It was not only incongruous, it was wrong. Either we were crazy or they were crazy. Either there was danger or there was no danger."[81]

Many would probably go with "No danger." Singapore was believed to be a rock in a turbulent ocean. This was where women and children fled when the situation in places like China became too explosive. Perhaps, some visitors thought, the safety that the colony's impressive defenses provided had resulted in a mood that might just be a little too laid-back. For *Life* correspondent Cecil Brown, 50 minutes with British Governor Sir Shenton Thomas served to show an administration woefully unprepared for war. "When I emerged from his sanctum in the white rambling Government House I had the strangest sensation of being immersed in an urbane sea of unreality. My first action was to look at the calendar to see if this was 1941, instead of 1931, and war was going on," Brown wrote.[82]

If the civilian administration was lulled into a false sense of security, the military was painfully aware of the dangers looming over the horizon. In April 1941, high-ranking officers representing the United States, Britain and the Dutch government in exile met in Singapore for a week of detailed discussions about contingency planning in case of a Japanese offensive in East Asia. The officers agreed that in the event of war, the two primary strategic objectives were to keep the sea lanes safe and to make sure Singapore did not fall into Japanese hands.[83] Recognizing that their capabilities were limited at a time when the efforts to contain Germany had to be the top priority, they also stated that they could not afford to ignore the need for coordination. "Our collective military strength can only be developed fully if our Governments agree to act together, should any of them judge that the Japanese have taken action which necessitated active military counteraction," said the final statement issued after the meeting, marked "Most Secret."[84]

The officers sounded committed, but there was one huge caveat hanging over everything they decided: American willingness to enter into a war with Japan. The United States could not, out of respect of its own Constitution, promise active military aid, since war would have to be declared by Congress. The lack of clarity had been the subject of British complaints for months, as Roosevelt's advisor Harry Hopkins had found when he had visited London early in the year and had long talks with Foreign Secretary Anthony Eden. "Eden asked me repeatedly what our country would do if Japan attacked Singapore or the Dutch East Indies, saying it was essential to their policy to know," Hopkins wrote. He could not give a good answer since, as he noted, "the isolationists and, indeed, a great part of the American people, would not be interested in a war in the Far East merely because Japan attacked the Dutch."[85] This uncertainty would hang like a dark cloud over contingency planning right until the final days before the Japanese attack in December.[86]

In the Dutch East Indies, the ultimate target of all of Japan's activities in the south, the military forces were hardly in a position to counter an invasion. Elliott Thorpe, a US military attaché to the Dutch colonial government and an intelligence operative, had obtained a first-hand look at the parlous state of the Dutch-led forces during autumn maneuvers in the Javanese countryside. "Two things struck me there," he wrote in his memoirs. "One was the almost complete lack of interest among the native enlisted men and the other was the tragic shortage of anything like modern equipment." The rifles carried by the men were from the turn of the century, tanks and machine guns were from World War I, and a coastal defense gun Thorpe was able to inspect had been salvaged from an American battleship junked after the Spanish-American War.[87]

In the Philippines, which was bound to be affected by any Japanese southward advance, US General Douglas MacArthur had helped build up the military since the mid-1930s. He had been assisted in his effort by Dwight D. Eisenhower, then a major. In this capacity, Eisenhower had been making statements on the defense against a potential Japanese invasion that eerily presaged his own role in the D-Day landing in Normandy half a decade later. "Successful penetration of a defended beach," Eisenhower had said, "is the most difficult operation in warfare." Anticipating the tactics that his German adversary Erwin Rommel would employ in defending Normandy in 1944, Eisenhower had also argued that the Japanese would have to be stopped at the coast.[88] This was embraced by MacArthur, who said in a plan for the defense of the Philippines that the beaches were to "be held at all costs."[89]

The job of throwing a Japanese invader back into the ocean was in the hands of the mixed assembly of American and Philippine soldiers under MacArthur's command. Reviewing hundreds of members of the Philippine Army Air Corps in 1941, the flamboyant general said with habitual martial eloquence that in case of war "you will write your own history, and write it in red, on your enemy's breast."[90] MacArthur also sent glowing reports to George Marshall in Washington about rapid progress in the ongoing training of the Philippine Army. In fact, the situation on the ground left much to be desired. MacArthur himself complained to a subordinate about finding "large groups of trainees and their officers standing and sitting around doing nothing ... some American officers were practically ignorant of what was going on, and a pall of inactivity was evident."[91]

There was only so much the likes of MacArthur and Eisenhower could do given the funding at their disposal, but a board on the future of US Naval bases set up by Congress in 1939 had come close to changing the basic rules of the game. Among its recommendations was a proposal to reinforce Guam in the Marianas and establish a fully equipped fleet base with facilities for aircraft and submarines. It would constitute a lifeline on the way to the Philippines and also strengthen the defense of the Dutch East Indies, creating "the most favorable conditions ... for the prosecution of naval operations in the western Pacific," the board's final report said. Congress, however, turned down the suggestions, fearing their implementation would offend Japan.[92] Anyway, the United States had Pearl Harbor, which General Marshall characterized as "the strongest fortress in the world."[93]

While a variety of factors were keeping the armed forces ill prepared for a Japanese onslaught, the American public was being fed a glowing image of a US Pacific defense force in a constant state of alert. *Collier's* weekly magazine carried a feature with the title "Impregnable Pearl Harbor." It exuded supreme confidence that any attack on the Pacific fortress would be a suicidal undertaking. "The Pacific Fleet of battleships, destroyers, cruisers, submarines and carriers are always within a few minutes of clearing for action," it said. "In the continental United States there may be some doubt about our readiness to fight. But none exists in Hawaii."[94]

In the evening of May 10, 1941, just before a dinner in Chongqing, Chiang Kai-shek pulled aside the US ambassador to Chongqing Nelson T. Johnson. Chiang had information from a reliable source, he told the American envoy, "that Germany plans [an] attack on Soviet Russia between end May and middle June." The generalissimo, who appeared to have received the report from the Chinese military attaché a few days earlier, candidly declared that he wanted the Soviet-German war to go ahead and warned against any action by the United States that risked dissuading Hitler from following through with the plan. In a rather cynical ploy, he wanted the United States to stay put and wait for events to unfold.[95]

To observers at the time, there might seem to be obvious reasons why Chiang would want a war between Germany and the Soviet Union, putting an end to the uneasy peace that had existed since the conclusion of a non-aggression pact between the two totalitarian powers nearly two years earlier. It might prompt Japan to attack the Soviet Union from the east, forcing the communist giant into a devastating two-front war. From the Chinese perspective, this would be a welcome development, since it would force Japan to divert troops away from the China front. Indeed, many in Chongqing believed at the time that Japan would react to a Nazi assault on Stalin by attacking Soviet forces in Siberia and Outer Mongolia.[96]

A Japanese war with the Soviet Union might have been a widespread hope in China, reflecting wishful thinking more than anything else, but it seems unlikely that Chiang belonged in this camp. In fact, according to Chiang's American advisor Owen Lattimore, the Chinese leader "was convinced … that as the Soviets would eventually defeat the Germans, the Japanese would not honor the Berlin-Tokyo Axis and attack Siberia from the east to help the Germans in the west."[97] It would appear, therefore, that Chiang was moved by a much subtler understanding of international affairs when pinning his hopes on a Nazi-Soviet confrontation.

In the preceding months, Chinese diplomats had been concerned that Japan might succeed in its quest for a coalition of revisionist powers, including not only itself along with Germany and Italy, but also the Soviet Union.[98] That scenario lost any plausibility with the Nazi attack, codenamed Barbarossa, and once millions of Axis troops poured across the Soviet frontier on June 22, Chiang acted fast. Just three days after the invasion, on June 25, the Chinese ambassador to Moscow met his American counterpart, pointing out there was no longer any reason to fear the Soviet Union might be driven into the Axis. Instead, Japan now saw itself surrounded on all sides by actual or potential hostile powers—China and the Soviet Union to the north, Australia and the British and Dutch colonial possessions to the south, and America to the east.[99] Arguably, it was Chiang's first step towards creating a new international constellation where the United States, the Soviet Union, Britain, and China formed the basis of a large global alliance against the Axis powers.

His next step came on July 2, when China broke off diplomatic relations with Germany and Italy, partly in retaliation for a decision by the two regimes announced just the day before to recognize Wang Jingwei's regime, and partly in order to underline the new division of the world into Axis powers and their adversaries.[100] On the same day, Chiang told an American representative in Chongqing that Japan was planning to declare war on the Soviet Union. "Japan now is only hoping that in this affair America will maintain [a] neutral attitude in which case she would take immediate action to attack Russia," Chiang said.[101] If he had hoped the information would prompt Roosevelt to consider an alliance with the Soviet Union and China, he was mistaken. Instead, the American president sent a message to Japanese Premier Konoe, stating bluntly: "We have information that Japan is starting military operations against the Soviets. We request assurance that this is contrary to fact."[102] The grand alliance pitting the Western powers with the Soviet Union against the Axis would have to wait another half year.

Not only was the Chinese government informed beforehand of Barbarossa, but Japan's leaders were, too. Tokyo's main source of information was the Japanese ambassador to Berlin, the strongly pro-German army officer Ōshima Hiroshi, who was briefed on several occasions by his German hosts. In one meeting, Luftwaffe chief Hermann Goering went into great detail about the planned invasion, "giving the number of planes and numbers and types of division to be used for this drive and that." In early June, Ōshima met with Hitler and Ribbentrop and reported back to Tokyo that "both men tell me that in every probability war with Russia cannot be avoided."[103]

The information was of great use to the US intelligence service, which read all Ōshima's cables, but in Japan his reports triggered an uneven response. Foreign Minister Matsuoka, who had only just visited Berlin and Moscow a few months earlier and was perhaps worried that his grand plan for a Soviet-Axis alliance was falling apart, maintained that if the Germans were indeed preparing an invasion, they would tell him directly.[104] Army officers, on the other hand, prepared contingency plans for a war against the Soviet Union.[105] However, when Hitler's armies did cross the border into the Soviet Union on June 22, Matsuoka immediately came around to the view that Japan should complement Barbarossa with an invasion of its own in the Soviet Union's eastern regions. Matsuoka even went so far as to tell the Soviet ambassador Constantin Smetanin that if he had known Germany was about to attack the Soviet Union, he would not have signed the Neutrality Pact in Moscow. "Japan is calm," Smetanin replied, "but nothing seems very clear."[106]

Japan's future direction was unclear even to the country's military and civilian leaders themselves, but it was gradually determined in the course of a series of tense meetings in late June and early July. Matsuoka repeatedly advocated war with the Soviet Union. "When Germany wins and disposes of the Soviet Union, we can't take the fruits of victory without having done something," he told a liaison conference bringing together ministers and senior officers on June 25. "We have to either shed blood or engage in diplomacy. It's best to shed blood."[107] His views were in a minority. The Navy, for one, feared having to eventually fight a war against the United States, Britain, and the Soviet Union at the same time. The painful memory of Nomonhan remained fresh. Instead the majority was in favor of taking advantage of the temporary Soviet weakness by diverting attention to Southeast Asia.

The discussions, which took place on a nearly daily basis over the next week, culminated in the adoption on July 2 of a masterplan for national policies in the radically changed international situation. While forces along the Soviet border would be strengthened, they were to undertake no aggressive moves and rather adopt a wait-and-see attitude. Invasion remained a possibility. Meanwhile, Japanese troops were to move into the southern part of Indochina, which had so far been under French control. "In carrying out the plans outlined above," stated the document resulting from the meeting, "our Empire will not be deterred by the possibility of being involved in a war with Great Britain and the United States."[108] Those were dire words, but the assessment in the Army was that the Western powers would not act. "Since the war situation is favorable to Germany, I do not believe that the United States will go to war if Japan moves into French Indochina," said Army Chief of Staff Sugiyama Gen.[109] He was right, in the sense that America was not ready to contemplate military action. Economic war was another matter, as events would soon show.

CHAPTER EIGHT

Countdown

Summer and fall of 1941

The city of Saigon was peeking into an uncertain future at the end of July 1941. The population knew that the Japanese military would arrive within just days, completing the takeover of French Indochina that had begun less than a year earlier in the north. As the Municipal Band was practicing for the welcoming ceremony in the city's main square, Japanese advance parties quietly moved into the best hotels, preparing for the arrival of much larger numbers of soldiers. The French officials had promised a peaceful occupation and pointed out that Saigon was lucky to escape the fate of Syria, another French possession, which had just recently been invaded by British and Australian troops.[1]

Despite the reassuring words from the officials, apprehension loomed everywhere. French and Japanese planes roared across the sky over Saigon, as if to symbolize rivalry between the two nations for mastery over the city. The government-controlled newspapers ominously warned people not to stage any protests against the city's soon-to-be masters, confirming that anti-Japanese feelings were running high, especially among ethnic Chinese and sympathizers of the Free French under General Charles de Gaulle. There were even runs on the British Hong Kong-Shanghai Bank, the Chartered Bank of India, and several Chinese banks, and they had all been forced to introduce temporary limits on the amount of money that could be withdrawn at a time.

The Japanese came on July 30. At 6:30 am a Japanese transport painted in dark gray touched the pier of Saigon harbor. The deck was loaded with barges and motorboats, and the masses of infantrymen in khaki ascended from the hull to get a first glimpse of the tropical city through the morning mist. Fifteen minutes later, the next transport arrived, and by the end of the day a total of 14 vessels had carried 13,000 Japanese troops to Saigon. Thousands of others were onboard 30 vessels anchoring at Cap St. Jacques at the mouth of the Saigon River. Soldiers also poured out onto the pier at the naval base at Cam Ranh Bay.

Over the next few days the soldiers worked around the clock to unload weapons and supplies onto the docks. Trucks were leaving incessantly for new barracks being set up on the outskirts of Saigon. Japanese officers with long traditional swords tied to their belts moved into private homes that had been requisitioned and ordered vacated, relegating the original inhabitants to passenger ships anchored in the river.[2] Several office buildings belonging to French and British firms were also taken over for military purposes. "The Japanese have landed, and the British threat to Indochina is ended," a local paper wrote, suggesting that Britain might have repeated its invasion of Syria here, although this was sheer fabrication.

Rather than a defensive move forestalling a British invasion, it was an offensive step with deep strategic implications. As the *New York Times* explained, "it will put a total of 40,000 Japanese troops in Southern Indo-China, will station Japanese planes within easy bombing range of British Malaya and Burma, within an hour's flight of Bangkok, Thailand, and will enable Japanese air patrols to cover the ship routes of the China Sea and complete Japanese air domination of all Indo-China. The five-year-old base of Cam Ranh Bay itself is virtually equidistant from the powerful American base of Cavite, guarding the approach of Manila Bay, and from the British bases of Hong Kong and Singapore. It is about 600 miles from the coast of the Netherlands Indies."[3]

In the French city of Vichy, half a world away, reports of the Japanese influx reached the weak German-tolerated government led by Marshal Philippe Pétain. The Vichy regime had acquiesced in the Japanese takeover, but only because it saw no other option.[4] Resistance similar to that offered in Syria, where French troops had fought vigorously against the British and Australians, was out of the question. The clashes with Thai troops in recent months had demonstrated the desperate weakness of France in Asia. Still, the Vichy officials were furious and frustrated, and prone to blaming the United States for the unbridled Japanese advance in Asia.

William Leahy, the US ambassador to Vichy, met with Pétain and his deputy and foreign minister, Admiral François Darlan on August 1. "It is always the same story," Darlan said. "The United States is too late."[5] The three men had met a fortnight earlier, and at that time Darlan had predicted the Japanese takeover of southern Indochina. "There has been no Japanese ultimatum," he had told the American envoy, explaining the backhanded manner of the Japanese. "They speak courteously of jointly occupying Indochina with us for common defense, but it amounts to a move by force."[6] What Darlan had been hoping for but failed to spell out at that earlier meeting was for a squadron of US warships from Manila to steam into Saigon harbor. This would have alleviated the Japanese pressure, Darlan said.[7]

The US government had in fact tried to prevent the Japanese invasion of southern Indochina, alerted not only by the Vichy leaders but also by its own ability to read secret Japanese communication in the form of intelligence that it had codenamed

MAGIC. In response, it had attempted a carrot-and-stick approach. Acting Secretary of State Sumner Welles had waved the stick and publicly warned the Japanese on July 24 against making the move, stating that it could only be seen as preparation for further conquest in the region.[8] On the same day, President Roosevelt had dangled a carrot, proposing in a meeting with Japan's Ambassador Nomura Kichisaburō a settlement that would turn Indochina into neutral territory where no outside power held sway to the exclusion of others, and all enjoyed equal access to its resources.

There had been some reason to believe that Japan would react positively to the American approaches. Japanese Prime Minister Konoe had fired Foreign Minister Matsuoka earlier in July, getting rid of the most prominent pro-Axis member of his Cabinet. Still, Konoe had continued to be constrained by the clout of the military, which had insisted that the prime minister stick to the original plan of invading southern Indochina.[9] Therefore, neither American appeal, the stick or the carrot, had been heeded—Ambassador Nomura had not even passed on the proposal to Tokyo—and the Japanese transports had set sail for southern Indochina on July 25.

Realizing that its warnings had fallen on deaf ears, the US government reacted by imposing the farthest-reaching economic sanctions to date, freezing all Japanese assets in the United States. What this meant in practical terms was that virtually all Japan's foreign trade was placed at the mercy of the US government. When Germany had attacked the Soviet Union the month before, it had the consequence of sealing off all Japanese commerce with Europe via the Trans-Siberian Railway. As a result, almost the entirety of Japan's imports became dollar-denominated overnight and had to be paid for with Japanese-owned assets kept in the United States, mostly in the form of bank deposits and securities.[10]

This had particular implications for Japan's vital imports of oil. By the summer of 1941, it had accumulated US licenses to buy a total of 21.9 million barrels of crude oil, or enough to last it until the end of 1943.[11] Freezing Japan's assets caused it all to be thrown back into limbo. The licenses were only any good if American authorities agreed to make US dollars available to pay for the fuel. The freeze had turned American oil exports into a potent but flexible weapon that the US government could use against Japan to reward or punish it for its behavior. It was an arrangement in keeping with a wish expressed by Roosevelt not to place Japan in a desperate situation where it might feel compelled to strike out.[12] Roosevelt "was still unwilling to draw the noose tight," his Secretary of the Interior Harold L. Ickes wrote in his diary. "He thought that it might be better to slip the noose around Japan's neck and give it a jerk now and then."[13]

American officials initially set out to implement the freeze in Roosevelt's spirit. "The exportation to Japan of oil, gas and petroleum products will be a matter to be dealt with on specific licenses ... although for the time being such licenses will be automatically granted," a memorandum from the Treasury Department stated.[14] In fact, the small group of officials charged with carrying out the policy, dominated by Assistant Secretary of State Dean Acheson, chose a much more Draconian interpretation of the new rules. "The Japanese tried every conceivable way of getting the precious crude oil," Treasury officials said later, "but to each proposal, the Division of Foreign Funds Control had an evasive answer ready to camouflage its flat refusal."[15] What was supposed to be a case-by-case release of oil shipments to Japan was replaced with a de facto full-blown embargo.[16]

Roosevelt was away from Washington in the first half of August, meeting with Winston Churchill in Newfoundland, and he may therefore have been largely unaware of the way the freeze was being managed. Once he returned, he realized that a decision to implement the freeze in the less rigorous manner originally envisaged could be interpreted in Tokyo as a sign of weakness and therefore opted for continuing the approach introduced by Acheson.[17] It is also possible that he was moved by opinion polls showing that the embargo was popular with the American public.[18] Whatever the exact motivations were, the complete oil embargo remained in place. "Whether or not we had a policy, we had state of affairs," Acheson, the embargo's chief architect, wrote in his memoirs.[19]

In Japan, editorial writers tried to put on a brave face. "Long ago Japan had made provision for its own self-support in anticipation of economic sanctions," the *Japan Times and Mail* wrote. "This country is able to take care of itself."[20] Privately, officials were much less sanguine. The empire "will shortly become impoverished," lamented the Cabinet's Planning Board, which coordinated Japan's war economy.[21] A consensus was spreading among military and civilian decision-makers that efforts had to be intensified to secure alternative sources of oil in the Dutch East Indies and other parts of Southeast Asia, even if it meant war with the United States. The situation, according to Premier Konoe, was "only a step this side of entering into a major war."[22] In other words, the American embargo, which was originally meant to deter Japan from further aggressive moves, in fact ended up having the exact opposite effect, setting the stage for Japan's advance south.

The Total War Research Institute, a think tank run by the Japanese government, performed a series of simulations for the economy in the summer of 1941 and subsequently issued reports that called for robust action. Japan, it said, ought to invade the Dutch East Indies in November, followed by the British and American possessions in Southeast Asia in December. The reports were distributed amidst a more belligerent mood in both Army and Navy ranks in the wake of the US decision to freeze Japanese assets, and they led to intensive discussions taking up the first half of August among senior military officials about different scenarios for a southward advance.[23]

Four alternative plans were up for discussion, including the Navy's favorite, a gradual advance proceeding clockwise from the Philippines to Borneo, Java, Sumatra, and finally Malaya. The Army vetoed this plan, since it would be too slow and elaborate, giving the defenders too much time to prepare a response. Finally, the two services agreed on a compromise plan, foreseeing the simultaneous attack against Malaya and the Philippines, using both areas as staging grounds for the subsequent rapid invasion of the Dutch East Indies. The plan had obvious weaknesses. It involved a lot of moving parts, and it would be a nightmare in terms of coordination. It also implied a risky division of forces. Still, it was the only plan that both services could agree on.[24]

The blueprint for the southward advance remained a contingency plan to be put into action only if diplomacy failed, but it gave both the Army and the Navy a solid basis for more detailed preparations. The discussions also served as an opportunity for Yamamoto to sell his plan for an attack on Pearl Harbor. During lengthy talks with Tomioka Sadatoshi, the Operations Section chief of the Navy General Staff, Yamamoto made his case for an early strike at the US Pacific Fleet before it could head west and hit the flank of Japan's southward offensive. Tomioka was not convinced, pointing out the difficulty of keeping a Japanese strike force secret while it sailed across half the Pacific to Hawaii. Being spotted by a single vessel or airplane was enough for the entire plan to come crashing down. "This Hawaii Operation is speculative and has little chance for success," he said.[25]

While the Pearl Harbor plan was left pending, with the possibility of being adopted at a later stage, another ambitious scheme was now given up: the attack on the Soviet Union from the east. Those in the Army who had advocated a strike north and war with Stalin now agreed that the southern advance and the likely conflict with the United States ought to be the top priority.[26] The fact that Barbarossa was not going as smoothly as hoped by Hitler and his generals also contributed to this decision. The Japanese Army General Staff's Soviet Intelligence Section had reported in early August that a Soviet surrender in 1941 was out of the question, and that Germany was in for a long war of attrition.[27]

Stalin had understandably been worried about the prospect of a Japanese assault in the rear while his soldiers were fighting for their lives against the ruthless Nazi war machine. He knew that the neutrality pact signed with Japan in the spring offered no real guarantee, and he was primarily relying on keeping the Japanese busy elsewhere. He had said as much when sending off General Vasilii I. Chuikov as military advisor for Chiang Kai-shek: "Your task, Comrade Chuikov, and the task of all our people in China, is to tightly bind the hands of the Japanese. Only when the enemy's hands are bound can we be free of a war on two fronts if the Germans attack our country."[28]

The Soviet Union was fortunate to have placed one of the war's most efficient agents in Tokyo. His name was Richard Sorge, a flamboyant renaissance man of Russo-German descent who had been in the Japanese capital for nearly a decade posing as a journalist. His primary assignment, his superiors in Moscow had told him, was to find out if and when Japan might invade the Soviet Union. "It would not be an overstatement to say that it was the entire purpose of my stay in Japan," Sorge said later."[29]

Sorge did not disappoint during the months after Barbarossa. In an encrypted message sent to Moscow in July, he wrote that Japan was boosting its military capability and would be able to wage war in August, "but only in the event the Red Army, in fact, suffers defeat from the Germans." A few weeks later, he updated this information, saying that "if Japan begins a war, it would be only in [Southeast Asia] where they could obtain raw materials—oil and metals." Finally, Sorge reported that "the Japanese government has decided not to advance against the USSR in the current year."[30]

While in the summer of 1941 the Japanese high command moved closer to a military solution of its resource straightjacket, doubts about the advisability of a war that would probably drag in the United States continued to linger. "We have no choice but to come out fighting," Nagano Osami, the chief of the Navy General Staff, told Hirohito immediately after the American freeze of Japanese assets had been announced, but then added: "I am even not sure whether we can win or not." That remark unnerved Hirohito: "This means embarking on a war of desperation, which is truly dangerous."[31] Premier Konoe, too, was hesitant and to introduce momentum into the dialogue with Washington, broached the idea of a summit with Roosevelt.[32]

Sober heads in Tokyo knew what was at stake. The United States was a continent-sized economy whose factories beat Japan's in every conceivable category, from trucks to radio receivers. Japan was a bigger player than America only in the construction of merchant ships, and here, too, the Americans could easily erase the gap once they put their minds to it.[33] The military significance of this imbalance was not lost on people like Admiral Inoue Shigeyoshi, who submitted a memo with the title "The New Defense Plan" to Navy Minister Oikawa. His conclusion sounded like a warning not to go to war: "Japan cannot invade the United States, occupy the US capital or blockade the US coastline. The United States can do all of the above to Japan."[34]

The Americans, too, tried on occasion to impress on the Japanese that peace would be in their own best interests. Admiral Harold Stark, the chief of Naval Operations, had a particularly frank conversation with Ambassador Nomura: "If you attack us," he stated bluntly and prophetically, "we will break your empire before we are through with you. While you may have initial success due to timing and surprise, the time will come when you too will have your losses but there will be this great difference. You not only will be unable to make up your losses but will grow weaker as time goes on; while on the other hand we not only will make up our losses but will grow stronger as time goes on. It is inevitable that we shall crush you before we are through with you."[35]

★   ★   ★

What kind of nation was Japan in 1941? Who were the 73 million people that would soon find themselves in the most devastating war in their island nation's long history? Foreign affairs writer Henry C. Wolfe visited Tokyo in the fall of 1941 and was shocked by the gloom and dreariness of life in the once vibrant city of 6.5 million inhabitants. Four years of war and accompanying austerity had turned it into a "capital of shadows" with long lines of customers waiting in front of stores selling low-quality products made from *ersatz* material. Shoes of real leather could not be found. Clothes were made from a little cotton mixed with bark and wood pulp and ripped easily. Wolfe described what happened when an American diner at a restaurant asked for a second helping of pudding, the only part of his meal that was somewhat palatable. The head waiter replied, "Do you want me to go to jail!"[36]

Wartime regulations had started out in a small way. Local governments had introduced rationing of sugar and matches in 1939, and it had become a national policy in 1940. Since then official controls had exploded, and by the fall of 1941 more than 100,000 goods and services were being regulated.[37] Energy shortages were particularly conspicuous. Many vehicles were converted to run on charcoal, although that fuel was also in short supply. Police were soon forced to stop all public vehicles from running between midnight and 5 am.[38] Adding to the woes, trams and trains were overloaded with people, since cars that had broken down could not be repaired due to a lack of spare parts.[39]

The American trade curbs worsened an already steep decline in the standard of living, but they did not cause it. The tougher conditions faced by the average Japanese were equally due to the priorities of the Japanese rulers, which allocated ever larger resources to military purposes, leaving the civilians to pay. The war in China had taken its toll. In 1931, military expenditures had taken up 31.2 percent of the government budget, but a decade later it had increased to a staggering 75.6 percent. Average wages dropped by more than 20 percent from the mid-1930s until 1941. Meanwhile, there was less and less to be had for the shrinking incomes. The light industrial sector, where consumer products were manufactured, saw its share of overall production drop precipitously over the same period.[40]

The finer things in life were, of course, virtually non-existent. Dance halls had been prohibited, despite their immense popularity, along with most jazz performances.[41] Foreign movies were strictly limited, and Japanese cinemagoers, who were once among the most ardent foreign fans of Hollywood and even copied manners and slang from major American releases, were now limited to grim German propaganda fare with titles such as *Victory in the West*.[72] The lights were out, also, in a quite literal sense. In Tokyo's Ginza shopping district, the famous glittering neon signs had been turned off to save electricity. Five-star hotels, too, were wrapped in gloom after they were urged to keep lighting at a minimum.[43]

Miyamoto Takenosuke, vice director of Planning Board, argued that "the people should be satisfied with the lowest standard of living." He went on: "The craving for a life of luxury must be abandoned. At this time, when the nation is risking its fate, there is no individual any more. What remains is the nation and the nation alone. The storm of economic warfare will become more furious. Come rain! Blow wind! We are firmly determined to fight against the storm."[44] Japan's largest candy maker Meijing Confectionary Company chimed in with an ad campaign featuring the slogan "Luxury is the Enemy!"[45] The National Defense Women's Association also did its part in imposing wartime rigor, posting members on street corners to stop women who were dressed too extravagantly, passing them handbills with stern admonitions about the need for thrift in light of the national emergency.[46]

At the same time, a thriving black market for regulated goods had emerged almost immediately, and a special economic police set up to rein in the activities made more than two million arrests within just 15 months. The vigorous law enforcement did not curb the illegal transactions, but simply encouraged them to be carried out in more ingenious ways. A modern historian gives an example of how it remained possible to trade coal at the black-market price of 1300 yen, well above the official 1000 yen price tag: "To secure the additional 300-yen profit without running afoul of the law, a vendor, for example, might arrange for a customer to 'accidentally' drop 3000 yen next to the vendor's stall. He would then take the money to the nearest official who would instruct the buyer to pay ten percent in thank-you money (300 yen) to the vendor."[47]

Despite the hardship, the Japanese government pretended it was in a position not only to care for its own population but for the peoples of all Asia. It marked the fourth anniversary of the Marco Polo Bridge Incident with the establishment of the "Great Japan-East Asia Construction League." It was an amalgamation of existing organizations promoting greater cooperation between Japan and other Asian nations, and it had Premier Konoe as its president. Following the slogan "Liberating East Asia from the shackles of white capitalism," it vowed to fight Anglo-American "encroachments on the lands and livelihood of the East Asiatic countries."[48]

To fill the region with soldiers and administrators, Japan also needed more people, some thought. An official advocated that the average age when Japanese women married should be lowered to 20 from 24, arguing the empire needed more people. "When Napoleon conquered Europe, France boasted of a high birth rate," he told a Western journalist. "The Roman Empire thrived also when its population increased. Japan likewise needs a large population to lead the Co-Prosperity Sphere in the Far East. At present, the country needs boys because the China war has cost us a large number of young men."[49]

The Japanese population was bracing for war in ways that visitors could not ignore. Since the late 1930s the authorities had carried out regular air raid drills in the big cities, always eliciting the earnest participation of men, women and children. "Foreigners in Tokyo have been caught unawares in drills and marked out as wounded," a Western correspondent wrote. "Thereupon, they were put on stretchers, into ambulances, and hurried to hospitals far across the city, despite loud protests. When the alarm was over, the victims were free to make their own way back."[50]

The conflict in China had brought numerous disadvantages, but it seemed that even after years of deprivation, the general population supported it. It was a paradox. A war that had left most families grieving for lost members was a main source of government legitimacy. There were 3,000 war correspondents with the armed forces in China, many of whom had died in their eagerness to get as close to the events as possible, and their reports from the frontline about a seemingly endless succession of victories filled the Japanese with nationalist pride. "The theory that the Japanese nation may not be behind its leaders in the war is not a sound one," a Western correspondent wrote.[51]

It was also not a sound assumption that everyday life in Japan on the eve of the Pacific War was one of unmitigated gloom. The reality had many facets. Certain classes of people actually prospered because of the hostilities. Kumagaya Tokuichi, a young man who had grown up in poverty and flirted with communism in his youth, found that the war created unheard-of job opportunities and even could afford to get married. "At the age of twenty-three, with a substantial income, I was independent enough to set up house," he said, "The happiest thing was that I didn't need to worry about finding a job."[52]

Yet, the few Japanese who were able to visit the United States were forced to acknowledge the immense wealth gap between themselves and the Americans. Mitsuharu Noda, a sailor in the Japanese Navy, passed through Honolulu during a training cruise in 1939. He was invited to visit an ethnic Japanese family of employees at the Dole Pineapple factory and was astonished to see that this household of moderate means nevertheless had three cars. "Just laborers at a pineapple factory—not noble offspring of immigrant barons—but each had his own automobile! What a grand country, I thought!"[53]

Unbeknownst to the Japanese public, war was moving closer by the day. In late August and early September, the Japanese Army and Navy engaged in a series of intense meetings which, in retrospect, put the empire on the track for war. Guidelines issued at the end of a pivotal conference on September 6 bringing together Hirohito with senior leaders from the military and the civilian administration set out the basic direction. It spelled out the Japanese insistence on retaining troops in China, and required of the United States and Britain that they not set up any obstacles to Japan's quest for resources in Southeast Asia. If there turned out to be no prospect of the demands being met, it said, "we will immediately decide to commence hostilities against the United States, Britain, and the Netherlands."[54] Realistically, there was next to no chance the United States would go along. A well-known Japanese historian has characterized the document as "a virtual declaration of war."[55]

Hirohito was not convinced that a war with the Western powers could be won easily or fast. He reminded his generals that they had promised him a quick victory in China, and he had no patience with their excuses that China took time because its interior was huge: "If the interior of China is huge, isn't the Pacific even bigger? How can you be sure that war will end in three months?"[56] At the end of the meeting on September 6, he pulled from his pocket a piece of paper containing a poem written by his grandfather, the Meiji emperor: "All the seas in every quarter are as brothers to one another. Why, then, do the winds and waves of strife rage so turbulently throughout the world?" It was a meditation on the absurdity of incessant strife among the nations despite the fundamental brotherhood of man and had been written at the start of the war with Russia, when Japan had been in a very similar situation. In response, the participants vowed to emphasize diplomacy.[57]

Negotiations with the United States continued, but with a major, seemingly unsolvable sticking point: the presence of Japanese troops on Chinese soil. To be sure, powerful members of the Japanese Army had worked for years to put an end to hostilities in China, but not at the cost of a humiliating retreat. They wished to maintain some level of presence in China as a source of strength and prestige.[58] However, a mere four days after the fateful meeting in Tokyo, on September 10, US officials made clear to Japanese diplomats that "a successive withdrawal of Japanese armed forces from China as speedily as possible until complete" remained an American demand.[59] American resolve in this respect was strengthened by Chinese fears of being shortchanged, and US negotiators did nothing to conceal to their Japanese counterparts the fact that talks had to be carried out in a way to preempt Chinese concerns.[60]

The Americans had one major underlying advantage: they were in no rush. The US Navy was only just beginning to build up its strength to a level where it could fight a war on two oceans, and it could expect its superiority vis-à-vis the Japanese Navy to grow steadily with each passing month. The Japanese military, on the other hand, was on a tight schedule as war, if unavoidable, should happen in 1941. Later than that, and the United States would be unbeatable. Moreover, Japan could not wait until too late into the year, when seasonal monsoons would complicate large-scale operations. In short, time had completely opposite implications for the two governments. In the words of a prominent historian of the origins of the war in Asia, "one did not mind its passing, while the other was crazed by the tick of the clock."[61]

Prime Minister Konoe was tormented by constant doubts about the wisdom of war against the Western powers, and received bad news on October 2. Hull informed him, through Ambassador Nomura, that Roosevelt had turned down his proposal for a summit, in large part due to Japan's intransigence on the issue of stationing troops in China.[62] Konoe decided for a last-bid effort to salvage the talks with the US government. In the afternoon of October 12, his 50th birthday, he hosted a meeting at his private residence on the outskirts of Tokyo with a picturesque view of Mount Fuji. Present were a small group of key decision-makers. Most of them were committed to one goal: convincing Army Minister Tōjō Hideki, a chief hawk, that negotiations with the Americans remained a viable option, and getting him to agree to a compromise on pulling the army out of China. The discussion was a prime example of the counterproductive way that Japan's leaders communicated and failed to speak their minds.

"If we were to say that we must determine on war or peace here, today, I myself would decide on continuing the negotiations," Konoe said. Tōjō fired back: "To carry on negotiations for which there is no possibility of a result, and in the end to let slip the time for fighting, would be a matter of the greatest consequence." Konoe then turned to Foreign Minister Toyoda Teijirō, asking for his assessment of the negotiations. Were they likely to be productive or not? Foreign Minister Toyoda hedged, saying it all depended on the Army: "The most difficult point in the problem today, I believe, is the matter of stationing troops in China, but if in this regard the Army says that it will not retreat one step from its former assertions, then there is no hope in the negotiations." Tōjō seemingly shot down all hope: "The problem of the stationing of troops in itself means the life of the Army," he said. "We shall not be able to make any concessions at all." [63]

The meeting ended long after the sun had set behind Mount Fuji. Four hours of discussions back and forth were not enough to move Tōjō one inch from his stubbornly held position. Fierce loyalty to the Army meant he would not give in on the issue of keeping troops in China, which was the generals' main claim to political influence. Still, war might have been averted, and millions of lives might have been saved if only that afternoon at the premier's residence the participants had been willing to speak their minds more openly. For example, the Navy remained just as reluctant as Konoe to rush into a war, but said so only vaguely. War Minister Tōjō was aware of the concern among the admirals and let Konoe know shortly afterwards that if the Navy would only come clear, he would be able to reconsider his whole attitude. The Navy, however, timidly kept a low profile and wanted Konoe to make the big decision about war or peace. Konoe would not or could not make that decision. The result was deadlock.[64]

Konoe handed in his resignation to Emperor Hirohito on October 16. In a letter signed "Your Majesty's Humble Servant, Fumimaro," Konoe explained that despite repeated attempts he had been unable to persuade War Minister Tōjō to continue negotiations with the United States, and therefore could no longer continue as prime minister. He resigned with regret, believing peace was still possible, while the alternative was so much worse: "To plunge into a great war, the issue of which is most uncertain, at a time when the China Incident is still unsettled would be something which I could not possibly agree to."[65]

Tōjō was picked as Konoe's successor. He was not the first choice, and it was obvious that it was fraught with risk to let an advocate of war take over the helm. Still,

Hirohito considered it a risk worth taking. "He who will not go into the tiger's den will not get the tiger cub," he told an advisor.[66] Tōjō was considered strong enough to curb the fierce proclivities of the armed forces. "Bear in mind, at this time, that cooperation between the Army and Navy should be closer than ever before," Hirohito told him.[67] Tōjō's appointment seemed to many foreign observers a beeline to war. A report prepared for the chief of Naval Operations in Washington predicted that "with the advent of the Tōjō Cabinet Japan swings back to closer Axis ties under the aegis of the jingoistic military clique."[68] Cordell Hull described him as "a typical Japanese officer, with a small-bore, strait-laced, one-track mind … rather stupid."[69]

In fact, the change of prime ministers gave peace another chance. Tōjō's loyalties shifted overnight, and he went from exclusively defending the Army's interests to serving what he considered to be the interests of the nation. He was now committed to a last-ditch effort to reach an agreement with the United States.[70] The most direct sign of this was his decision to appoint career diplomat Tōgō Shigenori, widely known as a dove, his new foreign minister. To keep control of the Army, Tōjō held onto his title as army minister and in addition took on the role of home affairs minister. This gave him the reins over the police force and enabled him to curb whatever protests might erupt if the Army or its supporters thought their demands were being ignored.[71]

Ironically, at this time Yamamoto's scheme for an attack on Pearl Harbor finally received a crucial stamp of approval. The admiral sent one his key staff officers to the Naval General Staff with yet more arguments in favor of the Hawaii Operations—and one trump card up his sleeve. If the plan was not adopted, Yamamoto would resign with his entire staff. This produced the official green light the admiral had been looking for. A few weeks later, the Pearl Harbor scheme was wrapped into the Combined Fleet Operation Order No. 1. Yamamoto, the gambler, had won the biggest bet of his career.[72]

★   ★   ★

Japan's reshuffled Cabinet went to work in a frantic manner, seeing senior military officers within the framework of the liaison conferences nearly every day in late October to early November. Those were grueling meetings, sometimes of marathon-type duration. The longest lasted an uninterrupted 17 hours.[73] Efficiency was low, however. A description of a typical session leaves the impression of near-chaotic procedures: "At times two men would start talking at the same time, or one member would be whispering to another while another one was speaking. Secretaries were constantly leaving or entering the room to make telephone calls, to call in subordinates who could provide detailed information, or to bring in documents."[74]

Further constraining the ability of the participants to make informed decisions, a tradition of secrecy was maintained, with minimal exchange of information between the civilian and military leaders. Newly-appointed Foreign Minister Tōgō found to his immense frustration that even the most basic statistics about his nation's situation were unavailable. "I keenly felt the absurdity of our having to base our deliberations on assumptions, since the high command refused to divulge figures on the numbers of our forces, or any facts relating to operations," he later said, looking back at the chaotic fall of 1941.[75] It was in this environment that Japan's decision-makers formed policies that would determine life and death for millions.

The result of the talks emerged in early November in the form of two Japanese proposals, referred to as A and B. Proposal A offered a partial Japanese withdrawal from China as well as a complete pullback from Indochina, once the China issue had been settled. It also offered to renegotiate Japan's Axis agreement, although the spirit of the pact was to remain the same. Proposal B simply called less ambitiously for Japan and the United States to muddle along, without going to war, in the hope of working out a permanent solution in the future. If both plans were rejected, Japan would go to war.[76] The Japanese saw this as an appropriate response to what they considered US intransigence. "The United States policy toward Japan had been strict and unsympathetic, revealing a determination to enforce their demands without compromise," Navy Minister Shimada Shigetarō said later. "It was a tight, tense and trapped feeling that Japan had at that time."[77]

Ambassador Nomura started out by handing Proposal A to the US government and was met with rejection. After all, MAGIC intelligence allowed US officials to read the Japanese diplomatic cables, and they knew an alternative had been prepared. Next in line was Proposal B, duly submitted by Nomura, who was now reinforced by career diplomat Kurusu Saburō as a "special envoy" in a sign from Tokyo that it wished to give the talks another chance. Roosevelt briefly entertained the idea of a somewhat similar counter-proposal, but thought better of it after meeting vehement protests from America's allies, especially China. Instead, he instructed Cordell Hull to send a 10-point note to Japan, listing the US demands, including a full Japanese withdrawal from China.

Even though Hull's note of November 26 was clearly marked as tentative, and even though no deadline was given for when the demands were to be met, the Japanese leadership considered it an ultimatum, and the last straw.[78] "This was a jarring blow," said Navy Minister Shimada. "The general view was that acceptance of this note would be tantamount to the defeat of Japan."[79] It further added to Japanese ire that the majority in Tokyo believed, mistakenly, that the reply from Hull also implied an American demand for Japanese withdrawal from Manchukuo. It would mean giving up everything Japan had gained in Northeast Asia since the war with Russia in 1904 and 1905, said Hara Yoshimichi, an elder statesman who at the age of 74 feared seeing all the triumphs of his lifetime come to naught.[80]

Through the deciphered diplomatic cables, the United States had been warned that Japan would commence hostilities if both proposals were turned down. Still, many in the West could not quite bring themselves to believe that Japan would actually embark on such a suicidal undertaking. Churchill voiced the opinion of many when he described the basic folly that Japan would exhibit in going to war: "It would seem a very hazardous adventure for the Japanese people to plunge, quite needlessly, into a world struggle in which they may well find themselves opposed in the Pacific by States whose populations comprise nearly three quarters of the human race."[81]

At the same time, there were ominous alerts that just could not be ignored. On November 22, US intelligence had received a warning: "Dutch authorities in the [Netherlands East Indies] have received information that a Japanese Expeditionary Force which is strong enough to constitute a threat against the [Netherlands East Indies] or Portuguese Timor has arrived in the vicinity of Palau." If that force entered into waters between the Philippines and the Dutch possessions, "the Governor General of the [Netherlands East Indies] will regard it as an act of hostility and will consider war to have begun."[82]

Both American and British decision-makers believed that if the Japanese did indeed attack, they would do so in Southeast Asia. US Secretary of War Henry L. Stimson recorded in his diary a Cabinet meeting on November 27 when Roosevelt read from an intelligence paper describing possible objectives of a Japanese advance: "It might develop into an attack on the Philippines, or a landing of further troops in Indochina, or an attack on the Dutch [East Indies] or on Singapore. After the President had read these aloud, he pointed out that there was one more. It might … develop into an attack on Rangoon."[83] By the time that Roosevelt met with his Cabinet, the Japanese fleet assigned to the attack on Pearl Harbor had already been on the way for 48 hours. Departing from Hittokapu Bay in the Kuriles north of the main Japanese islands, it had set a northern course where it was least likely to run into airplanes and vessels from other countries. No one encountering this assembly of ships could doubt it was assembled for a major endeavor—six aircraft carriers in addition to cruisers, destroyers, and various support vessels. Heading this mighty force, on board his flagship, the carrier *Akagi*, was Admiral Nagumo Chūichi. At heart, he doubted the operation's chances of success, but he was determined to carry out his mission with the utmost professionalism.[84]

General Sherman Miles, the head of the US Army's Intelligence Division, later claimed that Pearl Harbor had been considered as a possible object of Japanese attack, but it had been seen as unlikely because of the essential foolhardiness of such an undertaking. "We did grant the Japanese the best of good sense. We did very much question whether they would attack Hawaii, because such an attack must result from two separate decisions on the part of the Japanese, one to make war against the United States, which we thought at that time in the long run would be suicidal… and two to attack a great fortress and fleet, risking certain ships that they could not replace."[85]

Hirohito met with the Japanese military and political elite at 2:05 pm on December 1 to discuss the failure of negotiations and the resulting declaration of war against the United States, Great Britain, and the Netherlands.[86] The military and political leaders took turns speaking, declaring their preparedness to fight for Japan. War was decided not by a show of hands, but as a general understanding among the attendees, underlined by Hirohito's display of confidence, nodding in agreement at the various statements. "At the moment our Empire stands at the threshold of glory or oblivion," Tōjō said in conclusion. "We tremble with fear in the presence of His Majesty. We subjects are keenly aware of the great responsibility we must assume from this point on."[87]

By now, the Japanese Navy had already been on the move for days. The Pearl Harbor task force had covered half the distance to Hawaii. The Philippine invasion force, consisting of nearly 100 vessels, was anchored west of Taiwan, preparing its assault. Other fleets were on their way to Malaya and Guam. For those in the know, the mere thought of the enterprise now undertaken inspired awe. The Japanese Navy was at its height, and would never be stronger, relatively speaking. "The Navy was never confident of achieving victory over the United States, but we were confident that we were better prepared at that time to fight than we would have been at any later date," said Navy Minister Shimada.[88]

At 5:30 pm on December 2, Yamamoto's flagship, which had remained in Japanese waters, sent out the signal *Niitakayama Nobore 1208*, or "Climb Mount Niitaka 1208." It was the prearranged order to commence war against the United States on December 8, Japanese time. In the United States, beyond the dateline, that would be December 7.[89] It was seemingly irreversible, but some commanders scattered across the Pacific were still hoping for a negotiated solution at the last minute. Off the Philippine island of Mindanao, Rear Admiral Tanaka Raize assembled his officers and admonished them: "Remember that negotiations are still being carried on in Washington. We must be prepared at any moment to receive a message calling off the whole operation, if negotiations turn out to be successful. Then we do only one thing: turn around and return to Japan." Perhaps he knew he was dreaming, for he also ordered his men to sink any American submarine which might spot them in the period between then and December 8.[90]

The hectic Japanese movements indicated to the Western powers that some major operation was underway. The only questions were what the target was, how hard it would be hit, and for what purpose. Consultations between the US and British governments showed that they considered the most likely objective to be Malaya or the Dutch East Indies. A third possibility was a Japanese landing in southern Thailand near the strategic Kra Isthmus. In that case, the British would implement a plan to send troops across the border from Malaya.[91] In the Philippines, American forces were also bracing themselves. Pursuit pilots were being briefed about the Japanese fleet movements and received orders to complete their wills. A colonel summarized their situation: "You are not necessarily a suicide squadron, but you are Goddamn near it!"[92]

It was while discussing the various scenarios for a Japanese attack that the US government, in the last days of peace, finally gave the long-awaited assurance of active assistance to Britain and the Dutch if they were the targets of the Japanese operation underway. While meeting on December 3 with Lord Halifax, the British ambassador to Washington, Roosevelt made an explicit commitment to provide "armed support" to the British and the Dutch, even if it was in order to back a British violation of Thai territory to stop the Japanese.[93] The US pledge showed blissful ignorance of the fact that in just a few days' time, American garrisons across the Pacific would be fighting for their lives.

Shortly after midnight on December 7, Catalina flying boat W8417 with Warrant Officer William E. Webb and a crew of seven airmen of the 205th Squadron of the Royal Air Force took off from Seletar air field at Singapore. It headed north towards the Gulf of Thailand on a reconnaissance mission, looking for three Japanese convoys seen in the area within the preceding 14 hours, apparently with a course west towards Thailand or Malaya. After more than six hours in the air, the Catalina informed Seletar that it had still sighted nothing. It was to be its last signal.

At 8:20 am, the Catalina was spotted by Japanese Reserve Ensign Ogata Eiichi, the pilot of an E13A1 "Jake" reconnaissance plane from seaplane tender *Kamikawa Maru*, one of the three convoys. Although it was still officially peacetime, the Japanese pilots were under strict orders to down any Western airplane to keep their mission secret. Ogata fired twenty 7.7mm rounds from one of his machine guns into the hull of the Catalina, and started trailing it. After about 25 minutes, a group of Ki-27 fighter planes turned up, shooting up the already doomed RAF plane. It exploded in mid-air, the debris falling into the tropical sea beneath. The aircraft and its crew were the first combat casualties of the Pacific War.[94]

Thousands of miles to the east, the Pearl Harbor task force was approaching the Hawaiian islands. The officers in charge of the operation disagreed on what should be the main targets. The traditional surface ship officers wanted to get the American battleships. The officers from the naval air branch were more interested in the aircraft carriers. On the eve of the attack, they received intelligence that eight battleships were present in Pearl Harbor, but the aircraft carriers were out at sea. Genda Minoru, one of the chief planners of the aerial attack, found some comfort in a slim hope that the *Enterprise* and two other carriers might actually have slipped back into Pearl Harbor within the last few hours. "If that happens," said Genda, "I don't care if all eight of the battleships are away."[95]

On the same day, a message from Yamamoto was read to all participants in the task force: "The rise or fall of the Empire depends upon this battle. Everyone will do his duty to his utmost." It was an echo of Lord Nelson's signal to his fleet at Trafalgar, but it was also inspired by the order Admiral Tōgō Heihachirō had issued prior to the battle of Tsushima in 1905 when Japan had, with one blow, secured its position among the world's major nations. In similar pregnant symbolism, the very same flag that Tōgō had raised on his steam-driven battleship *Mikasa* thirty-six years earlier was now hoisted by the crew of aircraft carrier *Akagi*.[96] The technology had changed dramatically over the years, but the situation was very much the same: Japan was about to challenge a world power for predominance in the western Pacific.

Hawaii was "a world of happiness in an ocean of peace," Honolulu-based monthly *Paradise of the Pacific* said in its December issue.[97] For many of the sailors and soldiers at Pearl Harbor, the upcoming Christmas was the biggest concern, and there was time for some last-minute holiday shopping. "The captain told us that whoever wanted to go ashore to buy Christmas presents for our mothers, our families, our friends must do that this Saturday night," said Arles Cole, a 17-year-old sailor on the *West Virginia*.[98] In the Philippines, American soldiers were waiting for the arrival of the Clipper flying boat with "cheerful and newsy letters" from home. In Hong Kong, British servicemen went to the movies.[99]

In Washington, President Roosevelt sent a message to Emperor Hirohito, pointing out the threat felt from the growing numbers of troops in French Indochina and calling for their withdrawal. "I address myself to Your Majesty at this moment in the fervent hope that Your Majesty may, as I am doing, give thought in this definite emergency to ways of dispelling the dark clouds," Roosevelt wrote. "I am confident that both of us, for the sake of the peoples not only of our own great countries but for the sake of humanity in neighboring territories, have a sacred duty to restore traditional amity and prevent further death and destruction in the world."[100]

Roosevelt read his note to the Chinese Ambassador Hu Shi. "This is my last effort for peace," the president said. "I am afraid it may fail."[101] The message was delayed in transmission, and only around midnight was Ambassador Grew able to pass it on to the Japanese government. Despite the late hour, he insisted on handing it to Foreign Minister Tōgō immediately. Tōgō, who was informed in detail about the war plans, managed to put up a convincing act. "Why the hurry?" he asked in feigned bewilderment.[102] The sun was just about to rise over Hawaii, and only two more hours would pass before the first shots were fired.

CHAPTER NINE

Total War

December 7–8, 1941

Just before dawn on December 7, 1941, the destroyer USS *Ward* with a crew of naval reservists from St. Paul, Minnesota, was patrolling the entrance of Pearl Harbor. It looked like the beginning of a fine day, with just a few clouds caressing the green tropical mountain tops of the islands of Hawaii. At 6:37 am, with 20 minutes yet to go before sunrise, the unexpected happened. The *Ward's* captain, Lieutenant Commander William W. Outerbridge, was called to the bridge. His men had spotted the conning tower of a submarine, trailing the USS *Antares*, a cargo ship arriving from a cruise in the south Pacific with a 510-ton steel barge in tow.[1]

Outerbridge quickly decided that the submarine was hostile, and commenced an assault maneuver at 6:40 am, abruptly increasing his vessel's speed from 5 to 25 knots. Shortening the distance to 560 yards, at 6:45 am the captain ordered four depth charges to be dropped and the destroyer's guns no. 1 and 3 to be fired. No. 1 gun's 4-inch projectile narrowly missed the conning tower and exploded on impact with the water, showering the submarine with shrapnel. No. 3 gun scored a direct hit on the submarine at the waterline. The shell created a gaping hole in the conning tower, but failed to explode. Still, it was enough to doom the submarine, and it began to slow down and sink. At 7:05 am black oil bubbles appeared where it had vanished, in 1200 feet of water.

While the *Ward's* attack was still underway, Outerbridge sent a dispatch by radio to Rear Admiral C. C. Bloch, the commandant of the 14th Naval District inside Pearl Harbor: "We have attacked, fired upon, and dropped depth charges on a submarine operating in defensive sea areas." Outerbridge and his crew could not know it at the time, but they had just fired the first American shots of the Pacific War. They had sunk a 46-ton, 78-foot midget submarine with a crew of two, one of a fleet of similar vessels sent in advance of the massive strike on Pearl Harbor scheduled to kick off shortly.

At the exact time when the USS *Ward* began its attack on the submarine, Japanese infantry commenced their assault on beach defenses on the east side of the Malay

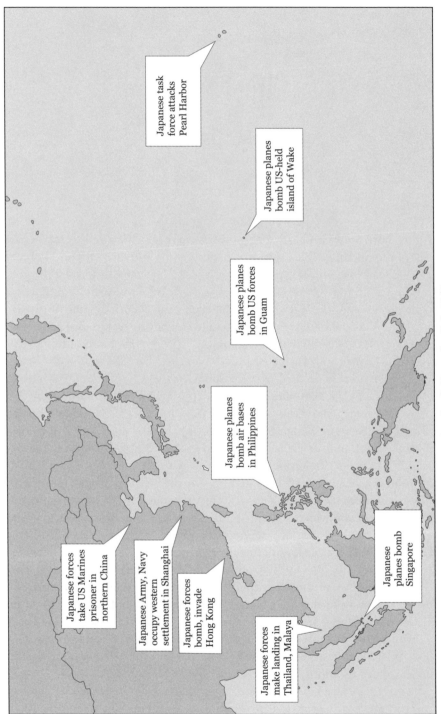

Asia-Pacific December 7–8, 1941.

peninsula. Here—at a distance of nearly 7,000 miles, across the dateline and six time zones away—it was already 12:45 am on December 8.[2] A Japanese amphibious force of 5,300 men disembarked from three transports into smaller landing-craft and made its way towards beaches near Kota Bharu, a town on the Malay border with Thailand. Their movements had not gone undetected. "We spotted there were lights being shown," said General Lewis Heath, commander of III Indian Corps. "They were apparently being operated by a Chinese smuggler whom we had tried to get arrested months previously but there was insufficient evidence."[3]

The attack began in a less than auspicious fashion. The seas were rough, and some of the craft capsized before reaching the shore.[4] As they approached the beach, the Japanese landing parties watched as guns from the naval escort started pounding the coastal defenses, tactically placed pillboxes protected by minefields and three rows of barbed wire. The bombardment had only a limited effect. When the wet Japanese soldiers hit dry land, they were met by hails of machine-gun fire from the entrenched defenders, Indians under British command, while artillery batteries near the coast rained down shells on them. The Japanese were stuck at the water's edge, unable to move. Instinctively, they dug with their hands into the wet sand, hiding their heads in the hollows, waiting for dawn to break.[5]

In this manner, the great war for supremacy in the Pacific had started, with sharp battles at the westernmost and easternmost edges of what the Japanese commanders, in their endless ambition, had chosen as their operations area. In the east, it was still Sunday, December 7. In the west, it had become Monday, December 8. For soldiers and civilians in all time zones, it would be a long day, one of the most momentous of the 20th century, with fighting at sea, in the air, and on land in locations thousands of miles apart, and when it was over, the world would be changed.

While the Japanese Marines stormed into Indian machine-gun fire on the beaches of Malaya, it was 7 am at Pearl Harbor. The first wave of Japanese planes, a total of 183 fighters, torpedo planes and bombers, was approaching Hawaii's main island of Oahu, with less than an hour to go before the scheduled attack. The wave was led by Commander Fuchida Mitsuo. Before take-off from aircraft carrier *Akagi*, the petty officer in charge of the maintenance gang had handed him a *hachimaki*, a headband with the rising sun for good fortune, and Fuchida had tied it around his flight helmet.[6] Ironically, at this point the Japanese almost ran out of luck.

The Pearl Harbor task force, which had miraculously made it the whole way from the Japanese home islands without being detected, was finally spotted. An operator at a US Army radar station near Kahuku Point at the northernmost tip of Oahu noticed the large blip from the approaching airplanes and phoned in the news to the radar information center on the outskirts of Honolulu. The officer in charge

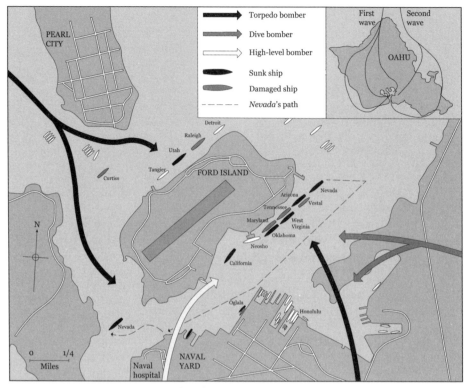

Pearl Harbor, December 7, 1941.

at the center listened patiently, but he knew a group of American B-17 Fighting Fortress bombers was expected to arrive the same morning and uttered four words that would haunt him for decades: "Don't worry about it."[7]

Consequently, Fuchida's dive bombers and torpedo planes swept unopposed across the northern shoreline of Oahu at about 7:50 am. As they passed by the island's green mountains and headed towards the island's more populated south, they could tell that the Americans still had no idea what was about to happen within just minutes. The only problem was when a Japanese reconnaissance plane reported having sighted only battleships and cruisers inside Pearl Harbor, confirming that there were no aircraft carriers.[8] At 7:53 am, Fuchida sent out the arranged message that complete surprise had been achieved: "*Tora! Tora! Tora!*" or 'Tiger! Tiger! Tiger!" This was the signal the entire task force had been waiting for. Surprise meant the difference between success and failure, perhaps even between life and death for each individual pilot.[9]

When the Japanese planes reached Honolulu, they flew past a messenger on a motorcycle who was on his way to US Army headquarters with a message from General Marshall, based on MAGIC intelligence, that some sort of Japanese action might be in the offing. The message had been delayed because the US Army had, for unknown reasons, decided to send it via the commercial telegraph service rather than via military communications, and it had not even been decoded yet. By the time it was read, thousands of Americans would already have lost their lives.[10]

"Pearl Harbor was still asleep in the morning mist," reminisced Lieutenant Commander Itaya Shigeru, who led the fighter planes in the first wave. "It was calm and serene inside the harbor, not even a trace of smoke from the ships at Oahu. The orderly groups of barracks, the wriggling white line of automobile road climbing up to the mountain-top; fine objectives of attack in all directions. In line with these, inside the harbor, were important ships of the Pacific Fleet, strung out and anchored two ships side by side in an orderly manner."[11]

What Itaya had spotted was eight battleships moored next to Ford Island, an islet in the middle of Pearl Harbor. Battleship Row, as it was called, had become the torpedo and dive bombers' main target in the absence of aircraft carriers. Like expert hunters, they had succeeded in sneaking up on their prey, making their presence known only at the very last moment. Rear Admiral William Furlong, commander of service vessels at Pearl Harbor, was pacing the deck of minelayer USS *Oglala*, waiting for breakfast to be announced, when he suddenly saw one of the Japanese planes fly by at low altitude, heading for the battleships. "I could have almost thrown something at it and I could have hit it," he said.[12]

The Japanese pilots themselves were puzzled that they had made it this far. They had been told by their superiors that probably half of them would be shot down even before having a chance to release their bombs.[13] Now their formations had arrived intact, and they split up into smaller groups, attacking the heaviest ships in the harbor. The long months of training and memorizing the details of their objective now paid off. The pilots knew exactly where to approach their targets in order to obtain the best avenue of attack. The torpedoes, specially designed for shallow water, worked perfectly.[14]

The men inside the ships in Battleship Row were caught completely by surprise. Ensign G. S. Flannigan onboard the USS *Arizona*, built shortly before America's entry into World War I, was awakened by the air raid siren shortly before 8 am. "I was in the bunk room and everyone in the bunk room thought it was a joke to have an air raid drill on Sunday. Then I heard an explosion," he said.[15] For many of the sailors it took just seconds to instinctively understand what was going on. The Rising Sun on the wings of the airplanes left no doubt. Cook Third Class "Dorie" Miller of the USS *West Virginia* had been sitting at his breakfast table when assembly was sounded. As he emerged on the quarter deck, the word was already being passed that "the Japs are attacking."[16]

The USS *Arizona* was hit by several bombs dropped from an altitude of nearly 10,000 feet. One of the bombs tore through the armored deck at the front end of the vessel, triggering an explosion in the forward magazines that severed its hulk in two. "Suddenly the whole bridge shook like it was in an earthquake," one of the survivors recalled. "Flame came through the bridge windows which had been broken by gunfire."[17] For a brief moment, the death throes of the *Arizona* dominated the entire scenery, and even attracted the attention of Japanese pilots engaged elsewhere. "A huge column of dark red smoke rose to one thousand feet and a stiff shock wave reached our plane," wrote Fuchida. "I called the pilot's attention to the spectacle, and he observed, 'Yes, Commander, the powder magazine must have exploded. Terrible indeed!'"[18]

The explosion cost the lives of 1,177 officers and men. "A hideous business altogether—over a thousand men burned to a crisp or trapped below until they drowned," wrote the US Navy's official historian Samuel Eliot Morison.[19] Adolph Czerwenka, a 22-year-old radioman third class, had been aboard the *West Virginia* at the start of the attack. After he was ordered to abandon ship, he had taken command of an empty motor launch, and watched as the *Arizona* exploded. The makeshift crew of the launch picked up survivors from the water, took them ashore and returned for more, all while Japanese planes were flying just above their heads, dropping torpedoes and strafing. "One pilot was so close I could see the big smile on his face," said Czerwenka. "Boy, was I angry!"[20]

While torpedoes and bombs left the vessels anchored in Pearl Harbor trapped in a blazing inferno, other groups of Japanese planes attacked Hawaii's airfields. There were six, spread across the southern part of Oahu. This was, in fact, an even higher priority than the ships, since the Japanese planners considered the American airplanes a serious threat and expected them to be airborne immediately, ready to inflict heavy losses.[21] Instead, they found the aircraft parked close together, in an effort to make it easier to guard them against sabotage. Within five minutes just before 8 am, the Japanese managed to destroy 188 American planes and damage another 159, out of a total of 394.[22] Arguably it was the greatest success of the entire attack.

The initial reaction in and around Pearl Harbor was disbelief. John Lacouture, an assistant engineer on the destroyer USS *Blue*, was sleeping at a private home in Honolulu when a member of the host family shook him violently: "Wake up, wake up! The Japanese are attacking Pearl Harbor!" He answered: "Are you crazy? Go away, I'm sleepy."[23] When Lieutenant Colonel George W. Bicknell, an intelligence officer, telephoned Fort Shafter with news that Pearl Harbor was being bombed, the reply he got from an anonymous voice at the other end was: "Go back to sleep, you're having a bad dream."[24]

Once the initial shock had receded, the Americans fought back, with whatever they could find. At Ewa airfield, angry Marine pilots, frustrated at seeing 33 of their 49 planes aflame, fired their pistols at the Japanese fighters.[25] An army chaplain at Hickam airfield had been preparing for an outdoor mass when the attack began.

He planted a machine gun on top of the altar and blasted back at the Japanese.[26] Ray Emory, a sailor on the cruiser USS *Honolulu*, was firing furiously at enemy airplanes zooming past and exposing themselves for just split seconds: "You've got tunnel vision. You don't have time to get scared or nervous. You are just doing what you are supposed to do."[27]

Fuchida Mitsuo was astonished by the swiftness and ferocity of the American response. "Had it been the Japanese Fleet, the reaction would not have been so quick because although the Japanese character is suitable for offensives, it does not readily adjust to the defensive," he said.[28] A doomed Japanese pilot, hit by anti-aircraft fire, may have decided to take as many Americans with him as possible and crashed near a battery on the ground. The plane struck a tree, leaving the dead pilot stuffed in the branches and then careened onwards, hitting several men on the way. "One man was completely decapitated. Another man apparently had been hit by the props, because his legs and arms and head were off, lying right on the grass," an eyewitness recalled.[29]

After a brief lull, the second wave of Japanese planes arrived over Oahu. Pearl Harbor was now shrouded in dense black smoke, and new targets had become harder to make out. Some ships that had already been thoroughly damaged were bombed again. Among the pilots trying to find their way through the evolving chaos was Lieutenant Abe Zenji, a 25-year-old dive bomber. He had put a photo in his inner pocket of his wife holding their six-month-old son, but even though he knew he might die, he was seized by a strange calm. "I didn't feel fear, or such excitement as 'I'm going to beat the Americans!' Instead I thought it was just like an exercise."[30]

Like many other pilots carrying just one big bomb, Abe only got a few seconds over Pearl Harbor. After he had fixed his sights on a target near Ford Island, he dove towards it, with the voice of his observer Warrant Officer Saitō Chiaki in his ear: "'800, 600 …!' Saitō shouted out the altitude through the voice tube. 'Ready!' With the target growing larger in the sight, I pulled the release at the instant of his cry, 'Fire!' Pulling the control lever which returned the dive brakes to their normal position, I grew giddy for a few seconds, but flew past the harbor, leveled out at 30-meter altitude … As I flew out towards the sea, I thought to myself, 'I am still alive!'"[31]

"This is war, mommy!" a young boy yelled, as he ran to his parents' house in a sleepy Honolulu neighborhood in the wake of the attack, seeing his mother on the porch, her arms full of laundry.[32] Not everyone reacted this quickly. Hawaii's civilian population only gradually realized what was taking place all around them. Daniel Inouye, the 17-year-old son of a Japanese immigrant, was putting on a necktie and preparing to go to church when the music on the radio was interrupted by reports of the attack. He initially believed it was a replay of Orson Welles' radio show *War of*

the Worlds, which had featured a Martian invasion, but the voice on the radio went on for so long that Inouye became suspicious and went outside. Puff of antiaircraft explosions could be seen over Pearl Harbor, and three gray aircraft flew by, with rising suns on the wings, telling Inouye what was happening: "I knew that it was no play, it was real."[33]

Many American shells fired at the Japanese airplanes landed in the Honolulu area with tragic results. John Garcia, a 16-year-old apprentice at Pearl Harbor Naval Yard, learned that his girlfriend's home had been hit during the attack. "At the time, they said it was a Japanese bomb. Later we learned it was an American shell. She was killed. She was preparing for church at the time," he said.[34] Altogether about 60 civilians lost their lives to friendly fire at Pearl Harbor. They included almost an entire family in a noodle shop and six local fishermen who were strafed near the coast by an American P-40 fighter mistaking them for the enemy.[35]

Numerous residents wanted to contribute, one way or the other. Richard Wrenshall, a World War I veteran living just outside Honolulu, had been writing a letter that morning but had been disturbed by the constant, heavy firing coming from the direction of Pearl Harbor. Then acquaintances called from downtown Honolulu asking if they could take their children to Wrenshall's home, since they were being bombed by the Japanese. "I thought this was some sort of hoax," he said, but turned on the radio and quickly understood it was for real. Unable to grasp the enormity of the events now unfolding, he sat down and smoked a cigarette, while deciding what to do. He then put on his old uniform and, armed with his Winchester rifle and 30 rounds of ammunition, turned up in Honolulu, but found there was little use for his services.[36]

Others found their services were almost too much in demand. Ruth Erickson, a nurse at the Naval Hospital, was talking over coffee with two of her colleagues when the attack started. "The 'fly boys' are really busy at Ford Island this morning," they told each other. Then the head nurse called: "Girls, get into your uniforms at once. This is the real thing!" The first patient arrived just minutes afterwards, bleeding profusely from a large opening in his abdomen. Everyone was terrified. The doctor's hand trembled as he picked up the needle. The patient died within the hour.

Soon the burn patients started streaming in. The USS *Nevada* ran aground near the hospital, and many sailors were able to swim to the shore. "The tropical dress at the time was white t-shirts and shorts. The burns began where the pants ended. Bared arms and faces were plentiful," Erickson said. "We gave these gravely injured patients sedatives for their intense pain."[37] Don Jones, a Marine who was hospitalized prior to the attack for minor surgery, helped out at the hospital: "It was a pretty gruesome sight. It was—you've all seen a hamburger that's stayed on the hamburger grill too long," he said.[38]

★ ★ ★

In Tokyo it was several hours before sunrise. The emperor's closest advisor, Kido Kōichi, was on his way to the Imperial Palace for what was likely to be a long day. He picked out the symbol of the Rising Sun on one of the buildings. "I thought it was symbolic of the destiny of this country now that we had entered the war against the United States and England," he wrote in his diary. "I closed my eyes and prayed for the success of our Navy planes making an attack upon Pearl Harbor at that time."[39] At 4:30 am Tokyo time, Tōjō received news from the Navy that the gamble had paid off and that the attack on Pearl Harbor had been successful. "I was enthusiastic and grateful for the miraculous success," he said.[40]

In fact, the success was less clear-cut than it would seem in faraway Tokyo. When the second wave of attack planes returned to the aircraft carriers off Hawaii, the question left for Nagumo, the commander of the First Air Fleet, was whether to launch yet another wave. Now that the battleships had been destroyed or damaged and a large part of Hawaii's air force disabled, the point would be to strike at Pearl Harbor's fuel supplies, dry docks, and other facilities that would underpin the enemy's longer-term ability to wage war. So far, the attack had exceeded all expectations. Only 30 planes had been lost. Nagumo decided not to push his luck and withdrew the task force.[41]

This happened over the objections of some of his younger and more aggressive officers. Among them was the aviator Genda Minoru, who had been responsible for much of the pre-attack training. He advocated staying in waters near Hawaii for several days in the hope of confronting the aircraft carriers that had escaped the first time around. Genda also argued in favor of further raids to destroy Pearl Harbor's infrastructure and had even advocated an invasion of Hawaii. "In my opinion, Japan had to neutralize American bases in the Pacific if she was to carry on the war successfully," he said later.[42]

History may have proven Genda right. One of the "missing" aircraft carriers, the USS *Enterprise*, had been scheduled to arrive in Pearl Harbor in the morning of December 7 from a cruise but had been delayed because of rough weather along the way. It was in the vicinity. More importantly, perhaps, an attack on Pearl Harbor's oil facilities could potentially have had a major impact on the conduct of the war in the months to come. Admiral Chester Nimitz, soon to be appointed the Navy's commander-in-chief in the Pacific, later pointed out that all the oil at Pearl Harbor was stored in surface tanks and could have been wiped out by later waves of Japanese aircraft: "We had about 4.5 million barrels of oil out there and all of it was vulnerable to .50-caliber bullets. Had the Japanese destroyed the oil, it would have prolonged the war another two years."[43]

At the time, however, Nagumo's decision seemed to make sense and may have been applauded by perhaps a majority of his men. "We did not realize we had destroyed planes to such an extent," Fuchida, the leader of the first wave, said after the war. "We thought that you would be re-supplied with planes from the other islands in the Hawaiian group, so it wouldn't pay to return."[44] Unlike Genda, many also considered the proximity of the carriers *Enterprise* and *Lexington* a risk rather than an opportunity. "We were told that the *Lexington* and the *Enterprise* were nearby and there was a possibility of an attack to the task force, so we had to be ready on the flight deck," said Muranaka Kazuo, a fighter pilot on board the aircraft carrier *Akagi*. There was no desire to go back to Pearl Harbor and finish the job: "Our concern at that time was the whereabouts of the *Enterprise* and *Lexington*."[45]

★   ★   ★

On the beaches of Malaya, the Japanese invasion force had been stranded at water's edge since shortly after midnight. Burrowing into the sand to avoid the machine guns of the defenders in their pillboxes, they had watched as the Royal Air Force had sent aircraft against the transport vessels while they were still unloading the last soldiers. Two of the transports had caught fire, and the soldiers on the deck had been forced to jump overboard. Kept afloat by their life jackets, they either crawled into the waiting landing barges or swam ashore.

As dawn approached on December 8, the soldiers on the beach slowly moved forward, digging their way with their helmets while staying as low as they could. When they reached the barbed wire, they cut holes with wire-cutters, but could get no further. The morning sun offered complete visibility for the Indian defenders, and any movement on the beach triggered a hail of machine-gun bullets. Some of the Japanese inadvertently detonated land mines. In this stalemate, one of the Japanese soldiers rose, rushed to the pillbox in front of him and threw himself on top of the loophole. This obstructed the view and allowed other soldiers to take the position with hand grenades and bayonets.[46]

In this way, little by little, the Japanese wrested control of the beach from the Indians. On the first day, a total of 26,000 Japanese troops landed on the Malayan peninsula. Only a minority disembarked on the bloody beaches of Kota Bharu. Most unloaded across the border with Thailand, near the towns of Singora and Patani.[47] In Thailand, most Japanese soldiers had the impression that they could simply wade ashore. Imoto Gunpei of the 106th Land Duty Company, had been on his vessel off Singora since midnight. "At 0300 hours, made preparations for opposed landing. Around 0600 hours an unopposed landing was made. Took the enemy completely by surprise," he wrote in his diary.[48]

There was some resistance from Thai forces, directed towards both belligerents. When Japanese officers attached to the Japanese consulate in Singora approached the local police station in their cars to discuss the practicalities of the ongoing occupation, men inside the building fired at them. The Japanese rushed out of their cars and crawled to the gate, shouting in bewilderment at the warm welcome: "The Japanese Army has come to save you."[49] Similarly, when British forces crossed the border into Thailand in the middle of the afternoon on December 8, they were stopped by a roadblock manned with 300 members of the Thai armed constabulary.

By nightfall, the British column had advanced no further than three miles north of the border.[50]

Further south, in Singapore, war brought Japanese air raids. A flight of 17 Japanese naval bombers took off from southern Indochina before dawn, targeting two airfields north of the city. They were detected at 3:30 am, when the Fighter Control Operations Room reported unidentified aircraft at a distance of 140 miles headed for Singapore. While the island's military units were alerted, the headquarters of the civilian air defense organization was unstaffed, and the population was given no warning. Blackouts and other air defense measures had not been implemented yet, and downtown Singapore appeared in full peace-time illumination. While some Japanese aircraft dropped their bombs on the two airfields, causing limited damage, others unloaded their deadly cargo over the center of the city, killing or injuring 200 civilians.[51]

British Malaya was ablaze. The Dutch East Indies understood that they would be next. Governor General Tjarda van Starkenborgh Stachouwer made a declaration by radio to the "People of the Netherlands East Indies" on December 8, describing the surprise Japanese attacks on US and British possessions, which, he warned, were aimed at establishing Japanese supremacy in the entire region. "These aggressions," he stated, "also menace the Netherlands East Indies in no small measure. The Netherlands government accepts the challenge and takes up arms against the Japanese Empire."[52]

At 12:15 pm on December 8 in the Philippines, Japanese bombers appeared over Clark Field, about 50 miles northwest of Manila. All but one of the airfield's B-17 bombers were lined up, as if for target practice. American fighters were also on the ground, just about to take off. The Japanese aircraft had achieved complete surprise despite their lengthy time in the air since departing from their bases on Taiwan, and dropped their bombs from an altitude of 22,000 to 25,000 feet. At that height, they could act with impunity, out of range of American antiaircraft batteries.[53] An eyewitness described a scenery of "flash fires and dense smoke that seemed to spread a pall of mourning over the area; clouds of dust that choked and clogged all vision."[54] Dozens of American aircraft were destroyed.

Shortly afterwards, Japanese Zero fighter planes descended over the airfield, strafing for more than an hour. Sakai Saburō, later nicknamed the Sky Samurai, had the first kill of an American fighter over the Philippines. He encountered a group of five P-40s. Four scattered and disappeared into the safety of the smoke from burning debris over Clark Field, leaving the fifth a lone target. Sakai approached it from below. He described what happened next: "At 200 yards the plane's belly moved into my sights. I rammed the throttle forward and closed the distance to fifty yards as the P-40 tried desperately to turn away. He was as good as finished, and a short burst of my guns and cannon walked into the cockpit, blowing the canopy off the plane. The fighter seemed to stagger in the air, then fell off and dove into the ground."[55]

American ground troops in positions at Clark Field watched with fury as the Japanese fighters swooped by mere feet above the ground. They were under strict orders not to fire at any aircraft, saving their ammunition for airborne troops that their commanders feared might follow after the initial bombardment. One tanker could no longer restrain himself but jumped on top of his tank, grabbing the turret's machine gun and firing at the aircraft. He managed to bring down a Japanese fighter.[56] "I felt a terrible hatred for the Japanese. People learn to hate quickly during war," wrote James Cowan, part of a B-17 crew on the ground. "One of the sergeants went to see one of the Japanese planes that had been shot down and immediately urinated on the dead pilot."[57]

When the first Japanese bomber returned to its base in Taiwan, the bewildered crew clambered down from their aircraft. "Are we really at war?" they asked, confused that they had met no opposition. "What is the matter with the enemy?" The lack of an effective response from the American defenses in the Philippines had taken all aback and for a brief moment even had the Japanese planners worried that the US side had cleared its airfields in advance.[58] After all, Pearl Harbor was several hours in the past, and the Americans ought to have had ample time to prepare. In Washington, General Marshall was just as dumbfounded. "I just don't know how MacArthur happened to let his planes get caught on the ground."[59]

In fact, the American aircraft had been airborne earlier in the day, as their commander Lewis Brereton, informed about the Pearl Harbor raid, wanted to prevent his aircraft becoming easy targets on the ground. Meanwhile, Brereton had attempted repeatedly to gain access to MacArthur for permission to launch bombing missions against Japanese bases on Taiwan. For reasons still not completely explained by historians eight decades later, MacArthur delayed the green light for a raid until it was too late.[60] The bombers and fighters were back at Clark Field for refueling exactly at the time when the Japanese struck. As a result of the debacle at Clark Field and a comparable disaster at the fighter base at Iba further to the west, the strongest American air force outside the United States lost half its planes.[61] According to the official American historian, the idea that Pearl Harbor was "the greatest military disaster in American history, is equally applicable to the Philippines."[62]

On December 9, MacArthur reported to Washington that Japanese forces had not yet landed in the Philippines. This was not entirely true. A small Japanese force had already disembarked two days earlier on the islet of Batan[63] midway between Taiwan and the Philippine island of Luzon, seizing a short airstrip there. Japanese engineers began work on expanding it in preparation for a lengthy campaign against the Philippines, but stopped after the triumph at Clark Field made it no longer necessary.[64] Along with Malaya, Batan was one of the only places where Japanese land forces were involved from day one of the Pacific War. A third place was Hong Kong.

★   ★   ★

The Japanese 38th Division crossed into Hong Kong, the British enclave at the Pearl River Delta, on December 8, moving through hilly countryside with the help of local guides. The British forces in the border area withdrew ahead of the Japanese, after having set off pre-prepared demolition charges to form obstacles along the Japanese route of advance.[65] The British troops were also expected to delay the Japanese by offering resistance at opportune moments. In the restrained phrase of an official British report written afterwards, "some failed to provide the measure of delaying action anticipated."[66] Hong Kong's defenses had been boosted by Canadian troops who had arrived just three weeks beforehand, and they were still only getting used to the alien new surroundings. Their vehicles, which had been transported separately across the Pacific, had not yet arrived when the Japanese attack began.[67]

In downtown Hong Kong, news about the Japanese offensive had set alarm bells ringing since early in the day. Barbara Anslow, a stenographer with the colonial government, had been told, without explanation, to come to work early. When she arrived, she was informed about the Japanese attack on Pearl Harbor. "We didn't know where Pearl Harbor was. All I could think of was the Pearl River," she told an interviewer later. "But as the morning wore on we discovered that the Japanese had attacked the Americans and war was expected to come to us. Just after 8 o'clock, air-raid sirens sounded."[68]

The reality of the Japanese invasion was brought home to the people of Hong Kong when at 8 am Japanese bombers attacked Kai Tak airport near the city center. "Shouts of delight came from onlookers when one or more planes were seen to be falling," the *South China Morning Post* reported. "But their delight died when the planes pulled out of their dives after releasing their bombs."[69] A civilian market was hit during the Japanese raid of Kai Tak. "The wounded and dead are still lying under the wreckage," according to an eyewitness account from the scenery. "The walls of the building and pavement are spattered with human blood and flesh and people are moving out of the houses that have been hit."[70]

Charles Barman, a 40-year-old battery quartermaster sergeant with the Hong Kong artillery, spent December 8 in a state of constant confusion as Japanese planes roared overhead, bombing and strafing seemingly at random. He had a problem with 30 Sikh recruits who had just been shipped in from India. "They became completely demoralized with the sudden attack, as of course did everyone," he said later. He found a temporary solution by mixing them with more experienced gunners and setting them to work loading lorries. It put their minds somewhat at ease, but as Barman remarked, "they still looked quite anxious."[71]

In Shanghai, the Japanese military moved in to take control of the International Settlement and the French Concession, which had been isolated enclaves since the Chinese Army had withdrawn from the city at the end of the battle four years earlier. In the city's Huangpu river, a Japanese boarding party attempted to take possession of the British gunboat HMS *Peterel*, and were startled by the greeting from the captain,

Stephen Polkinghorn: "Get off my bloody ship!" A short exchange of fire ensued, before Polkinghorn ordered his men to abandon ship. Six were killed, and the *Peterel* sank to the bottom of the river, becoming the first British vessel to be lost in the Pacific War.[72]

★   ★   ★

Further up north in China, the Japanese Army moved swiftly to ensure complete control, eliminating the few areas where Western powers maintained some authority. Colonel William W. Ashurst, the senior officer among the US Marines in China, was alerted to the outbreak of war by the Japanese in the morning of December 8, and was told to decide by noon if his men, in barracks in Beijing and Tianjin, would fight a hopeless battle or surrender. The Marines opted to give up any resistance, prompted by informal Japanese promises that they might be repatriated along with diplomatic staff. "When these rumors proved false, the opportunity had passed," the official Marine history of the war noted tersely.[73]

Elsewhere in the Asia Pacific where they found themselves on the first day of war, the US Marines were usually the underdog. On the large, jungle-covered island of Guam, 153 Marines were waiting for the arrival of the Japanese along with a small 300-member force consisting mostly of poorly equipped and poorly trained recruits. The only Japanese attack on December 8 was in the form of bombers that had taken off from the island of Saipan and sank the minesweeper USS *Penguin*. After nightfall, a Micronesian canoe landed on the northern end of Guam. On board where three islanders who presented themselves as being from Saipan and said ominously they had been sent in advance of a Japanese invasion force.[74]

Guam was supposed to be the next stop for the Pan American Clipper seaplane, carrying the letters eagerly anticipated by American servicemen in the Philippines, when it took off from the island of Wake, 1500 miles due east. It had only been airborne for ten minutes when it was instructed to return. As a result, it arrived just in time for the first Japanese air raid. The Japanese pilots approaching Wake encountered the same sight that was occurring throughout the Pacific during those fateful hours: American military defenses apparently lulling, oblivious to the war that had already broken out. Spotting eight Grumman F4F Wildcats lined up on the ground, one of the Japanese crew leaders commented: "The enemy is off his guard."[75]

The Japanese succeeded in completely destroying seven of the eight Wildcats then on the ground. They also killed or injured 23 of 55 aviation personnel. The Japanese were triumphant. "The pilots in every one of the planes were grinning widely," wrote Norio Tsuji, a Japanese observer during the raid. "Everyone waggled his wings to signify 'Banzai'."[76] Later that day, the Clipper was given permission to take off for Midway island further east, carrying civilian personnel deemed essential and all its passengers, except one who missed the flight. That unfortunate person, a US government official, eventually ended up in Japanese hands. "It struck me as a rather drastic lesson in the wisdom of punctuality," Colonel James Devereux, one of the top Marine commanders on the island, commented drily.[77]

As everywhere else, news of the attack on Pearl Harbor was greeted with disbelief in Washington. "My God, this can't be true," Secretary of the Navy Frank Knox said when receiving a report of the attack. "This must mean the Philippines." Admiral Stark, the chief of naval operations who was standing next to him and read the same signal, corrected him: "No, sir, this is Pearl."[78] Knox immediately called Roosevelt, who was having lunch in the Oval Office with his close advisor Harry Hopkins. "The President thought the report was probably true," Hopkins wrote the same evening, "and thought it was just the kind of unexpected thing the Japanese would do, and that at the very time they were discussing peace in the Pacific they were plotting to overthrow it."[79]

Ambassador Nomura and special envoy Kurusu came to see Cordell Hull at 2:20 pm, handing him a note from the Japanese government that officially broke off negotiations. The note did not directly declare war, but was nevertheless supposed to be delivered at the moment the attack began. Instead, there was a delay in decoding the message, and the two Japanese diplomats only brought it to Hull's apartment when the bombing had already been going on for over an hour. The reaction from the secretary of state, who in fact already knew the contents of the note from MAGIC, was scathing: "In all my fifty years of public service I have never seen a document that was more crowded with infamous falsehoods and distortions—infamous falsehoods and distortions on a scale so huge that I never imagined until today that any Government on this planet was capable of uttering them."[80] Nomura was about to speak, but Hull stopped him with a motion of his hand. He then nodded towards the door. The two Japanese left with bowed heads.[81]

Roosevelt summoned his Cabinet at 8:30 pm. This was the most important Cabinet meeting since the spring of 1861, when the American Civil War had broken out, the president told the participants at the start of his remarks.[82] He turned almost prophetic in his assessment of the way in which Japan would be brought to its knees: "The Japanese know perfectly well that the answer to her attack is proper strangulation of Japan—strangulation altogether," he said.[83] Secretary of War Stimson was somewhat surprised at this own initial reaction to the news: "My first feeling was of relief that the indecision was over and that a crisis had come in a way that would unite all our people," he wrote later the same day.[84]

In a similar vein, many Americans reacted with emotions ranging all the way to enthusiasm at the news. After years of painful uncertainty about the future, finally there was clarity about where their nation was heading. Edward C. Raymer, a naval diver at San Diego, was relaxing after a softball tournament when news of the Japanese attack arrived. "America is at war! A feeling of excitement welled up in me. By God, we'll kick their butts, I thought. I couldn't wait to get at the enemy. I had no idea of the horror I was so eager to encounter."[85]

At Pearl Harbor they were counting their losses. More than 2,400 had been killed in the attack, and another thousand had been injured. It was clear that more could have been done with the firepower at the American disposal. In the words of the official American historian, "a magnificent defense could have been interposed, sufficient to inflict on the raiders a proper penalty."[86] The debacle was due to oversights and errors on the US side, but in the immediate aftermath, many Hawaiians were looking for an explanation in the work of nebulous fifth columns. There were reports about swaths being cut in sugarcane and pineapple fields pointing to important objectives. The authorities probed these and other allegations of treachery and found nothing of substance.[87]

Hawaii had 160,000 residents of Japanese descent. The vast majority were as shocked as anyone else, and were disgusted with the rare signs of support of the raid, such as when a first-generation Japanese immigrant shouted out from his Honolulu home: "What a great job they did!"[88] Unlike the situation on the west coast of the continental United States, most Japanese Americans on Hawaii avoided detention. Still, about 1,000 were rounded up. Otani Akira, a young Japanese American, witnessed how his father, the owner of fish-wholesaling operation in Honolulu, was visited by FBI agents who stuck a gun in his gut and drove him away. Otani's father was suspected of subversive work, and even though no evidence was ever found against him, he spent the rest of the war in confinement.[89]

Fears were spreading among the Hawaiian population that the air raid had just been the prelude to a Japanese landing, and fantastical rumors were circulating about Japanese paratroopers poisoning the groundwater. The American commanders did not dismiss the possibility of a landing as they knew nothing about the location of the ships that had launched the attack, and they kept military personnel on Hawaii on high alert. "Everyone knew we would be invaded," said a Marine, who spent the night between December 7 and 8 on top of his barracks, scouting the sky. "We fired the machine gun in the air maybe every hour or so because it made a lot of smoke and it got rid of the mosquitoes."[90]

America was licking its wounds, and getting ready to fight. For some, it was literally as if they had been born again into a new life of struggle until the final victory. Electrician's Mate First Class Irwin H. Thesman had been trapped inside the battleship *Oklahoma* for more than a day before being rescued. "It was a deep, powerful feeling," he later said. "Like being dug up out of your own grave."[91] Some were not so lucky. When salvage crews restored the *West Virginia* in early 1942, they found the bodies of close to 70 sailors who had survived in air pockets, waiting in vain for rescue, in some cases for weeks. On a calendar that was found among the bodies, the last day that had been scratched off was December 23.[92]

★   ★   ★

"War Is On!" the *Japan Times and Mail* exclaimed on December 8 in oversized letters across its front page, even producing a short wire report datelined Honolulu.[93] In Japan, where anecdotal evidence had suggested a public less than eager to go to war with America, news about the sudden triumph at Pearl Harbor generated a brief bout of enthusiasm. In this respect it was similar to the mood in Germany, where apprehension at the start of the war in September 1939 had been followed by a certain sense of excitement after the speedy fall of France in 1940. The writer Hino Ashihei, a former soldier whose memoirs about the war in China had achieved a huge readership, was overwhelmed by visions of gods advancing in the skies over East Asia. "I am sure that I was not alone in this emotion," he said. "Was there anyone, I wonder, who did not weep with emotion on hearing the Rescript announcing the declaration of war?"[94]

As intelligence from across the Pacific arrived, Hirohito and his closest aides were briefed continuously about the successes of the operations going on in parallel across several time zones. "Throughout the day," one of his senior officials wrote in his diary, "the emperor wore his naval uniform and seemed to be in a splendid mood."[95] Premier Tōjō read the declaration of war on the radio. The announcement was followed by the popular song *Umi Yukaba* and its ill-boding lyrics:

> Across the sea, corpses in the water;
> Across the mountain, corpses in the field;
> I shall die only for the Emperor,
> I shall never look back.[96]

Otto Tolischus, a *New York Times* correspondent who had previously been deported from Germany for his reporting about the Nazis, was awakened at his home at 7 am on December 8 by four plainclothes police officers. They took him to the station, where he was accused of sending "political, diplomatic, and economic information to foreign agents harmful to Japan." Later, as he was driven through Tokyo, he was accompanied by a Japanese police officer, who seemed saddened by the uniformed guards and other signs of the war that had now broken out. "I am very sorry there is war between Japan and America," the officer said. Tolischus replied drily: "You can't be any sorrier than I am."[97]

Admiral Yamamoto, on board his flagship in Japanese waters, received congratulatory messages by the sackful in the days after the attack. He made a point out of answering each of them with handwritten notes, stating his belief as diplomatically as possible that tough battles lay ahead: "I swear I shall conduct further strenuous efforts and shall not rest on this small success in beginning the war."[98] A lingering thought may have formed in his mind that important chances had been missed at Pearl Harbor when the initial two attack waves were not followed up. In fact, less than 48 hours after the raid, Yamamoto ordered his staff to prepare a plan for the invasion of Hawaii.[99]

Some Japanese believed that any work left undone in Hawaii could easily be made up for later, and that in fact it was sound to focus on the more important campaign for resources in Southeast Asia. "In Japanese tactics, we are told when we have two enemies, one in front and one in the back, first we must cut in front by sword," Watanabe Yasuji, a member of Yamamoto's staff, said after the war. "Only cut and not kill but make it hard. Then we attack the back enemy and kill him. Then we come back to the front enemy and kill him. This time we took that tactic, having no aim to capture Pearl Harbor but just to cripple it. We might have returned to capture later."[100]

Even on the first days of war there were misgivings among Japan's professional soldiers. Aoki Taijirō, who was training future pilots at the Naval Aviation School at Tsuchiura at the start of the war, doubted it would be over soon. "They were all saying that it would be a long war, but nobody hazarded a guess as to the duration," he said in a post-war interrogation.[101] Fighter pilot Harada Kaname, who took part in the Pearl Harbor operation, remembered the idea of fighting "the huge superpower America" had triggered some misgivings. "Even at our level, whether we could go to war and win, there was some doubt," he said.[102]

In China, where it had all started in the preceding decade, the American advisor to Chiang Kai-shek, Owen Lattimore was awakened long before dawn with news about the Pearl Harbor attack. His reaction: to go back to sleep. "There will be a lot to do today," he thought to himself. "I'd better be fit for it." Once he woke up the second time, he was summoned to a meeting with Chiang Kai-shek. The Chinese leader was pleased because it meant complete American participation in the war. "He thought that though the Allies would suffer severe losses in the Pacific and Southeast Asia, in the end they, principally the United States, would recover and defeat Japan."[103]

For Chiang Kai-shek it was a time of quiet triumph. The moment he had been waiting for in the course of four long years of battle had finally arrived. Indeed, it was a turning point in Chinese history. For the first time in more than a millennium of history with Japan, China was not alone in a war against its arch enemy to the east. Chiang penned a brief message of solidarity to President Roosevelt: "To our now common battle we offer all we are and all we have to stand with you until the Pacific and the world are freed from the curse of brute force and endless perfidy."[104]

Endnotes

Preface

1   Jay Taylor, *The Generalissimo's Son: Chiang Ching-kuo and the Revolutions in China and Taiwan* (Cambridge MA: Harvard University Press, 2000), 101.

Chapter 1

1   The ancient name of today's Geum River.
2   Adapted from William Wayne Farris, *Population, Disease and Land in Early Japan 645–900* (Cambridge MA: Harvard University Press, 1985), 10–11.
3   June Teufel Dreyer, *Middle Kingdom and Empire of the Rising Sun* (Oxford: Oxford University Press, 2016), 9.
4   Robert E. Buswell and Donald S. Lopez, *The Princeton Dictionary of Buddhism* (Princeton NJ: Princeton University Press, 2014), 312–313.
5   F. Brinkley, *Japan: Described and Illustrated by the Japanese*, vol. 5 (Boston MA: J. B. Millet, 1897), 162.
6   Dreyer, *Middle Kingdom*, 17.
7   Samuel Hawley, *The Imjin War: Japan's Sixteenth-Century Invasion of Korea and Attempt to Conquer China* (n.p.: Conquistador Press, 2014), 262.
8   Wang Yong, "Realistic and Fantastic Images of 'Dwarf Pirates': The Evolution of Ming Dynasty Perceptions of the Japanese" in *Sagacious Monks and Bloodthirsty Warriors: Chinese Views of Japan in the Ming-Qing Period*, ed. Joshua A. Fogel (Norwalk CT: Eastbridge, 2002), 21.
9   Ibid., 22.
10   Ibid., 29.
11   *Ming Shi*, chapter 322. Adapted from Kwan-wai So, *Japanese Piracy in Ming China During the 16th Century* (Ann Arbor MI: Michigan State University Press, 1975), 180.
12   Wang Yong. "Dwarf Pirates," 28 and 40, n35.
13   *Ming Shi*, chapter 322. Adapted from So, *Japanese Piracy*, 169.
14   Joshua A. Fogel, "Introduction," in *Sagacious Monks and Bloodthirsty Warriors: Chinese Views of Japan in the Ming-Qing Period*, ed. Joshua A. Fogel (Norwalk CT: Eastbridge, 2002), 5.
15   Xue Jun's *Riben Kaolüe [A Comprehensive Study of Japan]*, quote adapted from Wang Yong, "Realistic and Fantastic Images," 29.
16   Fernão Mendes Pinto, *The Travels of Mendes Pinto* (Chicago IL: University of Chicago Press, 2013), 276–78. The veracity of Mendes Pinto's memoirs has been questioned and his tales in some cases debunked, but it is generally agreed that he did indeed visit Japan.
17   Alain Peyrefitte, *The Immobile Empire* (New York NY: Vintage Books, 2013), 291.

18 Angus Maddison. *The World Economy*. Paris: OECD, 2007. The view that China had roughly the same living standards as Europe until the early 1800s has recently been challenged by some economic historians, see, for example, Stephen Broadberry, Hanhui Guan, and David Daokui Li, "China, Europe and the Great Divergence: A Study in Historical National Accounting," *Discussion Papers in Economic and Social History*, no. 155, April 2017.

19 Peyrefitte, p. 465.

20 Julia Lovell, *The Opium War: Drugs, Dreams, and the Making of China* (London: MacMillan, 2011), 208.

21 Foster Rhea Dulles, *Yankees and Samurai* (New York NY: Harper and Row, 1965), 53.

22 Alexis de Tocqueville, *Democracy in America*, vol. 1 (Indianapolis IN: Liberty Fund, 2010), 637–41.

23 Dulles, *Yankees*, 59.

24 Ibid., 75.

25 *Japan Herald*, April 9, 1881. Quoted in Endymion Wilkinson, *Japan versus the West* (London: Penguin, 1991), 121.

26 Steven J. Ericson, *The Sound of the Whistle: Railroads and the State in Meiji Japan* (Cambridge MA: Harvard University Press, 1996), 71–72.

27 S. C. M. Paine, *The Japanese Empire: Grand Strategy from the Meiji Restoration to the Pacific War* (Cambridge: Cambridge University Press, 2017), 6–8.

28 Yŏn-suk Yi, *The Ideology of Kokugo: Nationalizing Language in Modern Japan* (Honolulu HI: University of Hawai'i Press, 2010), 8.

29 Marius B. Jansen, "The Meiji Restoration," in *The Cambridge History of Japan. Vol. 5: The Nineteenth Century.*, ed. Marius B. Jansen (Cambridge: Cambridge University Press, 1989), 335.

30 Quoted from Michael Green, *By More Than Providence: Grand Strategy and American Power in the Asia Pacific Since 1783* (New York NY: Columbia University Press, 2017), 58.

31 "Japan and Christianity," *New York Times*, April 20, 1879, p. 3.

32 "Christian Progress in Japan," *New York Times*, April 7, 1889, p. 4.

33 Dulles, *Yankees*, 69.

34 1 *li* = 1889 feet. In other words, Li was exaggerating the distance to Europe.

35 Teng Ssu-yu, *China's Response to the West: A Documentary Survey 1839–1923.* (New York NY: Atheneum, 1975), 119. The phrase "the weaknesses of our defense measures" is the translators' rephrasing of the expression "our emptiness and solitude" in the Chinese original.

36 Ericson, *Sound of the Whistle*, 8–9.

37 S. C. M. Paine. *The Sino-Japanese War of 1894–1895: Perceptions, Power and Primacy* (Cambridge: Cambridge University Press, 2003), 132–134.

38 Stewart Lone, *Japan's First Modern War: Army and Society in the Conflict with China, 1894–95* (New York NY: St. Martin's, 1994), 66.

39 Lone, *Modern War*, 65.

40 "The Destruction of Kowshing. Statement of the Survivors" in *The North-China Herald and Supreme Court & Consular Gazette*, August 10, 1894, 238. "The Sinking of the Kowshing" in *The North-China Herald and Supreme Court & Consular Gazette*, August 10, 1894, 209.

41 Lone, *Modern War*, 155.

42 Ibid., 156.

43 David C. Evans and Mark R. Peattie, *Kaigun: Strategy, Tactics and Technology in the Imperial Japanese Navy 1887–1941* (Annapolis MD: Naval Institute Press, 1997), 57–60.

44 Paine, *Japanese Empire*, 52–53.

45 Tadokoro Masayuki, "Why Did Japan Fail to Become the 'Britain' of Asia?" in *The Russo-Japanese War in Global Perspective: World War Zero*, ed. John W. Steinberg et al. (Leiden: Brill, 2005), vol. 2, 302.

46 Evans and Peattie, *Kaigun*, 139–140.

47 Ibid., 97.

48 Denis and Peggy Warner, *The Tide at Sunrise: A History of the Russo-Japanese War 1904–1905* (London: Angus & Robertson, 1974), 206.

49 Ibid., 520.

50 Ibid., 509.

51 Y. Tak Matsusaka, "Human Bullets, General Nogi, and the Myth of Port Arthur," in *The Russo-Japanese War in Global Perspective: World War Zero*, ed. John W. Steinberg et al. (Leiden: Brill, 2005), vol. 1, 183.

52 E. Pauline Johnson. *Flint and Feather: The Complete Poems of E. Pauline Johnson.* (n. p.: Leopold Classical Library, 2016), 158–159.

53 Philip A. Towle, "Japanese Treatment of Prisoners in 1904–1905—Foreign Officers' Reports" in *Military Affairs*, October 1975, vol. 39, issue 3, pp. 115–117.

54 Shimazu Naoko, "Love Thine Enemy: Japanese Perceptions of Russia" in John W. Steinberg et al. (eds.). *The Russo-Japanese War in Global Perspective: World War Zero* (Leiden: Brill, 2005), 368.

55 Theodore Roosevelt, *Letters*, vol. 4. (Cambridge MA: Harvard University Press, 1951–1954), 1079.

56 Sun Yat-sen, *China and Japan: Natural Friends—Unnatural Enemies.* Shanghai, 1941, p. 143. Quoted in Marius B. Jansen, *The Japanese and Sun Yat-sen* (Stanford CA: Stanford University Press, 1970), 117.

57 Edgar Snow, *Red Star over China* (New York NY: Grove Press, 1968), 138.

58 Zhou Qiqian, "Chinese Intellectuals' View of Japan in the Late Qing" in *Sagacious Monks and Bloodthirsty Warriors: Chinese Views of Japan in the Ming-Qing Period*, ed. Joshua A. Fogel (Norwalk CT: Eastbridge, 2002), 253.

59 "Tsingtau gefallen" in *Berliner Tageblatt*, November 8, 1914, p. 1.

60 Adapted from Luo Zhitian, "National Humiliation and National Assertion: The Chinese Response to the 21 Demands" in *Modern Asian Studies* 27, no. 2 (May 1993): 317.

61 Frederick R. Dickinson, "Japan Debates the Anglo-Japanese Alliance: The Second Revision of 1911," in *The Anglo-Japanese Alliance 1902–1922*, ed. Phillips Payson O'Brien (London and New York NY: Routledge, 2004), 102. Paine, *Japanese Empire*, 82.

62 Walter LaFeber, *The Clash: A History of US-Japan Relations* (New York NY: Norton, 1997), 131.

63 Robert H. Ferrell, American Diplomacy in the Great Depression: Hoover-Stimson foreign policy, 1929–1933 (New Haven CT: Yale University Press, 1957), 154.

64 "Fengtien Troops' Misconduct" in *The North-China Herald and Supreme Court & Consular Gazette*, December 20, 1924, p. 484.

65 Jonathan Fenby, *Chiang Kai-shek: China's Generalissimo and the Nation He Lost* (New York NY: Carroll and Graf Publishers, 2003), 114.

66 Donald A. Jordan, *The Northern Expedition: China's National Revolution of 1926–1928* (Honolulu HI: The University Press of Hawaii, 1976), 79.

67 C. Martin Wilbur, "The Nationalist Revolution: from Canton to Nanking, 1923–1928," *Cambridge History of China, Volume 12 Republican China, 1912–1949 Pt I*, ed. John K. Fairbank (Cambridge: Cambridge University Press, 1983), 702–706.

68 Hallett Abend, *My Life in China 1926–1941* (New York NY: Harcourt, Brace and Company, 1943), 80.

69 Jay Taylor, *The Generalissimo: Chiang Kai-shek and the Struggle for Modern China* (Cambridge MA: The Belknap Press of Harvard University Press, 2009), 82–83.

70 See for example, Lloyd E. Eastman, *The Abortive Revolution: China under Nationalist Rule, 1927–1937* (Cambridge MA: Harvard University Asia Center, 1990).

71 See for example Michael Walker, *The 1929 Sino-Soviet War: The War Nobody Knew* (Lawrence KS: University Press of Kansas, 2007).

72 John Powell. "Russia Storms China Trenches; Set Town Afire," in *Chicago Daily Tribune*, November 18, 1929, p. 18.

73 "Hailar Reported in Flames," in the *New York Times*, November 26, 1929, p. 1.
74 John Powell. "Tell How Babes Die in Massacre of 1,000 in China" in *Chicago Daily Tribune*, November 19, 1929, p. 4.
75 Iriye Akira, *The Origins of the Second World War in Asia and the Pacific* (Harlow: Pearson, 1987), 13.
76 S. C. M. Paine, *The Wars for Asia 1911–1949* (Cambridge: Cambridge University Press, 2012), 84.
77 Iriye, *Origins*, 2.
78 Justus D. Doenecke and John E. Wilz, *From Isolation to War, 1931–1941* (Chichester: John Wiley & Sons, 2015), 26.
79 Ronald H. Spector, *Eagle Against the Sun: The American War with Japan* (New York NY: Vintage Books, 1985), 54.
80 Evans and Peattie, *Kaigun*, 129, 142.
81 Mark R. Peattie, *Ishiwara Kanji and Japan's Confrontation with the West* (Princeton NJ: Princeton University Press, 1975), 49–74.
82 US planners had "color" codes for each potential enemy: black for Germany, red for Great Britain, green for Mexico.
83 Mark R. Peattie, *Sunburst: The Rise of Japanese Naval Air Power, 1909–1941* (Annapolis MD: Naval Institute Press, 2001), 53–54.
84 Evans and Peattie, *Kaigun*, 300.
85 Koshihiro Yukiko, *Imperial Eclipse: Japan's Strategic Thinking about Continental Asia before August 1945* (Ithaca NY: Cornell University Press, 2013), 65.
86 Alvin D. Coox, *Nomonhan: Japan against Russia, 1939, vol. 1* (Stanford CA: Stanford University Press, 1985), 19.
87 Richard H. Mitchell, "Japan's Peace Preservation Law of 1925: Its Origin and Significance," *Monumenta Nipponica* 28, no. 3 (1973): 339–340.
88 Nakamura Takafusa, "Depression, recovery, and war, 1920–1945" in *The Cambridge History of Japan, vol. 6,* ed. Peter Duus. (Cambridge: Cambridge University Press, 1988), 464–465.
89 "Opening of the National People's Convention," *The North-China Herald*, May 12, 1931, 182–83.
90 Shimada Toshihiko, "The Extension of Hostilities, 1931–1932" in *Japan Erupts: The London Naval Conference and the Manchurian Incident, 1928–1932,* ed. James William Morley (New York NY: Columbia University Press, 1984), 242.
91 Iriye, *Origins*, 5–7.

Chapter 2

1 The city is called Shenyang today.
2 Coox, *Nomonhan*, vol. 1, 31. Seki Hiroharu, "The Manchurian Incident, 1931," in *Japan Erupts: The London Naval Conference and the Manchurian Incident, 1928–1932,* ed. James William Morley (New York NY: Columbia University Press, 1984), 227–28. Seki mistakenly identifies Kawamoto as Komato.
3 League of Nations, Commission of Enquiry into the Sino-Japanese Dispute. *Appeal by the Chinese Government: Report of the Commission of Enquiry [Lytton Report]* (Geneva: League of Nations, 1932), 68.
4 "Eye-Witness Tells of Japan Mukden Invasion: Artillery Opened Fire On Airdrome; Police, Soldiers Clash," *The China Press*, September 26, 1931, 11.
5 James E. Auer, *Who Was Responsible? From Marco Polo Bridge to Pearl Harbor* (Tokyo: The Yomiuri Shimbun, 2006), 56. Seki, "Manchurian Incident,," 229.
6 Guo Daijun, *Chongtan Kangrishi [Revisiting the Second Sino-Japanese War, 1931–1945],* vol. 1. (Taipei: Linking Book, 2015), 69.

7 Peattie, *Ishiwara*, 101ff.

8 Shimada, "Extension of Hostilities," 242.

9 Coox, *Nomonhan*, 32. Meirion and Susie Harries, *Soldiers of the Sun: The Rise and Fall of the Imperial Japanese Army* (New York NY: Random House, 1991), 153–54.

10 Auer, *Responsible*, 54. Shimada, "Extension of Hostilities," 242–47.

11 Klaus Schlichtmann, *Japan in the World: Shidehara Kijūrō, Pacifism, and the Abolition of War*, vol. II (Landham MD: Lexington Books, 2009), 50.

12 Auer, *Responsible*, 57.

13 Guo, *Chongtan*, 66–67. Some sources claim the Chinese side had an even larger numerical advantage of 1:20, see Peter Calvocoressi, Guy Wint and John Pritchard, *The Penguin History of the Second World War* (London: Penguin, 1999), 702.

14 Taylor, *Generalissimo*, 93.

15 Shimada, "Extension of Hostilities," 289.

16 League of Nations, *Lytton Report*, 72.

17 John B. Powell, *My Twenty-Five Years in China* (New York NY: MacMillan, 1945), 186.

18 Coox, *Nomonhan*, 40–1.

19 Iriye, *Origins*, 15.

20 Ogata Sadako, *Defiance in Manchuria: The Making of Japanese Foreign Policy, 1932–1932* (Berkeley and Los Angeles CA: University of California Press, 1964), 150.

21 Coox, *Nomonhan*, 42.

22 Donald A. Jordan, *China's Trial by Fire: The Shanghai War of 1932* (Ann Arbor MI: The University of Michigan Press, 2001), 7.

23 Coox, *Nomonhan*, 44–45. Jordan, *Trial*, 7, 11–12. Shimada, "Extension of Hostilities," 307.

24 Shimada, "Extension of Hostilities," 309–10.

25 Abend, *My Life*, 189.

26 "The Bombing of Chapei," *North-China Herald*, February 2, 1932, 147.

27 Abend, *Life*, 190.

28 Jordan, *Trial*, 189.

29 Haruko Taya Cook and Theodore F. Cook, *Japan at War: An Oral History* (New York NY: The New Press, 1992), 212. Jordan, *Trial*, 146.

30 Jordan, *Trial*, 171–185.

31 Carroll Alcott, *My War with Japan* (New York NY: Henry Holt and Co., 1943), 154.

32 Jordan, *Trial*, 153.

33 US Department of States, *Papers Relating to the Foreign Relations of the United States* (hereafter *FRUS*), *1931, vol. 3: The Far East* (Washington, D. C.: Government Printing Office, 1931), 51.

34 LaFeber, *Clash*, 169.

35 "Friendly and Impartial," *New York Times*, October 14, 1931, 22.

36 Coox, *Nomonhan*, 50.

37 Quoted in Christopher G. Thorne, *The Limits of Foreign Policy: The West, the League, and the Far Eastern Crisis, 1931–1933* (London: Macmillan, 1972), 138.

38 Quoted in Michael P. Richards, *The Presidency and the Middle Kingdom: China, the United States, and Executive Leadership* (Lanham MD: Lexington Books, 2000), 88.

39 Quoted in Thorne, *Limits*, 159.

40 Doenecke and Wilz, *Isolation*, 41.

41 Lansing Warren, "League Sets Nov. 16 for Withdrawal of the Japanese Troops in Manchuria; Russia Ready to Protect her Interests," *New York Times*, October 25, 1931, 1.

42 Doenecke and Wilz, *Isolation*, 45.

43 Ferrell, *American Diplomacy*, 155–69.

44 Ibid., 161–62.

45 Iriye, *Origins*, 14.

46 Henry Pu Yi and Paul Kramer, *The Last Manchu: The Autobiography of Henry Pu Yi, Last Emperor of China* (New York NY: Skyhorse Publishing, 2010), 163–64.

47 Lytton Report, 71.

48 Ibid., 106, 111.

49 Coox, *Nomonhan*, 53. Ogara, *Defiance*, 173.

50 Hugh Byas, "Japan Quits League to 'Insure Peace'," *New York Times*, March 28, 1933, 1.

51 Ibid.

52 Bix, *Hirohito*, 262.

53 Quoted in Thorne, *Limits*, 224.

54 Peattie, *Ishiwara*, 136.

55 "Chaplin Welcomed like King in Japan," *New York Times*, May 15, 1932, 7.

56 David Bergamini, *Japan's Imperial Conspiracy* (London: Heinemann, 1971), 496–501.

57 Miriam Silverberg, *Erotic Grotesque Nonsense: The Mass Culture of Japanese Modern Times* (Berkeley and Los Angeles CA: University of California Press, 2006), 1.

58 John Toland, *The Rising Sun: The Decline and Fall of the Japanese Empire 1936–1945* (New York NY: Random House, 1970), 11.

59 Quoted in Maruyama Masao, "The Ideology and Dynamics of Japanese Fascism," in *Thought and Behavior in Modern Japanese Politics*, ed. Ivan Morris (Oxford: Oxford University Press, 1969), 45.

60 Quoted ibid., 67.

61 Auer, *Responsible*, 57. Calvocoressi, *Second World War*, 771–78.

62 Calvocoressi, *Second World War*, 782–83. Iriye, *Origins*, 32–33.

63 Ben-Ami Shilloney, *Revolt in Japan: The Young Officers and the February 26, 1936 Incident* (Princeton NJ: Princeton University Press, 1973), 136–37.

64 Herbert P. Bix, *Hirohito and the Making of Modern Japan* (New York NY: Perennial, 2001), 297–305.

65 Shilloney, *Revolt*, 198–206.

66 Sandra Wilson, *The Manchurian Crisis and Japanese Society, 1931–33* (New York NY: Routledge, 2002), 31–32.

67 Louise Young, *Japan's Total Empire: Manchuria and the Culture of Wartime Imperialism* (Berkely and Los Angeles CA: University of California Press, 1999), 62–64.

68 Annika A. Culver, *Glorify the Empire: Japanese Avant-Garde Propaganda in Manchukuo* (Vancouver: UBC Press, 2013), 112.

69 Ohbuchi Hiroshi, "Demographic Transition in the Process of Japanese Industrialization" in *Historical Demography and Labor Markets in Prewar Japan*, ed. Michael Smitka (New York NY: Garland, 1998), 178.

70 Warren L. Thompson, *Danger Spots in World Population* (New York NY: Knopf, 1930), 119.

71 Ohbuchi, "Demographic Transition," 184.

72 Young, *Japan's Total Empire*, 352–54.

73 Ibid., 364.

74 Shimada Toshihiko, "Designs on North China, 1933–1937" in *The China Quagmire: Japan's Expansion on the Asian Continent 1933–1941*, ed. James William Morley (New York NY: Columbia University Press, 1983), 13–14.

75 Ibid., 15.

76 Ibid., 11ff.

77 Ibid., 12.

78 Bix, *Hirohito*, 258.

79 Hallett Abend, "Planes Rake Lines; Kill Many Chinese," *New York Times*, March 3, 1933, 4.

80 Toshihiko, "Designs," 26–27.

81 Ibid., 30.

82 Ibid., 33–34.

83 Bix, *Hirohito*, 271–72. Toshihiko, "Designs," 54–55.

84 Taylor, *Generalissimo*, 99.

85 "Japan Warns Powers on China; Threatens Force to Put End to Aid," *New York Times*, April 18, 1934, 1.

86 Edwin L. James, "Japan Puts Soft Glove on Her New China Policy," *New York Times*, April 29, 1934, E1.

87 Evans and Peattie, *Kaigun*, 296–98.

88 Charles A. Selden, "Davis Says Japan Upsets Security of All in Pacific; Fears Costly Naval Race," *New York Times*, December 7, 1934, 1.

89 Evans and Peattie, *Kaigun*, 297–98, 354. B. J. C. McKercher, *Transition of Power: Britain's Loss of Global Pre-Eminence to the United States, 1930–1945* (Cambridge: Cambridge University Press, 2004), 224.

90 Memorandum by Harcourt Smith, January 2, 1934. *Documents on British Foreign Policy, 1919–1939*, 2nd Series, Vol. XX, eds. W. Medicott et al. (London: HMSO, 1984), doc. 72, 141.

91 McKercher, *Transition*, 228.

92 Summary by Sir V. Wellesley, January 18, 1934. *Documents on British Foreign Policy, 1919–1939*, 2nd Series, Vol. XX, doc. 77, 153.

93 Stephen Lyon Endicott, *Diplomacy and Enterprise: British China Policy, 1933–1937* (Manchester: Manchester University Press, 1975), 113.

94 John P. Fox, *Germany and the Far Eastern Crisis 1931–1938: A Study in Diplomacy and Ideology* (Oxford: Oxford University Press, 1982), 53.

95 Fox, *Germany*, 77.

96 Otto Tolischus, *Tokyo Record* (New York NY: Reynold & Hitchcock, 1943), 159.

97 Fox, *Germany*, 178–80.

98 Ibid., 207.

99 Ibid., 203–205.

100 Jonathan Haslam, *The Soviet Union and the Threat from the East, 1933–1941* (Pittsburgh PA: University of Pittsburgh Press, 1992), 50.

101 James MacGregor Burns, *Roosevelt: The Lion and the Fox* (New York NY: Harcourt Brace and Co., 1956), 51.

102 Robert Dallek, *Franklin D. Roosevelt and American Foreign Policy, 1932–1945* (Oxford: Oxford University Press, 1995), 75. John C. Walter, "Congressman Carl Vinson and Franklin D. Roosevelt: Naval Preparedness and the Coming of World War II," *Georgia Historical Quarterly* 64, no. 3 (1980): 296.

103 E. B. Potter, *Sea Power: A Naval History* (Annapolis MD: Naval Institute Press, 1981), 236.

104 Ibid., 236–237.

105 Evans and Peattie, *Kaigun*, 370–73.

106 Ibid., 304.

107 Ibid., 333–34.

108 Allan R. Millett, "Assault from the Sea: Development of Amphibious Warfare between the Wars" in *Military Innovation in the Interwar Period*, eds. Williamson R. Murray and Allan R. Millett (Cambridge: Cambridge University Press, 1996), 53–54.

109 Evans and Peattie, *Kaigun*, 443.

110 Millett, "Assault," 69–70.
111 Evans and Peattie, *Kaigun*, 291.
112 Iriye, *Origins*, 34–35.
113 Ibid.
114 Theodore H. White and Annalee Jacoby, *Thunder Out of China* (Cambridge MA: Da Capo Press, 1980), 129.
115 Jonathan Spence, *The Search for Modern China*, 2nd edition (New York NY: W. W. Norton, 1999), 393.
116 Stephen C. Averill, "The Origins of the Futian Incident" in *New Perspectives on the Chinese Communist Revolution*, eds. Tony Saich and Hans van de Ven (Armonk NY: M. E. Sharpe, 1995), 79ff.
117 Spence, *Search*, 397–403.
118 James B. Crowley, *Japan's Quest for Autonomy: National Security and Foreign Policy 1930–1938* (Princeton NJ: Princeton University Press, 1966), 214–217. Fox, 126–127.
119 The Xian incident has been subject of numerous historical accounts, for example Taylor, *Generalissimo*, 125–37 and John W. Garver, "The Soviet Union and the Xi'an Incident," *The Australian Journal of Chinese Affairs*, no. 26 (1991): 145–75. Although the rough sequence of events is well established, the details remain in dispute. A recent reassessment is Steve Tsang, "Chiang Kai-shek's 'secret deal' at Xian and the start of the Sino-Japanese War" in *Palgrave Communications*, no. 1, 2015.
120 Taylor, *Generalissimo*, 127.
121 Moscow's exact role in the incident is the subject of scholarly controversy. Tsang, "Secret Deal," argues that the Chinese communists decided against executing Chiang before being urged by Moscow to keep him alive.
122 When Chiang Kai-shek withdrew to Taiwan in 1949, the Young Marshal was moved to the island too, for continued house arrest. He was eventually freed and moved to Hawaii, where he died in 2001, aged 100.
123 "Dr. Kung's New Year Reflections," *The China Press,* January 3, 1937, 10.
124 "Arita Answers Critics in New Year Message," *The China Press*, January 1, 1937, 1.
125 Iriye, *Origins*, 38.
126 *FRUS 1937, vol. 3: The Far East*, 39–40.
127 Gerald E. Bunker, *The Peace Conspiracy: Wang Ching-wei and the China War, 1937–1941* (Cambridge MA: Harvard University Press, 1972), 19.
128 *FRUS, 1937, vol. 3: The Far East*, 594.
129 Peattie, *Ishiwara*, 283.
130 Bunker, *Conspiracy*, 19.
131 Iriye, *Origins*, 38.
132 Auer, *Responsible*, 69.

Chapter 3

1 Crowley, *Japan's Quest*, 324–38. Prior to Crowley's seminal research, it was generally assumed that the Japanese army in China engineered the Marco Polo Bridge incident. Hata Ikuhiko, "The Marco Polo Bridge Incident, 1937" in *The China Quagmire: Japan's Expansion on the Asian Continent 1933–1941*, ed. James William Morley (New York NY: Columbia University Press, 1983), 245ff.
2 The source for the troop strength numbers is Hattori Satoshi with Edward J. Drea, "Japanese Operations from July to December 1937" in *The Battle for China: Essays on the Military History of the Sino-Japanese War of 1937–1945* eds. Mark Peattie et al. (Stanford CA: Stanford University Press, 2011), 161. For the number of Japanese civilians, the source is Hata, "Incident," 251.

3 Guo, *Chongtan*, 246–47. Hata, "Incident," 247. Taylor, *Generalissimo*, 145.

4 Guo, *Chongtan*, 246–47. Hata, "Incident," 247–48.

5 Taylor, *Generalissimo*, 145.

6 Hata, "Incident," 248–49.

7 Ibid., 250.

8 Barbara W. Tuchman, *Stilwell and the American Experience in China 1911–1945* (New York NY: Random House, 2017), 202.

9 Guo, *Chongtan*, 259, 262–63.

10 Zhou Tiandu, "Cong Qiqi Shibian qianhou Jiang Jieshi riji kan ta de kangri zhuzhang ["A Look at Chiang Kai-shek's Position on Resisting Japan Based on His Diary Before and After the July 7 Incident"], *Kangri Zhanzheng Yanjiu [Journal of Studies of China's Resistance War Against Japan]*, no. 2 (2008): 138.

11 Hata, "Incident," 250–54.

12 Guo Rugui. Zhongguo Kangri Zhanzheng zhengmian zhanchang zuozhanji [China's War of Resistance against Japan: An Account of Frontline Battles], vol. 1 (Nanjing: Jiangsu Renmin Chubanshe, 2006), 335. Cui Zhenlun, "Langfang kangzhan shimo" ["The Langfang Battle from Beginning to End"], in *Qiqi Shibian: Yuan Guomindang jiangling Kangri Zhanzheng qinliji [The 7.7. Incident: Personal Recollections from the War of Resistance against Japan by Former Nationalist Commanders]* (hereafter: *Qiqi*) (Beijing: Zhongguo Wenshi Chubanshe, 1986), 102–105. Xing Bingnan. "Jizhan Langfang chezhan" ["Fierce Battle for Langfang Station"], in *Qiqi*, 110–113.

13 Hata, "Incident," 258.

14 Ibid., 254–60.

15 Cui, "Langfang," 104.

16 Ibid., 104–05.

17 Ibid., 105–06. Xing, "Jizhan," 111–12.

18 Hata, "Incident," 256.

19 Ibid., 260.

20 Guo, *Zhongguo*, vol. 1, 335.

21 Ibid., vol. 1, 339–40. Hata, "Incident," 260.

22 Bix, *Hirohito*, 321.

23 Guo, *Zhongguo*, vol. 1, 340. "Japanese Occupy Nanyuan After Short, Sharp Engagement," *The China Weekly Review*, August 7, 1937, 353.

24 "Piteous Scenes Witnessed in Nanyuan; Road, Ditches Filled With 500 Dead Bodies," *The China Press*, July 30, 1937, 1.

25 James Bertram, *North China Front* (London: MacMillan, 1939), 77–78.

26 Graham Peck, *Through China's Wall* (Boston MA: Houghton Mifflin, 1940), 322.

27 Guo, *Zhongguo*, vol. 1, 341.

28 Ibid., 341–344.

29 Frank Dorn. *The Sino-Japanese War 1937–41: From Marco Polo Bridge to Pearl Harbor* (New York NY: MacMillan, 1974), 42

30 Bix, 322.

31 International Military Tribunal for the Far East (hereafter IMTFE), *Transcript of Proceedings*, pp. 20,847–20,853.

32 Abend, *Life*, 247.

33 Peter Harmsen, *Shanghai 1937: Stalingrad on the Yangtze* (Havertown PA: Casemate, 2013), 13–43.

34 Ibid., 69–91.

35 Ibid., 45–67.

36 Percy Finch, *Shanghai and Beyond* (New York NY: Charles Scribner's Son, 1953), 255–256.

37 The name of the financier was Vandeleur Grayburn, the governor of the Hong Kong-Shanghai Bank, see John Haffenden, *William Empson: Among the Mandarins* (Oxford: Oxford University Press, 2005), 483, 659.

38 Zhang Fakui, *Reminiscences of Fa-K'uei Chang: Oral History, 1970–1980* (Columbia University Libraries, Oral History Research Office), 457.

39 Komatsu Keiichirō, "Misunderstanding and Mistranslation in the Origins of the Pacific War of 1941–1945: The Importance of 'Magic'," (paper delivered at Burma Campaign Society, on May 9, 2002), 7.

40 See for example "Chinese Reinforce Shanghai Defense; Morale Unbroken," *New York Times*, October 29, 1937, 1.

41 Li Junsan, *Shanghai Nanjing Baoweizhan [Defensive Battles for Shanghai and Nanjing]* (Taipei: Maitian chubanshe, 1997), 152.

42 Xu Fan and Zhen Rui, *Zhongri Zhuangiabing Quanshi 1918–1937 [A History of Armored Forces in China and Jaoan 1918–1937]* (Beijing: Zhongguo Changan chubanshe, 2015), 274–280, 300–312.

43 Leland Ness, *Rikugun: Guide to Japanese Ground Forces 1937–1945, vol. 2* (Solihull: Helion & Co., 2015), 263–64.

44 Ibid., *vol.2*, 269.

45 Geir Teitler and Kurt W. Radtke (eds.), *A Dutch Spy in China: Reports on the First Phase of the Sino-Japanese War 1937–1939* (Leiden: Brill, 1999), 162–163.

46 Evans and Peattie, *Kaigun*, 443–444.

47 Millett, "Assault," 92.

48 Robert P. Post. "Roosevelt Urges 'Concerted Action'," *New York Times*, October 6, 1937, p. 1.

49 Harold L. Ickes, *The Secret Diary of Harold L. Ickes. Vol. II: The Inside Struggle 1936–1939* (New York NY: Simon and Schuster, 1954), 213.

50 Dorothy Borg, *The United States and the Far Eastern Crisis of 1933–1938* (Cambridge MA: Harvard University Press, 1964), 382.

51 Samuel I. Rosenman, *Working with Roosevelt* (New York NY: Harper, 1952), 166.

52 Borg, 391.

53 Greg Kennedy, *Anglo-American Strategic Relations and the Far East 1933–1939: Imperial Crossroads* (London and New York NY: Routledge, 2002), 235.

54 Tsien Tai, *China and the Nine Power Conference at Brussels in 1937* (New York: St. John's University Press, 1964), 2.

55 For the full text of the Treaty, see *FRUS 1922, vol. I*, 276–281.

56 Tsien, *China*, p. 2.

57 *Brussels Conference Convened in Virtue of Article 7 of the Washington Treaty of 1922: Acts of the Conference* (hereafter *Brussels Conference*) (Brussels: A. Lesigne, n.d.), 40.

58 Borg, *United States*, 422–423.

59 Ibid., 427–430.

60 *Brussels Conference*, 79–80.

61 Borg, *United States*, 637–638.

62 Kennedy, *Anglo-American*, 238.

63 Ibid., 239.

64 Fox, *Germany*, 251–252.

65 Ibid., 265–272.

66 Hata, "Marco Polo Bridge," 456–457, note 97.

67 Cheng Siyuan, *Zhenghai Mixin [Behind the Scenes of Politics]* (Taipei, Li Ao chubanshe, 1995), 156.

68 FRUS, 1937, vol. 3: The Far East, 827.

69 Jiang Zhongzheng (Chiang Kai-shek), *Kunmian ji [Anthology of Encouragement amid Difficulties]* (Taipei: Guoshiguan, 2011), 569.

70 John W. Garver, *Chinese-Soviet Relations 1937–1945* (Oxford: Oxford University Press, 1988), 20–21.
71 Edward L. Dreyer, *China at War, 1901–1949* (London and New York NY: Longman, 1995), 213.
72 Satoshi and Drea, "Japanese Operations," 163.
73 Guo, *Zhongguo*, vol. 1, 398.
74 Dorn, *Sino-Japanese*, 109.
75 Satoshi and Drea, "Japanese Operations," 163.
76 Peck, *Wall*, 327.
77 The city of now known as Zhangjiakou.
78 Dorn, *Sino-Japanese*, 51.
79 Dreyer, *War*, 213–215.
80 Aaron William Moore, "The Peril of Self-Discipline: Chinese Nationalist, Japanese, and American Servicemen Record the Rise and Fall of the Japanese Empire 1937–1945" (PhD diss., Princeton University, 2006), 108.
81 Jiang Keshi, "Pingxingguan dajie Rijun sishangshu kaozheng" ["An Investigation of Japanese Casualties in the Pingxing Pass Victory," *Bunka Kyōseigaku [Studies in Cultural Symbiotics]*, no. 3 (2017): 61–62.
82 Anna Louise Strong, *One-Fifth of Mankind* (New York NY: Modern Age Books, 1938), 104.
83 Benjamin Yang, *Deng: A Political Biography* (Armonk NY: M. E. Sharpe, 1997), 86.
84 Peter Harmsen, *Nanjing 1937: Battle for a Doomed City* (Havertown PA: Casemate, 2015), 131–132.
85 Ibid., 189.
86 Ibid., 241.
87 Iriye, *Origins*, 52.
88 Ibid., 48.
89 Li Tsung-jen (Li Zongren) et al., *The Memoirs of Li Tsung-jen* (Boulder CO: Westview Press, 1979), 335.
90 Ruth Benedict, *The Chrysanthemum and the Sword* (Boston MA: Houghton Mifflin Harcourt, 1946), 2.

Chapter 4

1 F. P. Polynin, "Erfüllung einer internationalistischen Pflicht" ["Discharge of an International Duty"] in *Am Himmel über China: Erinnerungen sowjetischer freiwilliger Flieger [In the Sky over China: Memoirs of Volunteer Soviet Airmen]* (Berlin: Militärverlag der Deutschen Demokratischen Republik, 1986), 70–71.
2 Present-day Taipei.
3 Aleksandr Kalyagin, *Along Alien Roads* (New York NY: The East Asian Institute, Columbia University, 1983), 47–48.
4 "Navy Shows No Surprise Over Bombing of Taiwan; Creates Sensation Abroad," *Japan Times and Mail*, February 24, 1938, 1.
5 Zhang, *Reminiscences*, 504.
6 Ibid., 504.
7 Fox, *Germany*, 292–293.
8 Ibid., 293
9 Hata, "Incident," 283.
10 Auer, *Responsible*, 78.
11 Cowley, *Quest*, 374–375.
12 Hata, "Incident," 286.
13 Bix, *Hirohito*, 345–346.

14 Auer, *Responsible*, 78.

15 Bix, *Hirohito*, 345.

16 Hata, "Incident," 286.

17 Iriye, *Origins*, 53.

18 Hans van de Ven, *China at War: Triumph and Tragedy in the Emergence of the New China, 1937–1952* (London: Profile Books, 2017), 101.

19 Iriye, *Origins*, 58.

20 Garver, *Chinese-Soviet*, 29.

21 There are several conflicting versions of the circumstances surrounding Han's execution following his death sentence. See Diana Lary, "Treachery, Disgrace and Death: Han Fuju and China's Resistance to Japan," *War in History* 13, no. 1 (January 2006): 81–82. See also Stephen Mackinnon, "The Defense of the Central Yangtze" in *The Battle for China: Essays on the Military History of the Sino-Japanese War of 1937–1945* eds. Mark Peattie et al. (Stanford CA: Stanford University Press, 2011), 181.

22 Diana Lary, "Defending China: The Battles of the Xuzhou Campaign" in *Warfare in Chinese History* ed. Hans K. Van De Ven (Boston MA: Brill, 2000) 409–412.

23 Barbara Barnouin and Yu Changgen, *Zhou Enlai: A Political Life* (Hong Kong: Chinese University of Hong Kong, 2006), 71.

24 Meng Qisan, "Taierzhuang de xiangzhan" ["Streets Battles at Taierzhuang"] in *Xuzhou Huizhan: Yuan Guomindang jiangling Kangri Zhanzheng qinliji [Battle of Xuzhou: Personal Recollections from the War of Resistance against Japan by Former Nationalist Commanders]* (hereafter: *Xuzhou*) (Beijing: Zhongguo Wenshi Chubanshe, 1990), 179.

25 Li, *Memoirs*, 353–354.

26 Du Yuming, "Taierzhuang Dazhanzhong de zhanchefangyupao budui" ["An Anti-Tank Gun Unit at the Great Battle of Taierzhuang"] in *Xuzhou*, 206–207.

27 Li, *Memoirs*, 356.

28 F. Tillman Durdin, "Chinese Increase Shantung Victory," *New York Times*, April 9, 1938, p. 7.

29 For general descriptions of the battles at Xuzhou and Taierzhuang, the following are useful: Mackinnon, "Defense," 194–195. Paine, *Wars for Asia*, 138–140. Marvin Williamsen, "The Military Dimension, 1937–1941" in *China's Bitter Victory: The War with Japan 1937–1945* eds. James C. Hsiung et al. (Armonk NY: M. E. Sharpe, 1992), 139–142.

30 Xiong Xianyu, "1938 Huanghe jueti shiliao yizu" ["Historical Materials on Breaching the Yellow River Dykes in 1938"], *Minguo Dang'an*, no. 3 (1997): 11. See also Rana Mitter, *China's War with Japan 1937–1945: The Struggle for Survival* (London: Allen Lane, 2013), 155–167.

31 Ma Zhonglian, "Huayuankou jueti de junshi yiyi," *Kangri Zhanzheng Yanjiu*, no. 4 (1999): 212.

32 Diana Lary, "Drowned Earth: The Strategic Breaching of the Yellow River Dyke, 1938," *War in History* 8, no. 2 (2001): 206.

33 Lary, "Drowned," 205.

34 John Hunter Boyle. *China and Japan at War, 1937–1945: The Politics of Collaboration* (Stanford CA: Stanford University Press, 1972), 156–160. Zhang Bofeng, "Guanyu Kangri Zhanzheng shiqi Jiang Jiashi fandong jituan de jici tuoxie touxiang huodong" ["Regarding Several Appeasement and Capitulationist Activities by the Chiang Kai-shek Clique during the Anti-Japanese War"], *Jindaishi Yanjiu*, no. 2 (1979): 216.

35 Boyle, *China*, 156.

36 Iriye, *Origins*, 60. Bradford A. Lee. *Britain and the Sino-Japanese War, 1937–1939* (Stanford CA: Stanford University Press, 1973), 140.

37 Boyle, *China*, 156.

38 Wilfrid Fleisher. *Volcanic Isle* (Garden City NY: Doubleday, Doran and Co., 1941), 152.

39 Ibid., 145–146, 159.

40 Usui Katsumi, "The Politics of War," in *The China Quagmire: Japan's Expansion on the Asian Continent 1933–1941*, ed. James William Morley (New York NY: Columbia University Press, 1983), 331.

41 Boyle, *China*, 157.

42 Ibid., 158.

43 Ibid.

44 Iriye, *Origins*, 61.

45 Usui, "Politics," 330–331.

46 Lee, *Britain*, 142.

47 Ibid.

48 Ibid., 145.

49 Franco David Macri. *Clash of Empires in South China: The Allied Nations' Proxy War with Japan, 1935–1941* (Lawrence KS: University Press of Kansas, 2012), 73.

50 *FRUS, Japan: 1931–1941*, vol. 1, 781–790.

51 Edward S. Miller. *Bankrupting the Enemy: The U. S. Financial Siege of Japan Before Pearl Harbor* (Annapolis MD: Naval Institute Press, 2007), 77–78.

52 Du Longji. "Madang yaosai Changshan zhendi baoweizhan" ["The Defensive Battle for the Key River Barrier at Madang and the Position on Mount Chang"] in *Wuhan Huizhan: Yuan Guomindang jiangling Kangri Zhanzheng qinliji [The Wuhan Battle: Personal Recollections from the War of Resistance against Japan by Former Nationalist Commanders]* (Beijing: Zhongguo Wenshi Chubanshe, 1989), 31–32. Guo, *Zhongguo, vol. 2,* 795.

53 Guo, *Zhongguo*, vol. 2, 794.

54 Du, "Madang," 32.

55 Ibid., 33–34.

56 Ibid., 36. Guo, *Chongtan*, 463. Guo, *Zhongguo, Vol. 2,* 795.

57 Guo, *Zhongguo*, vol. 2, 796–797.

58 Ibid., vol. 2, 801.

59 Dorn, *Sino-Japanese*, 197–199.

60 Stephen Mackinnon. *Wuhan, 1938: War, Refugees, and the Making of Modern China* (Berkeley CA: University of California Press, 2008), 39.

61 Dorn, *Sino-Japanese*, 199.

62 Coox, *Nomonhan, vol. 1,* 128. IMTFE, *Transcript of Proceedings*, 7,807, 22,931, 38,291–38,292.

63 Hata Ikuhiko, "The Japanese-Soviet Confrontation, 1935–1939" in *Deterrent Diplomacy: Japan, Germany and the USSR 1935–1940*, ed. James William Morley (New York NY: Columbia University Press, 1976), 133.

64 Coox, *Nomonhan*, vol. 1, 120–122, 128–129.

65 Headquarters United States Armed Forces, Far East and Eighth United States Army Military History Section, *Japanese Night Combat* (n.p., 1955), part 3, 477–497.

66 Coox, *Nomonhan*, vol. 1, 134.

67 Haslam, *Soviet*, 118.

68 Coox, *Nomonhan*, vol. 1, 134.

69 Ibid., vol. 1, 135–136.

70 Iriye, *Origins*, 61–62.

71 Haslam, *Soviet*, 112.

72 Kuromiya Hiroaki, "The Battle of Lake Khasan Reconsidered," *The Journal of Slavic Military Studies* 29, no. 1 (2016):108.

73 Reuters, "China Sends Protest to Berlin Over Recognition, in *The China Press*, February 26, 1938, 1.

74 Hsi-Huey Liang. *The Sino-German Connection: Alexander von Falkenhausen Between China and Germany 1900–1941* (Amsterdam: van Gorcum, 1978), 134.

75 Quoted in Fox, *Germany*, 330.
76 Liang, *Sino-German*, 135.
77 Fox, *Germany*, 253.
78 Ōhata Tokushirō, "The Anti-Comintern Pact, 1935–1939" in *Deterrent Diplomacy: Japan, Germany and the USSR 1935–1940*, ed. James William Morley (New York NY: Columbia University Press, 1976), 55.
79 Dreyer, *War*, 231.
80 John R. Watt. *Saving Lives in Wartime China: How Medical Reformers Built Modern Healthcare Systems Amid War and Epidemics, 1928–1945* (Leiden: Brill, 2014), 133.
81 Fleisher, *Volcanic Isle*, 150.
82 Mackinnon, "Defense," 199.
83 Li, *Memoirs*, 374–375.
84 Dreyer, *War*, 231–232.
85 Zhang, *Reminiscences*, 505.
86 Dreyer, *War*, 230.
87 Zhang, *Reminiscences*, 501.
88 Teitler and Radtke, *Dutch Spy*, 269.
89 Ibid., 270.
90 Vincent K. L. Chang and Yong Zhou, "Redefining Wartime Chongqing: International capital of a global power in the making, 1938–46," *Modern Asian Studies* 51, no. 3 (2017), 583–584.
91 Quoted in Chang and Zhou, "Wartime Chongqing," 578–579.
92 Taylor, *Generalissimo*, 159–160.
93 Lary, *People*, 63.
94 Ibid., 64.
95 Joy Homer, *Dawn Watch in China* (Boston MA: Houghton Mifflin, 1941), 36–37.
96 Ibid., 39.
97 Bunker, *Conspiracy*, 108.
98 Ibid., 113–114.
99 Usui, "Politics," 383–385.
100 Bunker, *Conspiracy*, 120–121.

Chapter 5

1 Zhou Jun, "Banian Kangzhan zhong Guomindang Juntong de jingdian ansha zhiyi: Ansha Nanjing 'Zhonghua Minguo Weixing Zhengfu' Wajiaobuzhang Chen Lu" ["One of the classic assassinations carried out by the Kuomintang's Bureau of Investigation and Statistics during the eight-year War of Resistance: Killing Foreign Minister Chen Lu of the Nanjing Reformed Government of the Republic of China"], *Wenshi Yuekan* (September 2008): 29.
2 Oliver J. Caldwell, *A Secret War: Americans in China 1944–1945* (Carbondale Il: Southern Illinois University Press, 1972), 73. Frederic Wakeman Jr. *Spymaster: Dai Li and the Chinese Secret Service* (Berkeley CA: University of California Press, 2003), 1.
3 Milton E. Miles, *A Different Kind of War* (Garden City NY: Doubleday, 1967), 54.
4 Wen-Hsin Yeh, "Dai Li and the Liu Geqing Affair: Heroism in the Chinese Secret Service During the War of Resistance," *The Journal of Asian Studies*, 48, no. 3 (August 1989): 549–550.
5 Wen-Hsin Yeh, "Prologue: Shanghai besieged, 1937–45," in *Wartime Shanghai*, ed. Wen-Hsin Yeh (London: Routledge, 1998), 7.
6 Frederic Wakeman Jr., *The Shanghai Badlands: Wartime Terrorism and Urban Crime 1937–1941* (Cambridge: Cambridge University Press, 1996), 87.

7 Boyle, *China*, 285. Wakeman, *Shanghai Badlands*, 194n38. The story of Ding's assassination formed the basis of the 2007 thriller film *Lust, Caution* by director Ang Lee.

8 Ibid.

9 Brian G. Martin, "'In My Heart I Opposed Opium': Opium and the Politics of the Wang Jingwei Government, 1940–45," *The European Journal of East Asian Studies 2* (2003): 368–369.

10 Bunker, *Conspiracy*, 131–132.

11 Ibid., 135–150.

12 Tobe Ryōichi, "The Japanese Eleventh Army in Central China," in *The Battle for China: Essays on the Military History of the Sino-Japanese War of 1937–1945*, eds. Mark Peattie et al. (Stanford CA: Stanford University Press, 2011), 215.

13 Ibid., 215.

14 Ibid., 216.

15 Ibid.

16 Dorn, Sino-Japanese War, 255.

17 Edna Tow, "The Great Bombing of Chongqing and the Anti-Japanese War, 1937–1945," in *The Battle for China: Essays on the Military History of the Sino-Japanese War of 1937–1945*, eds. Mark Peattie et al. (Stanford CA: Stanford University Press, 2011), 259.

18 Ibid., 260–261.

19 F. Tillman Durdin. "Chungking Is Fighting Vast Fire, Started by the Japanese Bombings," *New York Times*, May 6, 1939, 4.

20 Claire Lee Chennault, *Way of a Fighter* (New York NY: G. P. Putnam's Sons, 1949), 88.

21 F. Tillman Durdin. "Hundreds Killed in Chungking Raid," *New York Times*, May 4, 1939, 16.

22 FRUS, Japan: 1931–1941, vol. 1, 800.

23 Bix, *Hirohito*, 349–350. Iriye, *Origins*, 67–68.

24 FRUS, Japan: 1931–1941, vol. 1, 818.

25 Ibid., *vol. 1*, 826.

26 Jonathan G. Utley, *Going to War with Japan, 1937–1941* (New York NY: Fordham University Press, 2005), 44–47.

27 E. B. Potter, *Nimitz* (Annapolis MD: Naval Institute Press, 1976), 169.

28 Wayne S. Cole, *Roosevelt and the Isolationists 1932–45* (Lincoln NE: University of Nebraska Press, 1983), 268–269.

29 Louis Morton, *Strategy and Command: The First Two Years. [United States Army in World War II: The War in the Pacific]* (Washington DC: Office of the Chief of Military History, Department of the Army, 1962), 22.

30 Ibid., 42.

31 Edward S. Miller, *War Plan Orange: The U. S. Strategy to Defeat Japan, 1897–1945* (Annapolis, MD: Naval Institute Press, 1991), 223–225.

32 Ibid., 351.

33 Thomas A. Fabyanic and Robert F. Futrell, "Early Intelligence Organization in the Army Air Corps," in *Piercing the Fog: Intelligence and Army Air Forces Operations in in World War II*, ed. John F. Kreis (Washington DC: Air Force History and Museums Program, 1996), 30.

34 Chennault, *Way of a Fighter*, 93.

35 "Japanese Aide Here to Plan Fair Exhibit," *New York Times*, June 7, 1938, 10. Helena Capkova. "Transnational Networkers—Iwao and Michiko Yamawaki and the Formation of Japanese Modernist Design," *Journal of Design History* 27, no. 4 (November 2014): 370–385.

36 "Japanese Shatter Record to London," *New York Times*, April 10, 1937, 9.

37 Lionel Wigmore. *The Japanese Thrust (Australia in the War of 1939–1945. Series I. Army, vol. 1)* (Canberra: Australian War Memorial, 1957), 5.

38 Sven Matthiessen. *Japanese Pan-Asianism and the Philippines from the Late Nineteenth Century to the End of World War II: Going to the Philippines Is Like Coming Home?* (Leiden: Brill, 2015), 59.

39 J. Calvitt Clarke III, *Alliance of the Colored Peoples: Ethiopia and Japan Before World War II* (Oxford: James Currey for the International African Institute, 2011), xv.

40 Ibid., 93.

41 Ibid., xii–xiii.

42 Ibid., 148–163.

43 Lawrence Fouraker, "Saito Takao and Parliamentary Politics in 1930s Japan," in *Sino-Japanese Studies* 12, no. 2 (2000): 11.

44 Iriye, *Origins*, 58.

45 Auer, *Responsible*, 83. Fouraker, "Saito," 13–14.

46 Fouraker, "Saito," 12.

47 Wm. Theodore de Bary et al. (eds), *Sources of Japanese Tradition, Volume Two: 1600 to 2000, Part Two: 1868 to 2000* (New York NY: Columbia University Press, 2006), 279.

48 Reuter, "Tientsin New Regime High Official Shot," *The North China Herald*, April 12, 1939, 53. AP, "Chinese Physician Slain," *New York Times*, April 11, 1939, 8.

49 Ding Wei, "Cheng Xigeng shijian zhenxiang" ["The Truth about the Cheng Xigeng Incident"], *Wenshi Jinghua*, no. 230 (2009): 53–58.

50 Lee, *Britain*, 183–185. "Japanese Tighten Tientsin Cordon," *New York Times*, June 15, 1939, 12.

51 Lee, *Britain*, 185–204.

52 The four were detained immediately upon the handover. There appears to be no known reference in the records to their further fates in Japanese-occupied China. See Ding, "Cheng Xigeng."

53 Usui, "Politics," 338.

54 Iriye, *Origins*, 76–77.

55 Auer, *Responsible*, 87–88.

56 Michael A. Barnhart, *Japan Prepares for Total War: The Search for Economic Security, 1919–1941* (Ithaca NY: Cornell University Press, 1987), 138–140.

57 Iriye, *Origins*, 75–76.

58 Barnhart, *Japan*, 140–141, 167–168.

59 Guo, *Zhongguo*, vol. 1, 930–933.

60 *Political Strategy Prior to the Outbreak of War [Japanese Monograph no. 144]* (Tokyo: Military History Section Headquarters, 1952), 46–47.

61 Arthur J. Marder, *Old Friends, New Enemies: The Royal Navy and the Imperial Japanese Navy* (Oxford: Clarendon Press, 1981), 45.

62 Lee, *Britain*, 176. Marder, *Friends*, 45.

63 Iriye, *Origins*, 76.

64 Lee, *Britain*, 187.

65 Miller, *Bankrupting*, 78–79.

66 Usui, "Politics," 348–349.

67 G. K. Zhukov, *The Memoirs of Marshal Zhukov* (New York NY: Delacorte Press, 1971), 147.

68 Coox, *Nomonhan*, vol. 1, 251.

69 Ibid., 191.

70 Stuart D. Goldman, *Nomonhan, 1939: The Red Army's Victory That Shaped World War II* (Annapolis MD: Naval Institute Press, 2012), 105.

71 Coox, *Nomonhan*, 175.

72 Kuromiya Hiroaki. "The Mystery of Nomonhan, 1939," *The Journal of Slavic Military Studies*, vol. 24, no. 4, 2011, 660–662.

73 Coox, *Nomonhan*, 284ff.

74 Zhukov, *Memoirs*, 151.
75 Coox, *Nomonhan*, 379. Goldman, *Nomonhan*, 118.
76 Goldman, *Nomonhan*, 120.
77 Coox, *Nomonhan*, 311.
78 Goldman, *Nomonhan*, 119.
79 Coox, *Nomonhan*, 340–341. Zhukov, *Memoirs*, 153.
80 Goldman, *Nomonhan*, 126.
81 Coox, *Nomonhan*, 546.
82 Goldman, *Nomonhan*, 132.
83 Ibid.
84 Zhukov, *Memoirs*, 155.
85 Ibid., 156–157.
86 Coox, *Nomonhan*, 705–706.
87 Zhukov, *Memoirs*, 161.
88 Coox, *Nomonhan*, 750–751.
89 Goldman, *Nomonhan*, 141.
90 Ibid., 148.
91 Coox, *Nomonhan*, 572.
92 Kuromiya, "Mystery," 670.
93 Iriye, *Origins*, 78.
94 Galeazzo Ciano, *The Ciano Diaries, 1939–1943* (Garden City NY: Doubleday and Company, 1946), 39.
95 Auer, *Responsible*, 88–89.
96 Paine, *Wars*, 164.
97 van de Ven, *War and Nationalism*, 237.
98 Ibid.
99 Ibid., 237–238.
100 Tobe, "Eleventh," 219.
101 Dorn, *Sino-Japanese War*, 281.
102 Ibid., 282–283.
103 Usui, "Politics," 367.
104 Ibid., 368.
105 *FRUS, 1939: The Far East*, 622.
106 Iriye, *Origins*, 86–88.
107 Ibid., 83–85.
108 Hosoya Chihiro, "The Tripartite Pact," in *Deterrent Diplomacy: Japan, Germany and the USSR 1935–1940*, ed. James William Morley (New York NY: Columbia University Press, 1976), 192.

Chapter 6

1 "Li Jiefu: Kunlunguan yige kang jiu maile 4500 ming xisheng zhanshi" ["Li Jiefu: At Kunlun Pass, 4500 Dead Warriors Were Buried in One Mass Grave"] https://www.thepaper.cn/newsDetail_forward_1902397

2 Academy of Military Science, *Zhongguo Kangri Zhanzhengshi [History of China's War of Resistance Against Japan]* (Beijing: Jiefangjun Chubanshe, 2000), vol. 2, 502. Cao Jianlang, *Zhongguo Guomindangjun Jianshi [An Outline History of the Kuomintang's Military Forces]* (Beijing: Jiefangjun Chubanshe, 2010), vol. 2, 754. Dorn, *Sino-Japanese War*, 287–288.

3 Zheng Dongguo and Zheng Tingji, "Kunlunguan gongjianzhan qinliji" ["A Personal Account of the Battle to Take the Fortified Positions at Kunlun Pass"], in *Yue Gui Qian Dian Kangzhan: Yuan Guomindang jiangling Kangri Zhanzheng qinliji [The War of Resistance in Guangdong, Guangxi, Guizhou and Yunnan: Personal Recollections from the War of Resistance against Japan by Former Nationalist Commanders]* (Beijing: Zhongguo Wenshi Chubanshe, 1995), 266–267.

4 Ibid., 268–270.

5 Ibid., 270–271.

6 Bai Chongxi, *Bai Chongxi Koushu Zichuan [Bai Chongxi's Oral Autobiography]* (Beijing: Zhongguo Dabaikequanshu Chubanshe, 2008), 175.

7 Paine, *Wars for Asia*, 148.

8 Zhu Pingchao, *Wartime Culture in Guilin 1938–1944: A City at War* (Lanham MD: Lexington, 2015), 142.

9 Cao, *Zhongguo*, vol. 2, 758–759.

10 Tobe, "Eleventh," 220.

11 Graham Peck, *Two Kinds of Time*, ed. Robert A. Kapp (Seattle WA: University of Washington Press, 2008) 29.

12 Iriye, *Origins*, 111.

13 Herbert O. Yardley, *The Black Chamber: An Adventure in Espionage* (London: New English Library, 1983), 169.

14 Bea Exner Liu, *Remembering China 1935–1945* (Minneapolis MN: New Rivers Press, 1996), 115–116.

15 "New Nanking Regime Installed," *The North-China Herald and Supreme Court & Consular Gazette*, April 3, 1940, p. 3.

16 Bunker, *Peace Conspiracy*, 225–226.

17 Ibid., 248.

18 Boyle, *China*, 294. "New Nanking Regime Defended," *North-China Herald*, April 10, 1940, 51.

19 Boyle, *China*, 296–297.

20 Ibid., 276.

21 Ibid., 279.

22 Martin, "Opium," 367–368.

23 Boyle, *China*, 289–293.

24 Ienaga Saburō, *Pacific War 1931–1945* (New York NY: Random House, 1978), 77.

25 Boyle, *China*, 292–293.

26 Kenneth J. Ruoff, *Imperial Japan at Its Zenith: The Wartime Celebration of the Empire's 2,600th Anniversary* (Ithaca, NY: Cornell University Press, 2010), 129, 146.

27 Mariko Asano Tamanoi, *Memory Maps: The State and Manchuria in Postwar Japan* (Honolulu HI: University of Hawaii Press, 2008), 41.

28 Ibid., 42.

29 Lee Chong-sik, *Counterinsurgency in Manchuria: The Japanese Experience, 1931–1940* (Santa Monica CA: Rand Corp., 1967), 44–45.

30 Ibid., 45.

31 Saitō Shohei, "Crossing Perspectives in 'Manchukuo': Russian Eurasianism and Japanese Pan-Asianism," *Jahrbücher für Geschichte Osteuropas* 65, no. 4 (2017): 597.

32 Sergei Smirnov, *Otriad Asano: Russkie voinskie formirovania v Manchzho-go 1938–1945 [The Asano Detachment: Russian Military Units in Manchukuo 1938–1945]* (Ekaterinburg: Izdatelstvo Uralskogo universiteta, 2012), 8–27. Sergei Smirnov, "The Russian Officer Corps of the Manchukuo Army," *The Journal of Slavic Military Studies* 28, no. 3 (2015): 557.

33 Smirnov, *Otriad Asano*, 28–41.

34 Ibid., 50.

35 Ibid., 55–57.

36 Snow, *Red Star*, 107.

37 Dagfinn Gatu, *Village China at War: The Impact of Resistance to Japan, 1937–1945* (Copenhagen: NIAS Press, 2007), 22.

38 James Bertram, *North China Front*, 303.

39 Lyman P. van Slyke (ed.), *The Chinese Communist Movement: A Report by the United States War Department, July 1945* (Stanford CA: Stanford University Press, 1968), p. 193.

40 *Peng Dajiangjun [Great General Peng]* (Beijing: Xiandai chubanshe, 2015).

41 Chalmers A. Johnson, *Peasant Nationalism and Communist Power: The Emergence of Revolutionary China 1937–1945* (Stanford CA: Stanford University Press, 1962), 57. Recently it has also been argued that the campaign was intended to divert attention away from another, slightly later offensive aimed at linking up the communist-controlled areas in north China with the New Fourth Army, see Sherman Xiaogang Lai, *A Springboard to Victory: Shandong Province and Chinese Communist Military and Financial Strength, 1937–1945* (Leiden: Brill, 2011), 104.

42 Johnson, *Peasant Nationalism*, 57.

43 Lyman P. van Slyke, "The Battle of the Hundred Regiments," *Modern Asian Studies* 30, no. 4 (October 1996): 993.

44 Kataoka Tetsuya, *Resistance and Revolution in China: The Communists and the Second United Front* (Berkeley and Los Angeles CA: University of California Press, 1974), 217.

45 Ibid., 218.

46 Johnson, *Peasant Nationalism*, 58. van Slyke, "Hundred Regiments," 994.

47 van Slyke, "Hundred Regiments," 998.

48 Johnson, *Peasant Nationalism*, 58.

49 Dreyer, *China at War*, 244.

50 Slyke, *Communist*, 111.

51 Kataoka, *Resistance*, 220.

52 Dreyer, *China at War*, 292–293.

53 Slyke, *Communist*, 112.

54 Hull, *Memoirs*, vol. 1, 902.

55 Iriye, *Origins*, 106.

56 *FRUS. 1940. The Far East*, 966–967.

57 Ike Nobutaka, *Japan's Decision for War: Records of the 1941 Policy Conferences* (Stanford CA: Stanford University Press, 1967), 186.

58 Auer, *Responsible*, 89–90.

59 Nagaoka Shinjirō, "The Drive into Southern Indochina and Thailand," in *The Fateful Choice: Japan's Advance into Southeast Asia, 1939–1941*, ed. James William Morley (New York NY: Columbia University Press, 1980), 134.

60 Jeremy A. Yellen, "Into the Tiger's Den: Japan and the Tripartite Pact, 1940," *Journal of Contemporary History*, 51, no. 3 (2016): 555–556.

61 Auer, *Responsible*, 90. Bix, *Hirohito*, 375. Iriye, *Origins*, 107–108.

62 Iriye, *Origins*, 107.

63 "The Matsuoka Draft Policy 'On Strengthening Cooperation between Japan, Germany and Italy,' July 30, 1940," Appendix 5 in in *Deterrent Diplomacy: Japan, Germany and the USSR, 1935–1940*, ed. James William Morley (New York NY: Columbia University Press, 1976), 285–286.

64 Auer, *Responsible*, 90. Iriye, *Origins*, 108.

65 Macri, *Clash of Empires*, 261.

66 Hata Ikuhiko, "The Army's Move into Northern Indochina," in *The Fateful Choice: Japan's Advance into Southeast Asia, 1939–1941*, ed. James William Morley (New York NY: Columbia University Press, 1980), 157.

67 Delphine Boissarie, "Indochina during World War II: An economy under Japanese control," in *Economies under Occupation: The Hegemony of Nazi Germany and Imperial Japan in World War II*, eds. Marcel Boldorf and Tetsuji Okazaki (London: Routledge, 2015), 233.

68 *FRUS, Japan 1931–1941*, vol. 2, 94–95.

69 John E. Dreifort, "Japan's Advance into Indochina, 1940: The French Response," *Journal of Southeast Asian Studies*, vol. 13, no. 2 (Sept. 1982): 282.

70 Ibid., 291.

71 David G. Marr, *Vietnam 1945: The Quest for Power* (Berkeley CA: University of California Press, 1995), 17.

72 *FRUS, Japan 1931–1941*, vol. 2, 291–292.

73 Hata, "Army's Move," 189–192.

74 Ibid., 192.

75 "Gentlemen's agreement," *Time*, October 7, 1940.

76 Marr, *Vietnam 1945*, 19. Murakami Sachiko, "Japan's Thrust into French Indochina, 1940–1945" (Ph.D. diss., New York University, 1981), 188–189. Hata, who writes that the crossing took place at midnight, refers to Tokyo time, which was two hours ahead of Indochina time, Hata, "Army's Move," 196.

77 Murakami, "Japan's Thrust," 191. King C. Chen claims that 800 soldiers were killed on the French side defending Dong Dang, King C. Chen, *Vietnam and China, 1938–1954* (Princeton NJ: Princeton University Press, 1969), 43.

78 Hata, "Army's Move," 196–198.

79 Claude Hesse d'Alzon, *La présence militaire française en Indochine 1940–1945* (Château de Vincennes: Publication du service historique de l'Armée de Terre, 1985), 74.

80 Ibid., 73.

81 Murakami, "Japan's Thrust," 191.

82 Ibid. See also d'Alzon, *Présence militaire française*, 74–75 for a slightly different version of the events.

83 d'Alzon, *Présence militaire française*, 75. Douglas Porch, *The French Foreign Legion: A Complete History of the Legendary Fighting Force* (New York NY: Skyhorse Publishing, 2010), 511.

84 FRUS, Japan 1931–1941, vol. 2, 222–223. Jonathan Marshall, *To Have and Have Not: Southeast Asian Raw Materials and the Origins of the Pacific War* (Berkeley CA: University of California Press, 1995), 85. Miller, *Bankrupting*, 92–93.

85 *FRUS, Japan 1931–1941*, vol. 2, 223–224.

86 Octane numbers describe the ability of fuel to withstand compression before igniting. The July restrictions did not have an immediate impact on the Japanese war effort, since Japan shifted to importing octane-86 gasoline, upgrading it in Japan. Miller, *Bankrupting*, 82, 88–89, 158. See also Herbert Feis, *The Road to Pearl Harbor* (New York NY: Atheneum, 1963), 158.

87 Present-day Jakarta.

88 Barnhart, *Japan Prepares*, 165–166.

89 María Emilia Paz Salinas, *Strategy, Security, and Spies: Mexico and the U.S. as Allies in World War II* (University Park PA: Pennsylvania State University Press, 1997), 41–44.

90 Anthony N. Stranges, "Synthetic Fuel Production in Prewar and World War II Japan: A Case Study in Technological Failure," *Annals of Science* 50, no. 3 (1993): 244.

91 Stranges, "Synthetic Fuel," 231.

92 "Synthetic Oil Manufacturing is Entering Industrial Stage," *Japan Times*, June 2, 1940, 4.

93 Barnhart, *Japan Prepares*, 146–147.

94 Stranges, "Synthetic Fuel," 232.

95 Barnhart, *Japan Prepares*, 146–147.

96 Hosoya Chichiro, "The Tripartite Pact, 1939–1940," in *Deterrent Diplomacy: Japan, Germany and the USSR 1935–1940*, ed. James William Morley (New York NY: Columbia University Press, 1976), 239.

97 Ibid., 230–234.

98 Auer, *Responsible*, 113.

99 Tsunoda Jun, "The Navy's Role in the Southern Strategy," in *The Fateful Choice: Japan's Advance into Southeast Asia, 1939–1941*, ed. James William Morley (New York NY: Columbia University Press, 1980), 266. Yellen, "Tiger's Den," 571–572.

100 Jost Dülffer, "The Tripartite Pact of 27 September 1940: Fascist Alliance or Propaganda Trick?" *The Australian Journal of Politics and History* 32, no. 2 (1986): 228.

101 The term "Axis" was first used by Italian dictator Benito Mussolini in 1936, but it only gained real currency in the Western democracies after the founding of the Tripartite Alliance. For example, President Roosevelt did not use it even once in public statements before November 1940, but 157 times after. See Kenneth Janda and Stefano Mula "Dubya, meet Il Duce: Who said 'axis' first?" *Chicago Tribune*, April 21, 2002.

102 *Akten zur deutschen auswärtigen Politik*, Series D (1937–1945), vol. 11/2 (Bonn: Gebr. Hermes KG, 1964), 177.

103 Yellen, "Tiger's Den," 555–556.

104 Breckinridge Long, *War Diary of Breckinridge Long*, ed. Fred L. Israel (Lincoln NE: University of Nebraska Press, 1966), 132.

105 Hosoya, "The Tripartite Pact," 255.

106 Yellen, "Tiger's Den," 556.

Chapter 7

1 James P. Duffy, *Hitler's Secret Pirate Fleet: The Deadliest Ships of World War II* (Lincoln NE: University of Nebraska Press, 2005), 22–23. Seki Eiji, *Mrs Ferguson's Tea-set, Japan, and the Second World War* (Kent: Global Oriental, 2007), 6–17.

2 Duffy, *Pirate*, 23.

3 Edward J. Drea, "Reading Each Other's Mail: Japanese Communication Intelligence, 1920–1941," *The Journal of Military History* 55, no. 2 (April 1991): 203. Chiefs of Staff Committee, "The Situation in the Far East in the Event of Japanese Intervention Against Us," C. O. S. (40), 592, National Archives, 4.

4 Drea, "Reading," 203. "The Situation in the Far East," 4.

5 Christopher J. Baxter, "A Question of Blame? Defending Britain's Position in the South China Sea, the Pacific and South-East Asia, 1991–1941," *RUSI Journal* 142, no. 4 (August 1997): 71.

6 Tsunoda, *Navy's Role*, 274.

7 Ibid., 276.

8 Ibid., 275.

9 Evans and Peattie, *Kaigun*, 475–477. Gordon W. Prange, *At Dawn We Slept* (New York NY: Penguin Books, 2001), 9–10, 16.

10 Evans and Peattie, *Kaigun*, 473–477.

11 Prange, *At Dawn*, 29.

12 *FRUS, 1941, vol. 4: The Far East*, 17. Prange, *At Dawn*, 30–31.

13 Ministry of Foreign Affairs of Japan, *Japan-China Joint History Research Report. Modern and Contemporary History*, vol. 1. (March 2011): 159.

14 *FRUS, Japan: 1931–1941*, vol. 2, 174.

15 Ibid., 181.

16 Dallek, *Roosevelt*, 255.

17 Morton, *Strategy and Command*, 76.

18 Chennault, *Way of a Fighter*, 89–90.

19 Feis, *Road*, 135.

20 Iriye, *Origins*, 121.

21 Marshall, *To Have*, 87.

22 *FRUS, 1940, vol. 4: The Far East*, 208.

23 d'Alzon, *Présence militaire française*, 92–93.

24 Nagaoka, "Drive," 209–210.

25 *FRUS, 1940, vol. 4: The Far East*, 164.

26 "Saigon Consulate Closed," *New York Times*, December 9, 1940, p. 4.

27 "More Bombing on Border," *New York Times*, December 9, 1940, p. 4.

28 d'Alzon, *Présence militaire française*, 93–94.

29 Ibid., 94.

30 Ibid.

31 Ibid., 95.

32 Ibid.

33 *FRUS, 1940, vol. 4: The Far East*, 146–147. Nagaoko, "Drive," 230.

34 Ellen J. Hammer, *The Struggle for Indochina, 1940–1955* (Stanford CA: Stanford University Press, 1966), 25.

35 Nagaoka, "Drive," 228.

36 Iriye, *Origins*, 131.

37 d'Alzon, *Présence militaire française*, 96. Iriye, Origins, 132.

38 David P. Chandler, *Brother Number One: A Political Biography of Pol Pot* (Boulder CO: Westview Press, 1992), 17.

39 Milton Osborne, "King-Making in Cambodia," *Journal of Southeast Asian Studies* 4, no. 2 (September 1973): 169–185.

40 Cordell Hull, *The Memoirs of Cordell Hull* (London: Hodder and Stoughton, 1948), 992.

41 Morton, *Strategy and Command*, 89.

42 Martha Gellhorn, *Travels with Myself and Another* (New York NY: Putnam, 1978), 51.

43 Ibid., 40–41.

44 Ibid., 51.

45 Theodore H. White, *In Search of History: A Personal Adventure* (New York NY: Harper and Row, 1978), 159.

46 Vasilii I. Chuikov, *Mission to China: Memoirs of a Soviet Military Advisor to Chiang Kaishek*, ed. David P. Barrett (Norwalk CT: Eastbridge, 2004), 15–16.

47 Gregor Benton, "The South Anhui Incident," *The Journal of Asian Studies*, vol. 45, no. 4 (August 1986): 681–682. Sherman Xiaogang Lai, "A War Within a War: The Road to the New Fourth Army Incident in January 1941," *Journal of Chinese Military History*, 2 (2013): 1–2.

48 Chuikov, *Mission*, 50–51.

49 van de Ven, *China at War*, 146.

50 Ibid., 147.

51 Taylor, *Generalissimo*, 175–177. van de Ven, *China at War*, 148.

52 Alexander Dallin and Fridrikh Igorevich Firsov (eds.), *Dimitrov and Stalin, 1934–1943: Letters from the Soviet Archives* (New Haven CT: Yale University Press, 2000), 140. Taylor, *Generalissimo*, 177.

53 John W. Masland, "American Attitudes Toward Japan, *The Annals of the American Academy of Political and Social Science* 215 (May 1941): 165.

54 Katō Masuo, *The Lost War: A Japanese Reporter's Inside Story* (New York NY: Alfred A. Knopf, 1946), 19.

55 *The Final Confrontation: Japan's Negotiations with the United States, 1941*, ed. J.W. Morley (New York NY: Columbia University Press, 1995), 12.

56 Feis, *Road*, 174–175.

57 Katō, *Lost War*, 21.

58 Feis, *Road*, 175. *FRUS, Japan: 1931–1941*, vol. 2, XXXIV, 387–389.

59 *FRUS, Japan: 1931–1941, vol. 2*, 389–396.

60 Hull, *Memoirs*, vol. 2, 989.

61 Ibid., 1030.

62 Morton, *Strategy and Command*, 86–89.

63 Nagaoko, "Drive," 230.

64 Iriye, *Origins*, 133.

65 Hosoya, "Tripartite Pact," 68–69.

66 AP, "Accord in Moscow," *New York Times*, April 14, 1941, 1. Hosyoa, "Tripartite Pact," 79. Iriye, *Origins*, 133–134.

67 Louis Allen, "Japanese Intelligence Systems," *Journal of Contemporary History* 22, no. 4 (October 1987): 551.

68 Takeo Yoshikawa and Norman Stanford, "Top Secret Assignment," *US Naval Institute Proceedings* 86, no. 12 (December 1960): 33.

69 Allen, "Intelligence," 551. Yoshikawa and Stanford, "Assignment."

70 Yoshikawa and Stanford, "Assignment."

71 US Congress, Joint Congressional Committee on the Investigation of the Pearl Harbor Attack, 79th Congress, Investigation of the Pearl Harbor Attack: *Report of the Joint Committee on the Investigation of the Pearl Harbor Attack* (hereafter *Pearl Harbor Attack*) (Washington DC: US Government Printing Office, 1946), part 40, 261. See also Gordon Prange et al. *Pearl Harbor: The Verdict of History* (New York NY: Penguin, 1991), 270.

72 *Pearl Harbor Attack*, part 12, 11.

73 Ibid., part 40, 261.

74 Prange, *At Dawn*, 102, 158.

75 Evans and Peattie, *Kaigun*, 477–478.

76 Tsunoda, *Navy's Role*, 292.

77 Paine, *Wars*, 176. H. P. Willmott, *The Barrier and the Javelin: Japanese and Allied Pacific Strategies, February to June, 1942* (Annapolis MD: Naval Institute Press, 1983), 8–9.

78 Kotani Ken, *Japanese Intelligence in WWII: Successes and Failures* (Tokyo: First Military History Research Office, n.d.), 12.

79 Ken Kotani, *Japanese Intelligence in World War II* (Oxford: Osprey, 2009), 116.

80 Wigmore, *Thrust*, 62.

81 Ibid., 63.

82 Cecil Brown, "Malay Jungle War: December 1941," in *Reporting World War II [Library of America]*, part 1 (New York NY: Penguin, 1995), 286.

83 *Pearl Harbor Attack*, part 15, 1558.

84 Ibid., part 15, 1564.

85 Robert E. Sherwood, *Roosevelt and Hopkins: An Intimate History* (New York NY: Harper, 1948), 259.

86 Raymond A. Esthus, "President Roosevelt's Commitment to Britain to Intervene in a Pacific War," *Mississippi Valley Historical Review* 50, no. 1 (June 1963): 33–34.

87 Elliott R. Thorpe, *East Wind, Rain: The Intimate Account of an Intelligence Officer in the Pacific 1939–49* (Boston MA: Gambit, 1969), 47.

88 Stanley Karnow, *In Our Image: America's Empire in the Philippines* (New York NY: Random House, 1989), 275–276.

89 Louis Morton. *The Fall of the Philippines [United States Army in World War II: The War in the Pacific]* (Washington DC: Office of the Chief of Military History, Department of the Army, 1953), 69.

90 Ricardo Trota Jose, *The Philippine Army 1935–1942* (Manila: Ateneo de Manila University Press, 1992), 196.

91 Jose, *Philippine Army*, 202.

92 Morton, *Strategy and Command*, 43.

93 Forrest C. Pogue, *George C. Marshall: Ordeal and Hope 1939–1942* (New York NY: Viking, 1966), 173.

94 Walter Daveport, "Impregnable Pearl Harbor," *Collier's*, June 14, 1941, 75, 78.

95 *FRUS, 1941, vol. 4, The Far East*, 971. Garver, Chinese-Soviet, 183.

96 Slyke, *Communist*, 215. Garver, *Chinese-Soviet*, 183.

97 Owen Lattimore, *China Memoirs: Chiang Kai-shek and the War Against Japan* (Tokyo: University of Tokyo Press, 1990), 149.

98 *FRUS, 1941, vol. 4: The Far East*, 281–282. Iriye, *Origins*, 140.

99 *FRUS, 1941, vol. 4: The Far East*, 281–282.

100 Garver, *Chinese-Soviet*, 184.

101 *FRUS, 1941, vol. 4: The Far East*, 289.

102 *Pearl Harbor Attack*, part 20, 3993. Dallek, *Roosevelt*, 279.

103 Carl Boyd, *Hitler's Japanese Confidant: General Oshima Hiroshi and MAGIC Intelligence, 1941–1945* (Lawrence, KS: University Press of Kansas, 1993), 21.

104 Eri Hotta, *Japan 1941: Countdown to Infamy* (New York NY: Alfred A. Knopf, 2013), 109.

105 Bix, *Hirohito*, 394–395.

106 Ike, *Decision*, 58.

107 Ibid., 60.

108 Ibid., 78.

109 Ibid., 88.

Chapter 8

1 The description of the Japanese takeover is based on a number of contemporary newspaper reports, including "Japan Occupies Indo-China Base," *New York Times*, July 30, 1941, 4. "Saigon Shows Apprehension," *New York Times*, July 29, 1941, 5. "Japan Pours Men into Saigon Base," *New York Times*, July 31, 1941, 3. "Japanese Influx at Saigon Goes On," *New York Times*, August 2, 1941, 5. "More Japanese Troops Land," *North-China Herald*, August 6, 1941, 208.

2 "Japanese Influx at Saigon Goes On," *New York Times*, August 2, 1941, 5.

3 "Japan Occupies Indo-China Base," *New York Times*, July 30, 1941, 4.

4 Murakami, *Thrust*, 331.

5 *FRUS, 1941, Vol. 5: Far East*, 246.

6 Ibid., 214.

7 Ibid., 246.

8 *FRUS, Japan: 1931–1941*, vol. 2, 315–317.

9 Iriye, *Origins*, 146.

10 Miller, *Bankrupting*, 172.

11 Ibid., 173.

12 Jonathan G. Utley. "Upstairs, Downstairs at Foggy Bottom: Oil Exports and Japan, 1940–41," *Prologue* 8, no. 1 (Spring 1976): 24.

13 Howard L. Ickes, *The Secret Diary of Harold L. Ickes. Vol. II: The Lowering Clouds 1939–1941* (New York NY: Simon and Schuster, 1954), 588.

14 "Memorandum of policy to be carried out in administering the freezing control order for Japan and China," July 25, 1941. *Morgenthau Diaries*, vol. 424, 268.

15 Utley, "Upstairs," 26.

16 Miller, *Bankrupting*, 195–203.

17 Dallek, *Roosevelt*, 275.

18 Miller, *Bankrupting*, 203. Some historians have argued that Roosevelt wanted a complete embargo from the outset and deliberately picked Acheson, known for his anti-Axis credentials, to manage the freeze. However, no sources provide definite evidence of this. Ibid. 203–204.

19 Dean Acheson, *Present at the Creation: My Years at the State Department* (New York NY: W. W. Norton, 1969), 26.

20 "Freezer Most Frozen in Trade Sanctions," *Japan Times and Mail*, August 1, 1941, 1.

21 Miller, *Bankrupting*, 225.

22 Iriye, *Origins*, 150.

23 Louis Morton, "Japan's Decision for War," in *Command Decisions*, ed. Kent Roberts Greenfield (Washington DC: Office of the Chief of Military History, Department of the Army, 1960), 105–106.

24 Morton, "Japan's Decision," 106.

25 Prange, *At Dawn*, 181–183.

26 Barnhart, *Japan*, 239.

27 *Final Confrontation*, 155.

28 Chuikov, *Mission*, 17.

29 Hotta, *Japan*, 119.

30 David M. Glantz, "The Impact of Intelligence Provided to the Soviet Union by Richard Zorge on Soviet Force Deployments from the Far East to the West in 1941 and 1942," *The Journal of Slavic Military Studies* 30, no. 3 (2017): 458.

31 *Final Confrontation*, 161–162.

32 Ibid., 179–180.

33 William D. O'Neill, *Interwar U.S. and Japanese National Product and Defense Expenditure* (Alexandria VA: CNA, 2003), 39.

34 Paine, *Japanese Empire*, 144.

35 Morton, *Strategy and Command*, 125.

36 Henry C. Wolfe, "Tokyo, Capital of Shadows," *New York Times*, October 26, 1941, SM6.

37 Owen Griffiths, "Need, Greed, and Protest in Japan's Black Market, 1938–1949," *Journal of Social History* 35, No. 4 (Summer 2002): 827.

38 John Goette, *Japan Fights for Asia* (New York NY: Harcourt, Brace and Company, 1943), 193.

39 Wolfe, "Tokyo," SM6.

40 Paine, *Empire*, 137–138.

41 Christine R. Yano, *Tears of Longing: Nostalgia and the Nation in Japanese Popular Song* (Cambridge MA: Harvard University Asia Center 2002), 37.

42 "German War Film Opens Here Today," *Japan Times and Mail*, May 15, 1941, 3. Goette, *Japan Fights*, 192.

43 Goette, *Japan Fights*, 192. Wolfe, "Tokyo," SM6.

44 Tolischus, *Tokyo Record*, 182.

45 Griffiths, "Need, Greed, and Protest," 830.

46 Thomas R. H. Havens, *Valley of Darkness: The Japanese People and World War Two* (Lanham MD: University Press of America, 1986), 20.
47 Griffiths, "Need," 828–829.
48 Otto D. Tolischus, "New Policy League Is Formed in Japan," *New York Times*, July 7, 1941, 1, 8.
49 Goette, *Japan Fights*, 185–186.
50 Ibid., 194.
51 Ibid., 195–196.
52 Cook and Cook, *Japan at War*, 49.
53 Ibid., 81–82.
54 Barnhart, *Japan Prepares*, 245. Ike, *Japan's Decision*, 135–136.
55 Iriye, *Origins*, 160.
56 Ike, *Japan's Decision*, 133.
57 Bix, *Hirohito*, 414. Ike, *Japan's Decision*, 151. *Pearl Harbor Attack*, part 20, 4005.
58 The fall of 1941 saw major battles between Chinese and Japanese forces at Changsha and Yichang, see Macri, *Clash of Empires*, 289-300.
59 *FRUS, Japan: 1931–1941*, vol. 2, 617.
60 Ibid., 595.
61 Feis, *Road*, 270.
62 *FRUS, Japan: 1931–1941*, vol. 2, 656–661.
63 Hotta, *Japan 1941*, 202. Ike, *Japan's Decision*, 184. *Pearl Harbor Attack*, part 20, 4009.
64 Ike, *Japan's Decision*, 184. *Pearl Harbor Attack*, part 20, 4009–4010.
65 *Pearl Harbor Attack*, part 20, 4025–4026.
66 Kido Kōichi's diary, October 20, 1941. IMTFE, *Transcript of Proceedings*, 10,295.
67 Ike, *Japan's Decision*, 185.
68 *Pearl Harbor Attack*, part 15, 1845.
69 Hull, *Memoirs*, vol. 2, 1054.
70 Iriye, *Origins*, 168–170.
71 Ibid., 169–170.
72 Prange, *At Dawn*, 295–299.
73 Ike, *Japan's Decision*, 184–207.
74 Ibid., xvi.
75 Ibid., 188.
76 Feis, *Road*, 195.
77 Affidavit of Shimada Shigetarō, IMTFE, *Transcript of Proceedings*, 34,658–34,659.
78 Bix, *Hirohito*, 428–429. *FRUS 1931–41: Japan, vol. 2*, 768. Iriye, *Origins*, 181–182.
79 Affidavit of Shimada Shigetarō, IMTFE, *Transcript of Proceedings*, 34,665.
80 Bix, *Hirohito*, 431–432.
81 Marder, *Friends*, 219.
82 *Pearl Harbor Attack*, part 17, 2648.
83 Quoted from Richard J. Aldrich, *Intelligence and the War Against Japan* (Cambridge: Cambridge University Press, 2000), 84.
84 Prange, *At Dawn*, 289–395.
85 Prange et al., *Verdict*, 269.
86 Ike, *Japan's Decision*, 262–283.
87 Ibid., 283.
88 Affidavit of Shimada Shigetarō, IMTFE, *Transcript of Proceedings*, 34,666–34,667.
89 Morton, *Strategy and Command*, 122.
90 Hara Tameichi, *Japanese Destroyer Captain* (Annapolis MD: Naval Institute Press, 1967), 43.

91 Esthus, "Roosevelt's Commitment," 33–34. S. Woodburn Kirby, *The War Against Japan, Volume 1: The Loss of Singapore* (London: Her Majesty's Stationery Office, 1957), p. 76–77. Llewellyn Woodward, *British Foreign Policy in the Second World War* (London: Her Majesty's Stationery Office, 1962), 186–187.

92 William H. Bartsch, *Doomed at the Start: American Pursuit Pilots in the Philippines, 1941–1942* (College Station TX: Texas A&M University Press, 1992), 41.

93 Esthus, "Roosevelt's Commitment," 33–34. Woordward, *British Foreign Policy*, 186–187.

94 Paul Maltby, "Report on the Air Operations During the Campaigns in Malaya and Netherlands East Indies From 8th December, 1941 to 12th March, 1942," *The London Gazette* (February 26, 1948): 1364. Jonathan Parkinson, *The Royal Navy, China Station: 1864–1941* (Leicester: Matador, 2018), 468.

95 Fuchida Mitsuo, "I Led the Air Attack on Pearl Harbor," *Proceedings* 78, no. 9 (September 1952): 595.

96 Dull, Japanese Navy, 14. John W. Dower, *Cultures of War: Pearl Harbor/Hiroshima/9–11/Iraq* (New York NY: W. W. Norton, The New Press, 2010), 53.

97 Steve Twomey, *Countdown to Pearl Harbor: The Twelve Days to the Attack* (New York NY: Simon & Schuster, 2016), xiv.

98 Henry Howard, "Dec. 6, 1941—A quiet day at Pearl Harbor," *American Legion*, December 6, 2016.

99 Kirby, *Singapore*, 118. Morton, *Fall of the Philippines*, 73.

100 828–830. US Department of State, *United States Foreign Policy, 1931–1941* (Washington DC: US Government Printing Office, 1943),

101 Feis, *Road*, 340.

102 Tolischus, *Tokyo*, 321.

Chapter 9

1 The account of the USS *Ward's* sinking of the Japanese submarine is based on the destroyer's after-action report, December 13, 1941. DD139/A16-3 (759) and Hawaii Undersea Research Laboratory, "Japanese midget submarine: sunk Dec. 7, 1941—found," Aug 2002.

2 See Kirby, *Singapore*, 96 for a useful compilation of the scheduled start of operations in different parts of the Asia Pacific on December 7/8.

3 Peter Thompson, *The Battle for Singapore: The True Story of Britain's Greatest Military Disaster* (London: Portrait, 2005), 132.

4 Paul S. Dull, *A Battle History of the Imperial Japanese Navy (1941–1945)* (Annapolis MD: Naval Institute Press, 1978), 37.

5 Tsuji Masanobu, *Japan's Greatest Victory, Britain's Worst Defeat* (Staplehurst: Spellmount: 1997), 75–77.

6 Abe Zenji, *The Emperor's Sea Eagle* (Honolulu HI: Arizona Memorial Museum, 2006), 40. Fuchida Mitsuo, "The Air Attack on Pearl Harbor," in David C. Evans (ed.), *The Japanese Navy in World War II: In the Words of Former Japanese Naval Officers* (Annapolis MD: Naval Institute Press, 1986), 54.

7 Dennis McClellan, "Kermit A. Tyler dies at 96; officer didn't act on radar warning about Pearl Harbor raid," *Los Angeles Times*, February 24, 2010. Walter Lord, *Day of Infamy* (New York NY: Henry Holt, 2001), 43–45.

8 Fuchida, "Air Attack," 58.

9 Prange, *At Dawn*, 504.

10 Morton, *Strategy and Command*, 123–124. Pogue, *Ordeal and Hope*, 230.

11 Samuel Eliot Morison, *The Rising Sun in the Pacific 1931–April 1942 [History of United States Naval Operations in World War II, vol. 3]* (Boston MA: Little, Brown and Co., 1948), 94–95.

12 *Pearl Harbor Attack*, Part 22, 595.

13 Oral History Interview No. 228, Matsumura Heita, December 8, 1991. nps.gov.

14 *Pearl Harbor Attack*, Part 1, 44.

15 USS *Arizona*, Report of Pearl Harbor Attack, BB39/A16/U. S. S. Arizona Receiving Barracks, Pearl Harbor, T. H. December 13, 1941. www.history.navy.mil.

16 Cook Third Class Doris Miller, USN. Enclosure F to USS *West Virginia*'s Action Report, 11 December 1941. www.history.navy.mil.

17 USS *Arizona*, Report of Pearl Harbor Attack, BB39/A16/U.S. S. Arizona Receiving Barracks, Pearl Harbor, T.H. December 13, 1941. www.history.navy.mil.

18 Fuchida, "Air Attack," 64.

19 Morison, *Rising Sun*, 108.

20 Adolph Czerwenka, "A Deadly Sunday Morning," *Newsweek*, March 8, 1999, Vol. 133, Issue 10, 42.

21 United States Strategic Bombing Survey (Pacific), Naval Analysis Division, *Interrogations of Japanese Officials*, vol. 1 (Washington DC: Government Printing Office, 1946), 122.

22 H. P. Willmott. *Empires in the Balance* (Annapolis MD: Naval Institute Press, 1982), 133–134.

23 Captain Lacouture, USN. Oral History of The Pearl Harbor Attack, 7 December 1941. www. history.navy.mil.

24 Prange, *At Dawn*, 525.

25 *Pearl Harbor Attack,* Part 1, 44.

26 Morison, *Rising Sun*, 123–124.

27 William Cole, "Reunion Turns Bittersweet," *Honolulu Star Advertiser*, December 8, 2010.

28 Fuchida, "Air Attack," 61–62.

29 *Pearl Harbor Attack*, Part 22, 265–266. Prange, *At Dawn*, 526.

30 Tanaka Miya, "Pearl Harbor was mistake: attack vet, 89," *Japan Times*, December 6, 2005, 3.

31 Abe, *Sea Eagle*, 54. According to Abe's autobiography, the ship he attacked was the USS *Raleigh*. However, in an oral history from 2001, he said the ship was the *Arizona*, which had already been fatally hit in previous waves. Oral History Interview No. 373, Abe Zenji, December 1, 2001. nps.gov.

32 Lily Rothman, "Powerful Stories of the Japanese-American Children Who Witnessed Pearl Harbor," *Time*, December 6, 2016.

33 "Sen. Daniel Inouye On Pearl Harbor, After 70 Years," *National Public Radio*, December 7, 2011.

34 Studs Terkel, *'The Good War'* (New York NY: The New Press, 1984), 19–20.

35 "Many lives taken by friendly fire," *Honolulu Star Advertiser*, November 30, 2016.

36 Testimony of Richard Wrenshall, John Toland Papers: December 7, 1941—Part Two (Folder 2). FDR Library.

37 Lieutenant Ruth Erickson, NC, USN. Oral History of The Pearl Harbor Attack, 7 December 1941. www.history.navy.mil.

38 Oral History Interview No. 269, Don S. Jones, December 7, 1998. nps.gov.

39 Kido Kōichi's diary, December 8 1941. IMTFE, *Transcript of Proceedings*, 10,684.

40 Testimony by Tōjō Hideki. IMTFE, *Transcript of Proceedings*, 36,409.

41 Prange, *At Dawn*, 541–550.

42 Angelo N. Caravaggio, "'Winning' the Pacific War: The Masterful Strategy of Commander Minoru Genda," *Naval War College Review* 67, no. 1 (Winter 2014): 99.

43 Gordon W. Prange et al., *Pearl Harbor: The Verdict of History* (New York NY: Penguin, 1986), 510.

44 Strategic Bombing Survey, *Interrogations*, vol. 1, 124.

45 Oral History Interview No. 321, Muranaka Kazuo, June 13, 1986. nps.gov.

46 Tsuji, *Japan's Greatest Victory*, 75–77.
47 Wigmore, *Japanese Thrust*, 135.
48 Japanese Demobilization Bureau Records (compiler), *Reports of General MacArthur: Japanese Operations in the Southwest Pacific Area*, Vol. II, part 1 (Washington DC: US Government Printing Office, 1994), 19.
49 Wigmore, *Japanese Thrust*, 135.
50 Kirby, *Singapore*, 186.
51 Ibid., 183.
52 H. J. van Mook, *The Netherlands Indies and Japan: Their Relations 1940–1941* (London: Routledge, 2011), 63.
53 Morton, *Fall of the Philippines*, 85–86.
54 E. B. Miller, *Bataan Uncensored* (Long Prairie MN: The Hart Publications, 1949), 67.
55 Sakai Saburō with Martin Caidin and Fred Saitō, *Samurai! The Autobiography of Japan's World War II Flying Ace* (n. p.: Uncommon Valor Press, 2015), 43.
56 Miller, *Bataan Uncensored*, 67.
57 James H. Cowan, *Bataan: A Survivor's Memoir* (Sacramento CA: Bella Vista Press, 1970), 2.
58 Shimada Kōichi, "The Opening Air Offensive against the Philippines" in David C. Evans (ed.), *The Japanese Navy in World War II: In the Words of Formers Japanese Naval Officers* (Annapolis MD: Naval Institute Press, 1986), 93.
59 Pogue, *Ordeal and Hope*, 234.
60 The most comprehensive historical account to date on the disaster befalling American air power in the Philippines places almost all the blame on MacArthur and his chief of staff Richard K. Sutherland. See William H. Bartsch, *December 8, 1941: MacArthur's Pearl Harbor* (College Station TX: Texas A&M University Press, 2003), 413–423.
61 Morton, *Fall of the Philippines*, 88. Spector, *Eagle*, 108.
62 Morton, *Fall of the Philippines*, 88.
63 Not to be confused with Bataan, the Philippine peninsula.
64 Morton, *Fall of the Philippines*, 100.
65 Kirby, *Singapore*, 119–120. 464–465. C. P. Stacey, *Six Years of War: The Army in Canada, Britain and the Pacific [Official History of the Canadian Army in the Second World War, vol. 1]* (Ottawa: Queen's Printer, 1955), 464–465.
66 Ibid., 465.
67 Ibid., 461.
68 "The Battle of Hong Kong through the eyes of people who survived it," *South China Morning Post*, December 16, 2016.
69 Quoted in Tony Banham, *Not the Slightest Chance: The Defence of Hong Kong, 1941* (Hong Kong: Hong Kong University Press, 2005), 28.
70 Banham, *Chance*, 28.
71 Charles Barman (ed. Ray Barman), *Resist to the End, Hong Kong 1941–1945* (Hong Kong: Hong Kong University Press, 2009). 6.
72 Mark Felton, *China Station: The British Military in the Middle Kingdom 1839–1997* (Barnsley: Pen & Sword, 2013), 123–124.
73 Frank O. Hough et al., *Pearl Harbor to Guadalcanal [History of U.S. Marine Corps Operations in World War II, Volume I]* (Washington DC: United States Marine Corps, 1958), 160–161.
74 Hough et al., *Pearl Harbor to Guadalcanal*, 75–76.
75 Gregory J. W. Urwin. *Facing Fearful Odds: The Siege of Wake Island* (Lincoln: University of Nebraska Press, 1997), 245.
76 Norio Tsuji, quoted in Hough et al., *Pearl Harbor to Guadalcanal*, 108.

77 R. D. Heinl, *The Defense of Wake [Marines in World War II: Historical Monograph]* (n. p.: Historical Section, United States Marine Corps, 1947), 14, n5.

78 Prange, *At Dawn*, 527.

79 Sherwood, *Roosevelt and Hopkins*, 430–431.

80 Hull, *Memoirs*, vol. 2, 1096. Testimony of Joseph W. Ballantine, IMTFE, *Transcript of Proceedings*, 10,849.

81 Hull, *Memoirs*, vol. 2, 1097.

82 Francis Biddle Papers: Cabinet Meetings, 1941. December 7, 1941. FDR Library.

83 Memorandum of remarks by Roosevelt at Cabinet meeting, December 7, 1941. General speech file, no. 1399a. FDR Library.

84 Prange, *At Dawn*, 554.

85 Edward C. Raymer, *Descent into Darkness: Pearl Harbor, 1941: A Navy Diver's Memoir* (Novato CA: Presidio Press, 1996), 11.

86 Mark Skinner Watson, *Chief of Staff: Prewar Plans and Preparations [United States Army in World War II: The War Department]* (Washington DC: Historical Division, Department of the Army, 1950), 519.

87 *Pearl Harbor Attack*, Part 35, 338. Prange, *At Dawn*, 561.

88 Franklin Odo, *No Sword to Bury: Japanese Americans in Hawai'i during World War II* (Philadelphia PA: Temple University Press, 2004), 104.

89 Odo, *Sword*, 112–113.

90 Oral History Interview No. 269, Don S. Jones, December 7, 1998. nps.gov.

91 Prange, *At Dawn*, 563.

92 Robert J. Martin, *USS West Virginia (BB-48)* (Paducah KY: Turner Publishing Company, 1997), 19.

93 "War Is On!" *The Japan Times*, January 8, 1941, 1.

94 Donald Keene, "Japanese Writers and the Greater East Asia War," *The Journal of Asian Studies* 23, no. 2 (February 1964), 212.

95 Bix, *Hirohito*, 437.

96 Morton, *Strategy and Command*, 124.

97 Tolischus, *Tokyo Record*, 322–324.

98 Cook and Cook, *Japan at War*, 82.

99 John J. Stephan, *Hawaii under the Rising Sun* (Honolulu HI: University Press of Hawaii, 1984), 1.

100 Strategic Bombing Survey, *Interrogations*, vol. 1, 65.

101 Ibid., 15.

102 Oral History Interview No. 379, Harada Kaname, December 5, 2001. nps.gov.

103 Lattimore, *China Memoirs*, 160–161.

104 Chiang Kai-shek, *All We Are and All We Have: Speeches and Messages since Pearl Harbor* (New York NY: The John Day Company, 1948), 1.

Bibliography

Literature in English

Abe Zenji. *The Emperor's Sea Eagle*. Honolulu HI: Arizona Memorial Museum, 2006.

Abend, Hallett. *My Life in China 1926–1941*. New York NY: Harcourt, Brace and Company, 1943.

Acheson, Dean. *Present at the Creation: My Years at the State Department*. New York NY: W. W. Norton, 1969.

Alcott, Carroll. *My War with Japan*. New York NY: Henry Holt and Co., 1943.

Aldrich, Richard J. *Intelligence and the War Against Japan*. Cambridge: Cambridge University Press, 2000.

Allen, Louis. "Japanese Intelligence Systems." *Journal of Contemporary History* 22, no. 4 (October 1987): 547–562.

Auer, James E. *Who Was Responsible? From Marco Polo Bridge to Pearl Harbor*. Tokyo: The Yomiuri Shimbun, 2006.

Averill, Stephen C. "The Origins of the Futian Incident." In *New Perspectives on the Chinese Communist Revolution*, edited by Tony Saich and Hans van de Ven, 79–115. Armonk NY: M. E. Sharpe, 1995.

Banham, Tony. *Not the Slightest Chance: The Defence of Hong Kong, 1941*. Hong Kong: Hong Kong University Press, 2005.

Barman, Charles. *Resist to the End, Hong Kong 1941–1945*. Edited by Ray Barman. Hong Kong: Hong Kong University Press, 2009.

Barnhart, Michael A. *Japan Prepares for Total War: The Search for Economic Security, 1919–1941*. Ithaca NY: Cornell University Press, 1987.

Barnouin, Barbara and Yu Changgen. *Zhou Enlai: A Political Life*. Hong Kong: Chinese University of Hong Kong, 2006.

Bartsch, William H. *December 8, 1941: MacArthur's Pearl Harbor*. College Station TX: Texas A&M University Press, 2003.

——, *Doomed at the Start: American Pursuit Pilots in the Philippines, 1941–1942*. College Station TX: Texas A&M University Press, 1992.

de Bary, Wm. Theodore et al. (eds). *Sources of Japanese Tradition, Volume Two: 1600 to 2000, Part Two: 1868 to 2000*. New York NY: Columbia University Press, 2006.

Baxter, Christopher J. "A Question of Blame? Defending Britain's Position in the South China Sea, the Pacific and South-East Asia, 1991–1941." *RUSI Journal* 142, no. 4 (August 1997): 66–75.

Benedict, Ruth. *The Chrysanthemum and the Sword*. Boston MA: Houghton Mifflin Harcourt, 1946.

Benton, Gregor. "The South Anhui Incident," *The Journal of Asian Studies*, vol. 45, no. 4 (August 1986): 681–720.

Bergamini, David. *Japan's Imperial Conspiracy*. London: Heinemann, 1971.

Bertram, James. *North China Front*. London: MacMillan, 1939.

Bix, Herbert P. *Hirohito and the Making of Modern Japan*. New York NY: Perennial, 2001.

Boissarie, Delphine. "Indochina during World War II: An economy under Japanese control." In *Economies under Occupation: The Hegemony of Nazi Germany and Imperial Japan in World War II*, edited by Marcel Boldorf and Tetsuji Okazaki, 232–244. London: Routledge, 2015.

Borg, Dorothy. *The United States and the Far Eastern Crisis of 1933–1938.* Cambridge MA: Harvard University Press, 1964.

Boyd, Carl. *Hitler's Japanese Confidant: General Oshima Hiroshi and MAGIC Intelligence, 1941–1945.* Lawrence, KS: University Press of Kansas, 1993.

Boyle, John Hunter. *China and Japan at War, 1937–1945: The Politics of Collaboration.* Stanford CA: Stanford University Press, 1972.

Brinkley, F. *Japan: Described and Illustrated by the Japanese.* Boston MA: J. B. Millet, 1897.

Broadberry, Stephen, Hanhui Guan, and David Daokui Li. "China, Europe and the Great Divergence: A Study in Historical National Accounting." *Discussion Papers in Economic and Social History*, no. 155, April 2017.

Brussels Conference Convened in Virtue of Article 7 of the Washington Treaty of 1922: Acts of the Conference. Brussels: A. Lesigne, n.d.

Bunker, Gerald E. *The Peace Conspiracy: Wang Ching-wei and the China War, 1937–1941.* Cambridge MA: Harvard University Press, 1972.

Burns, James MacGregor. *Roosevelt: The Lion and the Fox.* New York NY: Harcourt Brace and Co., 1956.

Buswell, Robert E. and Donald S. Lopez. *The Princeton Dictionary of Buddhism.* Princeton NJ: Princeton University Press, 2014.

Caldwell, Oliver J. *A Secret War: Americans in China 1944–1945.* Carbondale IL: Southern Illinois University Press, 1972.

Calvocoressi, Peter, Guy Wint and John Pritchard. *The Penguin History of the Second World War.* London: Penguin, 1999.

Capkova, Helena. "Transnational Networkers—Iwao and Michiko Yamawaki and the Formation of Japanese Modernist Design." *Journal of Design History* 27, no. 4 (November 2014): 370–385.

Caravaggio, Angelo N. "'Winning' the Pacific War: The Masterful Strategy of Commander Minoru Genda." *Naval War College Review* 67, no. 1 (Winter 2014): 85–118.

Chandler, David P. *Brother Number One: A Political Biography of Pol Pot.* Boulder CO: Westview Press, 1992.

Chang, Vincent K. L. and Yong Zhou, "Redefining Wartime Chongqing: International capital of a global power in the making, 1938–46," *Modern Asian Studies* 51, no. 3 (2017): 577–621.

Chen, King C. *Vietnam and China, 1938–1954.* Princeton NJ: Princeton University Press, 1969.

Chennault, Claire Lee. *Way of a Fighter.* New York NY: G. P. Putnam's Sons, 1949.

Chiang Kai-shek. *All We Are and All We Have: Speeches and Messages since Pearl Harbor.* New York NY: The John Day Company, 1948.

Chuikov, Vasilii I. *Mission to China: Memoirs of a Soviet Military Advisor to Chiang Kaishek.* Edited by David P. Barrett. Norwalk CT: Eastbridge, 2004.

Ciano, Galeazzo. *The Ciano Diaries, 1939–1943.* Garden City NY: Doubleday and Company, 1946.

Clarke, J. Calvitt III. *Alliance of the Colored Peoples: Ethiopia and Japan Before World War II.* Oxford: James Currey for the International African Institute, 2011.

Cole, Wayne S. *Roosevelt and the Isolationists 1932–45.* Lincoln NE: University of Nebraska Press, 1983.

Cook, Haruko Taya and Theodore F. *Japan at War: An Oral History.* New York NY: The New Press, 1992.

Coox, Alvin D. *Nomonhan: Japan against Russia, 1939.* Stanford CA: Stanford University Press, 1985.

Cowan, James H. *Bataan: A Survivor's Memoir.* Sacramento CA: Bella Vista Press, 1970.

Crowley, James B. *Japan's Quest for Autonomy: National Security and Foreign Policy 1930–1938.* Princeton NJ: Princeton University Press, 1966.

Culver, Annika A. *Glorify the Empire: Japanese Avant-Garde Propaganda in Manchukuo.* Vancouver: UBC Press, 2013.

Dallek, Robert. *Franklin D. Roosevelt and American Foreign Policy, 1932–1945.* Oxford: Oxford University Press, 1995.

Dallin, Alexander and Fridrikh Igorevich Firsov (eds.). *Dimitrov and Stalin, 1934–1943: Letters from the Soviet Archives*. New Haven CT: Yale University Press, 2000.

Dickinson, Frederick R. "Japan Debates the Anglo-Japanese Alliance: The Second Revision of 1911." In *The Anglo-Japanese Alliance 1902–1922*, edited by Phillips Payson O'Brien, 99–121. London and New York NY: Routledge, 2004.

Documents on British Foreign Policy, 1919–1939. London: Her Majesty's Stationery Office.

Doenecke, Justus D. and John E. Wilz. *From Isolation to War, 1931–1941*. Chichester: John Wiley & Sons, 2015.

Dorn, Frank. *The Sino-Japanese War 1937–41: From Marco Polo Bridge to Pearl Harbor*. New York NY: MacMillan, 1974.

Dower, John W. *Cultures of War: Pearl Harbor/Hiroshima/9–11/Iraq*. New York NY: W. W. Norton, The New Press, 2010.

Drea, Edward J. "Reading Each Other's Mail: Japanese Communication Intelligence, 1920–1941." *The Journal of Military History* 55, no. 2 (April 1991): 185–205.

Dreifort, John E. "Japan's Advance into Indochina, 1940: The French Response." *Journal of Southeast Asian Studies*, vol. 13, no. 2 (Sept. 1982): 279–295.

Dreyer, Edward L. *China at War, 1901–1949*. London and New York NY: Longman, 1995.

Dreyer, June Teufel. *Middle Kingdom and Empire of the Rising Sun*. Oxford: Oxford University Press, 2016.

Duffy, James P. *Hitler's Secret Pirate Fleet: The Deadliest Ships of World War II*. Lincoln NE: University of Nebraska Press, 2005.

Dülffer, Jost. "The Tripartite Pact of 27 September 1940: Fascist Alliance or Propaganda Trick?" *The Australian Journal of Politics and History* 32, no. 2 (1986): 228–237.

Dull, Paul S. *A Battle History of the Imperial Japanese Navy (1941–1945)*. Annapolis MD: Naval Institute Press, 1978.

Dulles, Foster Rhea. *Yankees and Samurai*. New York NY: Harper and Row, 1965.

Eastman, Lloyd E. *The Abortive Revolution: China under Nationalist Rule, 1927–1937*. Cambridge MA: Harvard University Asia Center, 1990.

Endicott, Stephen Lyon. *Diplomacy and Enterprise: British China Policy, 1933–1937*. Manchester: Manchester University Press, 1975.

Ericson, Steven J. *The Sound of the Whistle: Railroads and the State in Meiji Japan*. Cambridge MA: Harvard University Press, 1996.

Esthus, Raymond A. "President Roosevelt's Commitment to Britain to Intervene in a Pacific War." *The Mississippi Valley Historical Review* 50, no. 1 (June 1963): 28–38.

Evans, David C. and Mark R. Peattie. *Kaigun: Strategy, Tactics and Technology in the Imperial Japanese Navy 1887–1941*. Annapolis MD: Naval Institute Press, 1997.

Fabyanic, Thomas A. and Robert F. Futrell. "Early Intelligence Organization in the Army Air Corps." In *Piercing the Fog: Intelligence and Army Air Forces Operations in World War II*, edited by John F. Kreis, 11–56. Washington DC: Air Force History and Museums Program, 1996.

Farris, William Wayne. *Population, Disease and Land in Early Japan 645–900*. Cambridge MA: Harvard University Press, 1985.

Feis, Herbert. *The Road to Pearl Harbor*. New York NY: Atheneum, 1963.

Felton, Mark. China Station: *The British Military in the Middle Kingdom 1839–1997*. Barnsley: Pen & Sword, 2013.

Fenby, Jonathan. *Chiang Kai-shek: China's Generalissimo and the Nation He Lost*. New York NY: Carroll and Graf Publishers, 2003.

Ferrell, Robert H. *American Diplomacy in the Great Depression: Hoover-Stimson foreign policy, 1929–1933*. New Haven CT: Yale University Press, 1957.

The Final Confrontation: Japan's Negotiations with the United States, 1941. Edited by J. W. Morley. New York NY: Columbia University Press, 1995.

Finch, Percy. *Shanghai and Beyond.* New York NY: Charles Scribner's Son, 1953.

Fleisher, Wilfrid. *Volcanic Isle.* Garden City NY: Doubleday, Doran and Co., 1941.

Fogel, Joshua A. "Introduction." In *Sagacious Monks and Bloodthirsty Warriors: Chinese Views of Japan in the Ming-Qing Period,* edited Joshua A. Fogel, 3–14. Norwalk CT: Eastbridge, 2002.

Fouraker, Lawrence. "Saito Takao and Parliamentary Politics in 1930s Japan." *Sino-Japanese Studies* 12, no. 2 (2000): 3–28.

Fox, John P. *Germany and the Far Eastern Crisis 1931–1938*: A Study in Diplomacy and Ideology. Oxford: Oxford University Press, 1982.

Fuchida Mitsuo. "I Led the Air Attack on Pearl Harbor." *Proceedings* 78, no. 9 (September 1952): 595.

——, "The Air Attack on Pearl Harbor." In *The Japanese Navy in World War II: In the Words of Former Japanese Naval Officers,* edited by David C. Evans, 39–70. Annapolis MD: Naval Institute Press, 1986.

Garver, John W. *Chinese-Soviet Relations 1937–1945.* Oxford: Oxford University Press, 1988.

——, "The Soviet Union and the Xi'an Incident." *The Australian Journal of Chinese Affairs,* no. 26 (1991): 145–75.

Gatu, Dagfinn Gatu. *Village China at War: The Impact of Resistance to Japan, 1937–1945.* Copenhagen: NIAS Press, 2007.

Gellhorn, Martha. *Travels with Myself and Another.* New York NY: Putnam, 1978.

Glantz, David M. "The Impact of Intelligence Provided to the Soviet Union by Richard Zorge on Soviet Force Deployments from the Far East to the West in 1941 and 1942." *The Journal of Slavic Military Studies* 30, no. 3 (2017): 453–481.

Goette, John. *Japan Fights for Asia.* New York NY: Harcourt, Brace and Company, 1943.

Goldman, Stuart D. *Nomonhan, 1939: The Red Army's Victory That Shaped World War II.* Annapolis MD: Naval Institute Press, 2012.

Green, Michael. *By More Than Providence: Grand Strategy and American Power in the Asia Pacific Since 1783.* New York NY: Columbia University Press, 2017.

Griffiths, Owen. "Need, Greed, and Protest in Japan's Black Market, 1938–1949." *Journal of Social History* 35, No. 4 (Summer 2002): 825–858.

Haffenden, John. *William Empson: Among the Mandarins.* Oxford: Oxford University Press, 2005.

Hammer, Ellen J. *The Struggle for Indochina, 1940–1955.* Stanford CA: Stanford University Press, 1966.

Hara Tameichi. *Japanese Destroyer Captain.* Annapolis MD: Naval Institute Press, 1967.

Harmsen, Peter. *Nanjing 1937: Battle for a Doomed City.* Havertown PA: Casemate, 2015.

——, *Shanghai 1937: Stalingrad on the Yangtze.* Havertown PA: Casemate, 2013.

Harries, Meirion and Susie. *Soldiers of the Sun: The Rise and Fall of the Imperial Japanese Army.* New York NY: Random House, 1991.

Haslam, Jonathan. *The Soviet Union and the Threat from the East, 1933–1941.* Pittsburgh PA: University of Pittsburgh Press, 1992.

Hata Ikuhiko. "The Army's Move into Northern Indochina." In *The Fateful Choice: Japan's Advance into Southeast Asia, 1939–1941,* edited James William Morley, 155–208. New York NY: Columbia University Press, 1980.

——, "The Japanese-Soviet Confrontation, 1935–1939." In *Deterrent Diplomacy: Japan, Germany and the USSR 1935–1940,* edited by James William Morley, 113–178. New York NY: Columbia University Press, 1976.

——, "The Marco Polo Bridge Incident, 1937." In *The China Quagmire: Japan's Expansion on the Asian Continent 1933–1941,* edited by James William Morley, 233–286. New York NY: Columbia University Press, 1983.

Hattori Satoshi with Edward J. Drea. "Japanese Operations from July to December 1937." In *The Battle for China: Essays on the Military History of the Sino-Japanese War of 1937–1945*, edited by Mark Peattie et al., 159–180. Stanford CA: Stanford University Press, 2011.

Havens, Thomas R. H. *Valley of Darkness: The Japanese People and World War Two*. Lanham MD: University Press of America, 1986.

Hawley, Samuel. *The Imjin War: Japan's Sixteenth-Century Invasion of Korea and Attempt to Conquer China*. n.p.: Conquistador Press, 2014.

Headquarters United States Armed Forces, Far East and Eighth United States Army Military History Section. *Japanese Night Combat*. n.p., 1955.

Heinl, R. D. *The Defense of Wake [Marines in World War II: Historical Monograph]*. n. p.: Historical Section, United States Marine Corps, 1947.

Homer, Joy. *Dawn Watch in China*. Boston MA: Houghton Mifflin, 1941.

Hosoya Chihiro. "The Tripartite Pact." In *Deterrent Diplomacy: Japan, Germany and the USSR 1935–1940*, edited by James William Morley, 179–257. New York NY: Columbia University Press, 1976.

Hotta, Eri. *Japan 1941: Countdown to Infamy*. New York NY: Alfred A. Knopf, 2013.

Hough, Frank O. et al. *Pearl Harbor to Guadalcanal [History of U. S. Marine Corps Operations in World War II, Volume I]*. Washington DC: United States Marine Corps, 1958.

Hull, Cordell. *The Memoirs of Cordell Hull*. London: Hodder and Stoughton, 1948.

Ickes, Harold L. *The Secret Diary of Harold L. Ickes. Vol. II: The Inside Struggle 1936–1939*. New York NY: Simon and Schuster, 1954.

——, *The Secret Diary of Harold L. Ickes. Vol. II: The Lowering Clouds 1939–1941*. New York NY: Simon and Schuster, 1954.

Ienaga Saburō. *Pacific War 1931–1945*. New York NY: Random House, 1978.

Ike Nobutaka. *Japan's Decision for War: Records of the 1941 Policy Conferences*. Stanford CA: Stanford University Press, 1967.

International Military Tribunal for the Far East. *Transcript of Proceedings*.

Iriye Akira. *The Origins of the Second World War in Asia and the Pacific*. Harlow: Pearson, 1987.

Jansen, Marius B. *The Japanese and Sun Yat-sen*. Stanford CA: Stanford University Press, 1970.

Japanese Demobilization Bureau Records (compiler). *Reports of General MacArthur: Japanese Operations in the Southwest Pacific Area* (Washington DC: US Government Printing Office, 1994.

——, "The Meiji Restoration." In *The Cambridge History of Japan. Vol. 5: The Nineteenth Century*, edited by Marius B. Jansen. Cambridge: Cambridge University Press, 1989.

Johnson, Chalmers A. *Peasant Nationalism and Communist Power: The Emergence of Revolutionary China 1937–1945*. Stanford CA: Stanford University Press, 1962.

Johnson, E. Pauline. *Flint and Feather: The Complete Poems of E. Pauline Johnson*. n. p.: Leopold Classical Library, 2016.

Jordan, Donald A. *China's Trial by Fire: The Shanghai War of 1932*. Ann Arbor MI: The University of Michigan Press, 2001.

——, *The Northern Expedition: China's National Revolution of 1926–1928*. Honolulu HI: The University Press of Hawaii, 1976.

Jose, Ricardo Trota. *The Philippine Army 1935–1942*. Manila: Ateneo de Manila University Press, 1992.

Kalyagin, Aleksandr. *Along Alien Roads*. New York NY: The East Asian Institute, Columbia University, 1983.

Karnow, Stanley. *In Our Image: America's Empire in the Philippines*. New York NY: Random House, 1989.

Kataoka Tetsuya, *Resistance and Revolution in China: The Communists and the Second United Front*. Berkeley and Los Angeles CA: University of California Press, 1974.

Keene, Donald. "Japanese Writers and the Greater East Asia War." *The Journal of Asian Studies* 23, no. 2 (February 1964): 209–225.

Kennedy, Greg. *Anglo-American Strategic Relations and the Far East 1933–1939: Imperial Crossroads*. London and New York NY: Routledge, 2002.

Kirby, S. Woodburn. *The War Against Japan, Volume 1: The Loss of Singapore*. London: Her Majesty's Stationery Office, 1957.

Komatsu Keiichirō, "Misunderstanding and Mistranslation in the Origins of the Pacific War of 1941–1945: The Importance of 'Magic'." Paper delivered at Burma Campaign Society, on May 9, 2002.

Koshihiro Yukiko. *Imperial Eclipse: Japan's Strategic Thinking about Continental Asia before August 1945*. Ithaca NY: Cornell University Press, 2013.

Kotani, Ken. *Japanese Intelligence in World War II*. Oxford: Osprey, 2009.

——, *Japanese Intelligence in WWII: Successes and Failures*. Tokyo: First Military History Research Office, n.d.

Kuromiya Hiroaki. "The Battle of Lake Khasan Reconsidered." *The Journal of Slavic Military Studies* 29, no. 1 (2016): 99–109.

——, "The Mystery of Nomonhan, 1939." *The Journal of Slavic Military Studies* 24, no. 4 (2011) 659–677.

LaFeber, Walter. *The Clash: A History of US-Japan Relations*. New York NY: Norton, 1997.

Lai, Sherman Xiaogang. *A Springboard to Victory: Shandong Province and Chinese Communist Military and Financial Strength, 1937–1945*. Leiden: Brill, 2011.

——, "A War Within a War: The Road to the New Fourth Army Incident in January 1941." *Journal of Chinese Military History*, 2 (2013): 1–27.

Lary, Diana. "Defending China: The Battles of the Xuzhou Campaign." In *Warfare in Chinese History*, edited by Hans van de Ven, 398–427. Boston MA: Brill, 2000.

——, "Drowned Earth: The Strategic Breaching of the Yellow River Dyke, 1938." *War in History* 8, no. 2 (2001): 191–207.

——, "Treachery, Disgrace and Death: Han Fuju and China's Resistance to Japan." *War in History* 13, no. 1 (January 2006): 65–90.

Lattimore, Owen. *China Memoirs: Chiang Kai-shek and the War Against Japan*. Tokyo: University of Tokyo Press, 1990.

League of Nations. Commission of Enquiry into the Sino-Japanese Dispute. *Appeal by the Chinese Government: Report of the Commission of Enquiry [Lytton Report]*. Geneva: League of Nations, 1932.

Lee, Bradford A. *Britain and the Sino-Japanese War, 1937–1939*. Stanford CA: Stanford University Press, 1973.

Lee Chong-sik. *Counterinsurgency in Manchuria: The Japanese Experience, 1931–1940*. Santa Monica CA: Rand Corp., 1967.

Li Tsung-jen (Li Zongren) et al. *The Memoirs of Li Tsung-jen*. Boulder CO: Westview Press, 1979.

Liang, Hsi-Huey. *The Sino-German Connection: Alexander von Falkenhausen Between China and Germany 1900–1941*. Amsterdam: van Gorcum, 1978.

Liu, Bea Exner. *Remembering China 1935–1945*. Minneapolis MN: New Rivers Press, 1996.

Lone, Stewart. *Japan's First Modern War: Army and Society in the Conflict with China, 1894–95*. New York NY: St. Martin's, 1994.

Long, Breckinridge. *War Diary of Breckinridge Long*. Edited by Fred L. Israel. Lincoln NE: University of Nebraska Press, 1966.

Lord, Walter. *Day of Infamy*. New York NY: Henry Holt, 2001.

Lovell, Judith. *The Opium War: Drugs, Dreams, and the Making of China*. London: MacMillan, 2011.

Luo Zhitian. "National Humiliation and National Assertion: The Chinese Response to the 21 Demands." *Modern Asian Studies* 27, no. 2 (May 1993): 297–319.

Mackinnon, Stephen. "The Defense of the Central Yangtze." In *The Battle for China: Essays on the Military History of the Sino-Japanese War of 1937–1945*, edited by Mark Peattie et al., 181–206. Stanford CA: Stanford University Press, 2011.

——, Wuhan, 1938: *War, Refugees, and the Making of Modern China*. Berkeley CA: University of California Press, 2008.

Macri, Franco David. *Clash of Empires in South China: The Allied Nations' Proxy War with Japan, 1935–1941*. Lawrence KS: University Press of Kansas, 2012.

Maddison, Angus. *The World Economy*. Paris: OECD, 2007.

Maltby, Paul. "Report on the Air Operations During the Campaigns in Malaya and Netherlands East Indies From 8th December, 1941 to 12th March, 1942." *The London Gazette* (February 26, 1948): 1347–1415.

Marder, Arthur J. *Old Friends, New Enemies: The Royal Navy and the Imperial Japanese Navy*. Oxford: Clarendon Press, 1981.

Marr, David G. *Vietnam 1945: The Quest for Power*. Berkeley CA: University of California Press, 1995.

Marshall, Jonathan. *To Have and Have Not: Southeast Asian Raw Materials and the Origins of the Pacific War*. Berkeley CA: University of California Press, 1995.

Martin, Brian G. "'In My Heart I Opposed Opium': Opium and the Politics of the Wang Jingwei Government, 1940–45." *The European Journal of East Asian Studies* 2 (2003): 365–410.

Martin, Robert J. *USS West Virginia (BB-48)*. Paducah KY: Turner Publishing Company, 1997.

Maruyama Masao. "The Ideology and Dynamics of Japanese Fascism." In *Thought and Behavior in Modern Japanese Politics*, edited by Ivan Morris, 25–83. Oxford: Oxford University Press, 1969.

Masland, John W. "American Attitudes Toward Japan." *The Annals of the American Academy of Political and Social Science* 215 (May 1941): 160–165.

Matsusaka, Y. Tak. "Human Bullets, General Nogi, and the Myth of Port Arthur." In *The Russo-Japanese War in Global Perspective: World War Zero*, edited by John W. Steinberg et al., vol. 1, 179–201. Leiden: Brill, 2005.

Matthiessen, Sven. *Japanese Pan-Asianism and the Philippines from the Late Nineteenth Century to the End of World War II: Going to the Philippines Is Like Coming Home?* Leiden: Brill, 2015.

McKercher, B. J. C. *Transition of Power: Britain's Loss of Global Pre-Eminence to the United States, 1930–1945*. Cambridge: Cambridge University Press, 2004.

Miles, Milton E. *A Different Kind of War*. Garden City NY: Doubleday, 1967.

Miller, E. B. *Bataan Uncensored*. Long Prairie MN: The Hart Publications, 1949.

Miller, Edward S. *Bankrupting the Enemy: The U. S. Financial Siege of Japan Before Pearl Harbor*. Annapolis MD: Naval Institute Press, 2007.

——, *War Plan Orange: The U. S. Strategy to Defeat Japan, 1897–1945*. Annapolis, MD: Naval Institute Press, 1991.

Millett, Allan R. "Assault from the Sea: Development of Amphibious Warfare between the Wars." In *Military Innovation in the Interwar Period*, edited by Williamson R. Murray and Allan R. Millett, 41–95. Cambridge: Cambridge University Press, 1996.

Ministry of Foreign Affairs of Japan. *Japan-China Joint History Research Report. Modern and Contemporary History, vol. 1*. (March 2011).

Mitchell, Richard H. "Japan's Peace Preservation Law of 1925: Its Origin and Significance." *Monumenta Nipponica* 28, no. 3 (1973): 317–346.

Mitter, Rana. *China's War with Japan 1937–1945: The Struggle for Survival*. London: Allen Lane, 2013.

van Mook, H. J. *The Netherlands Indies and Japan: Their Relations 1940–1941*. London: Routledge, 2011.

Moore, Aaron William. "The Peril of Self-Discipline: Chinese Nationalist, Japanese, and American Servicemen Record the Rise and Fall of the Japanese Empire 1937–1945." PhD diss., Princeton University, 2006.

Morison, Samuel Eliot. *The Rising Sun in the Pacific 1931—April 1942 [History of United States Naval Operations in World War II, vol. 3]*. Boston MA: Little, Brown and Co., 1948.

Morton, Louis. *The Fall of the Philippines [United States Army in World War II: The War in the Pacific]* (Washington DC: Office of the Chief of Military History, Department of the Army, 1953.

——, "Japan's Decision for War." In *Command Decisions*, edited by Kent Roberts Greenfield, 99–124. Washington DC: Office of the Chief of Military History, Department of the Army, 1960.

——, *Strategy and Command: The First Two Years. [United States Army in World War II: The War in the Pacific]*. Washington DC: Office of the Chief of Military History, Department of the Army, 1962.

Murakami Sachiko. "Japan's Thrust into French Indochina, 1940–1945." PhD diss., New York University, 1981.

Nagaoka Shinjirō. "The Drive into Southern Indochina and Thailand." In *The Fateful Choice: Japan's Advance into Southeast Asia, 1939–1941*, edited by James William Morley, 209–240. New York NY: Columbia University Press, 1980.

Nakamura Takafusa. "Depression, recovery, and war, 1920–1945." In *The Cambridge History of Japan, vol. 6*, edited by Peter Duus, 451–493. Cambridge: Cambridge University Press, 1988.

Ness, Leland. *Rikugun: Guide to Japanese Ground Forces 1937–1945*. Solihull: Helion & Co., 2015.

Odo, Franklin. *No Sword to Bury: Japanese Americans in Hawai'i during World War II*. Philadelphia PA: Temple University Press, 2004.

Ogata Sadako. *Defiance in Manchuria: The Making of Japanese Foreign Policy, 1932–1932*. Berkeley and Los Angeles CA: University of California Press, 1964.

Ōhata Tokushirō. "The Anti-Comintern Pact, 1935–1939" in *Deterrent Diplomacy: Japan, Germany and the USSR 1935–1940*, edited by James William Morley, 1–111. (New York NY: Columbia University Press, 1976.

Ohbuchi Hiroshi. "Demographic Transition in the Process of Japanese Industrialization." In *Historical Demography and Labor Markets in Prewar Japan*, edited by Michael Smitka, 167–199. New York NY: Garland, 1998.

O'Neill, William D. *Interwar U.S. and Japanese National Product and Defense Expenditure*. Alexandria VA: CNA, 2003.

Osborne, Milton. "King-Making in Cambodia." *Journal of Southeast Asian Studies* 4, no. 2 (September 1973): 169–185.

Paine, S. C. M. *The Japanese Empire: Grand Strategy from the Meiji Restoration to the Pacific War*. Cambridge: Cambridge University Press, 2017.

——, *The Sino-Japanese War of 1894–1895: Perceptions, Power and Primacy*. Cambridge: Cambridge University Press, 2003.

——, *The Wars for Asia 1911–1949*. Cambridge: Cambridge University Press, 2012.

Parkinson, Jonathan. *The Royal Navy, China Station: 1864–1941*. Leicester: Matador, 2018.

Peattie, Mark R. *Ishiwara Kanji and Japan's Confrontation with the West*. Princeton NJ: Princeton University Press, 1975.

——, *The Rise of Japanese Naval Air Power, 1909–1941*. Annapolis MD: Naval Institute Press, 2001.

Peck, Graham. *Through China's Wall*. Boston MA: Houghton Mifflin, 1940.

——, *Two Kinds of Time*. Edited by Robert A. Kapp. Seattle WA: University of Washington Press, 2008.

Peyrefitte, Alain. *The Immobile Empire*. New York NY: Vintage Books, 2013.

Pinto, Fernão Mendes. *The Travels of Mendes Pinto*. Chicago IL: University of Chicago Press, 2013.

Pogue, Forrest C. *George C. Marshall: Ordeal and Hope 1939–1942*. New York NY: Viking, 1966.

Political Strategy Prior to the Outbreak of War [Japanese Monograph no. 144]. Tokyo: Military History Section Headquarters, 1952.

Porch, Douglas. *The French Foreign Legion: A Complete History of the Legendary Fighting Force.* New York NY: Skyhorse Publishing, 2010.

Potter, E. B. *Nimitz.* Annapolis MD: Naval Institute Press, 1976.

——, *Sea Power: A Naval History.* Annapolis MD: Naval Institute Press, 1981.

Powell, John B. *My Twenty-Five Years in China.* New York NY: MacMillan, 1945.

Prange, Gordon W. *At Dawn We Slept.* New York NY: Penguin Books, 2001.

Prange, Gordon W. et al. *Pearl Harbor: The Verdict of History.* New York NY: Penguin, 1991.

Pu Yi, Henry and Paul Kramer. *The Last Manchu: The Autobiography of Henry Pu Yi, Last Emperor of China.* New York NY: Skyhorse Publishing, 2010.

Raymer, Edward C. *Descent into Darkness: Pearl Harbor, 1941: A Navy Diver's Memoir.* Novato CA: Presidio Press, 1996.

Reporting World War II [Library of America]. New York NY: Penguin, 1995.

Richard, Michael P. *The Presidency and the Middle Kingdom: China, the United States, and Executive Leadership.* Lanham MD: Lexington Books, 2000.

Roosevelt, Theodore. *Letters.* Cambridge MA: Harvard University Press, 1951–1954.

Rosenman, Samuel I. *Working with Roosevelt.* New York NY: Harper, 1952.

Ruoff, Kenneth J. *Imperial Japan at Its Zenith: The Wartime Celebration of the Empire's 2,600th Anniversary.* Ithaca, NY: Cornell University Press, 2010.

Saitō Shohei, "Crossing Perspectives in 'Manchukuo': Russian Eurasianism and Japanese Pan-Asianism." *Jahrbücher für Geschichte Osteuropas* 65, no. 4 (2017): 597–623.

Sakai Saburō with Martin Caidin and Fred Saitō. *Samurai! The Autobiography of Japan's World War II Flying Ace.* n. p.: Uncommon Valor Press, 2015.

Salinas, María Emilia Paz. *Strategy, Security, and Spies: Mexico and the U. S. as Allies in World War II.* University Park PA: Pennsylvania State University Press, 1997.

Schlichtmann, Klaus. *Japan in the World: Shidehara Kijūrō, Pacifism, and the Abolition of War.* Landham MD: Lexington Books, 2009.

Seki Eiji. *Mrs Ferguson's Tea-set, Japan, and the Second World War.* Kent: Global Oriental, 2007.

Seki Hiroharu. "The Manchurian Incident, 1931." In *Japan Erupts: The London Naval Conference and the Manchurian Incident, 1928–1932,* edited James William Morley. New York NY: Columbia University Press, 1984.

Sherwood, Robert E. *Roosevelt and Hopkins: An Intimate History.* New York NY: Harper, 1948.

Shilloney, Ben-Ami. Revolt in Japan: The Young Officers and the February 26, 1936 Incident. Princeton NJ: Princeton University Press, 1973.

Shimada Kōichi. "The Opening Air Offensive against the Philippines." In *The Japanese Navy in World War II: In the Words of Formers Japanese Naval Officers* edited by David C. Evans, 71–104. Annapolis MD: Naval Institute Press, 1986.

Shimada Toshihiko. "Designs on North China, 1933–1937." In *The China Quagmire: Japan's Expansion on the Asian Continent 1933–1941,* edited by James William Morley, 1–230. New York NY: Columbia University Press, 1983.

——, "The Extension of Hostilities, 1931–1932." In *Japan Erupts: The London Naval Conference and the Manchurian Incident, 1928–1932,* edited by James William Morley, 119–230. New York NY: Columbia University Press, 1984.

Shimazu Naoko. "Love Thine Enemy: Japanese Perceptions of Russia." In *The Russo-Japanese War in Global Perspective: World War Zero,* edited by John W. Steinberg et al., vol. 1, 365–384. Leiden: Brill, 2005.

Silverberg, Miriam. *Erotic Grotesque Nonsense: The Mass Culture of Japanese Modern Times.* Berkeley and Los Angeles CA: University of California Press, 2006.

van Slyke, Lyman P. "The Battle of the Hundred Regiments." *Modern Asian Studies* 30, no. 4 (October 1996): 979–1005.

——, (ed.). *The Chinese Communist Movement: A Report by the United States War Department, July 1945.* Stanford CA: Stanford University Press, 1968.

Smirnov, Sergei. "The Russian Officer Corps of the Manchukuo Army." *The Journal of Slavic Military Studies* 28, no. 3 (2015): 556–566.

Snow, Edgar. *Red Star over China.* New York NY: Grove Press, 1968.

So, Kwan-wai. *Japanese Piracy in Ming China During the 16th Century.* Ann Arbor MI: Michigan State University Press, 1975.

Spector, Ronald H. *Eagle Against the Sun: The American War with Japan.* New York NY: Vintage Books, 1985.

Spence, Jonathan. *The Search for Modern China,* 2nd edition. New York NY: W. W. Norton, 1999.

Stacey, C. P. *Six Years of War: The Army in Canada, Britain and the Pacific [Official History of the Canadian Army in the Second World War, vol. 1].* Ottawa: Queen's Printer, 1955.

Stephan, John J. *Hawaii under the Rising Sun.* Honolulu HI: University Press of Hawaii, 1984.

Stranges, Anthony N. "Synthetic Fuel Production in Prewar and World War II Japan: A Case Study in Technological Failure." *Annals of Science* 50, no. 3 (1993): 229–265.

Strong, Anna Louise. *One-Fifth of Mankind.* New York NY: Modern Age Books, 1938.

Tadokoro Masayuki. "Why Did Japan Fail to Become the 'Britain' of Asia?" In *The Russo-Japanese War in Global Perspective: World War Zero,* edited by John W. Steinberg et al., vol. 2, 295–324. Leiden: Brill, 2005.

Tamanoi, Mariko Asano. *Memory Maps: The State and Manchuria in Postwar Japan.* Honolulu HI: University of Hawaii Press, 2008.

Taylor, Jay. *The Generalissimo: Chiang Kai-shek and the Struggle for Modern China.* Cambridge MA: The Belknap Press of Harvard University Press, 2009.

Teitler, Geir and Kurt W. Radtke (eds.) *A Dutch Spy in China: Reports on the First Phase of the Sino-Japanese War 1937–1939.* Leiden: Brill, 1999.

Teng Ssu-yu. *China's Response to the West: A Documentary Survey 1839–1923.* New York NY: Atheneum, 1975.

Terkel, Studs. *'The Good War'.* New York NY: The New Press, 1984.

Thompson, Peter. *The Battle for Singapore: The True Story of Britain's Greatest Military Disaster.* London: Portrait, 2005.

Thompson, Warren L. *Danger Spots in World Population.* New York NY: Knopf, 1930.

Thorne, Christopher G. *The Limits of Foreign Policy: The West, the League, and the Far Eastern Crisis, 1931–1933.* London: Macmillan, 1972.

Thorpe, Elliott R. *East Wind, Rain: The Intimate Account of an Intelligence Officer in the Pacific 1939–49.* Boston MA: Gambit, 1969.

Tobe Ryōichi. "The Japanese Eleventh Army in Central China." In *The Battle for China: Essays on the Military History of the Sino-Japanese War of 1937–1945,* edited by Mark Peattie et al., 307–229. Stanford CA: Stanford University Press, 2011.

de Tocqueville, Alexis. *Democracy in America.* Indianapolis IN: Liberty Fund, 2010.

Toland, John. *The Rising Sun: The Decline and Fall of the Japanese Empire 1936–1945.* New York NY: Random House, 1970.

Tolischus, Otto. *Tokyo Record.* New York NY: Reynold & Hitchcock, 1943.

Tow, Edna. "The Great Bombing of Chongqing and the Anti-Japanese War, 1937–1945." In *The Battle for China: Essays on the Military History of the Sino-Japanese War of 1937–1945,* edited by Mark Peattie et al., 256–282. Stanford CA: Stanford University Press, 2011.

Towle, Philip A. "Japanese Treatment of Prisoners in 1904–1905—Foreign Officers' Reports." *Military Affairs* 39, no. 3 (October 1975): 115–117.

Tsang, Steve. "Chiang Kai-shek's 'secret deal' at Xian and the start of the Sino-Japanese War." *Palgrave Communications*, no. 1, 2015.

Tsien Tai. *China and the Nine Power Conference at Brussels in 1937*. New York: St. John's University Press, 1964.

Tsuji Masanobu. *Japan's Greatest Victory, Britain's Worst Defeat*. Staplehurst: Spellmount: 1997.

Tsunoda Jun. "The Navy's Role in the Southern Strategy." In *The Fateful Choice: Japan's Advance into Southeast Asia, 1939–1941*, edited by James William Morley, 241–295. New York NY: Columbia University Press, 1980.

Tuchman, Barbara W. Tuchman. *Stilwell and the American Experience in China 1911–1945*. New York NY: Random House, 2017.

Twomey, Steve. *Countdown to Pearl Harbor: The Twelve Days to the Attack*. New York NY: Simon & Schuster, 2016.

United States Congress, Joint Congressional Committee on the Investigation of the Pearl Harbor Attack, 79th Congress. *Investigation of the Pearl Harbor Attack: Report of the Joint Committee on the Investigation of the Pearl Harbor Attack*. Washington DC: US Government Printing Office, 1946.

United States Department of State. *Papers Relating to the Foreign Relations of the United States*. Washington, D.C.: Government Printing Office.

——, *United States Foreign Policy, 1931–1941*. Washington DC: US Government Printing Office, 1943.

United States Strategic Bombing Survey (Pacific), Naval Analysis Division. *Interrogations of Japanese Officials*. Washington DC: Government Printing Office, 1946.

Urwin, Gregory J. W. *Facing Fearful Odds: The Siege of Wake Island*. Lincoln: University of Nebraska Press, 1997.

Usui Katsumi. "The Politics of War." In *The China Quagmire: Japan's Expansion on the Asian Continent 1933–1941*, edited by James William Morley, 289–435. New York NY: Columbia University Press, 1983.

Utley, Jonathan G. *Going to War with Japan, 1937–1941*. New York NY: Fordham University Press, 2005.

——, "Upstairs, Downstairs at Foggy Bottom: Oil Exports and Japan, 1940–41," *Prologue* 8, no. 1 (Spring 1976): 17–28.

van de Ven, Hans. *China at War: Triumph and Tragedy in the Emergence of the New China, 1937–1952*. London: Profile Books, 2017.

Wakeman, Federic Jr. *Spymaster: Dai Li and the Chinese Secret Service*. Berkeley CA: University of California Press, 2003.

——, *The Shanghai Badlands: Wartime Terrorism and Urban Crime 1937–1941*. Cambridge: Cambridge University Press, 1996.

Walker, Michael. *The 1929 Sino-Soviet War: The War Nobody Knew*. Lawrence KS: University Press of Kansas, 2007.

Walter, John C. "Congressman Carl Vinson and Franklin D. Roosevelt: Naval Preparedness and the Coming of World War II." *Georgia Historical Quarterly* 64, no. 3 (1980): 294–305.

Wang Yong. "Realistic and Fantastic Images of 'Dwarf Pirates': The Evolution of Ming Dynasty Perceptions of the Japanese." In *Sagacious Monks and Bloodthirsty Warriors: Chinese Views of Japan in the Ming-Qing Period*, edited by Joshua A. Fogel, 17–41. Norwalk CT: Eastbridge, 2002.

Warner, Denis and Peggy. *The Tide at Sunrise: A History of the Russo-Japanese War 1904–1905*. London: Angus & Robertson, 1974.

Watson, Mark Skinner. *Chief of Staff: Prewar Plans and Preparations [United States Army in World War II: The War Department]*. Washington DC: Historical Division, Department of the Army, 1950.

Watt, John R. *Saving Lives in Wartime China: How Medical Reformers Built Modern Healthcare Systems Amid War and Epidemics, 1928–1945*. Leiden: Brill, 2014.

White, Theodore H. *In Search of History: A Personal Adventure.* New York NY: Harper and Row, 1978.

White, Theodore H. and Annalee Jacoby, *Thunder Out of China.* Cambridge MA: Da Capo Press, 1980.

Wigmore. Lionel. *The Japanese Thrust (Australia in the War of 1939–1945. Series I. Army, vol. 1).* Canberra: Australian War Memorial, 1957.

Wilbur, C. Martin. "The Nationalist Revolution: from Canton to Nanking, 1923–1928." In *Cambridge History of China, Volume 12, Republican China, 1912–1949 Pt I,* edited by John K. Fairbank, 527–720. Cambridge: Cambridge University Press, 1983.

Wilkinson, Endymion. *Japan versus the West.* London: Penguin, 1991.

Williamsen, Marvin. "The Military Dimension, 1937–1941." In *China's Bitter Victory: The War With Japan 1937–1945,* edited by James C. Hsiung et al., 1135–156. Armonk NY: M. E. Sharpe, 1992.

Willmott, H. P. *The Barrier and the Javelin: Japanese and Allied Pacific Strategies, February to June, 1942.* Annapolis MD: Naval Institute Press, 1983.

——, *Empires in the Balance.* Annapolis MD: Naval Institute Press, 1982.

Wilson, Sandra. *The Manchurian Crisis and Japanese Society, 1931–33.* New York NY: Routledge, 2002.

Woodward, Llewellyn. *British Foreign Policy in the Second World War.* London: Her Majesty's Stationery Office, 1962.

Yang, Benjamin. *Deng: A Political Biography.* Armonk NY: M. E. Sharpe, 1997.

Yano, Christine R. *Tears of Longing: Nostalgia and the Nation in Japanese Popular Song.* Cambridge MA: Harvard University Asia Center 2002.

Yardley, Herbert O. *The Black Chamber: An Adventure in Espionage.* London: New English Library, 1983.

Yeh, Wen-Hsin. "Dai Li and the Liu Geqing Affair: Heroism in the Chinese Secret Service During the War of Resistance." *The Journal of Asian Studies,* 48, no. 3 (August 1989): 545–563.

——, "Prologue: Shanghai besieged, 1937–45." In *Wartime Shanghai,* edited by Wen-Hsin Yeh, 1–17. London: Routledge, 1998.

Yellen, Jeremy A. "Into the Tiger's Den: Japan and the Tripartite Pact, 1940." *Journal of Contemporary History,* 51, no. 3 (2016): 555–576.

Yi, Yŏn-suk. *The Ideology of Kokugo: Nationalizing Language in Modern Japan.* Honolulu HI: University of Hawai'i Press, 2010.

Yoshikawa, Takeo and Norman Stanford, "Top Secret Assignment." *US Naval Institute Proceedings* 86, no. 12 (December 1960): 27–29 and 33.

Young, Louise. *Japan's Total Empire: Manchuria and the Culture of Wartime Imperialism.* Berkely and Los Angeles CA: University of California Press, 1999.

Zhang Fakui. *Reminiscences of Fa-K'uei Chang: Oral History, 1970–1980.* New York NY: Columbia University Libraries, Oral History Research Office, n.d

Zhou Qiqian. "Chinese Intellectuals' View of Japan in the Late Qing." In *Sagacious Monks and Bloodthirsty Warriors: Chinese Views of Japan in the Ming-Qing Period,* edited by Joshua A. Fogel, 249–266. Norwalk CT: Eastbridge, 2002.

Zhu Pingchao. Wartime Culture in Guilin 1938–1944: A City at War. Lanham MD: Lexington, 2015.

Zhukov, G. K. *The Memoirs of Marshal Zhukov.* New York NY: Delacorte Press, 1971.

Literature in Chinese

Academy of Military Science. *Zhongguo Kangri Zhanzhengshi [History of China's War of Resistance Against Japan].* Beijing: Jiefangjun Chubanshe, 2000.

Bai Chongxi, *Bai Chongxi Koushu Zichuan [Bai Chongxi's Oral Autobiography].* Beijing: Zhongguo Dabaikequanshu Chubanshe, 2008.

Cao Jianlang, *Zhongguo Guomindangjun Jianshi [An Outline History of the Kuomintang's Military Forces].* Beijing: Jiefangjun Chubanshe, 2010.

Cheng Siyuan. *Zhenghai Mixin [Behind the Scenes of Politics]*. Taipei, Li Ao chubanshe, 1995.

Cui Zhenlun. "Langfang kangzhan shimo" ["The Langfang Battle from Beginning to End"]. In *Qiqi Shibian: Yuan Guomindang jiangling Kangri Zhanzheng qinliji [The 7.7. Incident: Personal Recollections from the War of Resistance against Japan by Former Nationalist Commanders]* (hereafter: *Qiqi*), 95–109. Beijing: Zhongguo Wenshi Chubanshe, 1986.

Ding Wei. "Cheng Xigeng shijian zhenxiang" ["The Truth about the Cheng Xigeng Incident"], *Wenshi Jinghua*, no. 230 (2009): 53–58.

Du Longji. "Madang yaosai Changshan zhendi baoweizhan" ["The Defensive Battle for the Key River Barrier at Madang and the Position on Mount Chang"]. In *Wuhan Huizhan: Yuan Guomindang jiangling Kangri Zhanzheng qinliji [The Wuhan Battle: Personal Recollections from the War of Resistance against Japan by Former Nationalist Commanders]*, 30–39. Beijing: Zhongguo Wenshi Chubanshe, 1989.

Du Yuming. "Taierzhuang Dazhanzhong de zhanchefangyupao budui" ["An Anti-Tank Gun Unit at the Great Battle of Taierzhuang"]. In *Xuzhou Huizhan: Yuan Guomindang jiangling Kangri Zhanzheng qinliji [Battle of Xuzhou: Personal Recollections from the War of Resistance against Japan by Former Nationalist Commanders]* (hereafter: *Xuzhou Huizhan*), 205–208. Beijing: Zhongguo Wenshi Chubanshe, 1990.

Guo Daijun. *Chongtan Kangrishi [Revisiting the Second Sino-Japanese War, 1931–1945]*, vol. 1. Taipei: Linking Book, 2015.

Guo Rugui. *Zhongguo Kangri Zhanzheng zhengmian zhanchang zuozhanji [China's War of Resistance against Japan: An Account of Frontline Battles]*. Nanjing: Jiangsu Renmin Chubanshe, 2006.

Jiang Keshi. "Pingxingguan dajie Rijun sishangshu kaozheng" ["An Investigation of Japanese Casualties in the Pingxing Pass Victory." *Bunka Kyōseigakū [Studies in Cultural Symbiotics]*, no. 3 (2017): 61–85.

Jiang Zhongzheng (Chiang Kai-shek). *Kunmian ji [Anthology of Encouragement amid Difficulties]* Taipei: Guoshiguan, 2011.

Li Junsan. *Shanghai Nanjing Baoweizhan [Defensive Battles for Shanghai and Nanjing]*. Taipei: Maitian chubanshe, 1997.

Ma Zhonglian. "Huayuankou jueti de junshi yiyi." *Kangri Zhanzheng Yanjiu*, no. 4 (1999): 203–213.

Meng Qisan. "Taierzhuang de xiangzhan" ["Streets Battles at Taierzhuang"]. In *Xuzhou Huizhan*, 178–181.

Peng Dajiangjun [Great General Peng]. Beijing: Xiandai chubanshe, 2015.

Xing Bingnan. "Jizhan Langfang chezhan" ["Fierce Battle for Langfang Station"]. In *Qiqi*, 110–113.

Xiong Xianyu. "1938 Huanghe jueti shiliao yizu" ["Historical Materials on Breaching the Yellow River Dykes in 1938"]. *Minguo Dang'an*, no. 3 (1997).

Xu Fan and Zhen Rui, *Zhongri Zhuangiabing Quanshi 1918–1937 [A History of Armored Forces in China and Jaoan 1918–1937]*. Beijing: Zhongguo Changan chubanshe, 2015.

Zhang Bofeng. "Guanyu Kangri Zhanzheng shiqi Jiang Jiashi fandong jituan de jici tuoxie touxiang huodong" ["Regarding Several Appeasement and Capitulationist Activities by the Chiang Kai-shek Clique during the Anti-Japanese War"]. *Jindaishi Yanjiu*, no. 2 (1979): 215–229.

Zheng Dongguo and Zheng Tingji. "Kunlunguan gongjianzhan qinliji" ["A Personal Account of the Battle to Take the Fortified Positions at Kunlun Pass"]. In *Yue Gui Qian Dian Kangzhan: Yuan Guomindang jiangling Kangri Zhanzheng qinliji [The War of Resistance in Guangdong, Guangxi, Guizhou and Yunnan: Personal Recollections from the War of Resistance against Japan by Former Nationalist Commanders]*, 266–273. Beijing: Zhongguo Wenshi Chubanshe, 1995.

Zhou Jun, "Banian Kangzhan zhong Guomindang Juntong de jingdian ansha zhiyi: Ansha Nanjing 'Zhonghua Minguo Weixing Zhengfu' Wajiaobuzhang Chen Lu" ["One of the classic assassinations carried out by the Kuomintang's Bureau of Investigation and Statistics during the eight-year War of Resistance: Killing Foreign Minister Chen Lu of the Nanjing Reformed Government of the Republic of China"], *Wenshi Yuekan* (September 2008).

Zhou Tiandu. "Cong Qiqi Shibian qianhou Jiang Jieshi riji kan ta de kangri zhuzhang ["A Look at Chiang Kai-shek's Position on Resisting Japan Based on His Diary Before and After the July 7 Incident"]. *Kangri Zhanzheng Yanjiu [Journal of Studies of China's Resistance War Against Japan]*, no. 2 (2008): 136–150.

Literature in other languages

Akten zur deutschen auswärtigen Politik, Series D (1937–1945). Bonn: Gebr. Hermes KG.

d'Alzon, Claude Hesse. *La présence militaire française en Indochine 1940–1945*. Château de Vincennes: Publication du service historique de l'Armée de Terre, 1985.

Smirnov, Sergei. *Otriad Asano: Russkie voinskie formirovania v Manchzho-go 1938–1945 [The Asano Detachment: Russian Military Units in Manchukuo 1938–1945]*. Ekaterinburg: Izdatelstvo Uralskogo universiteta, 2012.

Polynin, F. P. "Erfüllung einer internationalistischen Pflicht" ["Discharge of an International Duty"]. In *Am Himmel über China: Erinnerungen sowjetischer freiwilliger Flieger [In the Sky over China: Memoirs of Volunteer Soviet Airmen]*, 50–96. Berlin: Militärverlag der Deutschen Demokratischen Republik, 1986.

Newspapers, magazines

Berliner Tageblatt.
China Press.
China Weekly Review.
Chicago Daily Tribune.
Collier's.
Honolulu Star Advertiser.
Japan Times and Mail.
New York Times.
North-China Herald and Supreme Court & Consular Gazette.
National Public Radio.
Time.

Index